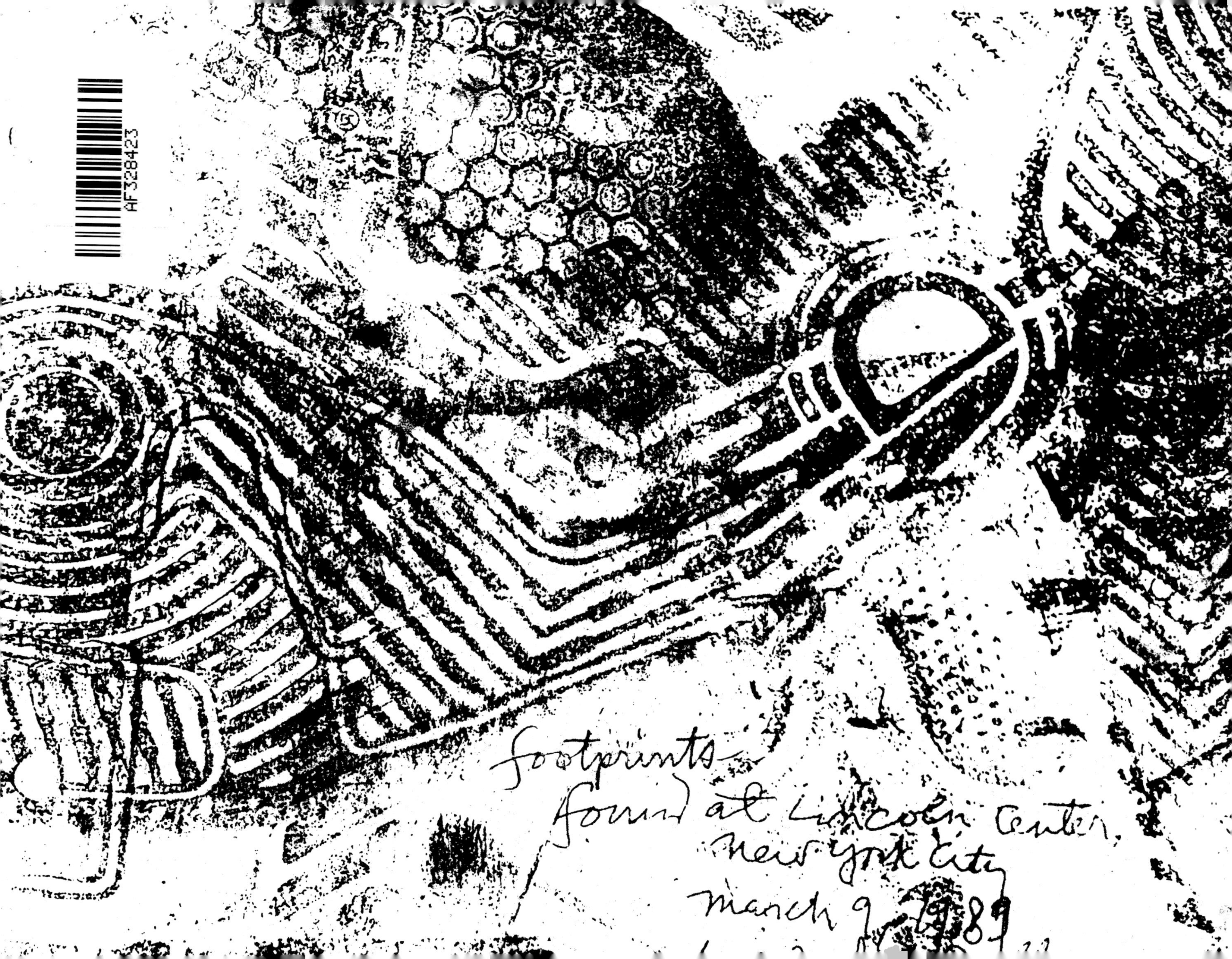

footprints
found at Lincoln Center,
New York City.
March 9 1989
AF328423

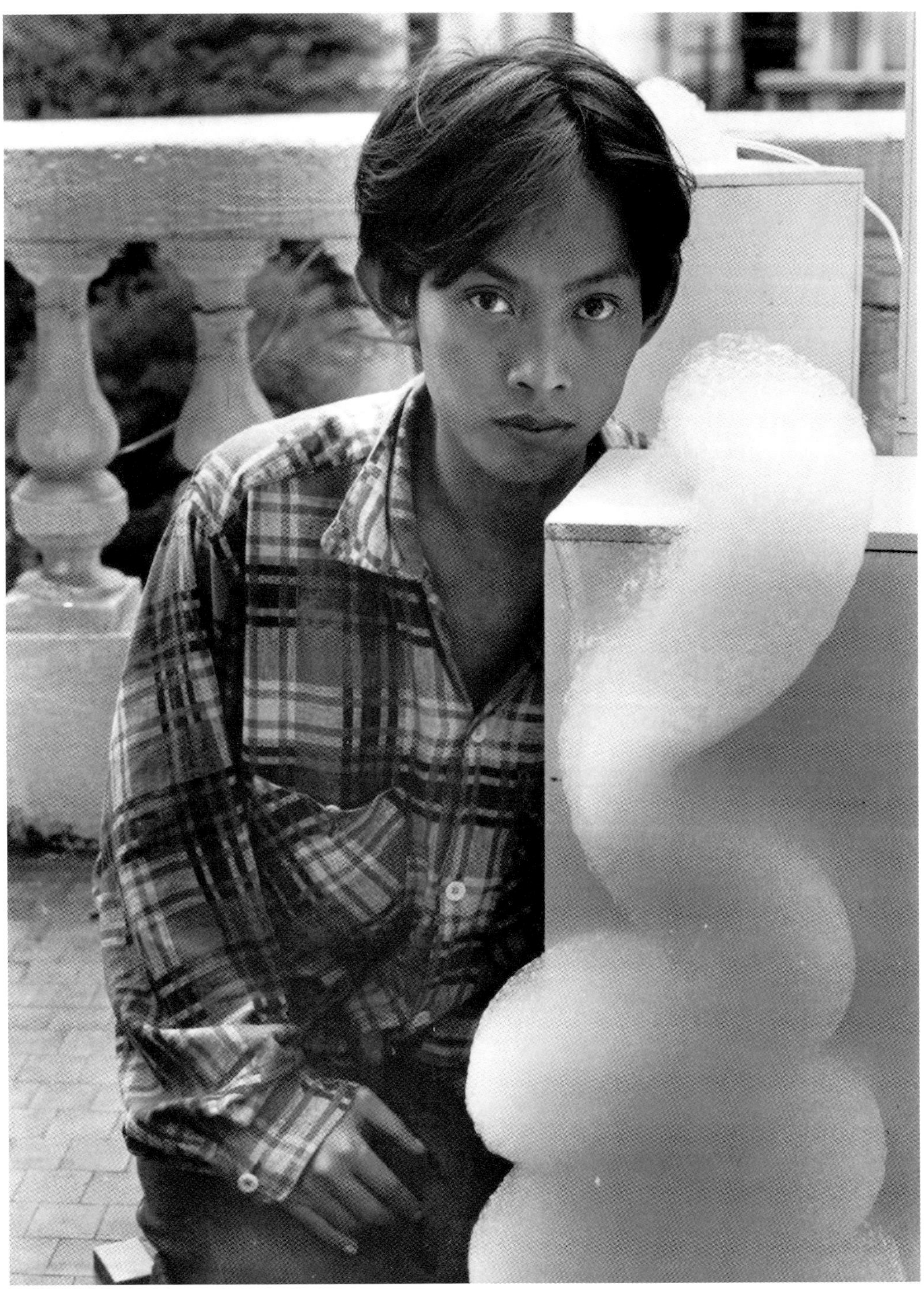

David Medalla with **Cloud Canyons no 2**, bubble machine, London, 1964.
Inside front cover: **Manhattan Footprints**, paper found on the street at the Lincoln Center, New York, 1989.
Collection of the artist.

EXPLODING GALAXIES
The Art of David Medalla

Guy Brett

foreword by
Dore Ashton

envoi by
Yve-Alain Bois

KALA PRESS
LONDON

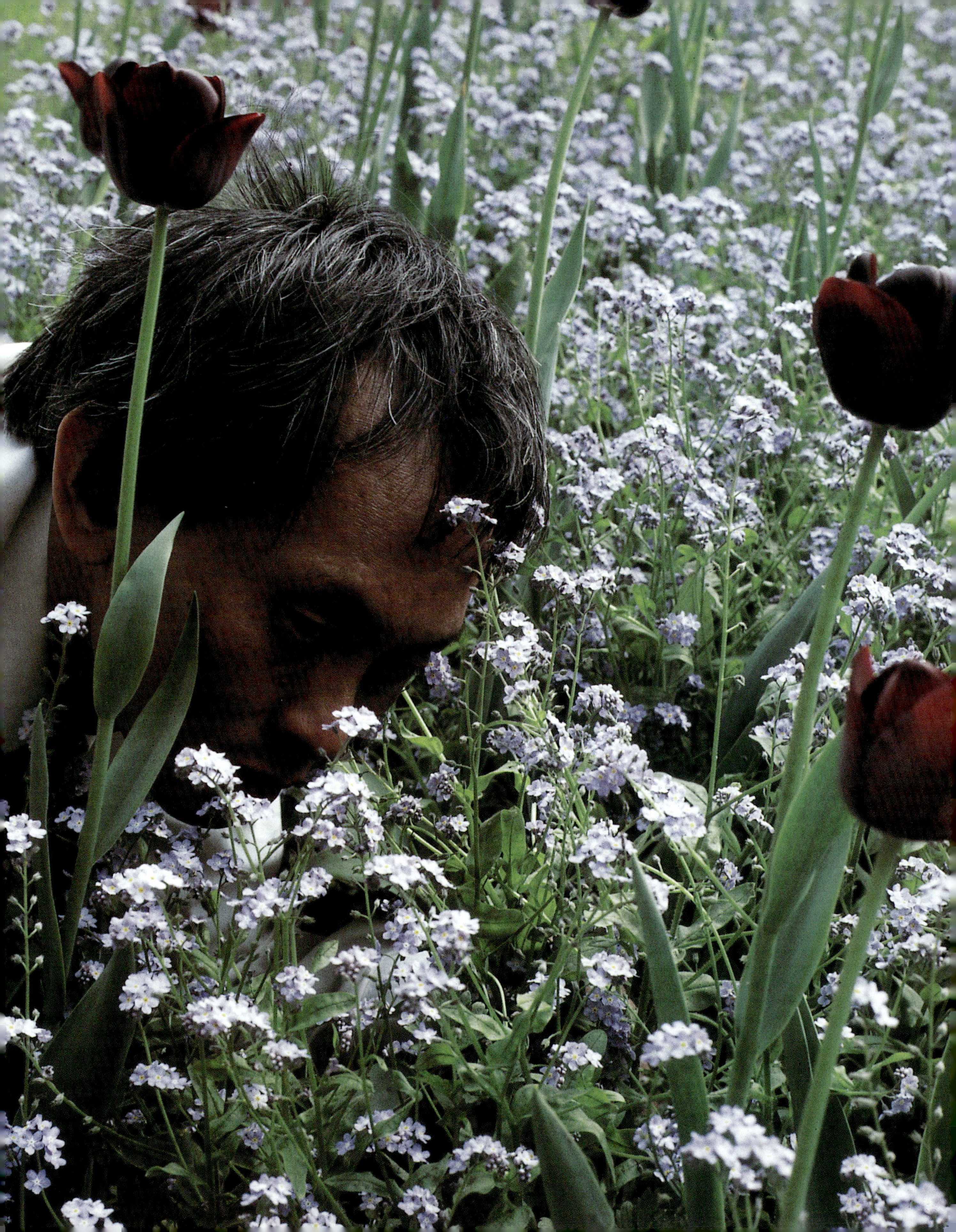

Think of me as a dream

Franz Kafka

First published in 1995 by

KALA PRESS
P O BOX 3509
LONDON NW6 3PQ

ISBN 0 947753 06 0

British Library Cataloguing in Publishing Data
A catalogue record for this book
is available from the British Library

This book is published under
The Arts Council of England's
Publishing Franchise for INIVA

Typeset and Designed by Zafar Abbas Malik
Printed by Arti Grafiche Roccia, Turin, Italy.

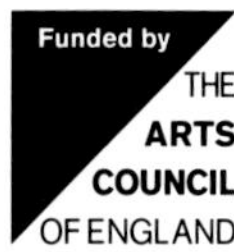

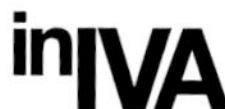

David smelling Forget-me-nots and Black Tulips, impromptu
at Finsbury Square, London, 1986.

contents

Foreword

An Impromptu
for David Medalla and Guy Brett

DORE ASHTON

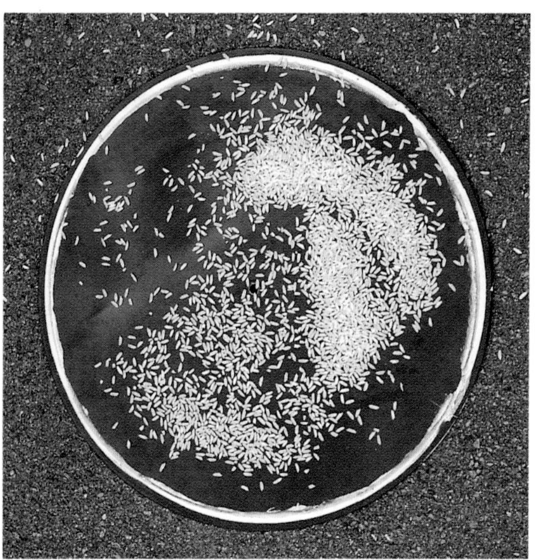

Somehow that indispensable word *luftmensch* has gotten a bad name. But I still find it serviceable. According to the OED, a *luftmensch* is an "impractical visionary". But was there ever a practical visionary? When I think of David Medalla, I think of him affectionately as one of the few authentic *luftmenschen* I have known. He comes with the wind. His spirit is airborne, but every once in a while he alights like a mythical bird, flutters about doing serious reconnaissance, and departs, leaving a feather or two. Over the years I have gathered evidence of his practical (or should I say practising?) existence. A letter arrives. A jumbled postcard. A greeting from some obscure village far from my everyday world. As there is never enough room for Medalla, each missive requires great attention to unscramble its many messages. As Guy Brett has now demonstrated, a little patience goes a long way. These fragmentary sightings, in London, in Paris, in New York, in Manila, in India, when painstakingly recorded,

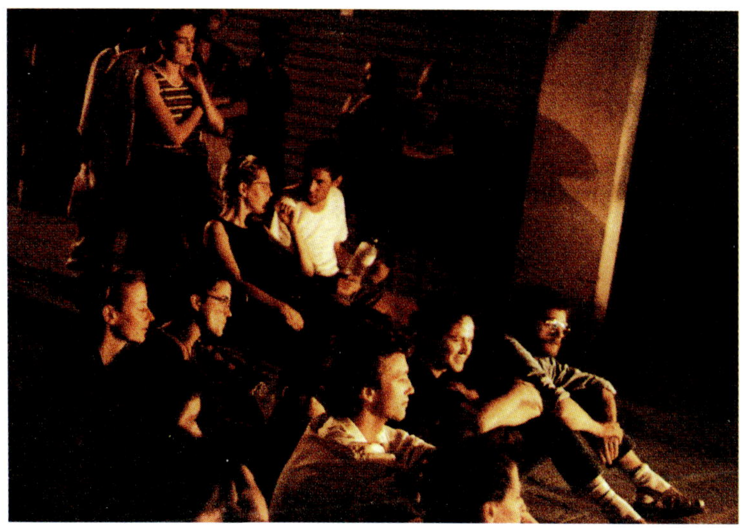

mount up and finally take shape as an extraordinary oeuvre. Impractical, it is true, but decidedly visionary.

During the glorious thousand or two thousand days just after the Russian Revolution, the artist later known as Iliazd founded one of the many short-lived movements that he christened 'Everythingism'.[1] While most avant-garde movements are pointedly exclusive, this was pointedly inclusive, and aimed to make use of everything, even the things of the past, in a resounding affirmation of diversity. Medalla is heir to this tradition – he who cherishes everything, from old master paintings to traditional masks to homemade tools to popular prints to Beethoven trios to *poètes maudits* to street performances, to scientific tracts, to political posters, to Buddhist chants, to… fill in the blanks.

While much of the time Medalla can be seen as *homo ludens* personified, some of the time he can be seen as *homo faber*, and all of the time he can be seen as a man of surpassing imagination. His approach to life is protean, which is to say, he is a versatile actor capable of playing many roles. In his role as dandy, he makes light of convention, and harks back to such 19th century prototypes as Beau Brummel or Oscar Wilde (in Wilde's own way – putting his art into his life, or, writing paradoxes that are profoundly serious). Knowing

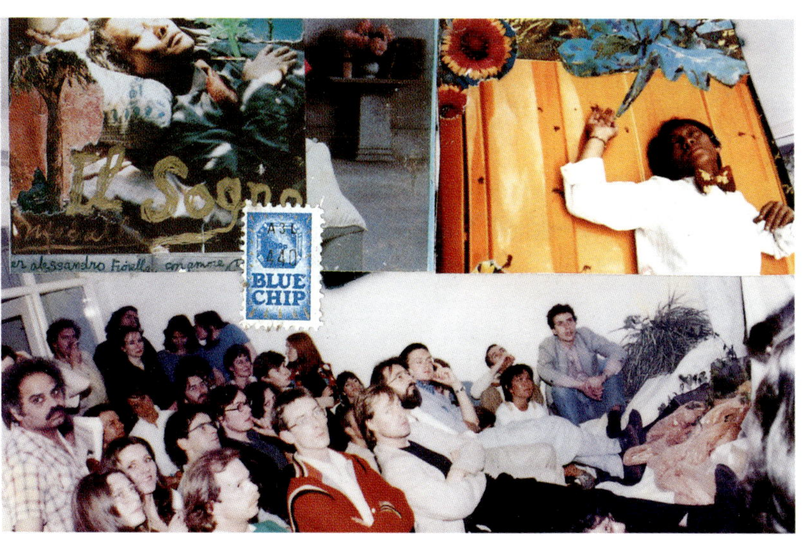

9

him, I am sure he studied Baudelaire's concept of the *flâneur* quite seriously and, in an almost scholarly way, went about testing Baudelaire's idea. I suppose that he also delved into the complex writings of Alfred Jarry whose commentary on modern technology, although couched in the language of parody, certainly holds today. Medalla's sortie in the world of machines during the years he created 'kinetic' art is far closer to Jarry's descriptions of fanciful machines than it is to the countless groaning contraptions that flooded galleries during the 1960s. But then, on the other hand, his machine effusions are not parodic so much as cosmic. After all, the *Bubble Machine*, which he says is not mystifying at all, since it involves just plain soap and water, produces the stuff of reverie – it reacts, as Medalla says, to wind, to sunlight, and all changes of phenomena in its environs. It is far more a lyrical metaphor than a machine-made product, and calls to mind the categories so beautifully described by the French philosopher Gaston Bachelard.[2]

Another side to Medalla's story is his conscientious activism: he has always known when to intervene in a perfectly straightforward, political level, and I once had the occasion to marvel at his swift and important response to an incident I myself witnessed. In the spring of 1965, I took myself up to the American Academy of Arts and Letters where I bravely (and with enormous and ignominious embarrassment) held aloft a hand-painted (by me) sign reproaching the august writers and artists for their shameful silence about the war in Vietnam. Then, to my great relief, Lewis Mumford, one of the few genuine, grand-scale intellectuals America has produced, made a stinging speech denouncing the war, and left the auditorium. With his usual alacrity, Medalla, who was then editing an important publication – important, that is, to those of us who thought so – immediately printed the address in *Signals*, and thereby enabled the peace movement to draw upon Mumford's clear reasoning and moral rectitude. Here and there during his many years of public acts, Medalla has been an organiser, or a kind of evangelical impresario, upholding the old ideal (impractical of course) of the artist as the conscience of society.

Although Medalla now calls himself a transcendental hedonist – a role he has sustained in all weathers even when he called himself a Buddhist or a Marxist – I think of him rather as a good old-fashioned surrealist. The most cherished criterion of the surrealists during the Aragon and Breton era was that of surprise. Medalla has never held to a single course, and one never knows what will come next. He holds surprise in reserve for the most surprising occasions. One can see on the faces of spectators at his various performance appearances their excited sense of anticipation. I often think that Diaghilev's famous command to Cocteau – *étonnez moi* – would have held no terrors for Medalla. I'm sure that just when Diaghilev would have expected Medalla to do something outrageous, Medalla might well have recited from Pushkin, or delivered himself of a lecture on Rembrandt or Vermeer (just as once, when I met Allen Ginsberg for the first time, he, to my surprise, earnestly lectured me on Shelley). Perhaps even more in the spirit of now-classical surrealism, Medalla's fundamental

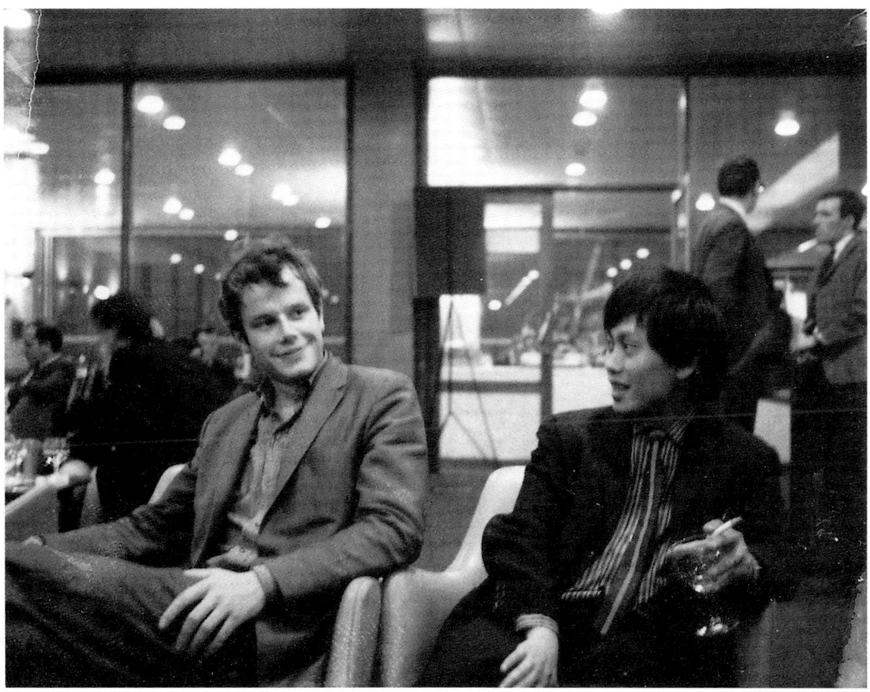

Guy Brett and David Medalla, Schiphol Airport, Amsterdam, 1964

point of view of existence is keyed to love. Not, of course, in the sentimental sense. What can it be other than love of experience, for its own sake, for its illuminating moment, that sponsors Medalla's boundless activity in the realm of the imagination. To put it more distinctly: although the writings of Georges Bataille, for whom, Octavio Paz wrote, "eroticism, death, and sin are interchangeable signs whose combinations repeat the same meaning again and again, with terrifying monotony: the nothingness of man, his irremediable abjection", are appallingly *en vogue* these days, spirits such as Medalla's do not give way. Breton's far more fecund notion of generation, through love, of imaginative life is consonant with his nature, to which he has remained true – another surrealist aspect of ethics.

Brett rightly sees Medalla as a bellwether – an inexhaustible imaginative artist whose clamorous existence has made its mark. Even more important, he has shown that Medalla's oeuvre in various periods has corresponded to significant way-stations on the well-travelled 20th century road of vanguard art. Although Brett appropriately demurs at the thought of 'placing' Medalla in history, it becomes apparent as we wander through this animated book that Medalla has a knack of appearing onstage precisely when a major turning point occurs. And, in fact, Brett has 'placed' him where he belongs: in that story of modern art that tells of liberty of imagination. Bravo Guy. Bravissimo David.

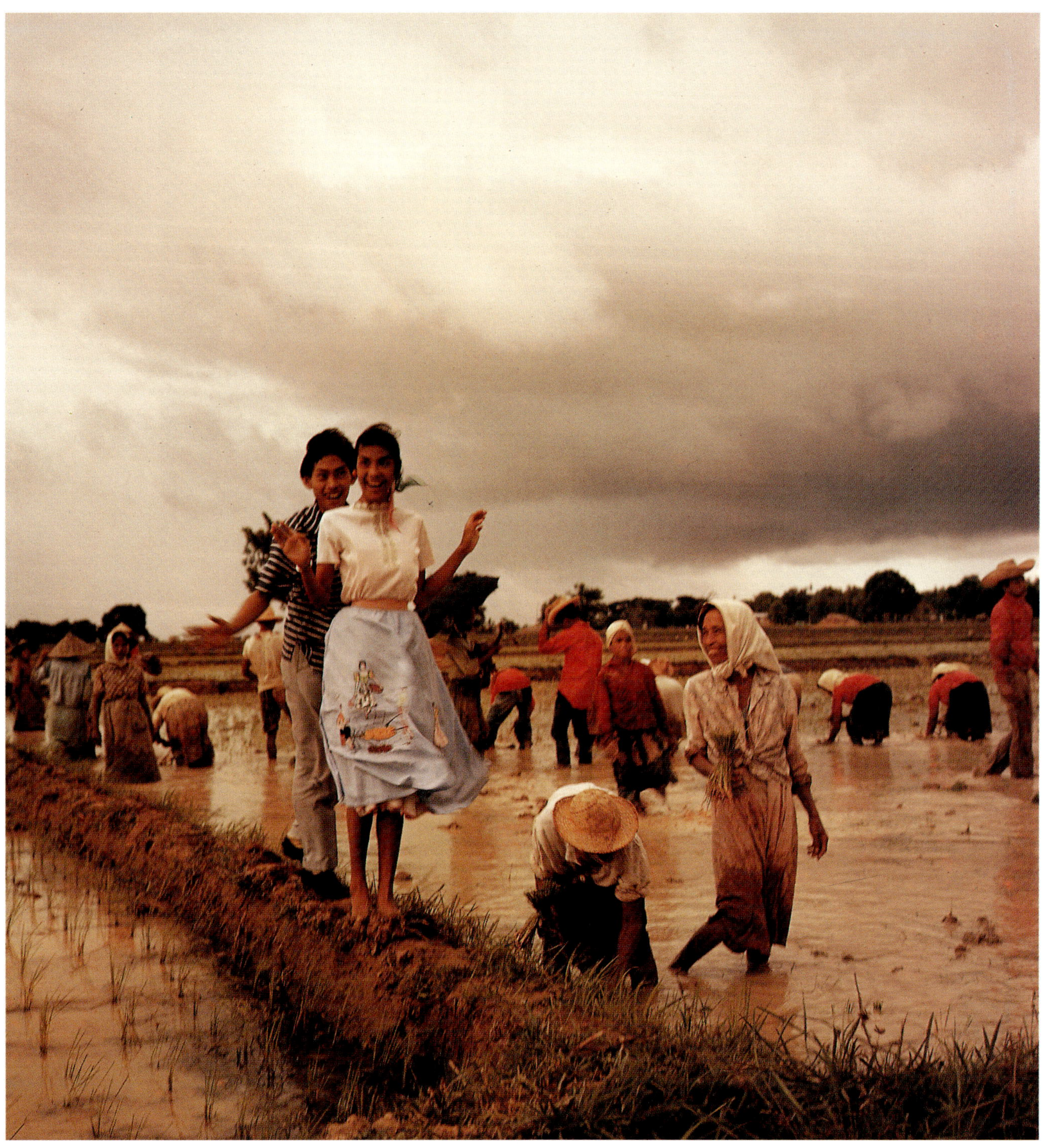

Impromptu before rice-planters, with Sonia Monillas, Rizal province, Phillipines, 1959

One

A Certain Way of Life

I have always thought the circumstances of my first meeting with David Medalla were both amusingly incongruous and strangely prophetic. I was seventeen and had been invited with my younger brother Sebastian to a dance at the village hall in Rotherfield Greys, near Henley-on-Thames in Oxfordshire. The party was in honour of the Yale University rowing team who were competing in the Henley Regatta, and was given by a family of near neighbours of ours, the Goyders. It so happened that David and Dan Goyder both attended a scholarship camp in the USA (Camp Rising Sun at Rhinebeck, New York, to be exact), and, since apart from a handful of relatives, he knew few people in England, having arrived only weeks previously from the Philippines, via East Africa, Egypt and France, decided to look him up. The Goyder family brought David to the dance. He gave a performance at the party, but what I remember best about the evening was his scintillating conversation about English poetry. I was attempting to produce poems at the time. His knowledge of all my favourites – Blake, Keats, Shelley, Crabbe, Hopkins, Eliot – astonished me. It is a very particular pleasure when someone from the other side of the world talks warmly and insightfully about your own culture. Only later I discovered he knew as much about French culture, and many others, as he did about English, and as much about art, music, dance and theatre as he did about literature.

I soon realised he was dividing his time between England and France. As soon as the stay allowed on his English visa expired he would go to France, and when his French visa expired, return again to England. Expiring and renewed visas have been a permanent feature of Medalla's life. As Petti Benitez says, "however unsettling, this situation created for Medalla the opportunity of opening his art to a breadth of ideas and possibilities not easily accessible to artists bound to, say, the London or St. Ives tradition."[1] The apparently incongruous circumstances of our meeting were a foretaste of the way Medalla has, throughout his life, made his own connections and artistic manifestations, often far from the routine channels of the art world, and how, with all his intimate knowledge of English culture, he has fostered an internationalism in England which has gone far beyond the narrow, nationalist priorities of the official British art establishment.

To understand this it is necessary to see his artistic work, the main subject of this book, in an indivisible, interwoven relationship with his activities as a catalyst and publicist of the work of others. The various strands are so intertwined that they can

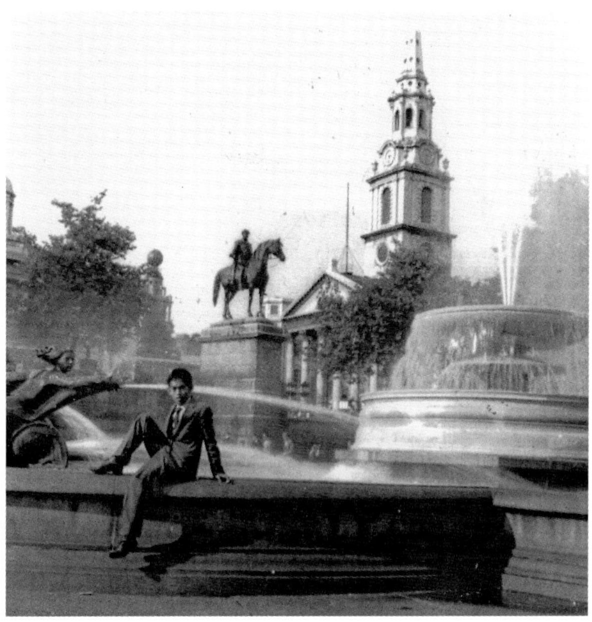
Trafalgar Square, 1960.

only be called a way of life rather than a single profession. Medalla's role as catalyst has always been carried on informally and individually, sometimes in partnership with one other artist and sometimes expanding and cohering into the formation of a group. Each group 'initiated' by Medalla has been unerringly at the vanguard of its time: Signals London, the centre for art/science experimentation and kinetics in the mid-1960s; The Exploding Galaxy, a live-together, work-together creative commune of the late 1960s; Artists for Democracy, an artists' group identified with a broad range of liberation movements in the 1970s; and in the 1980-90s various temporary, international clusters of multimedia artists such as Octetto Ironico, the Baroque Buddha Brotherhood, Synoptic Realists and the Mondrian Fan Club.

Monographs such as this concentrate on a person's 'production', as if it could be separated in time and space from that same person's 'reception', their intense pleasure taken in other people's work, company, and so forth. This convention is particularly inadequate to Medalla, who has always so unrestrainedly and energetically enjoyed, criticised, analysed and encouraged other people's art, whether in the visual arts, dance, poetry, theatre, music, film, or whatever (one could perhaps put this more broadly by saying he has encouraged the artist in others). He has often said he would just as soon be a collector, connoisseur or patron as an artist. 'Love of art' is a vapid phrase. But it is hard to imagine a person to whom it applies more genuinely, amounting to a 24-hour-a-day passion. To be an impresario of the arts is held in high esteem by Medalla, and he has been determined to live as if it was possible for him, within whatever material conditions he found himself, however precarious. If modern societies come low down on the scale of the genuine, disinterested value they give to artistic expression (compared to, say, ancient India, where great figures were remembered, even by ordinary people, as patrons of the arts before they were remembered as successful soldiers or conquerors), nevertheless there is always creative energy bubbling to be let loose. In this role Medalla himself appears as an incongruous mixture of Renaissance-type man and marginal, transnational nomad. There is nothing forced about the image. It is clearly a natural extension of his conviction that all creative work is dialogic, and that every person is multi-faceted.

The same principles apply to what can more specifically be called his artistic work. David Medalla has never represented one style, one problem, one current in art. He has managed to be both elegantly, even ironically, detached from art movements and at the same time to be deeply into them – an ambivalence by which he has maintained his intense individuality and mobility of mind. His work is itself partly a search for a way in which insights may resist institutionalisation and remain at their most active, most able to inspire others. This is why his work has often been ephemeral, or taken the form of 'propositions'. He coined the phrase "*cosmic propulsions*" to describe his artistic propositions.

Although he has worked in Britain for more than thirty years (and for periods in other countries such as France, Holland, Germany, Italy, Spain and the USA) Medalla is not readily perceived as belonging to the British, nor for that matter to the Filipino, art world. This again can be seen as something he might welcome, another outcome of his attempt to find for his work something other than a commercial or museum destiny. Today, all art institutions are structured along national lines. There are as yet no art institutions which represent the mobility, physical and mental, which many artists in fact live today, institutions which do not attempt to tie such mobility to a national identity. 'Not belonging' can be seen as an accursed state, or a blessing, according to a psychic orientation which goes very deep. Medalla, for his part, has never seen displacement from one's native land as a state of exile: "I've always felt at home wherever I was, wherever I found myself at any given moment of time."

How has this affected his outlook as an artist? The position of the artist vis-à-vis the institutions of the art world, and contemporary society in general, is often described in terms of a dilemma between two antagonistic alternatives. Either artists adopt a marginal position in the face of an increasingly consumerist and standardised society, proclaiming their freedom and refusing to be bound by the logic of the art market, in which case they lose any possibility of having a public; or they claim their place within the mainstream, they accept the position and the identity given to the artist in capitalist society, and risk losing their critical independence and freedom to innovate. Naturally, by presenting reality in terms of polarised opposites, such an analysis assumes that an artist can only be part of the mainstream of society by submitting to the art market, just as it assumes the artist cannot be independent and also have a public. The terms themselves imply fixed, exclusive positions. One suspects, in any case, that 'marginal' is a designation given to the artist by the institutions and not by the artists themselves.

Along with this designation go associations of deprivation, eccentricity, even amateurishness. From the point of view of the artist the freedom sought is not an idealist abstraction, nor a retreat from society; on the contrary it is a positive thing, a lived, experimental practice and the invention of new conceptual categories which connect across barriers that are supposed to divide society and intellectual life. For the artist it is an aspiration towards greater movement, rather than fulfilling the rather narrow obligations and proprieties of the art circuit, which is administered increasingly according to bureaucratic norms, much the same as any other institution or corporation.

◆   ◆   ◆

For nearly 40 years, David Medalla has worked more or less outside this system. He has had exhibitions but never signed up with a dealer or gallery. He has collaborated with artists in many countries without being inscribed into a national art history. He has performed in venues from the most venerable to the most marginal (for him, the

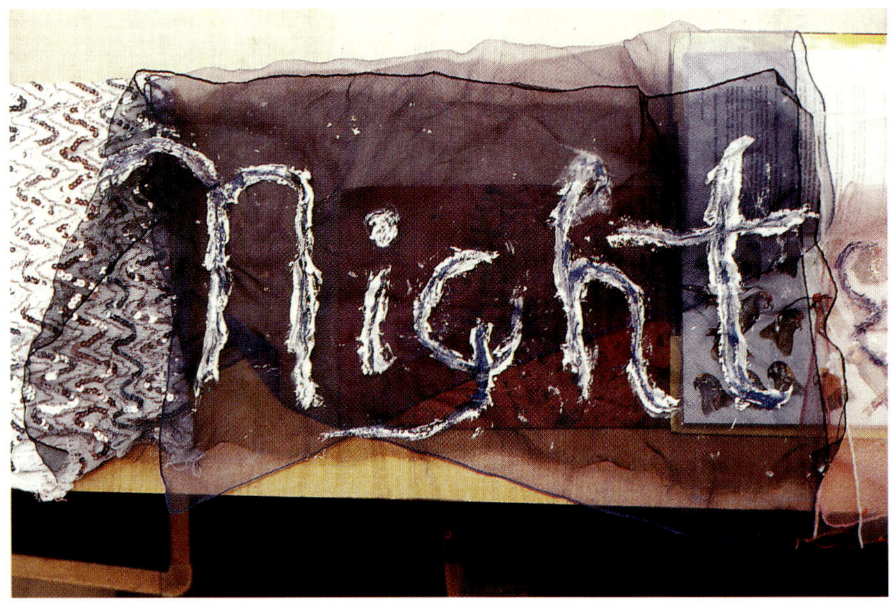

Night and Day, kinetic scroll collage, First Festival of Performance Art, Bracknell, England, 1983. (continues to page 25)

kudos of one is not threatened by the other).[2] Not as fluidly as he would like, of course, and not without sacrifice. He has lived and worked with whatever possibilities were available, but nevertheless exerting a considerable influence. There is as yet no term 'independent art' as there is 'independent film', perhaps because art has no mass commercial production base, no 'Hollywood', as film does. Nevertheless, artists are increasingly finding themselves dependent on winning the approval of the art world equivalent of movie backers and distributors: museum directors, dealers, sponsors, media, funding bodies, etc. Outside the system one survives by mysterious means. Medalla's methods have had something in common with those that Maya Deren, one of the pioneers of independent film in the USA in the 1950s, described as the key to freedom in film making: "To use one's imagination as a means of independence."[3]

It is only later that a name may be found for such a use of time, and an experimental practice may be recognised and cohere into a new definition of 'the artist'. Trying to write about David Medalla, Rasheed Araeen has said, "is like putting an elephant in a bird cage".[4] Once, after printing excerpts from the statements of various artists in the first issue of *Signals*, 1964, Medalla ended by adding his own comment: "As for me, I do not subscribe to any theory. I have no theories, only a certain way of life." He quoted Walt Whitman: "Do I contradict myself? Very well then, I contradict myself. I am large, I contain multitudes." The nomadic and

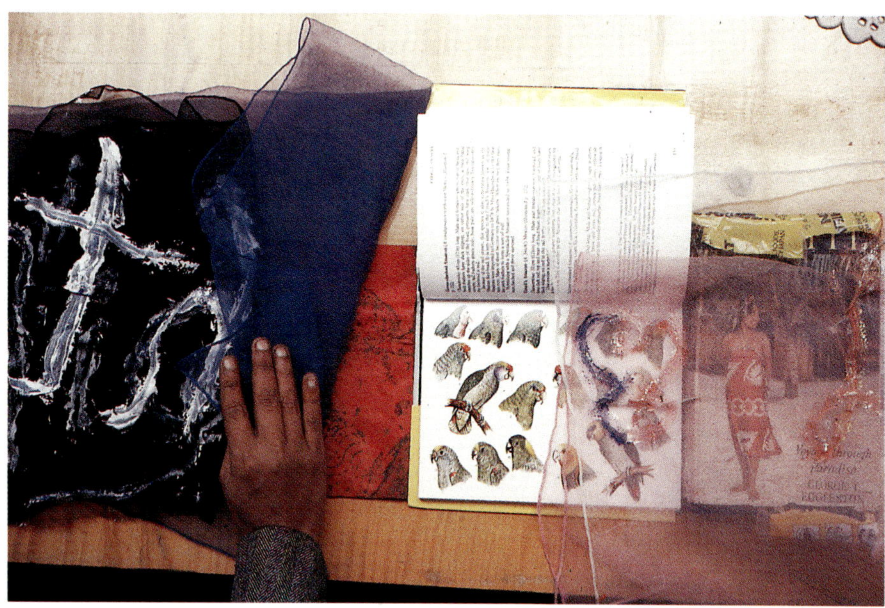

improvisatory pattern of Medalla's life, and the aesthetic and philosophical principles of his work, are both expressions of a vision of continuous movement, flux and change. Art and life as process. This, I believe is where Medalla's great originality lies, both as an artist and a person. The investigation of the contemporary cultural reality, from a somewhat ironic position of not-belonging and yet not feeling alienated, by which one becomes acutely aware of the mass of contradictory human phenomena which are "consciously or unconsciously coexisting"[5] – at the level of nations and of neighbourhoods – links up with the artist's investigations into the transformations of material. These material experiments are in turn rediscovered in the social world.

Objects have both a material existence and a socially conventional sign: for the artist neither is fixed and immutable. The unlikely, incongruous aspects of our first meeting were simply an instance of an endlessly proliferating web of kinetic connections. In reading the artist's interviews, one continuously finds that descriptions of the work he is doing are prefaced by some ambulatory experience. As for example:

I was listening to some kids at a Bracknell bus stop... I was hanging around near the Audubon Ballroom in Manhattan... I was walking one day near Astor Place and was handed a flyer...[6] I came across a photograph in a crumpled magazine thrown away on a skip near the Centre Pompidou...[7] I was visiting a fortuneteller in Montmartre and I was a bit early, so I went down to the Place Clichy to watch a striptease show...[8] I took the night train from Rome and they give you a disposable blue bedsheet to sleep on, a beautiful blue bedsheet which I wound round myself as a turban and used next day in my performance *Piranesi and the Mother Scorpion*.[9]

Sometimes, into this endlessly expanding narrative of people and things, enters a celebrity. The saga of Medalla's 'chance encounters', many of them in the street, with such figures as Edith Piaf, Wanda Landowska, Pablo Neruda, Gaston Bachelard, Caresse Crosby, Salvador Dali, James Baldwin, Lee Miller, Louise de Vilmorin, Jean Genet, Marlon Brando, Man Ray, Meret Oppenheim, Walt Disney, Louis Aragon, Gloria Swanson, Jorge Luis Borges, Edward James, William Burroughs, Elias Canetti or James Dean, is told in various interviews and reminiscences. Some see these as tall stories. More likely they are simply a spin-off of the immense ease with which Medalla gets talking with strangers (he once told me he reckoned he met twelve new people a day). He is able to place them quickly, by some elastic circuits of memory, in the complex web of their relationships. This is sometimes a surprise even to the people themselves, since they may have only a hazy idea of their own real connections. The temptation for digression is enormous (is it digression or the desire to reveal a little more of the web?). Interviewers always have a job to keep their discussions with Medalla on course:

[Walt Disney] spoke to me at the Café de la Paix while I was busy sketching the passers-by in front of the Opéra. I told Walt Disney I loved his film of *Alice in Wonderland*. He said the film met censorship troubles because of the scene with the caterpillar smoking opium through a hookah. I learned from him that the scriptwriter of the film was Aldous Huxley, author of *The Doors of Perception*. I told Walt Disney I also loved the film *Pinocchio*, especially the section with the Swiss mechanical clocks. Walt Disney told me there was a small museum of automata in Neuilly just outside Paris which I should visit. He gave me the address and then paid for my coffee...[10]

Today, information technologists are talking of their 'superhighways' and 'world wide webs', computer networks where, supposedly, every piece of information is linked to every other and instantly accessible. They speak of 'navigating through' it. I sometimes think that Medalla has operated for years this kind of web, with the difference that instead of dealing with conventional facts and already-established relationships, his idea of navigation is to open oneself to the unexpected and the random. This, for him, is the only way to catch a glimpse of the 'whole' which is invisible and which our knowledge, even if brought together in one vast, immediately-accessible store, cannot help us to know. For Medalla the momentary insight brought about by chance is the connecting thread between lived-life and the work of art. He makes this clear in a concentrated statement, amounting almost to his credo as an artist, written in Holland in 1985:

I personally believe that the invisible is the totality of what we call life in all its manifest forms: the unity of the microcosmos and the macrocosmos. We apprehend this unity only at certain inspired moments. These moments come to us in random ways: by way of memory (whereby we get in touch once more with our past) and by way of intuition (whereby we make a bridge into our future). Because we live only in the moment, 'past' and 'future' will always be invisible to us.

Art works can sometimes be the substance and sometimes the shadow of our varied and various inspired moments. These moments can come to us in dreams, reveries or during our awakened hours, they can be self-generated or they can be provoked by external factors: by an object, a person or an event. They can even be provoked not only by the presence but also by the absence of these things; witness Proust and Mallarmé in literature, Mondrian and Malevich in the visual arts.

I believe our capacity to generate inspired moments (or to be inspired by the moment) contracts and expands in proportion relative to, consonant with, our ability to love and to our individual 'luck' to be loved or unloved.

By opening my mind to the random and chance events of existence, I have avoided, in the practice of my art, the cul-de-sac of formalism. In art, formalism substitutes atrophied schema (empty formulae) for the immediacy of the inspired moment, the free flow of dreams and reveries, and the fragrance of memory. In life, formalism imposes dogmas, in place of adventure and risks.[11]

David Medalla has conspicuously lived out this ideal. He has allowed himself the freedom, even perversity, to follow the inspiration of the moment in day-to-day existence, and to follow up many different lines of enquiry in the problematics of art. As a result his work has changed radically during his lifetime and at first sight has an almost chaotic diversity. Ideas pour out, some intensively developed, others abandoned; some surviving in physical objects, drawings, collages, photos or pieces of writing, others lost. Many ideas have been left at a rudimentary stage of execution, where another artist would have gone on to polish and present them to great advantage. In all this the purposeful rejection of a conventional artistic career is quite evident since Medalla is as aware as anyone that the institutions of the art world prefer a product which can be clearly identified, packaged and marketed. He realised that this kind of simplistic demand is in the end self-defeating and produces the conditions of its own boredom.

Therefore, as if in subtle recognition of this irony, Medalla has always clearly and provocatively identified both his work and himself. It is simply that the labels have changed so many times they have appeared at first sight to be capricious and even self-contradictory. During the period of his 'biokinetics', Medalla liked to call himself a 'hylozoist' ('one who believes that matter is alive', following a definition of the pre-Socratic Greek philosophers). During the period of the Exploding Galaxy he became a Buddhist. When the Galaxy ended, his extended travels in Asia and Africa politicised

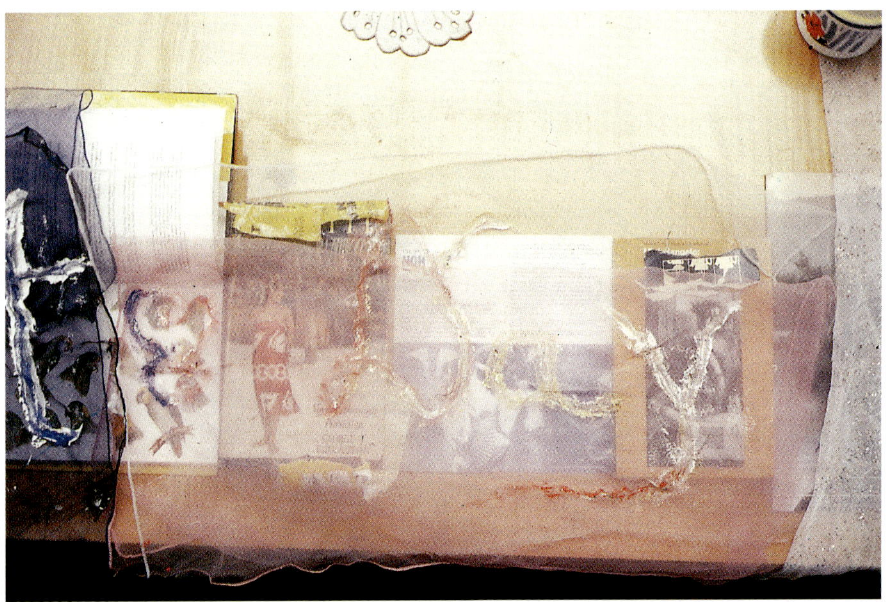

Night and Day

him, and an intense involvement with Marxism characterised his participatory works during the Artists for Democracy period of the Seventies. The performances and paintings of the 1980s were the productions of a 'Synoptic Realist', and most recently, as if in flagrant contradiction of his Marxism, Medalla has described himself as a 'Transcendental Hedonist'. Do such chameleon changes represent more than the artist's desire to be one step ahead of those who would wish to define him?

To impose a schema on the 'chaos' of Medalla's life and art is exactly what he himself set out to avoid. And therefore any ordering interpretation runs the risk of merely drawing attention to its own desire for tidiness and its poverty of imagination.

Nevertheless, it has long seemed to me that there was a compelling logic in the succession of changes that Medalla's work has passed through ('succession' is perhaps a misleading word since the changes or diversity have often been simultaneous). His work has played in a highly individual fashion around several movements in the recent history of art, and as it has done so, a thread has emerged of a coherently conducted investigation which keeps spreading its net according to a broader brief. There is one common identity between the Hylozoist, Buddhist, Marxist, Synoptic Realist and Transcendental Hedonist incarnations of the artist. All represent different aspects of a 'kinetic' vision. The connecting thread is essentially a dynamic one which sees reality in terms of multi-dimensionality and transformation. Not that this was planned, or

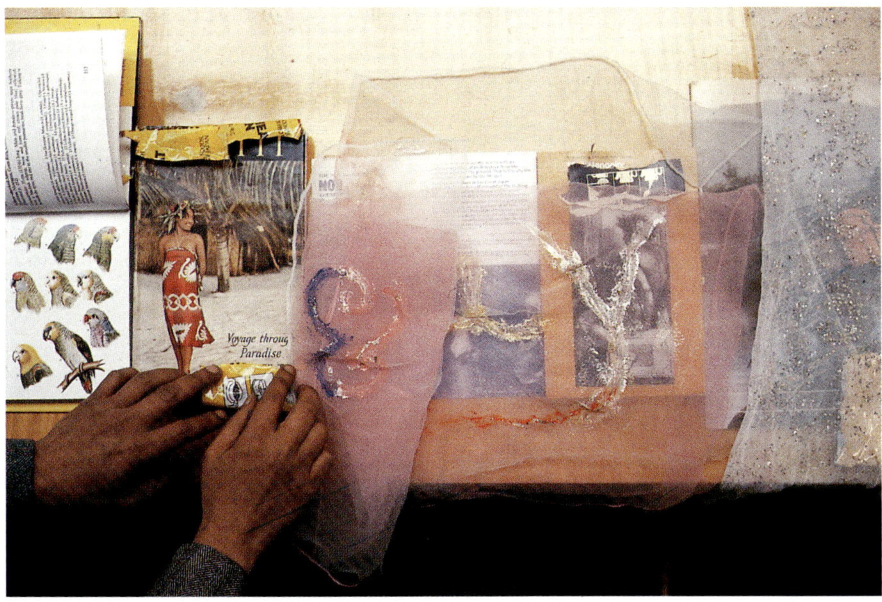

forseeable in advance. Medalla's approach has always been one of experiment based on personal experience, finding out for oneself rather than trusting to established or dogmatic truths.

Put in the most schematic terms, the chapters which follow divide Medalla's work into four main stages:

1. The period of kinetics, or 'biokinetics' to use the artist's own term, 1963-67. *The Bubble Machines*, 1963 on, *Sand Machine*, 1964, *Mud Machine*, 1964-67, etc. Concentrating on the relationship with nature in an elemental form. Natural processes and transformations as a means to

explore aesthetic experience and philosophical enigmas: the relationship between mechanical and organic rhythms, between order and chaos, between monumentality and ephemerality, between the artist's sense of beauty and random forms.

2. The period of participation art, 1967-76. Concentrating on the relationship with other people, and the interaction of nature and culture, art and society. The kinetic model of growth, change and random form transferred from an elemental to a social field of reference. 'Participation-Production' works: *A Stitch in Time*, 1968, *Down With the Slave Trade!*, 1971, *Games of the Sea and Tides*, 1972, *Porcelain Wedding*, 1973, *Alchemical Wedding*, 1975, *Eskimo Carver*, 1977, etc. Propositions which allow, which grow from, an infinite number of contributions from an infinite number of people. These works explore the possibility of interplay between phenomena traditionally considered, in western society at least, as firmly opposed: the creative artist and passive spectator, communal and individual production, instrumentality and fantasy (play), work and leisure, the part and the aggregate, the 'street' and the 'museum' views of culture, and so on. Playful analogies of social basics: production, exchange, festivity, marriage, enslavement. Raw materials of these collective works were either the most ancient and primary (earth/clay, thread), or contemporary, all-pervading and worthless (refuse and waste).

3. The period of performance (the mid 1970s up to today). A move from centering on other people towards himself, his place in the world. The staging of himself – artist, individual – in an everchanging masquerade touching history, culture, identity and sexuality. His relationship to other artists past and present, to places, to friends/lovers, and the interweaving of the subjective with the objective conditions, contingencies, constraints and freedoms within which people live. Again, the 'kineticism' consists in the crossing of inherited conceptual barriers which divide experience. The performances and impromptus propose a fluid structure of 'chance' meetings bringing together past and present, the living and dead, the mundane and cosmic, great art and kitsch, male and female, local and distant, the possible and impossible, etc. Hundreds of performances given all over Europe, in Africa and Asia, and in New York: composite collages combining painting, sculpture, music and theatre within the limits of his own resources and nomadic lifestyle. Development of the concept of Synoptic Realism linking his work in performance with his painting.

4. Painting. This cannot be confined by a period since Medalla has always continued to paint, draw and make collages. However, a more intense involvement with painting began in the early 1980s and has continued up to today, perhaps in conscious contra-distinction, as well as in secret affinity, with performance. The 'ephemerality' of performance may paradoxically be complemented by the fixing of the transitory in painting. Enigmatic relationship between stasis and kinesis. Persistence of the historical genres of painting - still-life, portrait, interior, landscape - in the face of the flux of contemporary life. Cycles of paintings: *Parables of Friendship*, 1985, *Filipiniana*, 1986, *New York Epiphanies*, early 1990s, the paintings celebrating Mondrian, 1994-5, and individual works: *A Prophecy*, 1989, *Mr Morley's Harp Shop*, 1989, *The Phoenix's Breakfast*, 1991, *Orpheus Enchanting the Animals with his Songs*, 1993, etc.

In these encapsulated descriptions, relationships between opposed pairs keep constantly coming up. There is a huge range of them, and they arise only to have the rigid dichotomy between them subtly questioned. Each phase of Medalla's work can be seen as a different way of approaching 'the multiple levels of reality'. Although one approach can never tell the whole story, each continues to reveal new connections with the others. The different philosophies and personas David Medalla has adopted at different periods can also be seen as facets of the same "desire and pursuit of the whole".[12] The Hylozoist and the Buddhist are apparently expressions of opposed conceptions of reality originating in the West and East. Yet there are considerable affinities between the Heraclitian and the Buddhist-Taoist notions of the universal flux (the bigoted idea of an irreconcilable difference between East and West was largely an invention of western empire-builders intent on proving their right to rule the rest of the world, and erroneously identifying their theories with ancient Greece).

Some of Medalla's own 'isms' are combinations of opposites. He began to call himself a Transcendental Hedonist in the 1970s, partly to counter the self-denying puritan streak in left-wing politics, and in British culture generally (he had already said in the 1960s that, for him, kinetic art produced the possibility of "making people sensuously alive once more"). And yet, at the same time, the 'transcendental' part of the label suggests that a true work of art aims for something beyond sheer sensuous beauty. In fact we keep coming back to a dialectical play, or point of dynamic equilibrium, between supposedly exclusive categories.

So far this dialectic has been traced as the thread of a kinetic vision running through the chronological development of Medalla's work. Yet it also concerns the nature, or concept, of 'a work'. The idea of a tidy line of discrete objects constituting the work of David Medalla would be absurd. What has been labelled as a work is often itself only a stage of some larger concept which is essentially unpredictable and open-ended. It is hard to say if it has been, or could be, finished. In fact, Medalla's are by nature unfinished propositions. This distinction is more than simply sophistry. Take, for example, Medalla's *Eskimo Carver* (p. 103,110-117).

The photographs that survive record some of the knives visitors made out of local garbage. This part of the work is itself endless, since "there is no end to people coming in and making knives". Its authorship is fluid, not only as regards the numbers and identity of its makers but also its physical limits in time and space. The participatory part of *Eskimo Carver* was interwoven with other parts which have not been recorded: the artist's drawings and transcriptions of Eskimo poetry, a performance, entitled *Alaska Pipeline*, about the despoliation of the Arctic, and documentary exhibits. Medalla planned, but did not execute, further transformations of the multiplicity of people's knives. One scheme was to work them into a computer-generated synthesis of a single, vast 'cosmic' knife to be projected into the night sky. Medalla has always defended the 'process' nature of his work, maintaining that its real vitality lies there and not in any final product. For him, *Eskimo Carver* was a "cosmic propulsion". This is his generic term for many of his works: something that propels the mind and imagination and that links the everyday with the universal. It may function as a sign or a metaphor. It may even propose in words the making of something which it is not necessary to make, only to imagine (I can hear David's often-repeated "Why bother?" when faced with an artist's laborious fabrication of something which would have been better left as a written note or an idea). On the other hand, a 'propulsion' may be very much connected with 'making', as *Eskimo Carver* was. At one level this work was a brilliant re-evaluation of the early modernist polemic against identifying art with the unique and hand-made. This in turn had created a fashion for the mechanical, the 'ordered by telephone', and the conceptual. *Eskimo Carver*

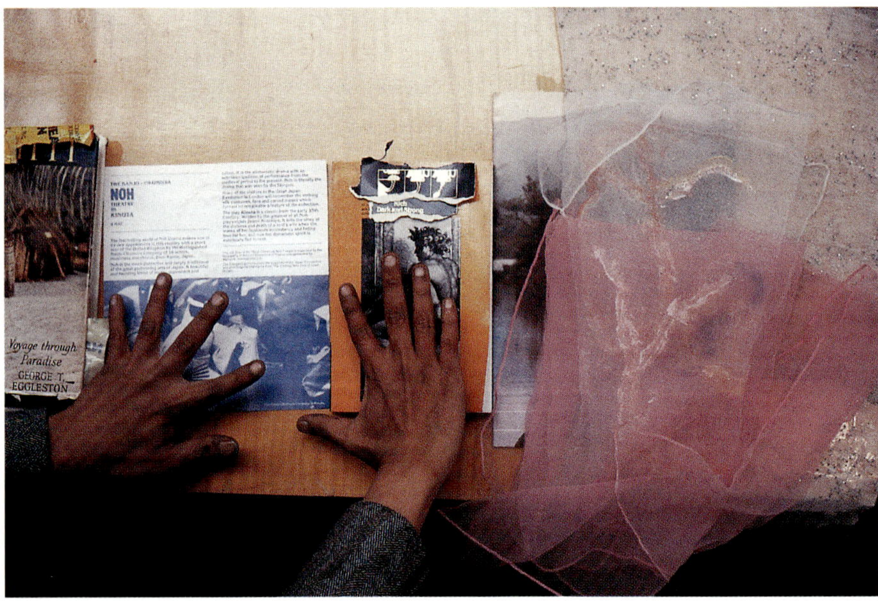

Night and Day

returned to the artisanal only to expose again, in a new and expanded way, the relativity of the whole question of choice, taste, uniqueness and multiplicity.

To make one further point about *Eskimo Carver* here: the titles people gave their knives, and wrote on the wall, were as important as the objects themselves. This suggests the close relationship which has always existed in Medalla's work between the literary and the visual. It would not be unusual for him to use a literary conceit to play against the intractability of material, the inescapable coordinates of present time and space. He would also, in the contrary sense, bring poetic dreams down to the most humble thrown-away material object. In the *New Projects* and the *MMMMM.....Manifesto* of his kinetic period, for example (p.60-1), literary licence became a means of wittily affirming the agility of imagination, and of mocking the rather pedestrian seriousness of some proposals by kinetic artists for linking art and science. Later, the titles of his performances are often poems in themselves. But then Medalla's dual visual/literary identity goes back to his earliest days.[13]

◆   ◆   ◆

When asked why he first came to Europe, David has always answered: "to retrace the footsteps of Rimbaud". On his first journey to Europe, which ended in England in

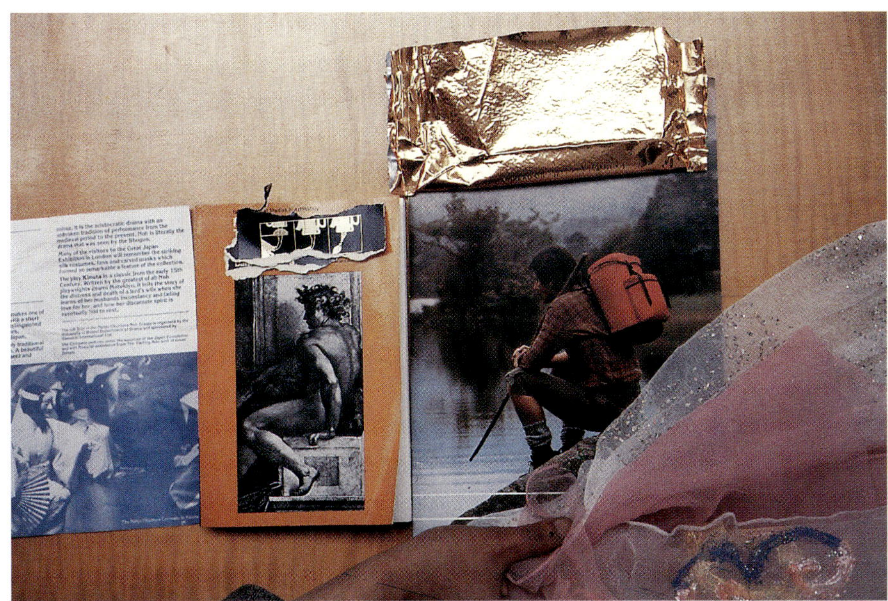

1960, he stopped at Djibouti, at Addis Ababa in Ethiopia and at Aden, where Rimbaud worked as an importer/exporter and explorer after he abandoned poetry. He also passed through Marseilles, visiting the Hôpital de l'Immaculé Conception where Rimbaud died. A few months later he visited Charleville in north-east France, Rimbaud's birthplace, even staying in a room in which the poet had lived as a boy. Aside from loving his poetry, Medalla believes Rimbaud, in the conduct of his life, reached a "visionary stage". It took a generation or two for this to become clear. "In his relationship with Verlaine, he gave the first tentative signs that two men can share real equality and camaraderie. Before that it was only a father with his son or a master with

David Cortez Medalla Jr.
Little Boy With Big Ideas

DAVID Cortez Medalla Jr. parried all questions, some he thought inane ("What is your idea of girls?") some too generalized ("What is the world coming to?") with a deftness born of much practice. Students at the UP English 12 class he spoke before one whole hour recently had prepared themselves for a "genius." It is a word David

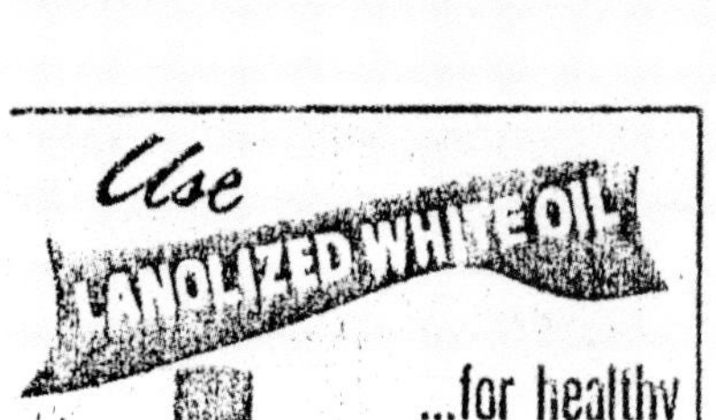

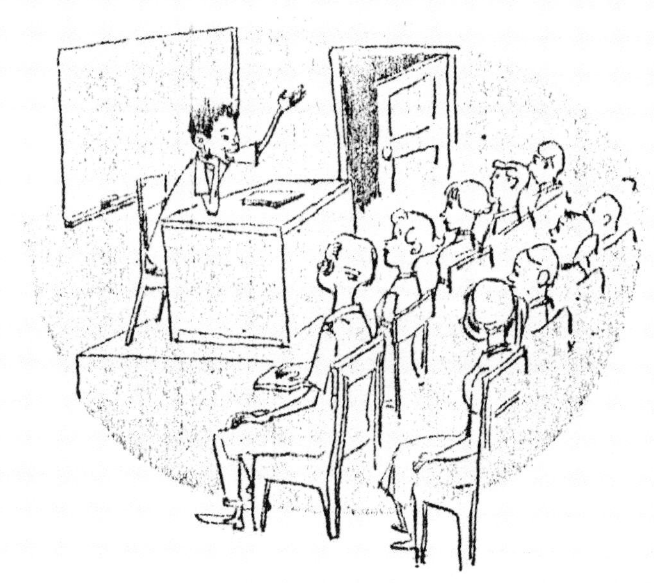

crinkles his nose at, he does   are talking about." His lit-

From the **Saturday Mirror**, Manila, 1954.
Opposite page from top: From the **Manila Chronicle**, Manila, 1952. Reading his poem about Arthur Rimbaud to Gaston Bachelard, Chartres Cathedral, 1960. Place Saint Michel, Paris, 1960.

his servant (even if affectionate as with Don Quixote and Sancho Panza). Rimbaud transcended the morals of his class and period. All of us are his children. It is foolish to try to destroy his myth. Myths are created by everybody. His life became an allegory of freedom."[14]

There must have also been an identification, on Medalla's part, of Rimbaud's childhood with his own. In one of his essays, the French philosopher Gaston Bachelard has written of Rimbaud as "...a childhood in search of a personal culture, a schoolboy prodigy determined to break with all schools"; and, further, that "Rimbaud's poetry... shows the possibility of a superchildhood, a childhood in possession of self-awareness".[15] Both sentences ring remarkably true of Medalla. They seem to pinpoint, on the one hand, his own history as a child prodigy and so called *enfant terrible* in the Philippines, and on the other, the particular tone of a 'self-aware childhood' – the mixture of innocence and sophistication, the playfulness, the easy accessibility which is never simplistic – which runs throughout his work.

Almost all my references to Medalla's childhood come from what the artist has told me, or told others in interviews. He grew up as part of a large, extended family. In

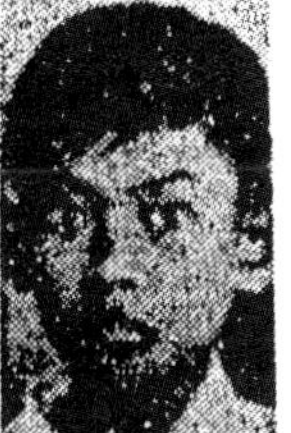

in order that the controversial reparations issue in the Dulles treaty draft, may be satisfactorily settled.

● Boy Sleeps, Finds Himself in Hong Kong

A high school student who went out to buy some textbooks fell asleep in one of the cabins of the SS President Wilson last Saturday and woke up later to find himself in Hong Kong, returned to Manila aboard a PAL plane.

D. Medalla

David Medalla. Jr.,12, of 18 A Mabini, a first year high school student of

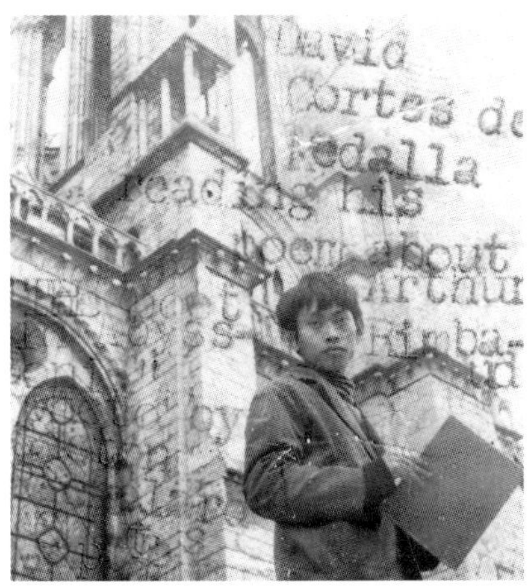

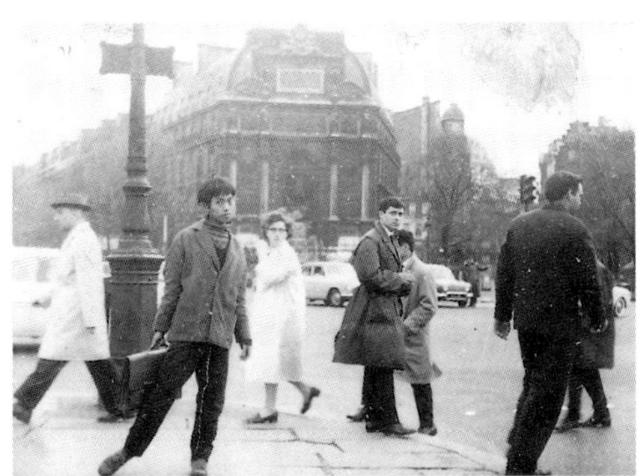

a Third World, pre-television, aristocratic ambience, the brothers and sisters entertained and partly educated one another. Poetry, painting, music, plays and puppet shows were made at home and performed in the garden of the big family house in the Ermita district of Manila. David describes his father as a jack-of-all-trades and a *bon viveur*, also a freethinker and strong believer in Philippine independence (he was a friend of Gregoria Agoncillo, one of the three sisters who sewed the Filipino flag in Hong Kong, when the government of the First Filipino Republic was in exile there). His mother maintained an inexhaustibly hospitable home. There was always food for the ceaseless flow of friends and acquaintances David brought to the house. Convinced of the fortunate nature of his birth and youth, David likes to see in himself a fusion of the different characters and origins of his parents: his father from Batangas, where "the Tagalog character is very sharp and analytical", and his mother from a peasant family in Cebu, with the "Visayan love of the good life, having *joie de vivre* (though hardworking), always interested in singing, dancing and eating".[16]

The family, consequently, had relatives all over the Philippines. Summer trips to stay with distant relatives were revelations of tropical nature. Unlike many Filipinos at the time, who either stayed close to home or went abroad, Medalla even as a child travelled extensively around his country. Manila too was an experience of shifting realities. It had long been one of the great *mestizo* cities, in human beings and in culture, a mixture of East and West. Influences from the long Spanish colonial domination – in European terms stretching from the period of the Baroque to that of Art Nouveau – vied with Chinese influences, and every aspect of Philippine life was becoming

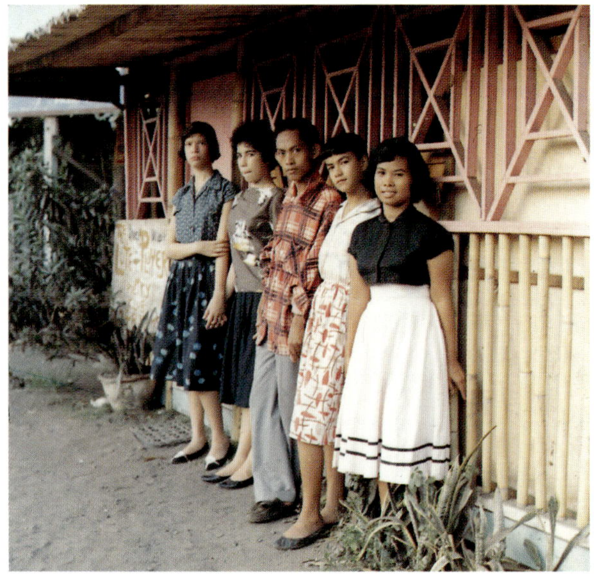

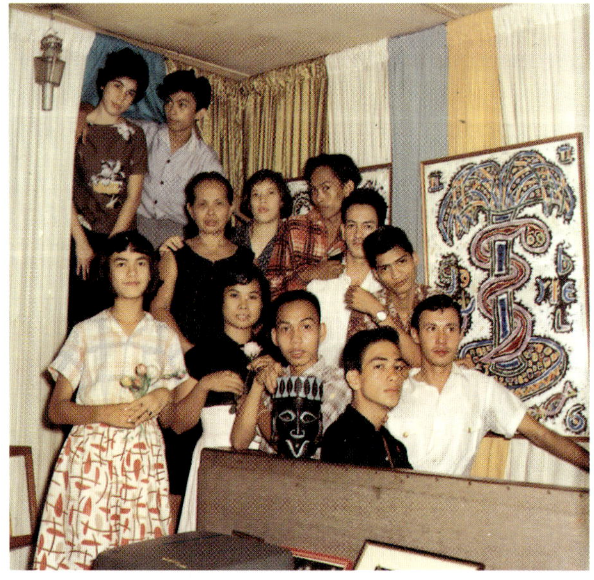

Outside and inside the Lute Player Poetry Club, founded by Medalla in Manila in the late Fifties. The artist appears in a check shirt. His mother is fourth from left in the lower photo.

increasingly Americanised. Like every other Third World capital, Manila was socially and economically polarised. Right next to the wealthy district of Ermita was a shanty-town which David crossed every day to take organ lessons in the Baroque church of San Agustin in Intramuros. The inhabitants were poor country people who had come to Manila looking for work. Immediately after the war the entire city was covered in ruined buildings, bombed by the American 'liberating' forces, and littered with pieces of abandoned military equipment. "A strange mixture of *la belle époque* and Kurt Schwitters", is how Medalla describes Manila in the late 1940s.[17] The port was crowded with foreign ships and the young Medalla liked to hang around there to practice his English and talk to sailors about their home countries.

A school friend's father was a captain on the American President Line and allowed the boys to roam over the ships when in port. One day, when he was ten or eleven, David fell asleep while reading in the library of the SS President Wilson. When he woke up the ship was already at sea on its way to Hong Kong. By the time he had been met at Hong Kong and escorted back to Manila, David found himself a celebrity. But he was also becoming famous for his precocity. His education had always been an erratic affair due to his father's dislike of religious schools and his own impulses. One of the schools he attended was in the

Mountain Province, St Mary's School, run by American missionaries in the town of Sagada. There he met an American anthropologist, H. Otley Beyer, who was studying the Igorots, a Filipino indigenous tribal mountain people. Medalla became fascinated, lived with the Igorots for a time, learned their language, and helped Otley Beyer translate some of their epic songs into English. This work brought him to the attention of the University of the Philippines (UP), and, in 1953, he was invited to give special lectures there by the then University President, Dr. Vidal A. Tan, and the Board of Regents. The exuberant and opinionated talks of "the boy genius", the poetry readings he organised in his blue bamboo studio, his flamboyant persona, were a staple of Philippine society columns in the early 1950s.

Arthur & Co, impromptu on the pavement outside an abandoned shop, Notting Hill Gate, London, 1993. Collection of the artist.

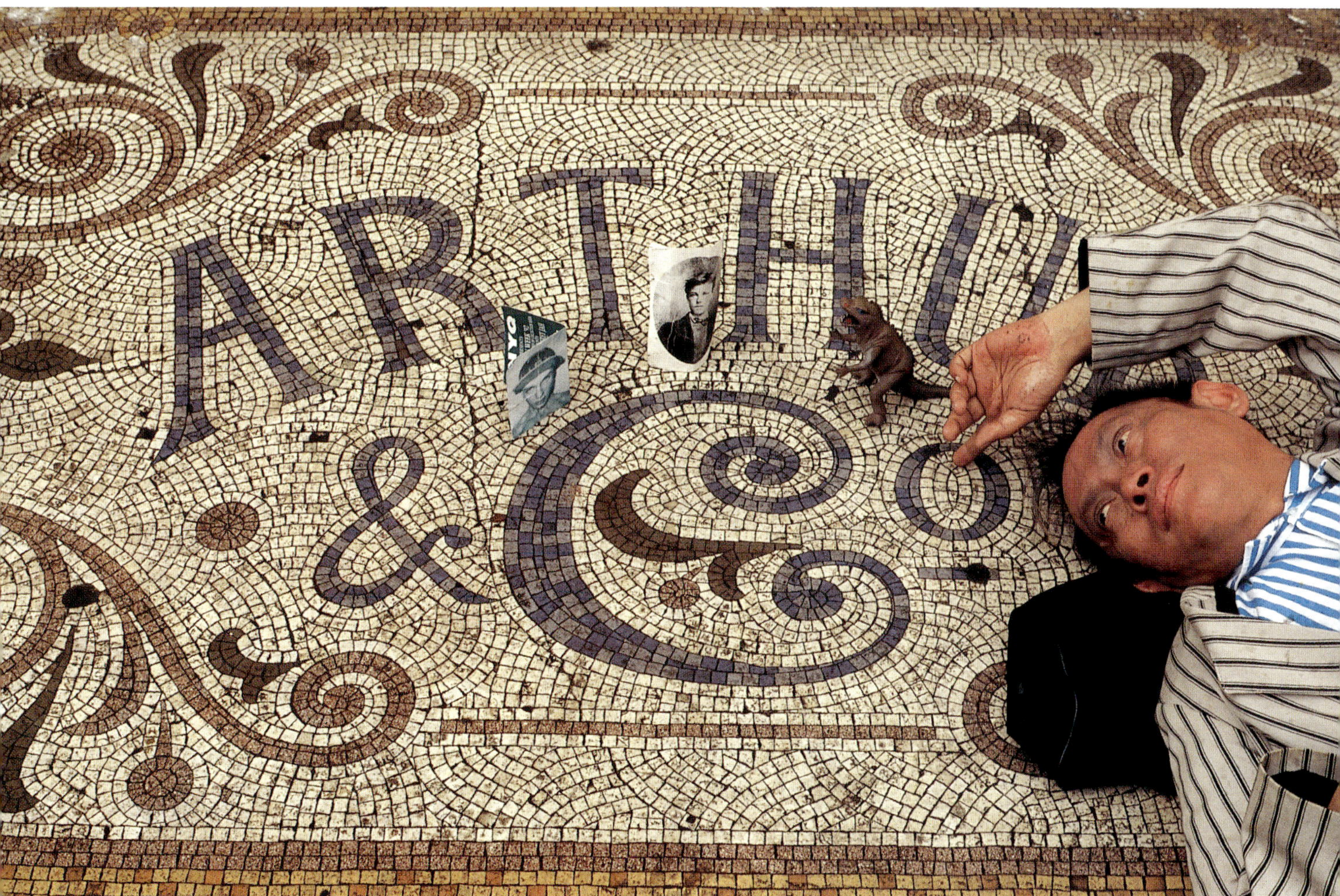

It was suggested by his UP professors that David attend Camp Rising Sun, at Rhinebeck, New York, a summer scholarship camp for internationally selected students, and this was how he first came to the US in 1954. After camp he was invited by Professor Mark van Doren to attend Columbia University in New York as a special student and he enrolled, aged 14, in the course on classical Greek literature under Moses Hadas. Truant as always, he spent much of his time in the cafés of Greenwich Village. In the Village he met Milton Avery, Franz Kline, Willem de Kooning, Mark Rothko, Ad Reinhardt and Jackson Pollock. Encouraged by José García Villa, the Filipino expatriate poet, by the young actor James Dean and by the American poet e. e. cummings, he started to paint in New York: the first great European, and indeed oriental, works of art were those he saw in New York museums at this time. Returning to the Philippines in the late 1950s, he attended lectures on art given by the painter and connoisseur Fernando Zobel de Ayala (later founder of the first Spanish museum of abstract art in the Casas Colgadas, the hanging houses of Cuenca, Spain), and made friends with the small Filipino avant-garde. Several of them were already followers of Abstract Expressionism. Although it was still an obscure experimental movement far away in New York, it was known to them through the Filipino painter Alfonso Ossorio, who was a friend of Jackson Pollock. In 1955 Medalla gave his first solo exhibition of paintings at La Cave d'Angely, a cultural centre he founded in Ermita, Manila.

Since arriving in Europe in 1960 Medalla has made only two return visits to the Philippines. Both were extensively reported in the local press and David's opinions on art, and especially on the Philippines cultural scene, were eagerly solicited. He plunged immediately into local controversies. A long interview (actually made in

Opposite: **On My First Sculpture**, collage, 1964. Collection of the artist.

Homage to Shih Tao, congealed rice from a saucepan, London, 1976.

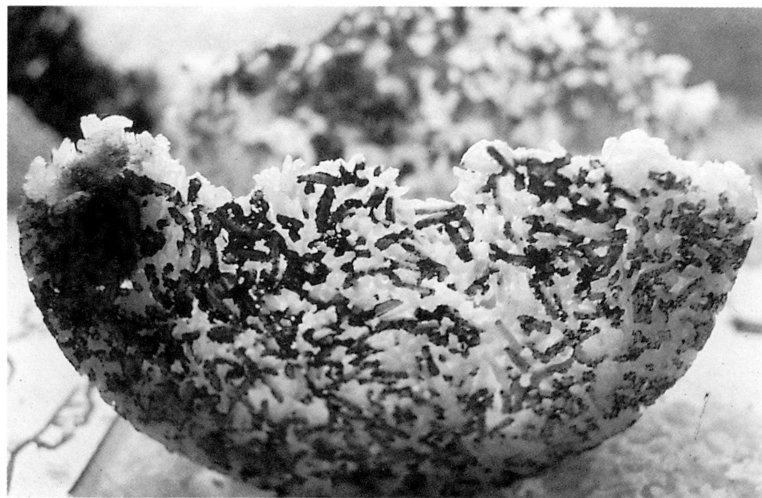

ON MY FIRST SCULPTURE

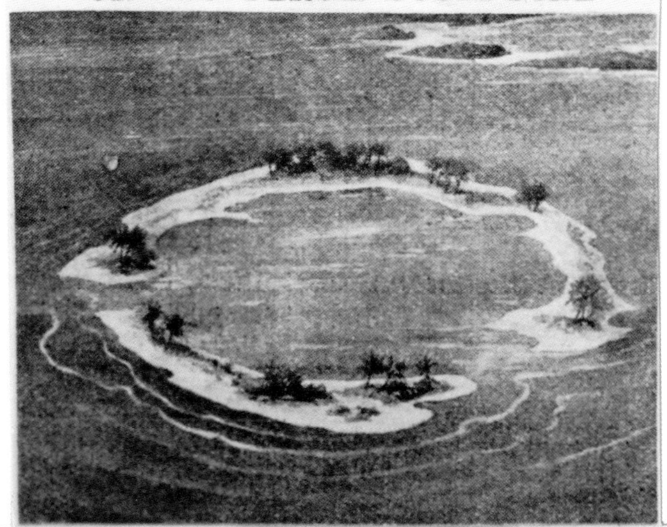

When I was 9 years old my family
went on holiday to Cebu, Philippines. We vacationed with my mother's relatives, half of whom
were farmers, while half were
fishermen, in the coastal town of
Dalaguete. While there I discovered a clay deposit in the barrio of Kawayan. I played with the
clay and made shapes of different
animals. One day I showed my clay
'sculptures' to an older cousin.
I told him, 'Wouldn't it be fun if
we can transform a small coral is
-land off the shore of our barrio
into a large sculpture shaped
like a tortoise (one of my clay
'sculptures)? My cousin greeted
my idea with great enthusiasm. In
no time he mobilised all our able
relatives who comprised practical
-ly the entire population of the
town and who were equally enthu-
siastic with my idea. Together we
cleaned the small coral island of
weeds. Afterwards we shaped it in
to a large sculpture resembling
my little clay tortoise. At high
tide the entire coral island-scul
-pture disappeared in the foam.
At night it glowed because of the
phosphorescent polyps and fishes.
This entire coral island-sculptu-
-re has since changed shapes many
times. It is now overgrown with
vegetation and palm trees. It belongs to all the people in the
town.

DAVID MEDALLA 1964.

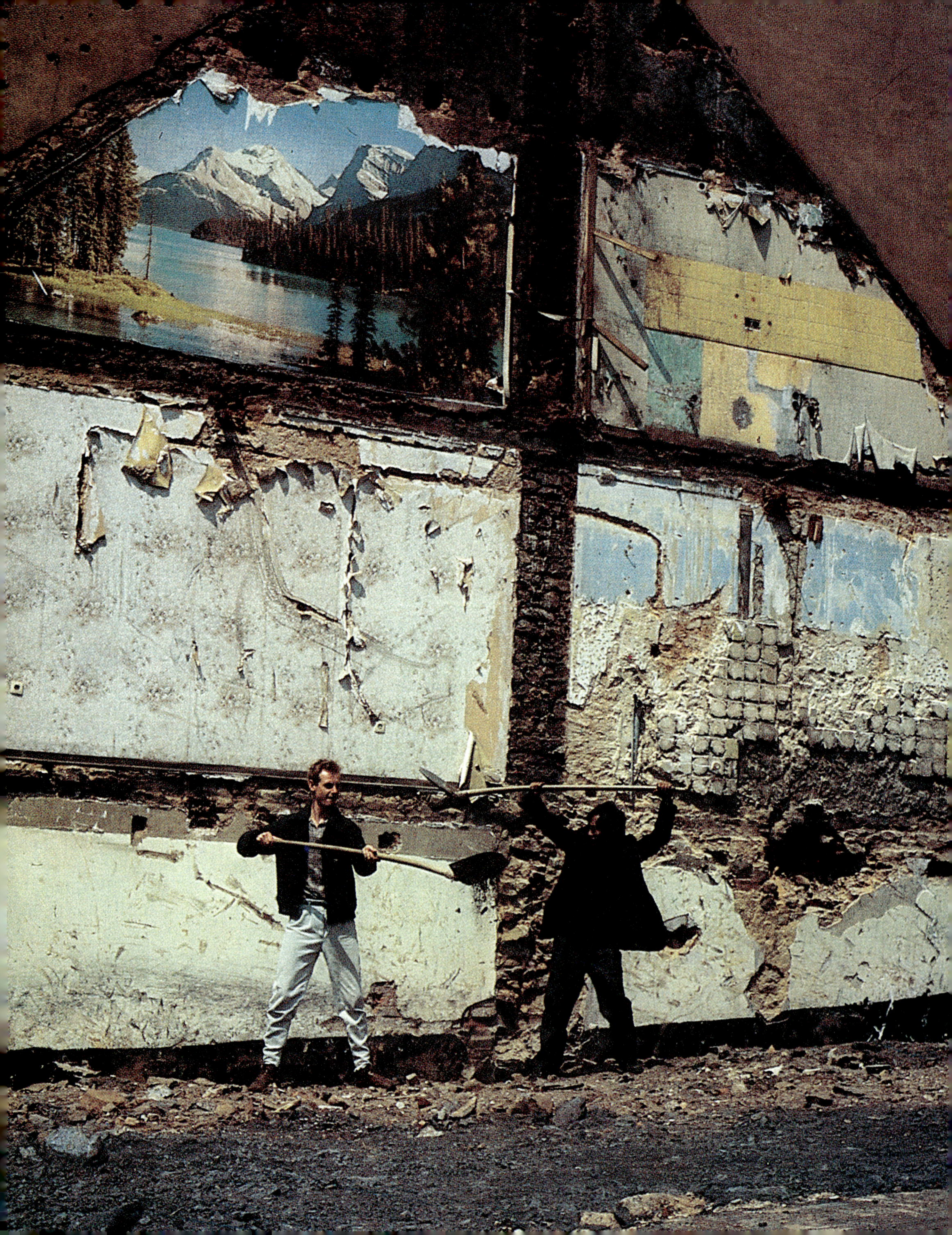

London in 1975) with the Filipino writer Cid Reyes, for his book *Conversations on Philippine Art*, caused Medalla to give some carefully considered reflections on the paradoxes – both the liberating and the crippling aspects – of cultural identity. Again, in New York in the early 1990s, asked to write a weekly column for the *Filipino Express*, a newspaper of the US Philippine community, he returned to certain aspects of Filipino culture and identity, this time counterpointed by his roving intake of New York's fantastic cultural and linguistic mix. These thoughts were elicited by circumstances, or by the interests of particular interlocutors in a dialogue. No European interviewer had asked Medalla about his ethnicity, and he himself rarely mentioned it in his writings on his own art, except in recounting the facts of his curriculum vitae, as if, for him, that was where it belongs, as part of a temporal process in which origins/childhood/roots interweave the later thinking of someone who continuously opened himself to new experiences, new places, new knowledge. This is not the same thing as the close concern he has always had for the socio-political and cultural predicament of the Philippines. Later experiences – the distance given by residence abroad and so on – sharpened his perception of what he really loved and valued in his own culture.

Identity is a multi-temporal and multi-directional process, since one continually reconstructs what one was from what one has become, just as one evaluates what one now experiences in the light of what one has known. Medalla himself certainly seems "equally at home in East or West", at ease with both. As an artist, he is truly avant-garde but also Third World. His experimentalism has not evolved at the expense of a 'Third World perspective', nor vice versa. This is one of the reasons why his groups and friendships have always brought together Third World artists with western artists dissatisfied with the status quo. He epitomises the artist in a period of the accelerating mix-up of cultures, without exclusivity or a new 'centrism'. The thought of David Medalla adhering to any ethnocentrism, say Filipino-centrism or Asia-centrism, would be absurd. In a way, he has represented in his way of life for many years a position eloquently defined recently – if we can allow another 'world' metaphor – by the artist Guillermo Gómez–Peña:

I... oppose the old colonial categories of First/Third World with the much more pertinent notion of Fourth World, a conceptual place where the indigenous peoples meet with deterritorialised peoples. The members of the Fourth World live between, around and across various cultures, communities, and countries and our identities are constantly being reshaped by this kaleidoscopic experience.

In the Fourth World, there is no place for static identities, fixed nationalities or sacred cultural traditions. Everything is in constant flux, including this text.[18]

David Medalla and Kai Hilgemann, 'The Signs and Wonders of David and Kai', in **The Song of Milarepa**, impromptu at Saarbrücken, 1985. Collection of the artist.

On the other hand Medalla has never given up his Philippine passport. He has retained his nationality despite the endless visa problems this has given him as a peripatetic artist. One could enumerate some of the aspects of Filipino culture David deeply admires: the dislike of monolithic and dogmatic structures ("7000 islands!", he exclaims in explanation); the beauty of a culture vested in everyday forms of sociability and presentation rather than in monuments ("very South Pacific", he would say); the multi-ethnicity of the Philippines; and for what he called, in one of his *Filipino Express* articles, "tropical stoicism":

Filipinos are rarely stoic in their temperament. We are too hedonistic, too fun-loving for the kind of sombre demeanour prescribed by certain philosophers of ancient Greece and Rome. Nevertheless, because of our long history of suffering under various imperialisms and, more recently, under the philistine dictatorship of an avaricious couple (the notoriously greedy Marcoses), because we Filipinos are born and nurtured in an environment which, for all its beauty, is often ravaged by natural disasters and visited as well by man-made calamities, we have developed a certain form of tropical stoicism which expresses itself succinctly in the phrase *Bahala na!* which has no precise equivalent in any other, foreign language I know. *Bahala na!* is a devil-may-care attitude of mind, as well as a rallying cry for our improvisations in the face of the unknown. As an expression of the recklessness of our often shy (if not timid) spirits, it transgresses the moral rigidities of other more codified cultures. It is the key to the irrepressibility of our character and a component part of our psychic survival as a people.[19]

These values are threaded into his own work. They become part of the material inflections and nuances of his kinetic machines, his participatory propositions, his performances and paintings, in a way which cannot necessarily be put into words. They are indivisibly woven together with 'western' nuances. At another level, therefore, his work makes one reflect again upon the history of modern art. The true transcultural, or intercultural, nature of 20th century art is only beginning to be discerned.[20] It has partly been obscured by the tendency, conscious or unconscious, to identify art narrowly with the existing power relations of the world, in all their inequality and injustice. This reductionism tends to have the same effect, whether one actively or passively goes along with existing relationships or actively or passively resists them. In other words, to give one example, to say that artists outside Europe or North America have been 'marginal' to the development of 20th century art movements, amounts to the same as saying that they have made 'important contributions' to those movements, if the image and the values of those movements continue to be identified with a single, dominant and homogenising culture. What is lost is the belief in art, which the artist Susan Hiller has expressed "as a critique of existing culture and as a locus where futures not otherwise possible can begin to shape themselves".[21] If we allow art this relative freedom we begin to see how the avant-garde movements are themselves scenes of dialogue and dispute over civilisational values, where no one 'culture' is sole protagonist.

Equally paradoxical, reciprocal and dialogic – rather than mutually exclusive – have been the relationships between modernity and tradition, and between 'fine' and 'popular' art in the 20th century. It has often been pointed out that many of the leading European avant-garde figures of the early 20th century came from remote, rural, even feudal surroundings. They migrated from countryside to metropolis (Brancusi,

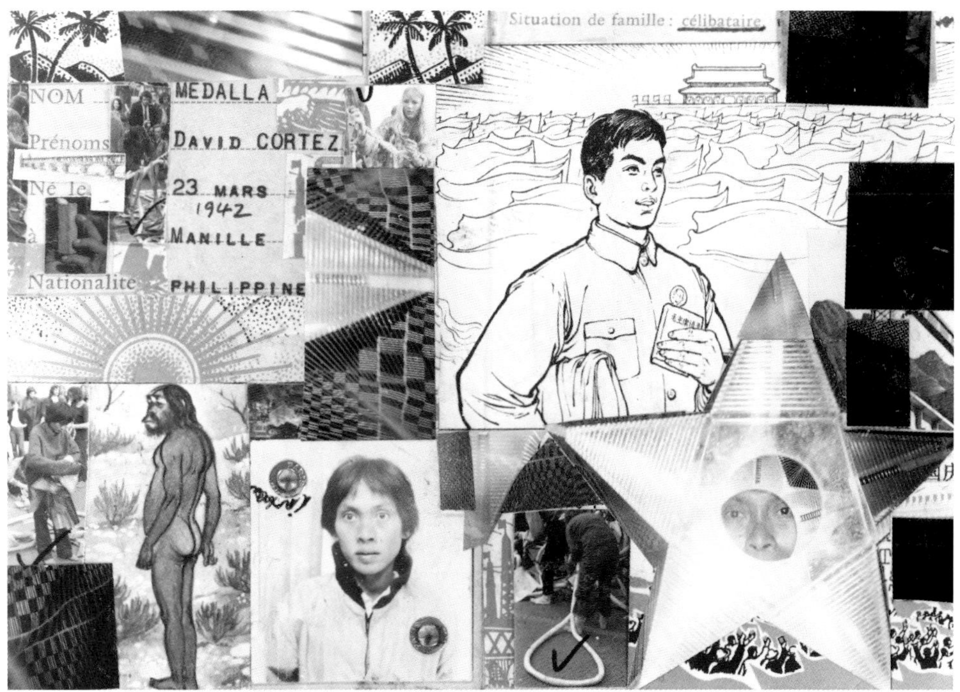

Carte d'Identité, collage, 1972. Collection of the artist.

Malevich, Moholy-Nagy, Buñuel, are examples). The urban modernity of Brancusi was inextricably interlaced with the archaic. After the Second World War this paradox took an even broader scope with the virtual creation of movements like Kinetic Art by artists of Third World origin, or artists from the European periphery, of whom, of course, Medalla is one.

If these movements reflected an aspiration by peoples of formerly marginalised or supposedly backward countries to be 'absolutely modern', to take on and surpass the innovations of the European vanguard, they soon, in the work of the most challenging artists, passed this stage and entered into a much more complex and critical relationship with modern culture. Among the Third World artists this inevitably meant a reabsorption in, reassessment of, the traditional and popular aspects of their native cultures in order better to understand and answer to the dilemmas of contemporaneity. Something of this process can be seen in the work of the Brazilians Lygia Clark and Hélio Oiticica, who will be mentioned later for their considerable affinity with Medalla's art. This process could be called a new modern art (rather than 'post-modernism'), which is critical of many aspects of modernity in the name of a fresh definition of freedom and beauty.

An example of this process in Medalla's work may be briefly suggested here. At one level we are convinced by certain descriptions of the way in which modern conditions have obliterated traditional categories and differences, so that they no longer have any meaning, and instigated a global totalitarian system. Thus, as Michel Foucault has written, "Our society is not one of spectacle but surveillance. We are neither in the amphitheatre nor on the stage but in the panoptic machine".[22] In other words, the stage/world, illusion/reality distinction is irrelevant in a system which incorporates everything under the rationalised surveillance of a 'super power'. But isn't Foucault's model simply another image deriving from the western patriarchal myth of the 'God's-eye view'? It seems to me that Medalla's wandering, ephemeral performances, his creation of instant stages here and there, sidestep the alternatives of both spectacle and surveillance. He recreates those categories of amphitheatre and stage freshly in the midst of life, and with a fluid, dialogic ambivalence, which defies such a crude and monolithic destiny.

But I hardly want to slip into another positivist or prescriptive definition. I am sure David Medalla would be happy to escape from all the definitions I have offered of him. Out of perversity, out of ego perhaps, or, alternatively, out of a modest understanding of the common basis from which we all begin:

I mean I'm an enigma to myself... I don't know why I'm here. You can always have a construct: I'm here to pay my taxes, to please my parents, to have children. Thomas Aquinas said the animals were here in order to praise God. You see, the constructs are always changing...

I believe art should investigate reality and bring out its enigmas.[23]

Opposite: **The Secret Portrait of ...** , 1954, typographic version.

"The Secret Portrait of..."

an art work conceived in 1954 in New York City
dedicated to James Dean
(whose other name is Byron)

There are questions, questions, about the artist and the art work,
about the subject of the art work, about the art work's provenance,
about the mysterious process whereby the art work came into being,
about the secret ways of the art work's becoming...
There are questions, questions. Here are some of them:
Is the artist male or female? Is he or she young or old?
Is the subject of the portrait a stranger or a friend?
Was the portrait painted in the city or the countryside?
Was the portrait painted in one room or several rooms?
In one place or several places? Was there only one portrait painted
from place to place in different cities? Or were there, are there, several
portraits of the same subject by the same artist? Was the portrait painted from memory?
Is the primary portrait full-length, half-length, or just a close-up
of the subject's face? Was the portrait painted in daylight?
Or was it painted under artificial light? Or was it painted in darkness?
Was the subject of the portrait naked? Or was the subject clothed?
Was the subject standing, or seated, or reclining on a bed?
Was the subject awake when the portrait was painted? Or was the subject asleep?
Was the subject dreaming? Or was it the artist who dreamt
the subject of the portrait? Was the portrait painted in a single sitting?
Or was it painted over several days, weeks, months, years?
Did the artist and the subject converse while the portrait was being painted?
Or was the portrait painted in silence? Or was the portrait painted
while music was being played while the artist painted the subject in silence?

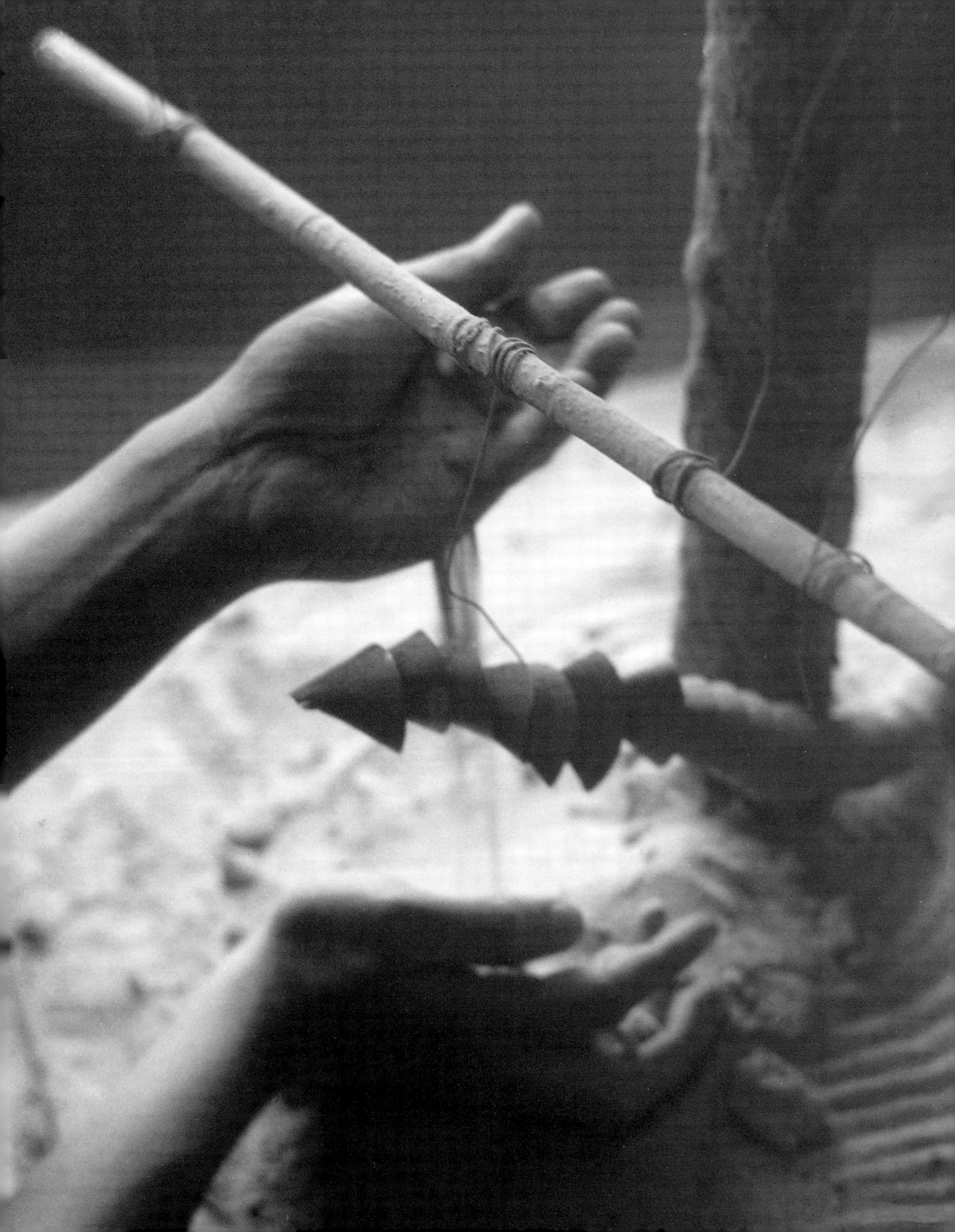

Two

Biokinetics

The movement known as Kinetic Art is in need of a reappraisal. It is often treated as an interlude or sideshow in recent art which has sunk back into history without ever entering, as terms like Pop Art or Minimal Art have done, into discussions of the mainstream of art. This is partly because there is very little of this work on view today. Museums favour the static. It is only very occasionally that one can get a glimpse of the new sensibility, in the true meaning of a new formation of the senses, which was introduced into art by the use of actual movement and internal sources of light. When one does, it is always a revelation. In the work of the best artists, movement emerges as a fully-articulated and inflected language, able to range from sublime beauty and tender sensuality to the carnivalesque. The art called 'kinetic' was simultaneously a technical development in the use of materials and media, and a new stage in the investigation of certain problematics which have always haunted art: particularly the relationship between movement and rest, light and dark, matter and energy.

As such, kinetic art could be interpreted either within a narrow framework of technique, or with a much broader focus. Both are valid. The narrow focus defines kineticism's specific characteristics as an art movement but is liable to dogmatism and a literal interpretation of the nature of movement. The broader focus is particularly pertinent to David Medalla, enabling one to see the relationship between his 'biokinetics' and the long-term concerns of his art as a whole.

Museums have only grudgingly accepted kinetic art not only because it makes unusual technical and conservational demands, but for conceptual reasons too. Museums (together with galleries and the commercial system of the art world) are themselves an expression of a static conception of seeing and understanding and they impose this upon everything in their care. Since, in its broader sense, 'kineticism' is a way of knowing reality as a process of continuous change, it implies a new take upon all phenomena, including the past history of art, and including art works which have always been presented as static entities. When the emphasis shifts to change and 'process', the work itself is redefined in many senses. Ancient sculptures and paintings, for example, are seen as part of performative ritual practices, not as self-sufficient monuments. The relationship between the conceiving of a work, its execution, and its final exposure in public is seen as a process. The dichotomy, in the western tradition, between rough sketch and finished work may be contrasted with other notions, like the fusion of the premeditated and the spontaneous in Chinese calligraphy, for example. In

20th century art, Matisse's transition from the brush to cut paper in his last works, Mondrian's continuous rearrangement of panels of primary colour on his studio walls, Schwitters's *Merzbau*, Tatlin's *Monument to the Third International*, Klee's "taking a line for a walk", Pollock's action-painting: all of these episodes could be included within a general kinetic concept of an evolution in modern art towards overcoming rigidity, lightening the material element, moving "from mass towards motion", as Moholy-Nagy expressed it.

Moholy-Nagy's experiments with light, transparency and movement, Duchamp's optical machines, Gabo's vibrating wire, Calder's mobiles – the examples usually given in attempts to trace a genealogy for kinetic art as such – would then fit within a larger picture of experiment. 'Orders' in art history tend to be linear and chronological. But movements can also be understood in the way they spread out sideways or in all directions. The term 'kinetic art' then comes to represent one nexus in shifting and overlapping fields of experiment which characterised the 1950s and 1960s. The 'kinetic' nexus, strictly defined, incorporates work connected with visual and perceptual research, processes of material transformation, use of the elements light, fire, electricity and magnetism, and so on. But beside and around it, touching it at many points, were other sorts of nexus: concrete poetry, non-composition or random composition, Fluxus events, happenings, spectator participation, neo-Dada, assemblage. Monochrome painting, for example, shared a permeable boundary with kinetic art in the 1950s and 1960s, a basic feature of the work of Yves Klein, Aubertin, Soto, Otero, Fontana, Calderara, Li Yuan-chia, von Graevenitz, Takis, Camargo, Lygia Clark, Hélio Oiticica, and extending to Medalla's foam sculptures and mud machines. The monochrome was expressive of the *tabula rasa*, the degree zero, out of which the new space-time would arise. All in all, a more sophisticated understanding is needed of the way in which ideas are 'in the air' at any given moment – an understanding, in fact, of the kind of 'meta', or even 'telepathic', communication implied by this common phrase.

When it is considered in this way, one is powerfully struck by two features of this fluid scene of experimentation: its internationalism and its interdisciplinarity. A list of both major and minor figures would include people born in widely different parts of the world, with a high proportion of these artists coming from Third World countries. The kinetic nexus was particularly cosmopolitan. Its origins cannot be associated with any one country, especially not the USA whose local conditions have always been considered (probably exaggeratedly) so important in the formation of Pop Art or Minimal Art. In fact, after the Second World War, kineticism was one powerful focus for the aspirations felt by young artists from colonised, 'developing' or marginalised countries to be 'absolutely modern'. It was the means of catching up and then surpassing the development of modernism in Europe, and of assuming the right to speak in visionary, utopian, even cosmic terms. The more profound the artist, the more these 'universal' terms incorporated the particularities of local experience and

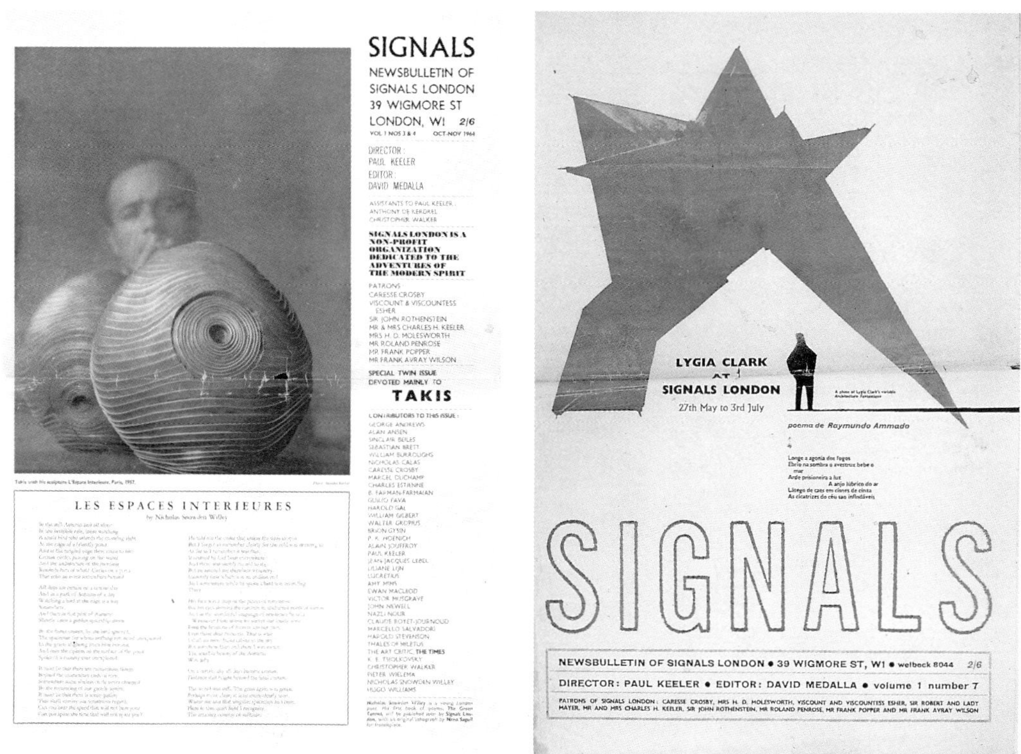

Signals Newsbulletin, edited by David Medalla. Left: special Takis issue, vol 1 no 3/4, October-November 1964. Right: special Lygia Clark issue, vol 1 no 7, April-May 1965.

history, as we mentioned in the first chapter. Therefore, although often present in western metropolises, these artists did not identify with the notion either of 'national schools', or of a European–North American alliance (and rivalry), but maintained a genuine internationalism. This was the position which Medalla adopted within the British context throughout the 1960s.

Another peculiarity of kinetic art was its relationship with science and technology. It is hard to imagine today the optimistic spirit there was then for a collaboration between art and science. Kinetic art itself was embedded in a wider culture, which included, among other things, the studies in formal and structural morphology by excellent but now unfashionable writers such as Hermann Weyl, Eugen Herrigel, Gyorgy Kepes, Siegfried Giedion, D'Arcy Wentworth Thompson and Henri Focillon. Again, it is not a question of crude causation but of ideas 'in the air'. Among the practitioners of kinetic art there were people who had more of a technical or scientific background and those who had an artistic background. Sometimes a person with an advanced scientific background had only a conventional notion of painting. This often resulted in work which did little more than set in motion traditional formal

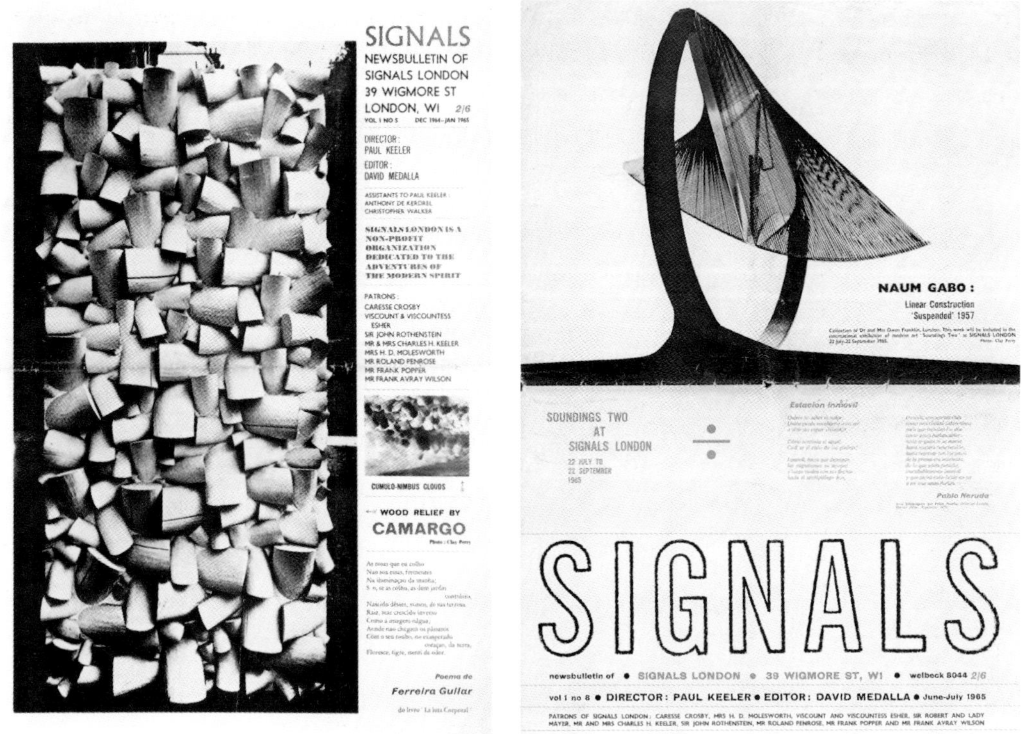

Signals Newsbulletin. Left: special Camargo issue, vol 1 no 5, December 1964 - January 1965. Right: 'Soundings Two' special issue, vol 1 no 8, June - July 1965.

structures. In other cases a generalised notion of painting was not a problem because what the experimenter had discovered was a new relationship between nature, technology and the science of optics.

The 'Robot Painter' of the Israeli artist P.K. Hoenich is an example of the latter. Hoenich devised a system of mobile reflectors to work directly with sunlight, producing beautiful projections on the walls of a darkened room. In doing so he renewed the wonder of sunlight in contemporary terms as a fusion of macroscopic/microscopic imagery. Hoenich's work is forgotten today because only those parts of kinetic art which could be assimilated within the conventional limits of the art world have been remembered. He himself had little interest in that set-up, regarding his work not as a personal expression but as a means, "a gift to artists all over the world", as he wrote to David Medalla when Medalla featured his work in *Signals Newsbulletin* in 1965.[1]

Some artists arrived at a kinetic art through a rigorous investigation of the pictorial or sculptural order, consciously working forward from positions reached by Mondrian, Malevich, or Albers. The Brazilians Lygia Clark's and Hélio Oiticica's, and the Venezuelan Soto's, discoveries were of this kind. For them, the pictorial order was a kind of paradigm of the cosmic order.[2] Takis's invention of the *Telemagnetic* sculpture, 1959, and Medalla's 'auto-creative art', beginning with his *Bubble Machines*, 1963, on the other hand, were in the nature of a sudden breakthrough, a fresh and unprecedented reformulation in aesthetic terms of the relationship between matter and energy. But these 'leaps' also involved a summing-up of previous pictorial and sculptural history, as will become clear from the evolution of Medalla's own 'biokinetics'.

◆   ◆   ◆

David Medalla had spent the early part of the 1960s travelling between England and France. He made his European landfall at Marseilles in March 1960. After visiting

Mailing **Signals Newsbulletin**, Cornwall Gardens,1964. Clockwise: GB, Sergio Camargo, Paul Keeler, Christopher Walker, DM, Gustav Metzger.

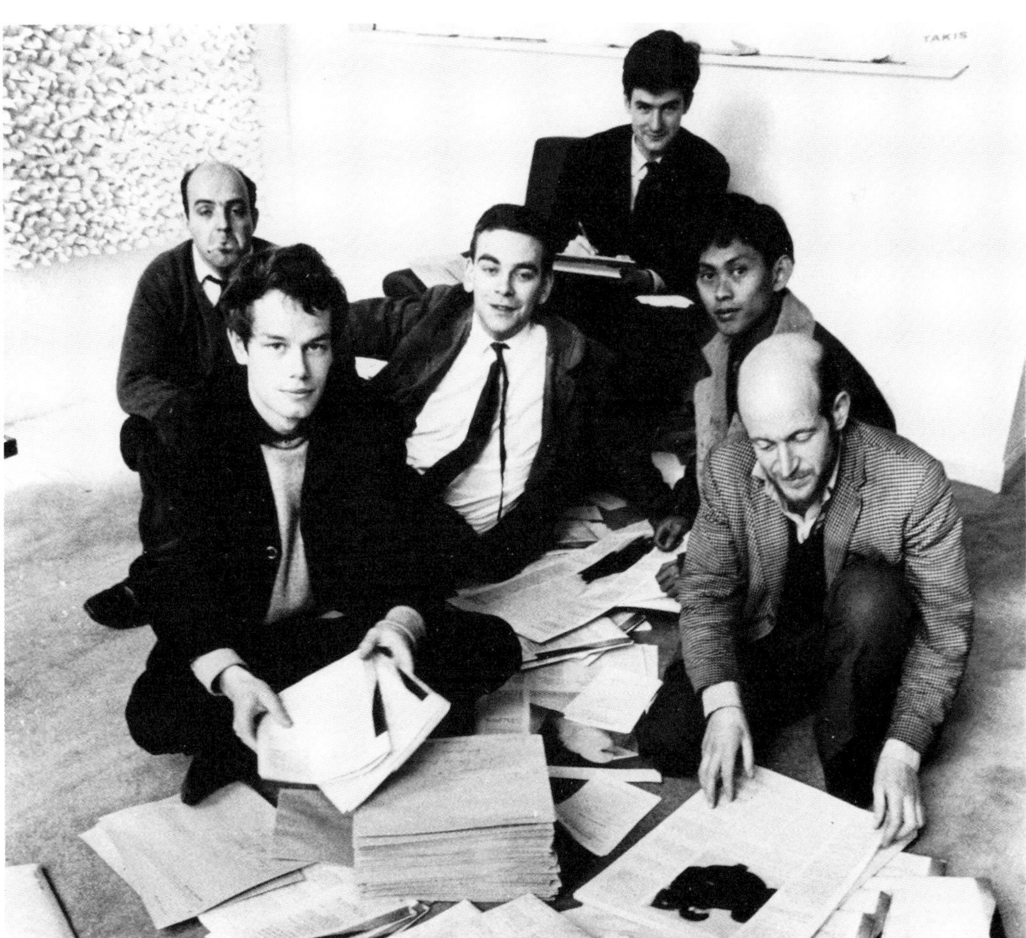

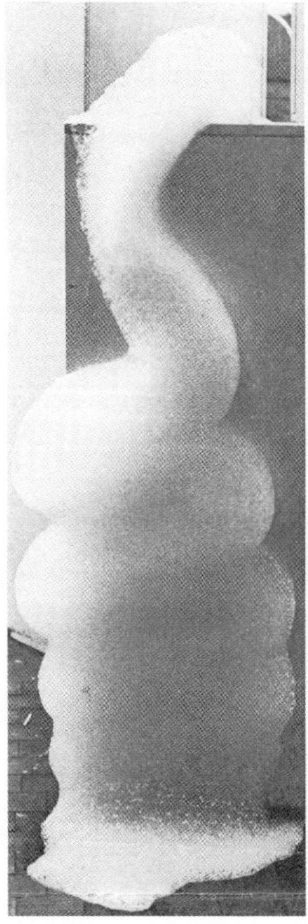

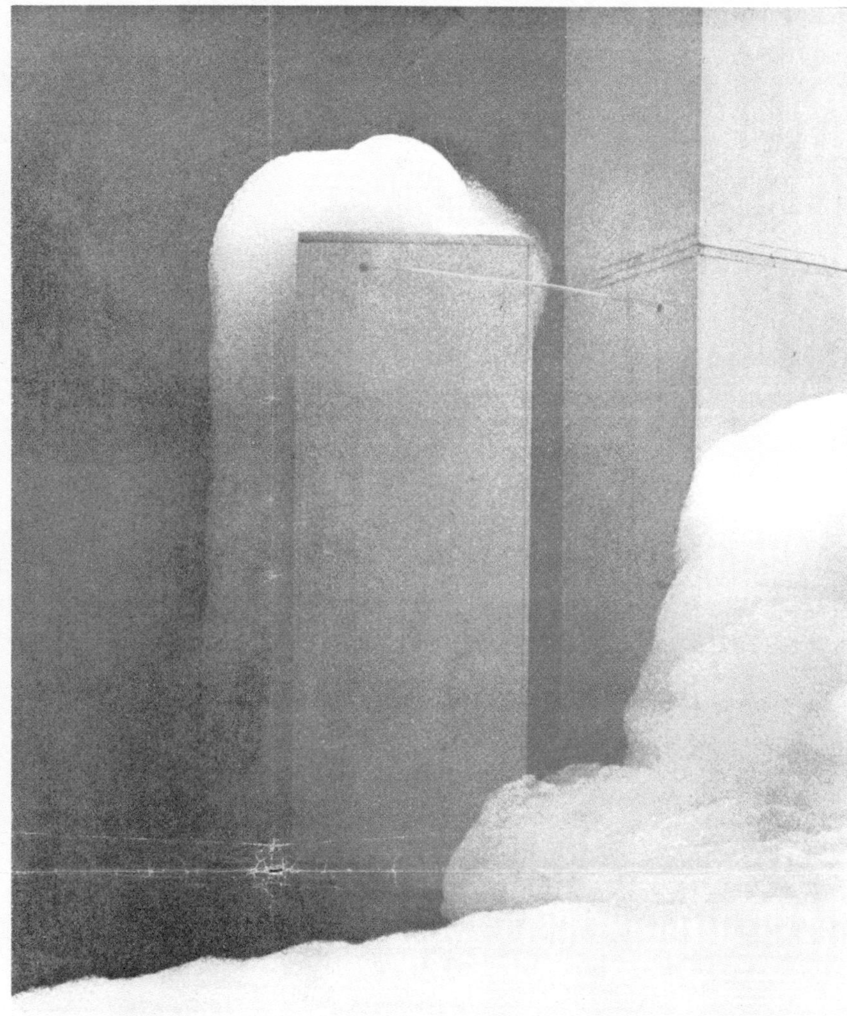

**DAVID MEDALLA: CLOUD CANYONS:
BUBBLE MOBILES 1964.**

PHOTOGRAPHS BY CLAY PERRY.

*". . . the universe begins to look more like a great
thought than like a great machine . . The old
dualism of mind and matter . . . seems likely to
disappear, not through matter becoming in any way
more shadowy or insubstantial than heretofore, or
through mind becoming resolved into a function of
the working of matter, but through substantial
matter resolving itself into a creation and manifestation of mind . . .
A soap bubble with irregularities and corrugations
on its surface is perhaps the best representation,
in terms of simple and familiar materials, of the
new universe revealed to us by the theory of
relativity."*

—Sir James Jeans.

"IF YOU LIKE I SHALL GROW

IRREPROACHABLY GENTLE,

NOT A MAN, BUT A CLOUD

IN TROUSERS. . ."

Vladimir Mayakovsky.

With the five bubble machines exhibited this
year in London **David Medalla** has achieved a
leading position in art.
A quarter million forms continuously changing,
reflecting, growing, disintegrating.
Random activity is at present among the most
crucial questions in art.
Apart from other contributions his works have
made, **Medalla** has shown conclusively that
random activity in material/transforming art is
capable of achieving not only the most complex
forms and motions but also an aesthetic content
of the highest order.

—Gustav Metzger.

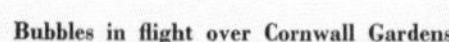

Bubbles in flight over Cornwall Gardens

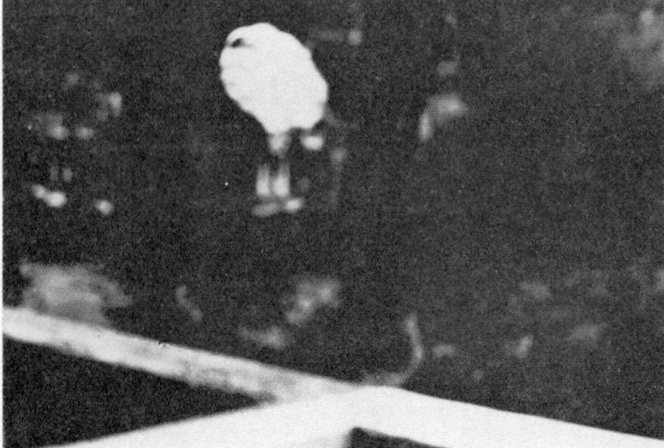

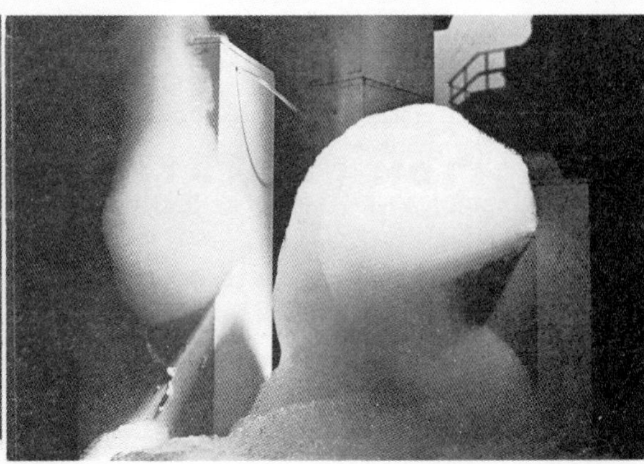

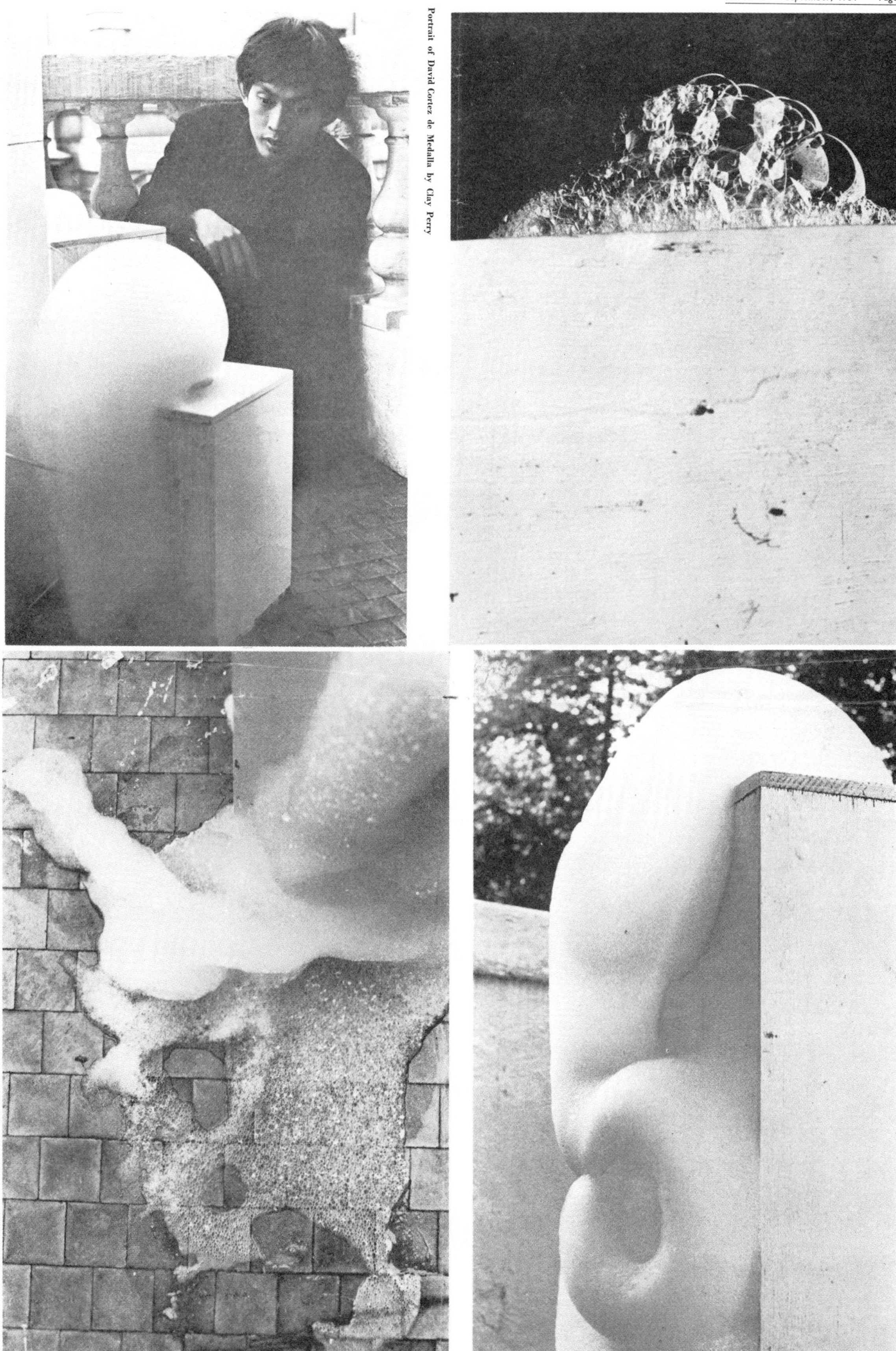

Portrait of David Cortez de Medalla by Clay Perry

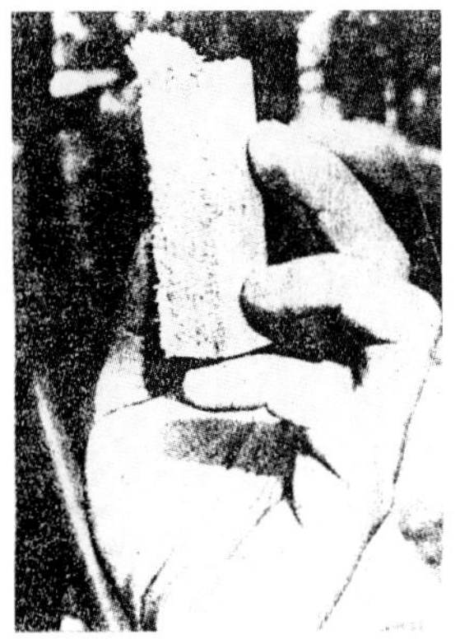

For Smokey, the First Bubble Machine, Paris, 1963.

Paris and staying there to the end of his three-month French visa, he crossed to England. He was writing and painting with equal emphasis, and he continued to give the occasional performance as he had done in Manila and New York (Medalla's first performance in Paris was in the theatre of the Raymond Duncan Academy, run by the brother of Isadora Duncan). In London he painted the church of St. Mary Magdalene near his room in Little Venice, Paddington, and in 1962 was working on a religious composition, including a madonna, after moving to a flat in Islington he shared with Paul Keeler. Keeler, a young ex-actor who had started a small business priming canvases, was also eager to organise exhibitions. In 1963 he arranged Medalla's first exhibition in England of paintings and drawings at the Mayflower Barn at Seer Green and Jordans in Buckinghamshire, an ancient building made from the timbers of the original Mayflower, the ship which took the Pilgrim Fathers to the New World. During one of his Paris visits Medalla saw for the first time the *Telemagnetic* sculpture of Takis, the 'vibration' paintings of Soto, and Yves Klein's *Anthropometries* (his paintings using women's bodies as 'living brushes'). They made a profound impression on him, whose effects began to be felt immediately. 'Soundings 1', a group show Paul

Left to right: **Cloud Canyons no 2**, ensemble of bubble machines, London, 1964. Collection of the artist.
Cloud Messenger, bubble machine, Indica Gallery, London, 1967. Collection of the artist.
Megha Sutta: The Cloud Discourse, bubble machine, 1971. Collection of the artist.

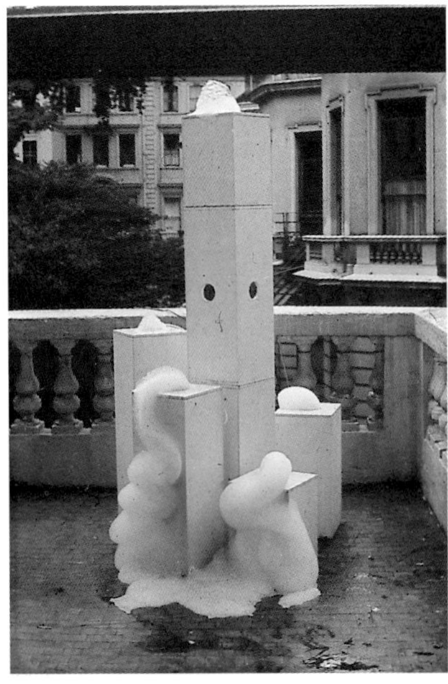
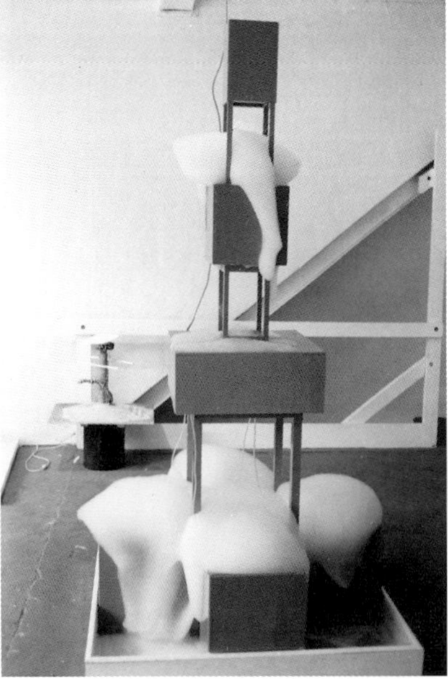
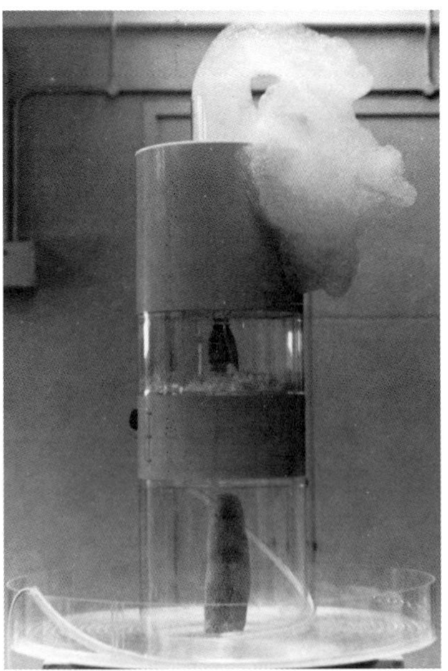

Keeler organised at the Ashmolean Museum in Oxford in 1964, included pieces by Soto, Takis and Pol Bury alongside works in many different styles. More encounters were made in Paris: the white wood reliefs of Camargo and, through him, the work of other Brazilians living in Rio de Janeiro and São Paulo, Lygia Clark, Hélio Oiticica and Mira Schendel. Medalla began making his own kinetic experiments in 1963 and exhibited his first *Bubble Machine* and *Smoke Machine* in 'Structures Vivantes: Mobiles/Images', effectively the first survey of kinetic and optical art held in Britain, organised by Paul Keeler at the Redfern Gallery in 1964.[3]

A group of likeminded artists began to coalesce. Keeler and Medalla moved to a spacious flat in Cornwall Gardens, South Kensington, and the Centre for Advanced Creative Study was founded there in 1964 by Keeler, Medalla, artists Gustav Metzger and Marcelo Salvadori, Christopher Walker and myself. *Signals Newsbulletin* (its title inspired by a series of tensile sculptures by Takis) was started, edited and designed by Medalla, and Signals London became the name of the group, and of the 'showroom', when it was moved, in late 1964, to a large four-storey building at the corner of Wigmore Street and Welbeck Street in central London. The building was made available by Keeler's father, an optical instruments manufacturer.

By the time they joined Signals, Salvadori's and Metzger's interests were already clearly defined. Salvadori, who was born in Florence and came to England in

Left to right: **Cloud Canyons no 10**, bubble machines, 1985. Collection of the Aukland City Art Gallery, New Zealand. **Cloud Canyons no 11**, bubble machines, 1989. Installed at "The Other Story" exhibition, Hayward Gallery, London. Collection of the artist. **Cloud Gates**, ensemble of four bubble machines, 1994. Installed at Medalla's exhibition, 'The Secret History of the Mondrian Fan Club', 55 Gee Street, London, 1994-5. Collection of the artist.

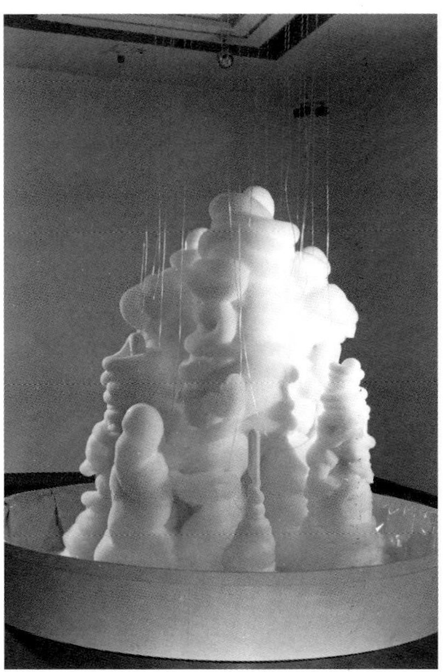
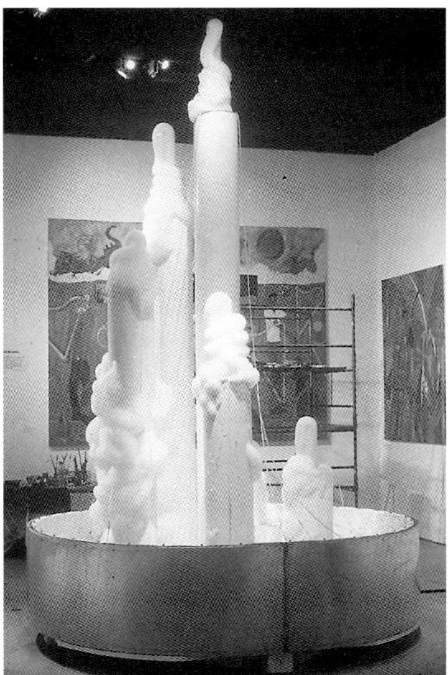
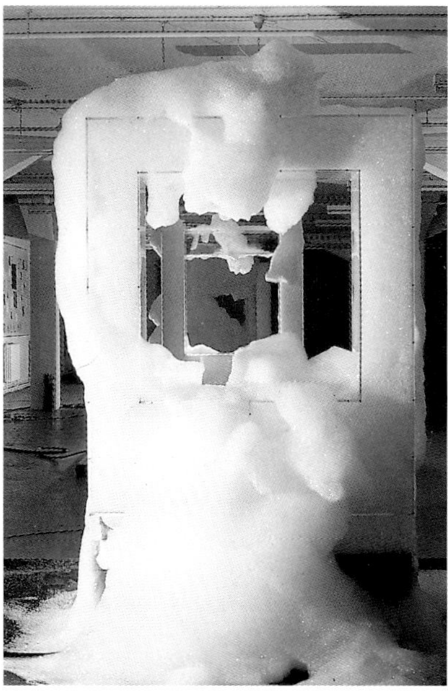

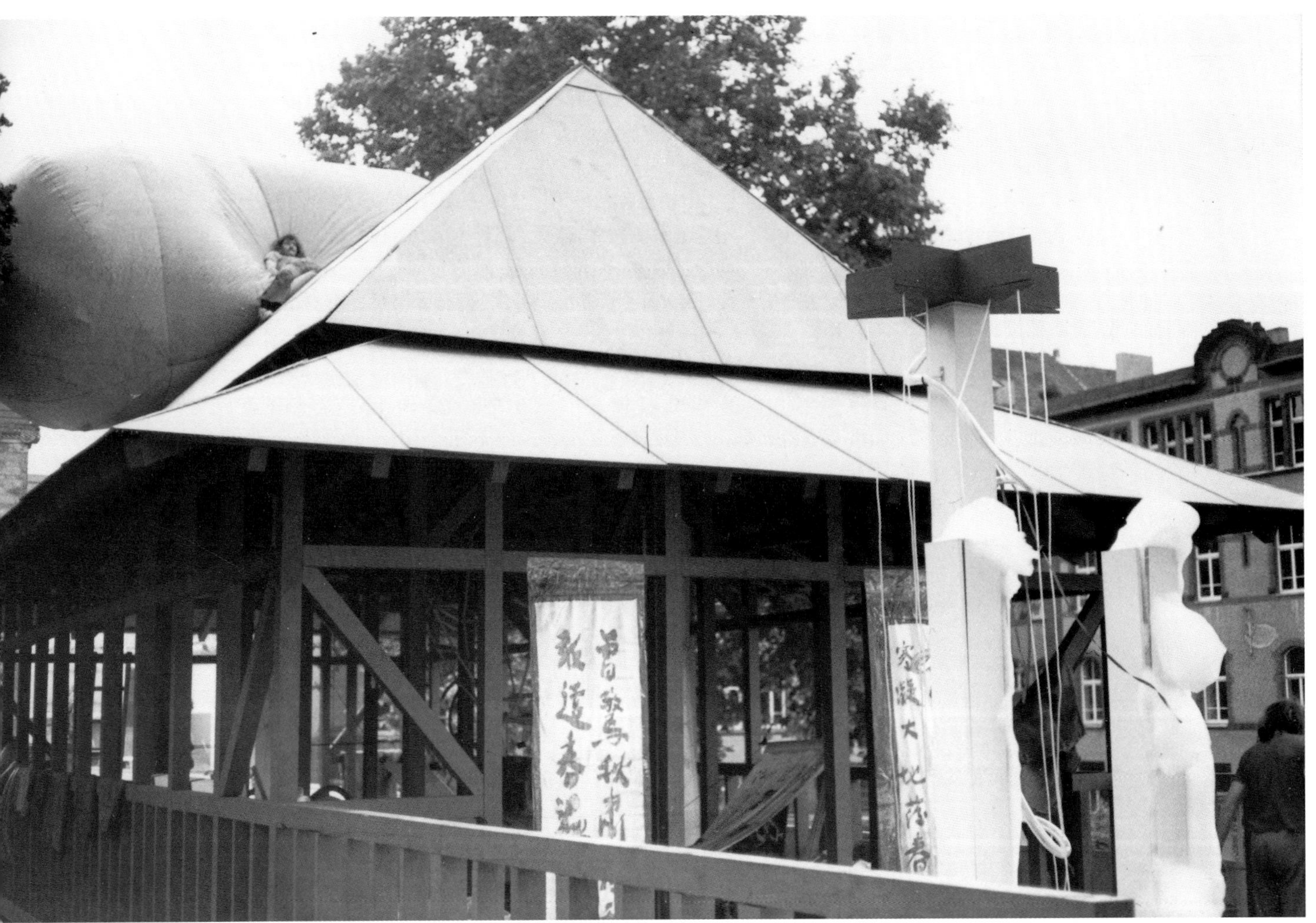

Cloud Towers: Homage to Lu Xun, bubble machines forming part of **Peoples' Participation Pavilion,** Medalla's and John Dugger's contribution to Documenta 5, Kassel, 1972. Behind the bubble machines are scrolls with poems by Lu Xun. On the roof of the pavilion, inflatable by Graham Stevens.

1955, was looking for a close collaboration between artists and scientists based on the model of a research institute (the original name of the group was his). He thought of his own works using plastics and foam rubber as maquettes for a transformation of the environment. Metzger was the apostle of 'auto-destructive art'. He combined a pioneering interest in self-generated and random forms in art with a wide-ranging critique of contemporary society. These interests mainly took the form of written manifestos, since, in his view, the theory of 'auto-destruction' was ten years ahead of practice.

Medalla's approach was broader. As an artist he was completely committed to the ideas he had adopted, plumbing them to the depths so to speak. At the same time he always maintained a certain attitude of free-floating, uncommitted openness. As an organiser and publicist he pursued a non-dogmatic and non-exclusive policy. His statement defining the aims of Signals, in its newspaper-format periodical, said only that it was "dedicated to the adventures of the modern spirit",[4] and encouraged experiment in art. *Signals Newsbulletin* printed poems, political discussions, a digest of scientific discoveries and personal news as well as extensive documentation of the artists exhibiting in the gallery (the quality of information on each artist was outstanding in a period before large catalogues).[5] He always gave poems as much prominence as critical essays in the interpretation of an artist's work. Both Keeler and Medalla commissioned artists to produce a new large-scale environmental work for their Signals shows.[6] In a curious way, Medalla combined an eminently pragmatic sense, as an organiser, of what could actually be created out of a meeting of specific people, with the wildest flights of fantasy in his kinetic projects and 'propulsions', whose playfulness and poetic licence showed up a sometimes pedestrian strain in the more earnest attempts by other artists to link art and science.

From 1964-66 Signals London was a major showroom of the international avant-garde. Its premises were bigger than the old Institute of Contemporary Arts in Dover Street and its *Newsbulletin* was far more lavish than the ICA's small publication. Artists like Takis, Camargo, Soto, Otero, Kenneth and Mary Martin, Li Yuan-chia, Gerhard von Graevenitz and Lygia Clark had opportunities to exhibit on a large scale, and to experiment, which they did not yet have in London or in Paris. An international and diverse public sought out the gallery. The first two small-scale 'Pilot Shows' held at Cornwall Gardens, even before the move to Wigmore Street, were attended by 6,854

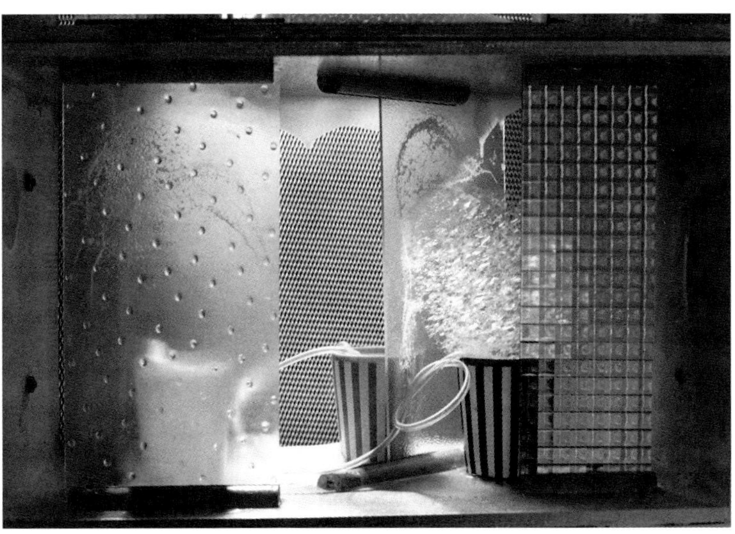

Bubble Wall, bubble machines built in situ at Cornwall Gardens, London, 1964 (detail).

people, according to records kept by Medalla, and these included, besides artists and students, "architects, engineers, writers, scientists, technologists, designers, industrialists, doctors, nurses and teachers".[7]

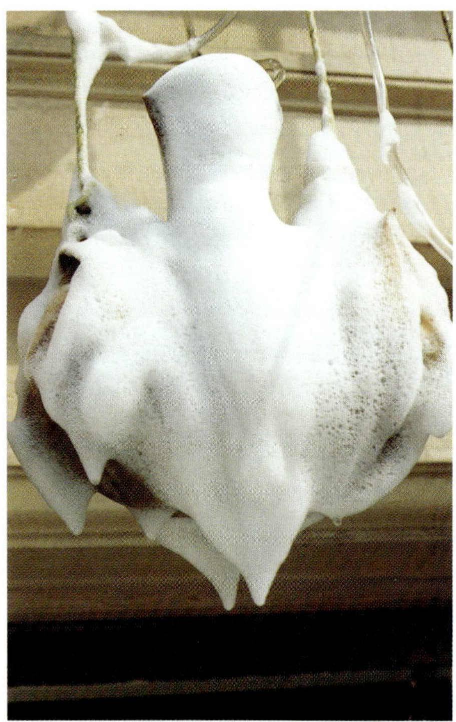

Opposite page and above: **Cloud Fruits**, bubble machine, the facade of Gallery House, Goethe Institute, London 1972.

In fact Signals encapsulated the character of the London-based avant-garde for the period. Like the ICA (originally founded in 1947 by Roland Penrose, Herbert Read, Peter Watson and others), which had a far longer life than Signals, and venues of the early 1960s such as Victor Musgrave's Gallery One and Denis Bowen's and Kenneth Coutts-Smith's New Vision Centre, the character of Signals was cosmopolitan, experimental and interdisciplinary. These qualities have never been recognised by British art history. In fact the entire mainstream historical writing and exhibition-making has been concerned with constructing a national image of British art, wedded to a traditionalist, beaux-arts view of practice, ignoring or excluding the work of those foreigners which cannot be assimilated within the national canon. By the cruel logic of chauvinism, official aspirations to make London an international art centre have only resulted in obliterating London's cosmopolitan reality and the actual ferment of its cultural life.

◆   ◆   ◆

Those who like to trace the 'migration of symbols', and the renewal of metaphors, would probably notice that the snake motif, which is common in Medalla's earliest paintings, reappears in his biokinetic works. By chance or design, or by a deeper process which unifies both, the foam in the *Bubble Machines*, the metal and sand in the *Sand Machine*, the thin, flexible rods which delve sponges into the liquid mud in the *Mud Machine* take on sinuous, serpentine forms. When I first saw these machines in the 1960s I was deeply struck by the quality of their movements. "A complex and tender expression of energy which before had not existed in mechanical sculpture", I wrote at the time.[8] This intimate response was somehow mixed together with amazement at the works' conceptual audacity as artistic propositions in the context of their time.

Medalla himself, when describing the origins of the Bubble Machines, likes to

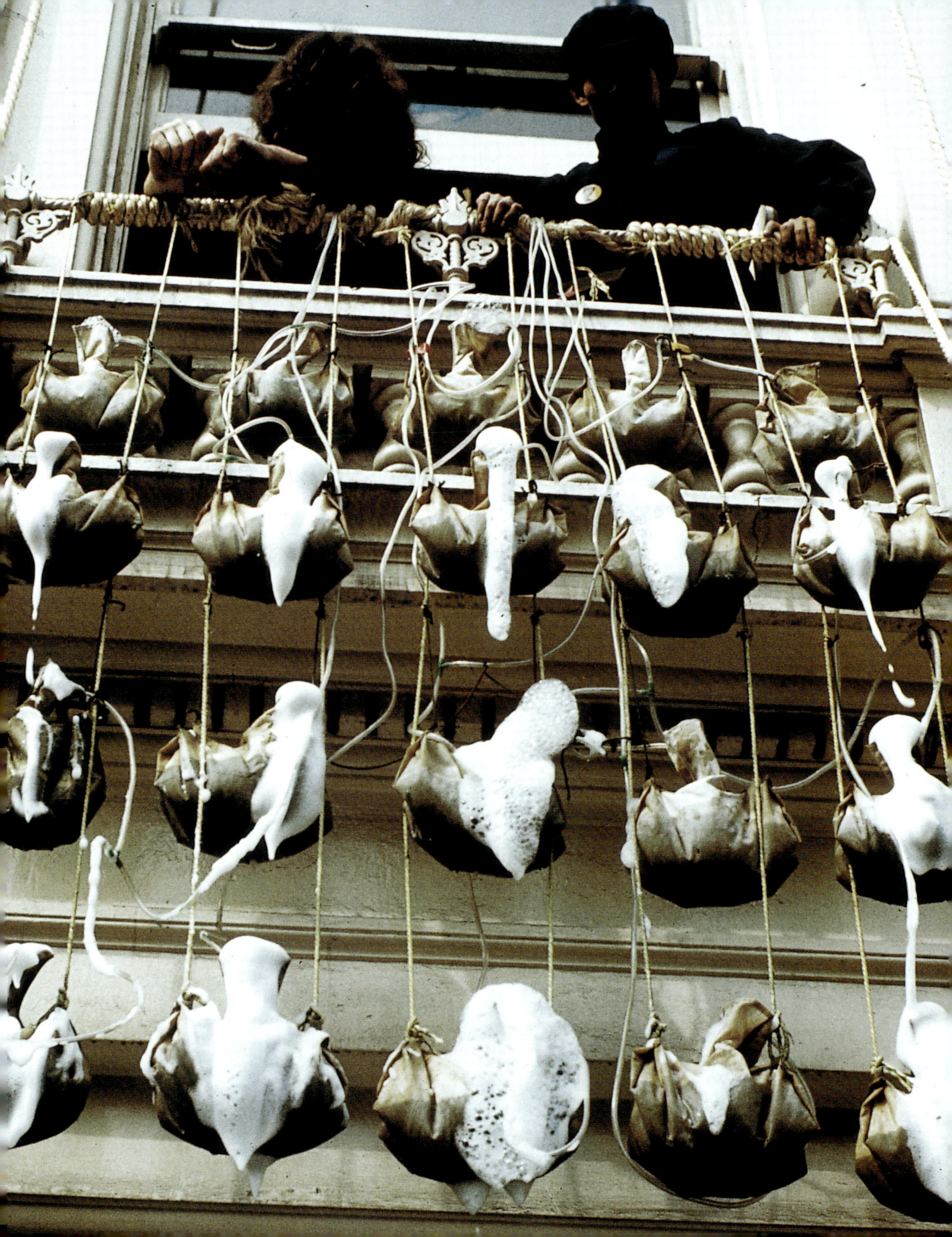

mix artistic and scientific aspirations with an assortment of personal memories. From 1960 to 1963 he was consciously experimenting to find a way to give "tangible form to invisible forces....to find a model which would show the transformation of matter into energy".[9] This search re-awakened childhood memories. On a grand scale, he remembered the fantastic colours and shapes of the clouds in the tropical sunsets over Manila Bay; on a homely scale, watching his mother cook *guinataan* with *bola bola*, a bubbling coconut delicacy. Later, in 1961, he made a visit to an Edinburgh brewery with the writer and musician Viv McCorry. After looking at the enormous vats of foaming beer, they climbed up to the top of the hill at King Arthur's Seat and lay on the ground watching the clouds race overhead. Occasionally Medalla mentioned a more disturbing memory: at the age of three he stared fascinated at the frothing mouth of a young resistance fighter who lay shot and mortally wounded in the family garden. He had been shot by the Japanese occupation forces' savage military police, the *Kempetai*, while attempting to warn Medalla's father, who was fighting in the resistance, of an impending Japanese attack.

There was, too, Medalla's appraisal of developments within kinetic art itself. All movements produce pedestrian work. In kinetic art there was a particularly sharp distinction between those artists who were content merely to 'motorise' already existing formal structures, anecdotal caricatures or other whimsicalities, and artists

John Dugger with **Megha Sutta: The Cloud Discourse** in the basement of the Tate Gallery, London, 1971.

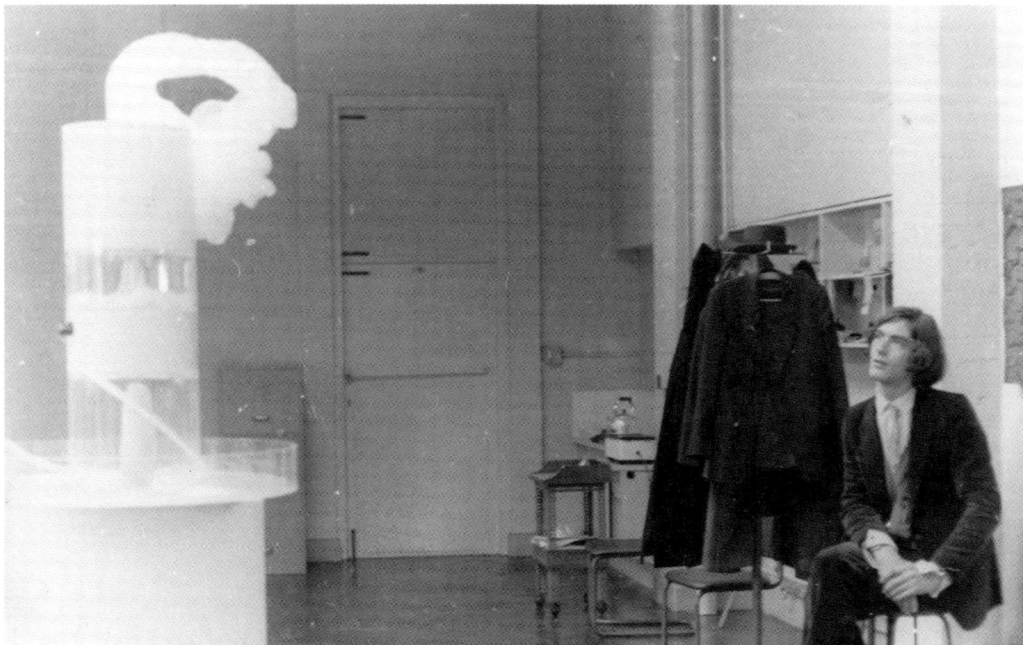

who were searching for a new structure of
material transformation, and a new space.
What was at stake was to make visible the
equivalence of matter and energy, and it
seemed a point of honour to accomplish this
with the greatest possible economy and wit.
To do so laboriously was a contradiction in
terms. The new structure would achieve
greater freedom and depth by being
transparently simple, being both ordinary and
cosmic at the same time.

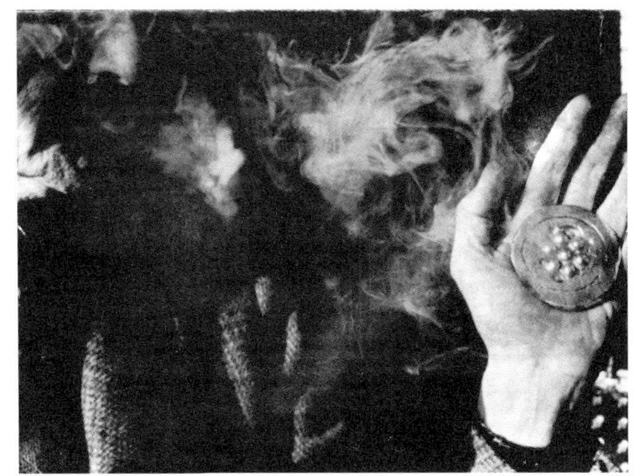
Marcel Duchamp with his **Medallic Sculpture**, 1968.

This was the beauty of *Cloud Canyons*, as Medalla's early ensembles of Bubble
Machines were called. The foam was allowed to follow its aleatory paths, emerging and
forming according to its own energies interacting with gravity, air currents,
atmospheric pressure, and the shape of the containers. The genius of the Bubble
Machine was that a conceptual logic went together with an extraordinary subtlety of
luminosity and texture, for which the analogy with clouds was no exaggeration. It was
never the same two days in a row. When *Cloud Canyons* was mounted on the balcony at
Cornwall Gardens in the summer of 1964, the photographer Clay Perry remembers
being called sometimes in the middle of the night by Medalla to come over and capture
a particular effect.

At another level, the Bubble Machines offered a provocative critique of the
position reached by Minimalist sculpture. Minimalism had freed itself to some degree
from the element of individual expression and taste by cultivating various systems of
cellular, serial, uniform and repetitive structure. The plain white boxes of Medalla's
early foam machines acknowledged this tenet of Minimalism, but the emerging foam
disturbingly exceeded these orderly and static forms and introduced a completely new,
kinetic and organic understanding of the cellular and repetitive. In fact the structure of
the Bubble Machine was dialectical at both formal and philosophical levels. Creation
proceeded inseparably from destruction, the fullness and monumentality of form was
accompanied by its complete evaporation, it was simultaneously a material 'something'
and an immaterial 'nothing'. A seething activity went together with an overall calm.
Chaos and order coexisted. Motion and rest.

Medalla considered these and the other machines he made as facets of an
exploration of the sculptural possibilities of pulverised, elastic and soluble materials:
"Water, grains of rice, gold and silver dust, sand, fire, powdered coal, granulated
coffee-beans, dried seeds, rubber, gum, mud, ice, salt, oil, steam, mist, smoke, etc... I
was looking for materials that, in sculpture, would be analogous to the smallest
biological unit, the cell; materials that would be capable of multiplication."[10]

The import of Medalla's innovation was immediately recognised by his peers.
Gustav Metzger wrote: "The foam kinetics stand at the peak of a development started

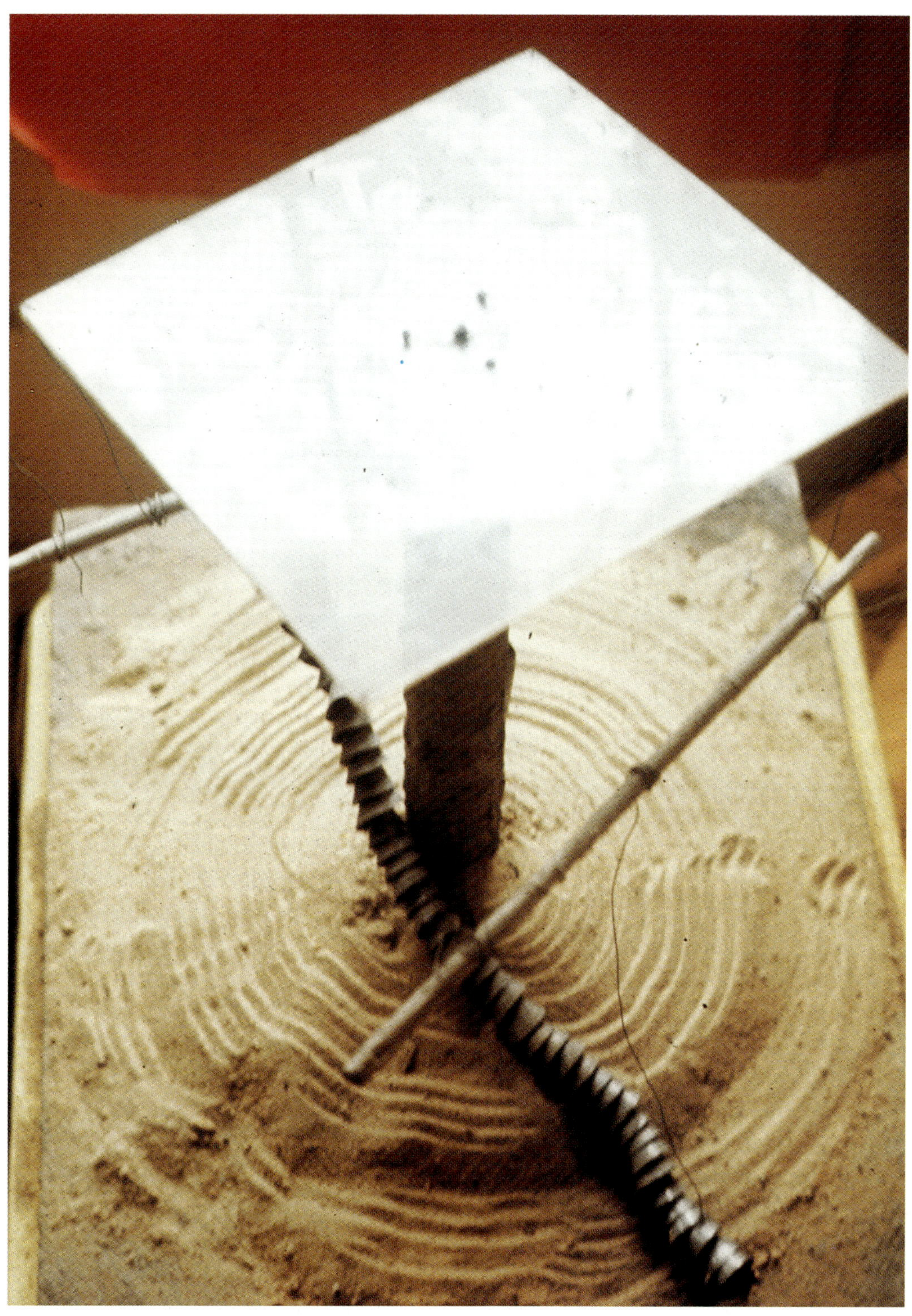

Lament, Sand Machine, 1964. Collection of the artist.

at the end of the last century. Gabo, Moholy-Nagy, Brancusi, Arp, Calder and others produced theories and works that lead to Medalla."[11] Metzger called Medalla "the first master of auto-creative art", a term Metzger had introduced, along with 'auto-destruction', in a theoretical manifesto of 1961. Among others, Hans Haacke, then a young artist in Germany, wrote the artist with "admiration for what you did in this field".[12] Scientists responded too. Medalla received a letter from Werner Heisenberg (he had published the great physicist's text on indeterminacy in *Signals Newsbulletin*), praising his demonstration of the poetic interactions between human-made technology and natural phenomena. J. D. Bernal, the crystallographer, writer and friend of Picasso, who visited Signals several times, also expressed a keen interest. On a visit to New York, Paul Keeler showed photographs of the Bubble Machines to Marcel Duchamp. It was intriguing to see, given the French artist's love of wordplay, that a short while later Duchamp issued a multiple he called *Medallic Object* (1968). This was a silver medal erupting with bubblelike forms which Duchamp was photographed holding in the palm of his hand surrounded by swathes of cigar smoke.

The mainstream world of British art, however, ignored the Bubble Machines. Despite the fact that this was the period when the new sculpture of Anthony Caro, Philip King, William Tucker and others was emerging, few in that milieu were able to see the greater daring and wit of Medalla's reprise of sculptural history. For as well as being a model of the "transformation of matter into energy", the Bubble Machines provided a startling development of the problematics explored by sculptors like Arp, Gabo and Brancusi (the latter often used as a touchstone in discussions of sculpture by the younger generation in the 1960s). Medalla felt that Brancusi had come as close as he could to the idea of dematerialisation, within the limits of a static and solid sculptural object, by polishing the smooth metal skin of his *Bird in Space* and egg-shaped *Beginning of the World*. In his use of plastics, Gabo also went as far as he could "to destroy the traditional idea of mass in sculpture". In Gabo's work "the experience of sculptural space becomes synonymous with the experience of continuous depth".[13] Similarly it could be said that Arp's *Concretions* reached static sculpture's limits in suggesting a polymorphic biological energy which all organisms have in common. The Bubble Machines seemed to take up the latent implications in these works and recast them in a new, freer spatio-temporal structure, or paradigm. Perhaps just for these reasons Medalla's work was seen as disturbing, for the ephemerality of mere foam threatened the laboured craft traditions which have always had such a hold on British art.

Medalla himself had no intention of leaving the Bubble Machine as a historical marker. The foam was a metaphor for expansion and growth which naturally exceeded its own bounds. There was no reason to declare it finished in the geometric and minimal framework in which he presented it in the mid-1960s, or to repeat it. It could continue to grow. As Medalla became increasingly absorbed by Buddhism in the late 1960s, and then by Marxism in the early 1970s, he produced a number of new Bubble

Machines in which the basic metaphor can be seen in beautiful and subtle reincarnations. For example, there was the philosophical, even cosmological, stupa-like mode of *MeghaSutta: The Cloud Discourse*, 1971,[14] and the delectable, sensuous structure of the hanging *Cloud Fruits*, 1972.

The first Bubble Machine (a single box) was exhibited in the 'Structures Vivantes' exhibition at the Redfern Gallery in 1964.[15] Later in the same year Medalla made the Sand Machine, quite a different sort of structure. In place of liquidity and flow there was something brittle and dry. A flimsy motor-driven structure dragged a suspended metal snake or helix slowly around a circular patch of sand. The Sand Machine was called *Lament*: it was "the death of metal, stone, all the materials of the past".[16] At the same time it suggested the possibility of growth. "I also see the sand machine", Medalla said, "as a metaphor for the future, when technology will be able to use solar power to help irrigate the world's deserts".[17] The sand imprinted by the metal was never still and "returned energy to it". Medalla saw the work as "like a three-dimensional mandala – it turns around".[18] Although revolving repetitively, the Sand Machine was in every other way reminiscent of non-mechanical technology, like a rudimentary plough suspended by wires, or "like the outriggers of Philippine canoes".[19] At the same time it was a snake, a penis, or a chrysalis about to discharge its contents.[20]

If Medalla's kinetics generally refer to sculptural traditions, the *Mud Machine*, 1964-67, is undoubtedly a 'painting machine'. As such it belongs to a small sub-genre within kinetic art. It invites comparison with certain of Jean Tinguely's *Metamatics*, machines which contain a roll or sheet of paper, a crank holding a pen, and produce wild automatic drawings one after another. In one sense painting machines were kinetic art's wry comment on the automatism of action painting. But the connections go deeper than that, for the drawing or painting machine is also analogous to the seismograph, encephalograph (and equivalents): devices for obtaining graphic traces of vital or cosmic energies. The 'painting machine' was another way of approaching the enigmatic borderline between aesthetic form and the forces of nature, between matter and meaning, between volition and chance, between pure play and intelligible signs, the domain of language. Medalla's *Mud Machine* is very elegantly poised on this borderline. By means of revolving discs, red-painted and mounted on a red panel, sponges on the end of wires delve with

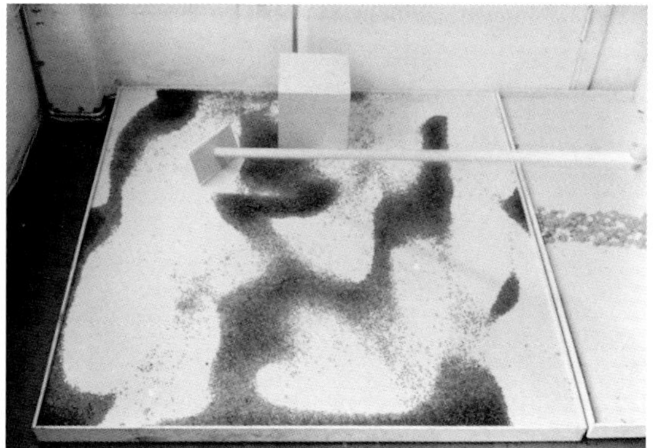

Glue Pearls Machine, 1967. Collection of the artist.

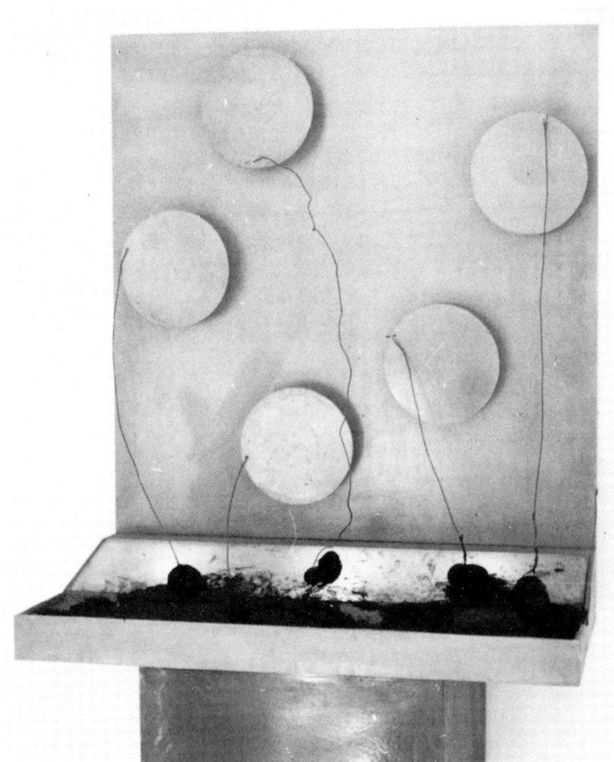

Mud Machine, 1967. Collection of the
artist.

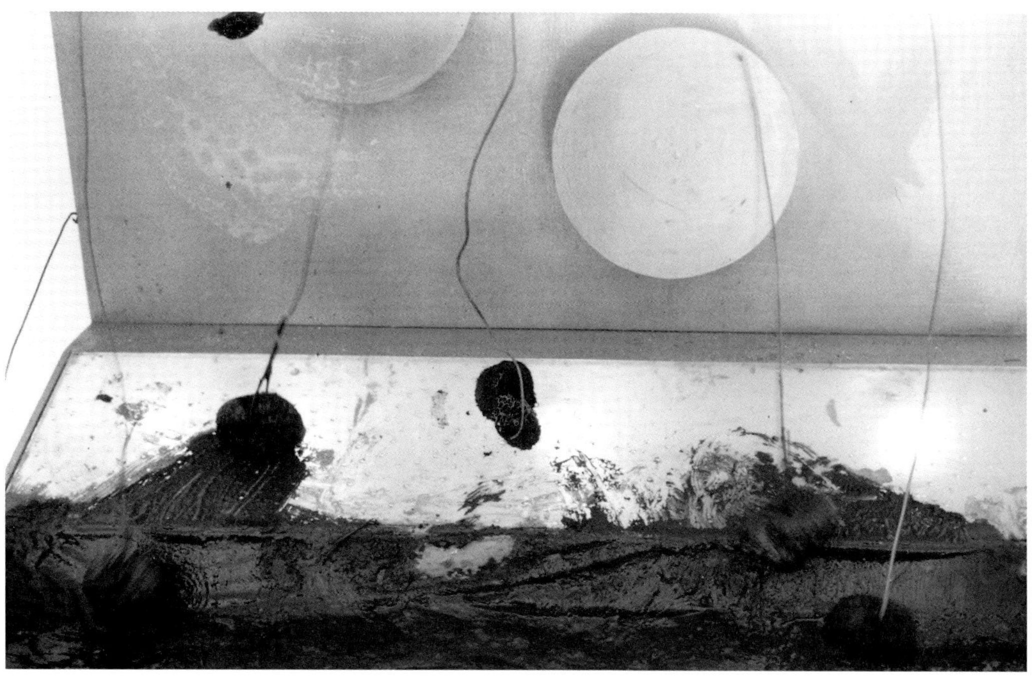

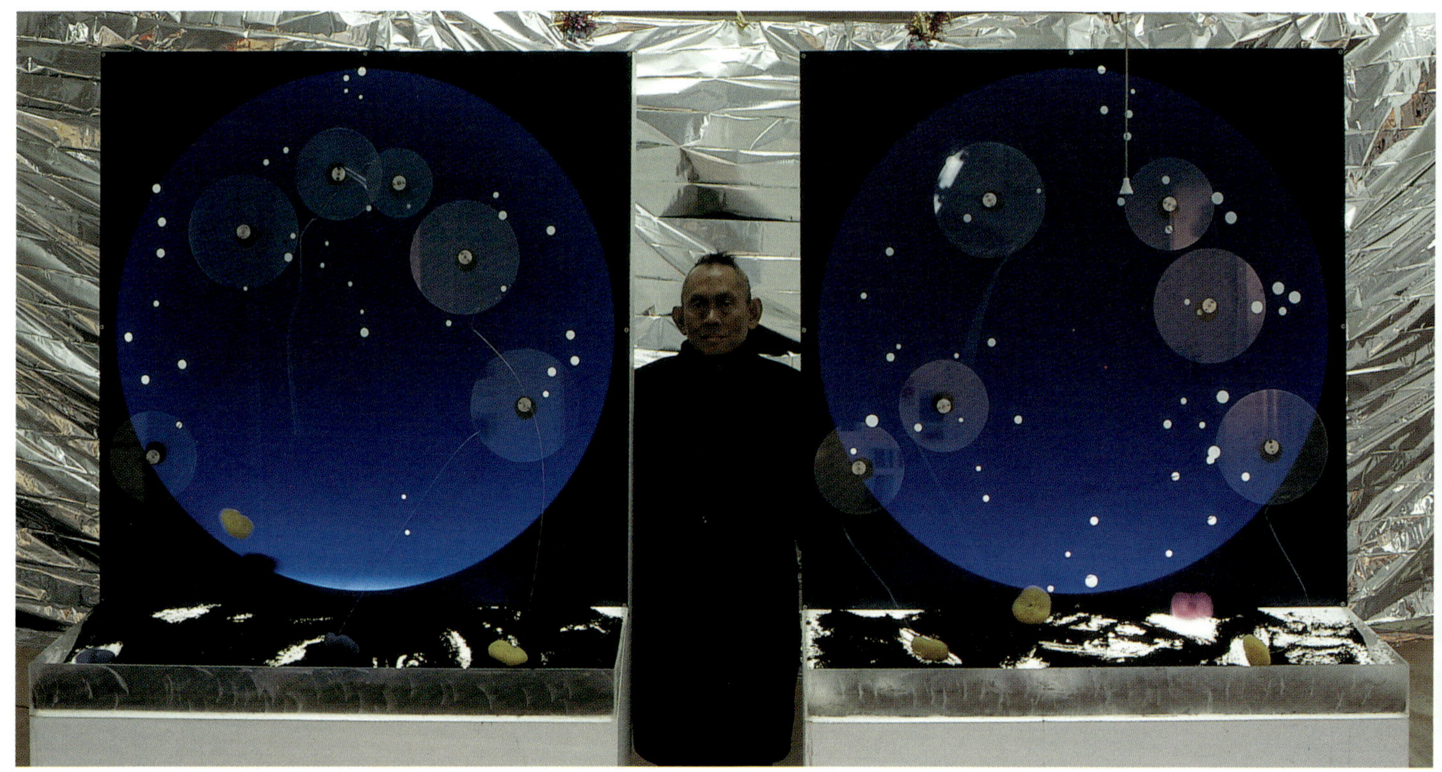

Medalla with a pair of Mud Machines, made in 1994 and exhibited during the 'Secret History of the Mondrian Fan Club', 55 Gee Street, London, 1994-5. The light apertures in the blue discs follow the patterns of the constellations, one of the southern hemisphere, the other of the northern.

Opposite: Study for **Audio-Capillary Mobiles,** 1968. Crayon on paper, 25.5 x 22 cms. Collection Guy Brett.

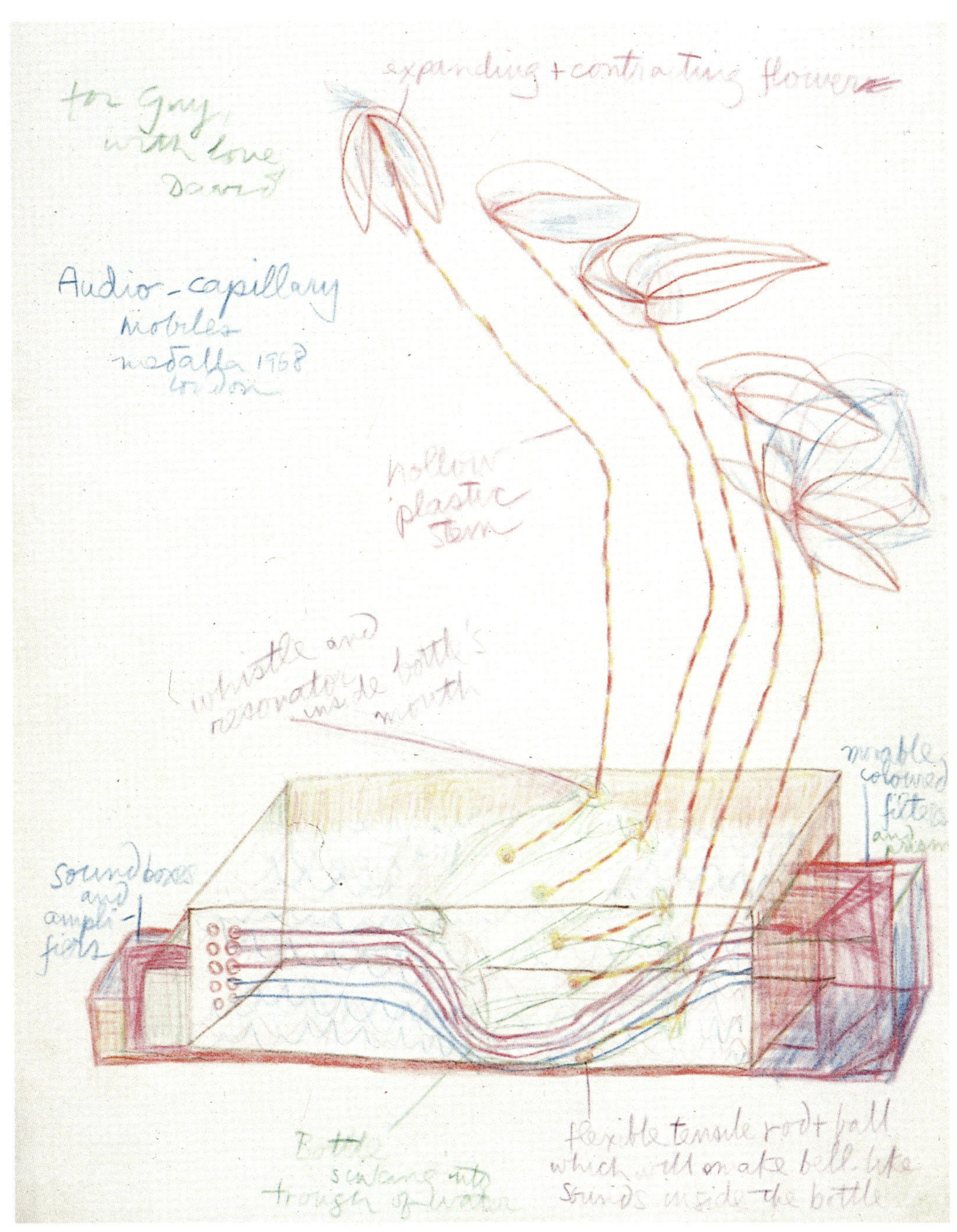

for Guy, with love David
Audio-capillary mobiles metalfa 1968 London
expanding + contracting flowers
hollow plastic stem
whistle and resonator inside bottle's mouth
marble coloured filter and prism
soundboxes and amplifiers
Bottle sinking into trough of water
flexible tensile rod + ball which will make bell-like sounds inside the bottle

Mondrian

Pruned his palette to
   Primary colours and his
     Design mechanisms to
     Verticals and horizontals:—
       Finally he

Reached a point at which
   He could not abide
     Green and changed seats
   At tables to avoid
     Seeing trees:

This magician who in
   His early work did some
     Of the most sensitive
   Studies of trees over achieved:
     Advancing

The degree of abstraction
   From example to
     Example until they
   Vanished in squares and
     Rectangles.

        José Garcia Villa,
          (New York)

Medalla : New Projects

David Medalla, the Filipino artist, has embarked on a series of new projects. David describes himself as " an **hylozoist** " (in reference to the Old Ionian pre-Sokratik philosophers)—" one of Those-who-think-Matter-is-Alive." Medalla introduced *into* sculpture the use of actual elements, not merely as adjuncts of objects but the elements themselves forming the major part of his truly original objects. David's main interest is matter in all its living manifestations. " I am not a physicist," he says, " but I like to think of myself as a poet who celebrates physics,"

Julio Herrera described David as " a boy of wisdom, the ferocity of whose wraths is tempered always with the tenderness of his loves." An apt description, say those who know David personally.

In Paris last month fellow-artist **Takis,** upon seeing David's sand machine, hailed him as a genius. " If other artists understand what Medalla has discovered," said Takis, " then they too will be geniuses like Medalla himself."

A number of David Medalla's new work is a direct continuation of his " **thermal sculptures.**" The first of these thermal sculptures was the bubble machine which was included in last month's pilot show at the Centre's headquarters. Other new developments are the following projects, small models of which will be included in the second pilot show and in subsequent exhibitions of the Centre for Advanced Creative Study.

1. Smoke machines with flickering lights in which the smoke itself, with its varying shapes, colours and densities, is the *actual* sculpture.

2. Artic columns: a series of sculptures in which water turns into icicles; the icicles dance, crackle and refract sunlight into a thousand rainbows; the icicles then melt into water and the process outlined above is repeated in an infinity of variations.

3. Floating sculptures which produce musical sounds when they hit each other while creating " pelagic pictures " under water with electric lights. A small study for this project was exhibited at last month's pilot show.

4. Whirlpool sculptures: leaves and other floating things whirling in *actual* whirlpools.

5. Machines for making Instant-Poetry. With a twinkle in his eye David says that these machines should provide " a sort of un-unified field theory of poetry somewhat analogous to the still missing unified field theory in physics which physicists have been trying to find in the last two or three thousand years."

6. Sand, wind and rain sculptures: further developments of Medalla's sand mobiles. In these constructions sand is blown by winds in different directions while raindrops and running water, make continuous patterns on sand. (Several people incidentally have noted the similarity of this concept to those of the sand gardens of Japan like the Ginkakuji in Kyoto and to the sand paintings of the Tacos Indians of North America.)

7. Hydrophonic rooms: rooms with ceilings planted with a million edible mushrooms, rooms with melting walls of milk and butter, rooms with transparent floors containing herbariums.

8. Collapsible sculptures and sculptures in components incorporating actual living things such as snails, shrimps, ants. In one construction, snails pass over sensitive plates of metal which trigger off certain modulated sounds. In another, ants travel in space through different lenses, the lenses magnifying and fragmenting into abstract patterns the ants' shapes. A third construction will present an underwater ballet of shrimps. In this set of projects living things are encouraged to express

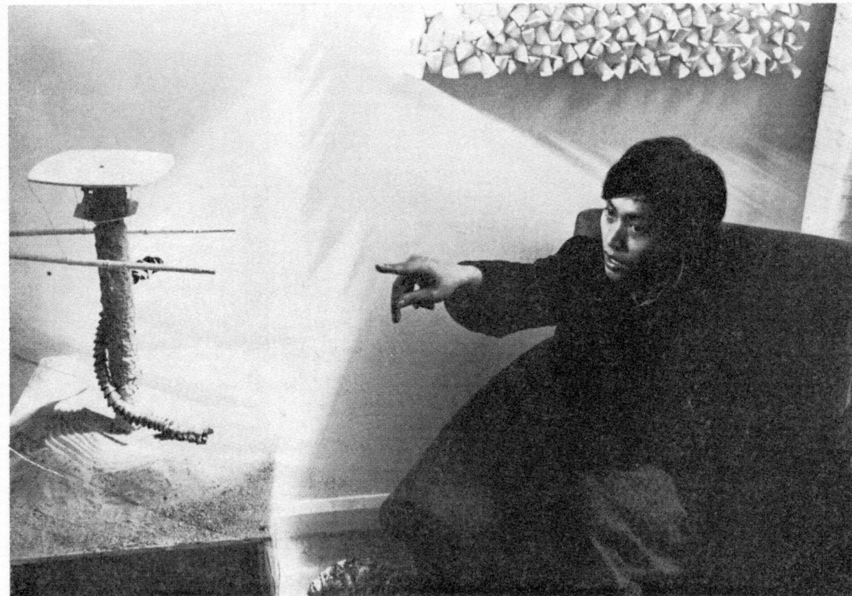

David Medalla with his Sand Machine. 1964

themselves. Medalla will thus confer the titles of " musicians to the snails, artists to the ants and dancers to the shrimps."

9. Radio-controlled flying sculptures, in which objects fly from a sort of gigantic " hive " into different parts of a room, different parts of a house, and into the streets. The " vagabond objects " will return to the hive at different intervals, at different hours of the day, even different days and months, from all parts of a city and may-be also the countryside, bringing with them all sorts of things such as envelopes, handkerchiefs, banners, buttons, banana peelings.

10. Lightning-rod sculptures: sculptures to be set in the open air and on top of sky-scrapers. The electricity which is " picked " by the lightning rods is conducted and transmitted into picture-making machines.

Finally there are

11. The thermo-paintings, in which pictures on frost- and mist-covered glass are made and unmade purely by the warmth of human breath, . . .

12. The machines for making mud pictures and sculptures.

13. The Braille sculptures : sculptures to be felt in the dark emitting incense, marjoram, thyme, mint, laurel, benjamin and other fragrances.
and

14. Transparent sculptures that sweat and perspire. When the spectator fans these sculptures, they cool down, reduce their volumes, change their colours, sizes, shapes. These perspiring sculptures also palpitate with the changing intensities of darkness and light.

David Medalla is also a poet, a mime, and a dancer. At the age of 12 Medalla was appointed lecturer on the humanities at the state University of the Philippines. By that time he had already written anthropological studies on the remaining primitive tribes of the Philippines as well as the first translations into Tagalog, the Filipino national language, of the works of Shakespeare, Milton and Walt Whitman.
At 15, upon the recommendation of the American poet **Mark Van Doren,** Medalla was admitted as a special scholar at Columbia University. At Columbia David studied Greek drama under Professor **Moses Hadas** who was also appointed Medalla's tutor. It was in New York that David took up painting seriously under the encouragement of the poet **José Garcia Villa.**
When David returned to the Philippines he was invited to deliver a set of lectures on Dante's *Commedia* before the Poetry Club of Manila. Shortly afterwards, David delivered another set of lectures, **The Ironical Discourses,** parodying the pomposities of Manila's social and cultural life, before a herd of carabaos (water-buffaloes) and a flock of white-legged herons in the rice-fields of his father's home province.
David is the author of a comic biography in verse of Arthur Rimbaud entitled **The Poet in Abyssinia,** and of several black fairytales including one about the love life of a daylight-bat and another on " the memoirs of an Irish trombone in the Chicago days of the gangster Al Capone." A third fairytale, **The Floating Pagoda,** was successfully translated into a dance drama for children.

David has given many lectures before schools and clubs in England on behalf of the Freedom from Hunger campaign (" the only movement," he says, " in which I truly believe."). This year **David Medalla** is designing an **Heraclitean Ballet** in which dancers will perform on a smoking stage while spirals, squares, cones, cubes, and pyramids of fire whirl in space.

New Books

Next year should see the publication of several interesting books on kinetic art. **Frank Popper** is completing a history of movement in art which he hopes to publish soon in paperback form. Popper's informative article " Movement and Light in Today's Art " in *The Unesco Courier*, September 1963, may be said to have sparked the present worldwide interest in this subject.
Reg Gadney of Cambridge is also preparing a full-length study of art in motion. Gadney wrote an article on kinetic art for *Granta*, November 1963, and he has just finished another essay with especial emphasis on the aesthetic problems of this movement which will appear soon in *The London Magazine*.
Guy Brett, youngest and in many ways the most dynamic of London's art critics, is writing a book on individual kinetic artists. Brett is personally acquainted with the leading artists of this movement and should be able to report first-hand their ideas, plans, thoughts and projects. Brett is the author of three full-length articles in *The Guardian* on the immense possibilities of kinetic art in relation to our environment.
Jack Burnham and **Willoughby Sharp** are two art historians from America who will also be writing on kinetic art in the next few months. Both came to London last month to attend the first pilot show of the Centre for Advanced Creative Study and to gather material for their work. Willoughby Sharp is a graduate of Columbia University and writes for American art magazines. Jack Burnham is with the art department of Northwestern University, Illinois, where he is now preparing a study of kinetic art with especial emphasis on artists like **Medalla** and **Yves Klein** who have broken the artificial " boundaries " between nature and the so-called art object.
Most recent book to discuss (along with other subjects) aspects of kinetic art is **Frank Avray Wilson's** *Art as Understanding*, Routledge and Kegan Paul, 1963. *Signalz* recommends Mr. Wilson's book for its detailed and intelligent exposition of the different trends in today's art.

Many Thanks

The Centre thanks **Miss H. Swift** and the Central Office of Information for the loan of their documentary film on *structures vivants*, and **Mr. Simon Watson Taylor,** *pataphysicien,* for the loan to the first pilot show of two small *erectiles* by **Pol Bury.** Many thanks also to the anonymous donor who gave the Centre its first gift : an Isokan pengiun donkey mark 2. Thanks also to the Couper Gallery for the loan of works by **J. M. Cruxent** to the second pilot show; to the McRoberts and Tunnard Gallery for the loan of a work by **Otto Piene;** to **Willoughby Sharp** for bringing over from Europe works by **Hans Haacke** and **Aubertin;** to **Clay Perry** for the photographs in this issue; to **Julie Lawson** of the Institute of Contemporary Arts for her encouragement and cooperation; and to the following for their gift of a book (*Kunst und Naturform*, Basilius Presse, Basel): **Brian Stones, Keith Potts, Philip Smythe** and **Stephen Knott.**

Book on Nena Saguil

Mme. Suzanne de Coninck, directress of the *Centre d'Art Cybernetique* and of the Galerie de Beaune in Paris, has announced the publication for autumn of a book on the art of **Nena Saguil.**
The book was begun last year by the late **Professor Ernest Fraenkel,** author of a monograph on the Russian expatriate painter **Schraga Zarfin** and of a remarkable *critique cinétique* on Stephane Mallarme's **Un coup de dès n'abolira pas le hasard.** Professor Fraenkel died last spring a month after he wrote the note on Saguil for the catalogue of the **Soundings One** exhibition which **Paul Keeler** organised at the Ashmolean Museum in Oxford. Fraenkel's unfinished essay on Saguil is now being completed by the French critic and art historian **M. Waldemar George.** In M. George's opinion the essay on Saguil was Professor Fraenkel's most beautiful work.
The book when completed will contain over fifty black-and-white illustrations and half a dozen colour reproductions tracing the development of Nena Saguil's art from her early geometric abstractions to her present explorations into " the fourth dimension in painting."

BBC Film, Interview

The film unit of BBC's **Town and Around** under producer **David Hartsilver** made a 3-minute film on the Centre's first pilot show. **Michael Noakes** interviewed **David Medalla** who discussed some of the work on view including **Salvadori's** *Eclipses,* **Camargo's** *Wooden Reliefs,* **Soto's** *Vibrations,* and the *Ballet Magnetique* by **Takis.**
Last June 21st, **John Newell,** BBC science correspondent, interviewed **Paul Keeler** on the BBC home service about the aims and activities of the Centre.

Vasarely Journals

The cultural bureau of the *Ecole Nationale Superieure des Beaux Arts,* Paris, has just published the journals of **Victor Vasarely.** Mimeographed on green paper with an original cover by Vasarely himself, this handsome volume contains notes and reflections on life and art by this profound and fecund artist. Translations of the journal will appear soon in *Peacock,* a new literary magazine in Oxford.

Metzger Film

Centre members recently attended a private showing of a film on **Gustav Metzger's** demonstration of auto-destructive art.

Telescope

A medium-range telescope will be installed in the balcony of Flat 4, 92 Cornwall Gardens this summer for the use of Centre members and their guests.

Printed by Luff & Sons Ltd., Windsor

abandon and also considerable delicacy into a mixture of mud and oil and drag it onto an electrically-lit glass screen.

A comparison between Tinguely's and Medalla's machines is quite revealing. Tinguely's are considerably more frenetic, noisy and draw attention to their own exertions. They lurch about like clowns, but they are very much clowns at the court of King Machine, completely imbued with the mechanical ethos. Tinguely, after all, was Swiss, from a country with a long-standing culture of the machine, whereas the Philippines, according to Medalla, traditionally had no concept of the machine. Medalla's are machines made by a non-mechanical person. It is also a curious and revealing fact that, whereas Tinguely's machines keep an exclusive mechanistic integrity into which one would not dare to insert a hand (like the machine in Chaplin's *Modern Times*), Medalla's welcome the hand.

Thus, although both artist's works are ultimately propelled by the same type of electric motor, with its uniform and repetitive motion, the expression is quite different. The painting simile in the Tinguely is close to the Baroque, in the Medalla to oriental calligraphy. Medalla himself noted the difference: "In western sculpture, in Baroque art for instance, there is no balance between active and passive. There is pure emphasis on dynamic movement: no point of rest and no point of meditation".[21] By inclination, and fuelled by the study he was then making of Buddhism and Indian and Chinese art, Medalla was looking for a kind of movement which would also contain stillness, "a movement which is elastic and very still and calm... without frenzy such as you find in Baroque art".[22] He later said of his Bubble Machines that "there is a certain slowness in motion,

MMMMMMM . . . MANIFESTO

(*a fragment*)

Mmmmmmm . . . Mmmedalla! What do you dream of?

I dream of the day when I shall create sculptures that breathe, perspire, cough, laugh, yawn, smirk, wink, pant, dance, walk, crawl, . . . and move among people as shadows move among people. . . . Sculptures that will retain a shadow's secret dimensions without a shadow's obsequious behaviour. . . . Sculptures without hope, with waking and sleeping hours. . . . Sculptures that, on certain seasons, will migrate *en masse* to the North Pole. Sculptures with a mirror's translucency minus the memory of a mirror!

Mmmmmmm . . . Mmmedalla! What do you dream of?

I dream of the day when I shall go to the centre of the earth and in the earth's core place a flower-sculpture. . . . Not a lotus, nor a rose, nor a flower of metal, . . . nor yet a flower of ice and fire. . . . But a *mohole*-flower, its petals curled like the crest of a tidal wave approaching the shore. . . .

Mmmmmmm . . . Mmmedalla! What do you dream of?

I dream of a day when, from the capitals of the world, London Paris New York Madrid Rome, I shall release missile-sculptures. . . . to fly — at nine times the speed of sound . . . to fall — slim as a stork on a square in Peking . . . bent, crushed — like a soldier's boot after an explosion — on an airport in Ecuador . . . in splinters — on the fields of Omaha. . . . A few — to cross interstellar space . . . accumulating, as they wing along, asteroids, meteorites, magnetic fields, interstellar germs . . . of a new life . . . on their way from our galaxy to the Spiral Nebula. . . . *Mmmmm-mmmmmmmmmmmmmm. . . .*

David Medalla
London, 1965

MMMMMMM..... Manifesto, 1965, published in Signals Newsbulletin, Vol 1 no 8, June-July 1965.

Opposite: **New Projects** published in Signals Newsbulletin vol 1 no 1, August 1964.

quite different from the dizzying and frenetic kind of kinetic art".[23] The exploration of movement in Medalla's sculpture took forms which sometimes bring to mind the eroded stones used in Taoist cosmology as symbols of the universal flux, or the "growing and expanding" sense of form which the German scholar Heinrich Zimmer,

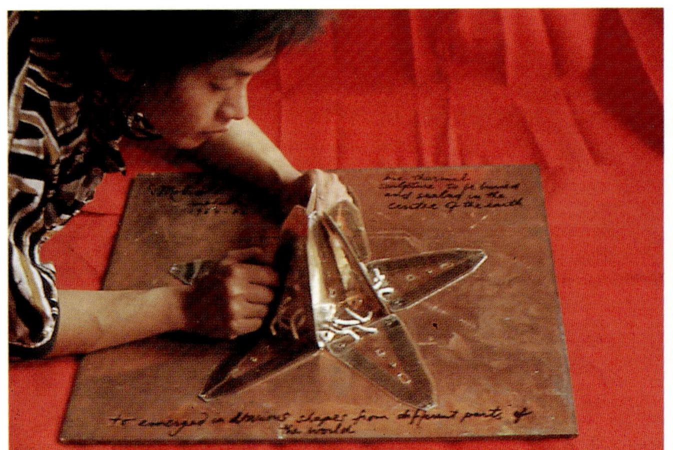
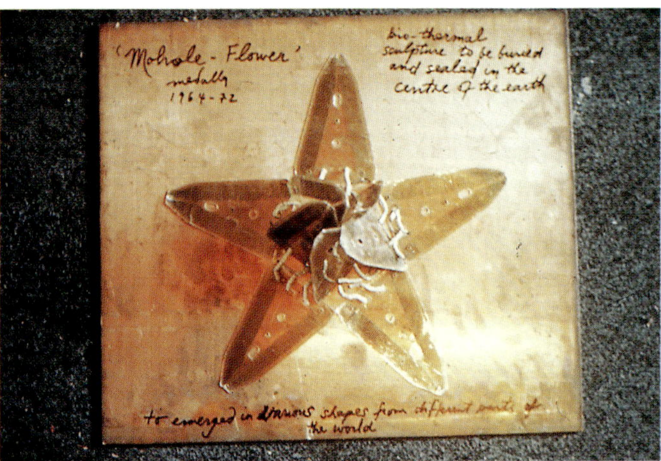

Above and opposite: **The Mohole Flower**, 1964-72, project for a "biothermal sculpture to be buried and sealed in the centre of the earth to emerge in various shapes in different parts of the world." Collection of the artist.

in a seminal book, *Myths and Symbols in Indian Art and Civilization*, identified as characteristic of Indian sculpture. Thus was the internationalism of kinetic art mixed with distinct cultural traditions.

Medalla produced a rather small number of kinetic machines. Each had a distinct identity. He made one when the possibility or the need arose, but equally striking at this period is the relationship he posed between the sensuous experience given by a physical object, and the imaginative experience given by words. Direct exposure to the Bubble Machine is essential: there is no other way to experience the quality of its movement, its translucency, even the sound of its millions of tiny bursting bubbles. For the artist this kinetic experience was a way of overcoming a gulf between spectator and work: "The most important thing I think is to give life to materials, so that instead of finding ourselves separate from them we find a complete dialogue with the material."[24] "For me, interior space and exterior space are mutually interchangeable... and access from one to the other is made possible through rhythm."[25] He had constructed the group of boxes in *Cloud Canyons* according to the proportions of his own body: he was looking for a correspondence between the play of elemental forces in the work and in the spectator's body, very much in the manner Moholy-Nagy had prophesied forty years before for a future kinetic art:

Dynamic construction... must be evolved, in which material is employed as the carrier of forces... A dynamic-constructive system... is attained whereby man, hitherto merely receptive in his observation of works of art, experiences a heightening of his own faculties, and becomes himself an active partner with the forces unfolding themselves.[26]

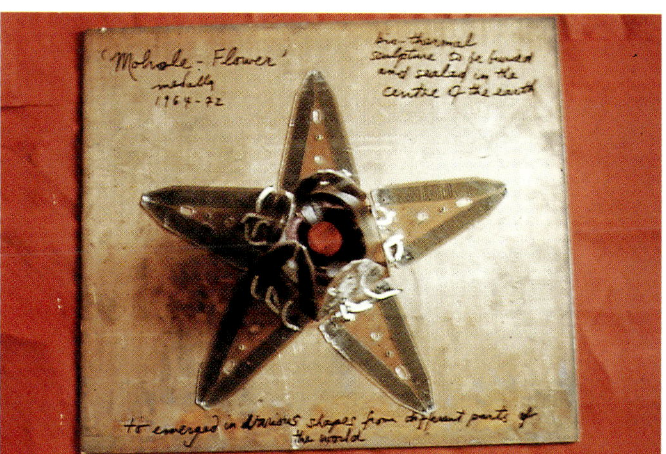

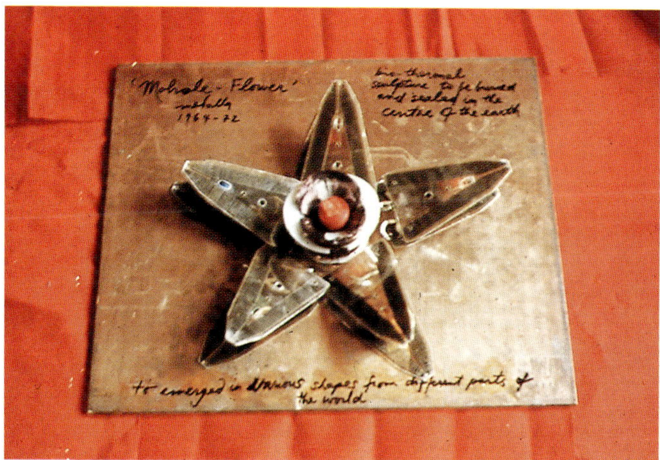

Medalla believed that biokinetics offered new possibilities of "making people sensuously alive once more",[27] at a time when the senses were undervalued in favour of the intellect. His kinetic objects were intended to bridge the gap between our expanding scientific knowledge of the universe, including ourselves, and our psychic awareness of it, the sensory experience with its complex of instincts and reflexes, memories and suppressions, unique to each individual, with which art is concerned.

At the same time Medalla remained very much the writer. His physical art objects may be said to represent the tangible portion of a larger intangible reality which was in some sense a poetic reality, a boundless reality, a longing for the impossible. His kinetic machines were accompanied by a great outpouring of ideas in the form of fantastic projects for sculpture. These make a playful use of the conceits of literary style. As in the list of *New Projects* published in the first issue of *Signals Newsbulletin*, or the *MMMMM.....Manifesto*, 1965, published in *Signals Newsbulletin* 8, Medalla contrived to weave together the roles of pragmatic 'maker' and unrestrained 'dreamer'. Later he gave the name of *Cosmic Propulsions* to these foci for imaginative reverie, which could both take a verbal and/or a physical form. They became a constant vehicle for his thinking, even while the style of his work changed and he experimented with various media. One model for his notion of the *Cosmic Propulsion* he found in the kind

63

of metaphors the Buddha would use in his discourses in answer to the questions which obsessed people at the time:

...pedants were trying to determine the length of one kalpa - the life span of one cosmic system - but the Buddha had more wisdom and imagination than these scholastics and he proposed a metaphor: if you imagine a cube of solid rock which is four metres square, and at the end of every century a man were to stroke it once with a fine piece of Benares muslin, the rock would be worn away before the kalpa came to an end...

This kind of metaphor is incredible! It shows what a metaphor is. First, you have two separate elements: a piece of solid rock and a piece of the finest Benares muslin - two almost incongruous elements. The equation between these two produces an image which is almost boundless. If I aspire to anything in art, I aspire for that kind of proposition. It doesn't matter if it is only a proposition if it inspires others. Confronted with such a metaphor, your mind will be able to grasp the mysteries of life. A metaphor also has the capacity for continuous growth. It grows all the time you think about it. It transcends the elements which constitute it...[28]

Medalla's written kinetic projects draw upon visual art as a metaphorical structure. 'Sculpture' becomes an elastic concept or a designation to celebrate the richness of nature, and its micro/macrocosmic unity. Some of these projects were based on the human body (*Capillary Environments*, 1964, *Astroacupuncture Man*, 1964, or sculptures which "move among people as shadows move among people... [retaining] a shadow's secret dimensions without a shadow's obsequious behaviour", (*MMMMMM.....Manifesto*). Others were based on the globe itself: *The Mohole Flower*, 1967, a sculpture to be placed at the core of the earth to grow towards the surface in the heat and darkness – an opposite of the Bubble Machine's "quiet celebration of the beneficence of sunlight and water"; *Listen to the Sonar Trees*, 1969, where electronic trees on the daylight side of the world would receive and broadcast the nocturnal sounds of people sleeping on the other side; *Sweeping the Sounds of the Sea*, at various ports (Venice, Barcelona, Dakar, Mombassa, Karachi, Bombay, Cochin, Madras, Colombo, Singapore, Bangkok and Manila) and putting them in a crystal box which the artist dropped into the Marianas Trench in the Pacific, 1968-69; *The World as a Migrant Microdot*, 1964, images of every face in the world condensed into a microdot and launched into outer space, and so on. In *Go to Work on a Poem*, 1965, the 'poem' is submitted to the same treatment.[29] Such projects provided a precedent and pioneered an atmosphere in which artists later could think of taking a walk, cooking food, digging a hole or building an aeroplane as 'sculpture'.

As Medalla's kinetic work progressed the overall theme of an interaction between human beings and materials, between human beings and nature, was increasingly given a social and a psychological dimension. The Brazilian sculptor Sergio de Camargo considered Medalla's Bubble Machines as modern-day fountains (albeit proposing a more subtle form of mutability than the graphic patterns of waterjets). The Bubble Machines are public, communal amenities, enjoyable as a simple form of recreation as well as a radical proposition in the discourse of sculpture.[30] Medalla speculated on the possibility of bringing together the themes of kinetic sculpture, the transformation of materials, social amenity, and the participation of the spectator, in unrealised projects like his *Monumental Breadmaking Machines* of 1967 (environmental urban sculptures incorporating ovens in which people could bake bread in any shape they chose). These interrelated themes were to become of increasing importance in the next phase of his work.

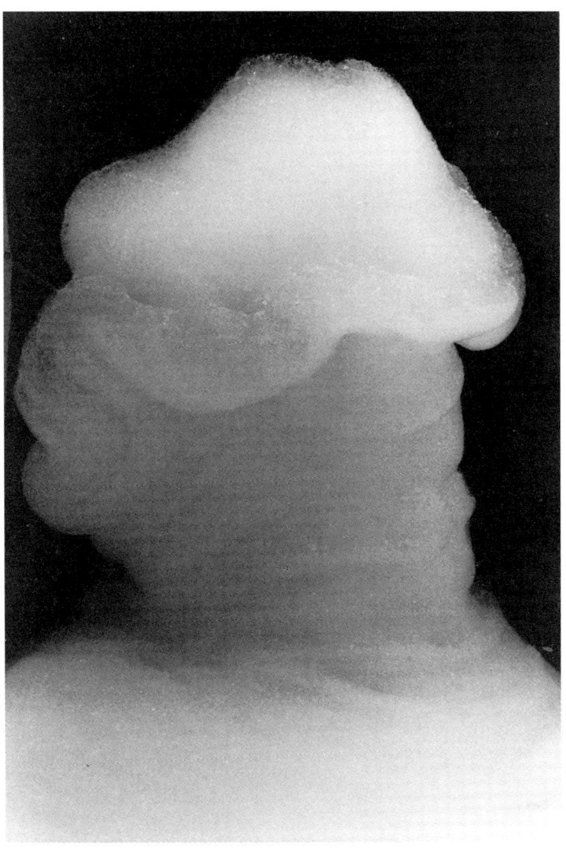

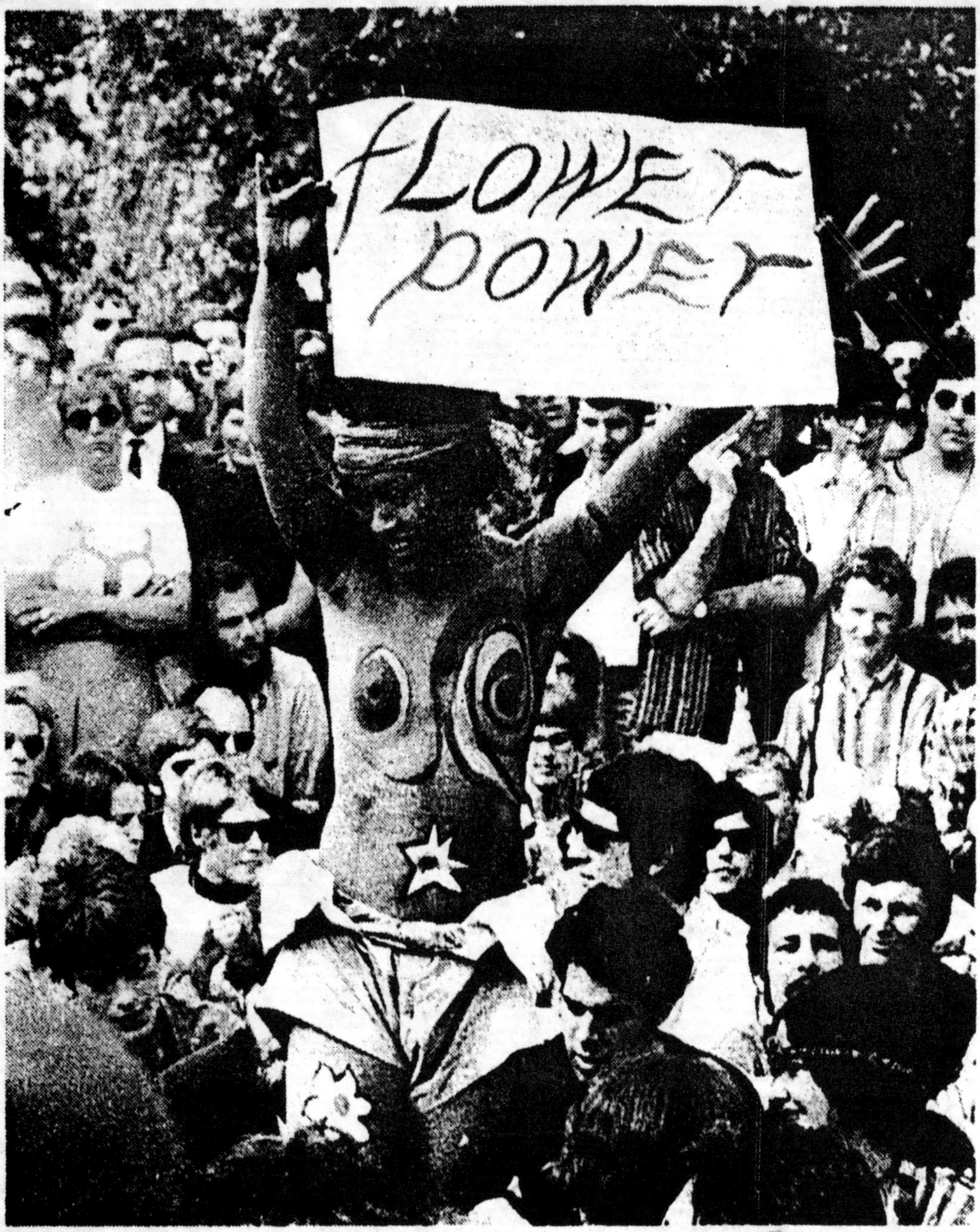

The hippy look in Hyde Park . . . painted Philippine sculptor David Medalla leads the dancing.

March of the Flower (Pot) men

Story: Mirror Reporter

Picture: Eric Piper

EVEN the regulars down at Speakers' Corner, who are well versed in eccentricities, had to admit that yesterday was quite something.

To put it psychedelically, it was a rare old happening.

Hundreds of young "Hippies" wandered into London's Hyde Park to spread their love-thy-neighbour beliefs.

And, in passing, they

flowers. They are used to this sort of thing in San Francisco, of course, where the Hippie cult started, but police had to step in only twice yesterday.

The first time was when American beat poet Alan Ginsberg chanted

an Indian prayer accompanied by an accordion.

A policeman reminded him he could not play a musical instrument in public without a licence.

The long-haired poet thanked the officer and handed him a red rose.

Another Hippie was

booked for leaving his car (registration letters LOVE) in a no-waiting area. All in all . . . a very loving afternoon.

And with the temperature in the eighties, the Hippies rounded it off with a dip in the Serpentine. Real cool.

By MIRROR REPORTER

HE'S daring. Pow! He's resolute. Wow! He's . . . Frugalman.

He's the comic-strip hero specially dreamed up for American Servicemen and their families in Britain.

But the tough new crusader, modelled on the bold Batman, won't be fighting petty villains like the Riddler and the rest.

Holy small fry, no! He'll be campaigning to stop the American families spending dollars in Britain.

For Frugalman and his

T

chum, K part of a mick to US gold

The da posters man, is that d foreign being exc instead buy Ame

The de

Warning c cartoon d

DANTE, the champion police children not to take sweets

He is the star of a strip-cartoon Sussex police will hand out to 30,00

Dante children pictures to bewa and to are hor

The an atte crimes

Mr. G Constab said yer tribution has bee cide wit days, w more li risk."

Dant police touring the con

NANCY TO MAKE A COME-BACK

From DENIS MARTIN, Vienna, Sunday

ACTRESS Nancy Kwan is coming back to the bright lights of London— to look for a job.

She left Britain and her part in "The World of Suzie Wong" three years ago to help her Austrian husband Peter Pock run a hotel near Innsbruck. At the time she said: "We are staying here for ever." But the hotel itself cost them much more to build than they expected. Avalanches upset the winter sports prospects — and holidaymakers didn't turn out in force. Now Nancy hopes to make enough to pay off their debts. She will be contacting her film friends when she arrives in London.

"Then," she says, "as soon as I have made enough money I will go back home."

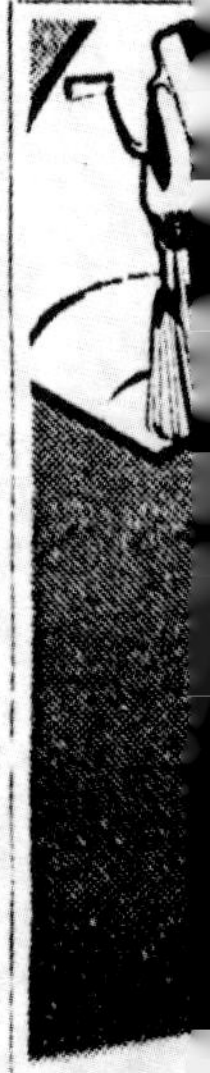

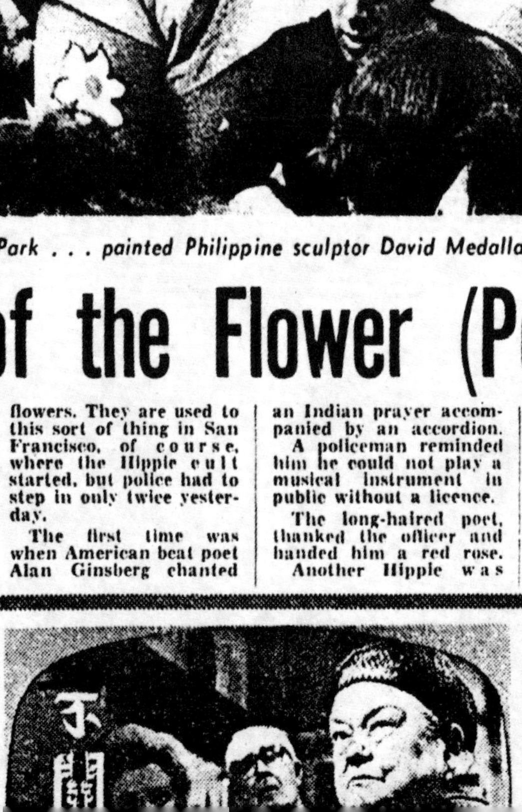

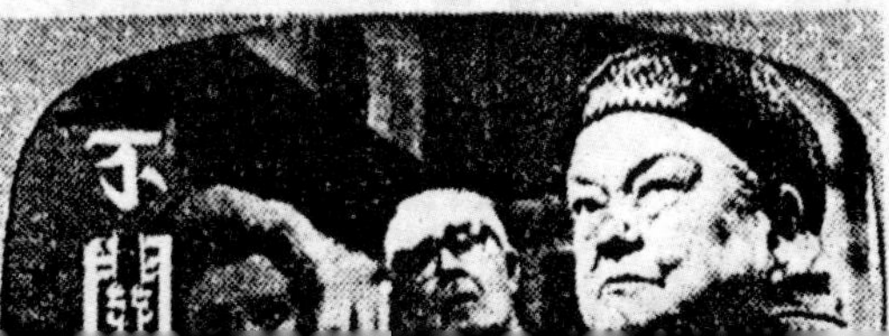

NOW ENA SAYS IT WITH CANTONESE SUB-TITLES

GIMLET eyes, thin-lipped smile. It's Ena

of her twice-weekly serial "Coronation Street" have sold 156 episodes to Hong

Great

Three

Agitation and Festivity

In 1966 Signals' main backer (Paul Keeler's father, Charles Keeler) withdrew his support and the gallery went into liquidation. Mr Keeler charged financial incompetence; Medalla, that Paul's father, a business man, had strongly disapproved of his, Medalla's, publication in *Signals Newsbulletin* of Lewis Mumford's 1965 address to the American Academy of Arts and Letters. Mumford had used this prestigious occasion to criticise publicly the American involvement in Vietnam, and *Signals* also published the American poet Robert Lowell's letter declining an invitation to the White House for the same reasons.[1] In keeping with a decision I have taken for the book as a whole, I will not try here to untangle the details of the demise of Signals. Like that of later groups Medalla formed, the ending was a painful shock to all concerned. There were several exhibitions in preparation and Medalla had a mass of material for future issues of the magazine. But at this distance it is impossible not to be struck by the logic of the metamorphosis of Signals, 1964-66, into The Exploding Galaxy, 1967-69, Artists' Liberation Front, 1970-74, and Artists for Democracy, 1974-77. Each group corresponded precisely to its period and to those great underlying cultural and historical changes which touched in some way almost everyone on the planet.

Signals' ambience was scientific, research-oriented, and was inspired by the visionary belief that there could be an imaginative fusion between technology, art and nature. The Exploding Galaxy, to all appearances, was the typical anarchic hippy commune everyone associates with the 1960s. Artists' Liberation Front was like a radical cell or party branch, with regulated meetings, agitational programmes and ideological struggle. Artists for Democracy was a broad-front organisation, beginning with an agitational mode of operation in which individuals cooperated on an agreed cultural task, and later relaxing its boundaries to become an avant-garde venue which welcomed early experiments in performance, video, installation and the aesthetics and politics of identity. The connecting thread is that all these were artists' groups, and a changing notion of artistic practice can be traced through them.

Of course the agenda of Signals, and kineticism, was far from finished. Many artists would continue along the path they had chosen, with better or worse results. Medalla's position was a paradoxical mixture. He continued with his kinetic machines, as we have seen, but also chose to plunge into each cultural change as it came along – in fact to be one of the instigators of change. Therefore it is hard to know whether the speed with which the appearance of The Exploding Galaxy followed the disappearance of Signals represented Medalla's capacity to recover from a serious setback, or expressed an unexpected liberation from a pattern which was becoming constricting. It would fit with both interpretations that Medalla proceeded to initiate a new phase, precisely placed at the vanguard. This must be recognised as a courageous act since it would have been easy for him to have used the success of his kinetic work to launch a career in the art world. As it was, the formation of The Exploding Galaxy represented a decisive turn away from the recognised art world.

The analysis he was making about the development of his own work coincided with what he observed going on around him:

London in the beginning of 1967 was full of fermenting creativity, of signs of renewal. The public became aware of the sudden appearance of what the press immediately labelled 'The Flower People'. Mostly young people, disappointed with the values of a morally bankrupt society. A colourful mixture of people who experimented sometimes wisely sometimes not so wisely with various means to reach consciousness of their oppressed egos. They searched for different ways to live honestly, free of the destructive pressures and obligations of the consumer society.[2]

He saw clearly that the kinetic processes in his machines, "which respire and perspire, grow and decay in the same way as other organisms in nature", could be extended to the world of people:

I felt at that time a deep dissatisfaction towards all art that derives solely from one single person, and is determined by one person's ideas and wishes. True, in my biokinetic works I gave up my role as creator for the benefit of an auxiliary function: that of 'transmitter' or 'initiator'. Ultimately what became the true creators were: electrochemical forces, the elements in motion, light. A total submission to the acts of chance, a complete acceptance of every incident, this has characterised my works since 1961...

I wanted to share my thoughts and feelings with the spectator, who has been kept at an almost unreachable distance by the established art of our time. I wanted to break down the invisible barrier between 'creator' and 'spectator', [for art to become] a living process in which one, two or several people formulate suggestions that others take up and develop in different directions.

I thought: why not create a situation where dance, poetry, singing, painting and sculpture could cooperate and penetrate each other as they did in the great historical cultures? Yes, why not! And with that intention I went round London in the beginning of 1967, among strangers and friends and invited all interested to join me in the creation of such a dynamic climate. I called my original suggestion 'The Exploding Galaxy' as I thought this name sufficiently flexible to contain and inspire all sorts of activities.[3]

A comparable trajectory was also being followed by two Brazilian artists, associated with Signals but based in Rio de Janeiro, Lygia Clark (1920-1988) and Hélio Oiticica (1937-80). Because of the parallels and mutual influences, and because the connections between a Filipino and two Brazilians forged in Europe represent a kind of creative axis which is still invisible to our art history, it is necessary here to say a little more about it.

An exhibition of Lygia Clark's reliefs and articulated metal sculptures had been held at Signals in 1965, with a special issue of *Signals Newsbulletin* devoted to her work. Works by Oiticica were already in Britain waiting for a show when the gallery closed in 1966. They were kept and later added to in a special environment designed by the artist for his celebrated 'experiment' at the Whitechapel Gallery in 1969. Medalla wrote an appreciation of Lygia Clark's work in the Paris publication *Robho* and met her several times when Clark was living and working in Paris in the late 1960s and early 1970s. For her part, Lygia Clark considered Medalla a "great artist and innovator".[4] Medalla and Oiticica never met, although they corresponded. Oiticica looked forward to work (or to play) with the Exploding Galaxy when he came to London in 1969 (by that time half the Galaxy, including David, were in India but other members became regular visitors and Oiticica's helpers at the Whitechapel). In many ways the Galaxy, for Oiticica, represented the *Barracão*, place/community of experiment and creativity (the term derived from the sacred communal dance space in Afro-Brazilian *candomblé*), which Oiticica dreamed of initiating in Rio de Janeiro. When Oiticica died in 1980, David described him as "my spiritual twin". There are many parallels between their

First Legalise Pot Rally, Hyde Park, London, 1967.

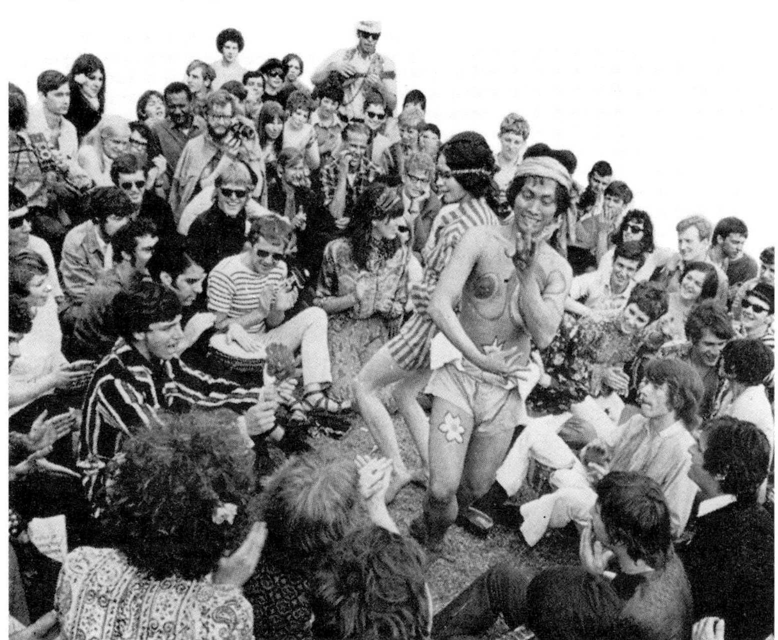

personalities, ideas and way of life. One example would be the link between Oiticica's *Delirium Ambulatorium*, 1978 and Medalla's *London Walks* and *Impromptus*. Both were a sort of systematisation of the delight of discovering new meanings in the everyday environment, suddenly, like an 'epiphany'.

Both Lygia Clark and Hélio Oiticica first appeared in the context of the powerful modernising drive which arose in several of the wealthiest Latin American countries after World War II. European modernism was studied to the depths in art, architecture, theatre, music, poetry and film. Earlier stages in Latin American modernism were revived. Clark and Oiticica moved rapidly to the most radical positions reached in European abstraction, of which Mondrian and Malevich were for them the key representatives. The work of Mondrian and Malevich they saw not as an end, the achievement of a pictorial language or a style, but as a stage in an aesthetic-philosophical exploration of reality which could be extended. They had a dual position which was very significant. On the one hand they accepted Mondrian's break with traditional representation, with illusionistic picture-space and figuration; on the other hand they gradually moved from the rational rigidities of the geometricisation of space towards something more sensuous and organic.

They conceived of the work of art not as a 'machine' or as an 'object', but as a 'quasi-body'. This was stated in the manifesto of their Neo-Concrete Group (founded in Rio in 1959), in which they stressed their differences with constructivism and concrete art. An early work like Lygia Clark's *Egg*, 1958, (of which David Medalla owns the original) perfectly expresses their position at that time. This is a circular black relief about 12 inches in diameter with a narrow white indented circumference line that, at one point, is left open. The black void leaks out, the surrounding space filters in. The whole is the cosmic egg of 'full-emptiness'. Lygia herself said that she "began with geometry but was looking for an organic space where one could enter

Opposite: David Medalla as the yellow wagtail bird.

The Exploding Galaxy in **The Bird Ballet**, Round House, London, October 1967. Left: Jocelyn de Warren Waller as stork, Audrey Vipond as sacred ibis, Eve Ridoux as flamingo.

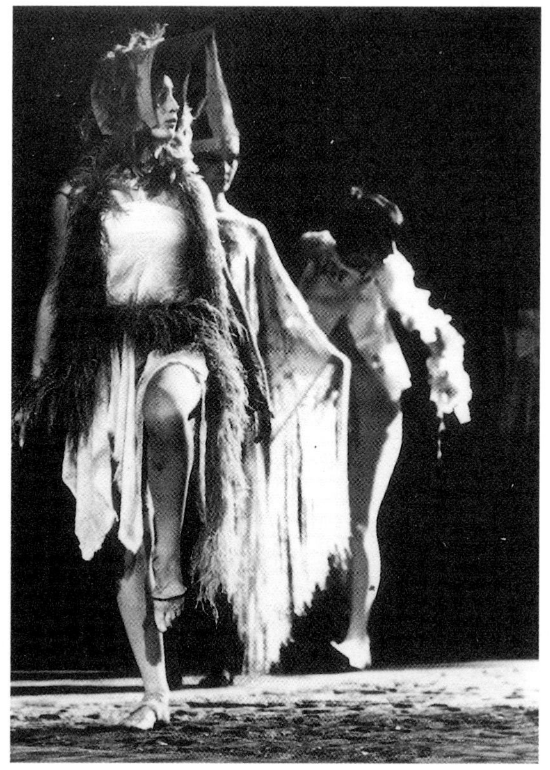

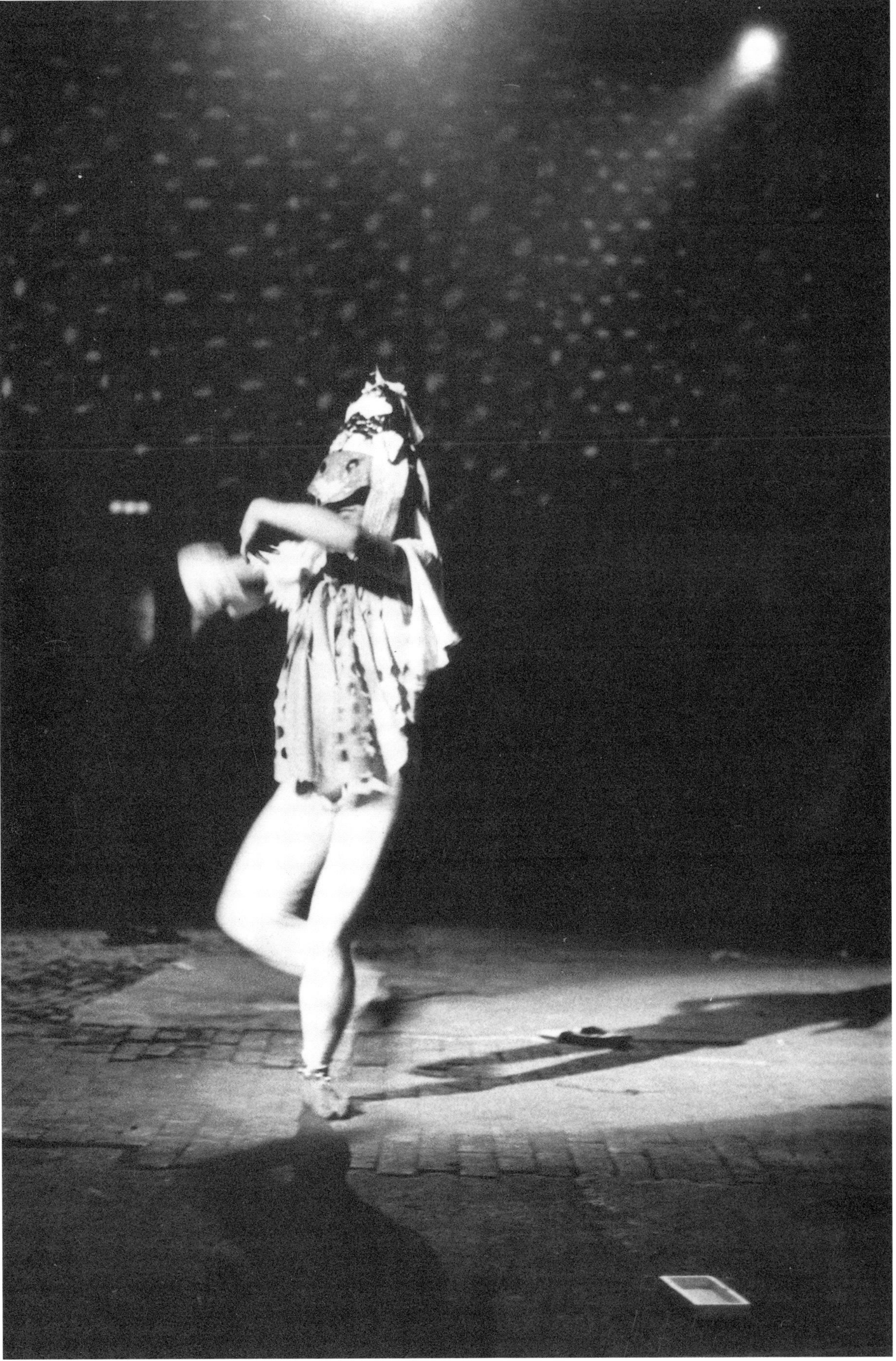

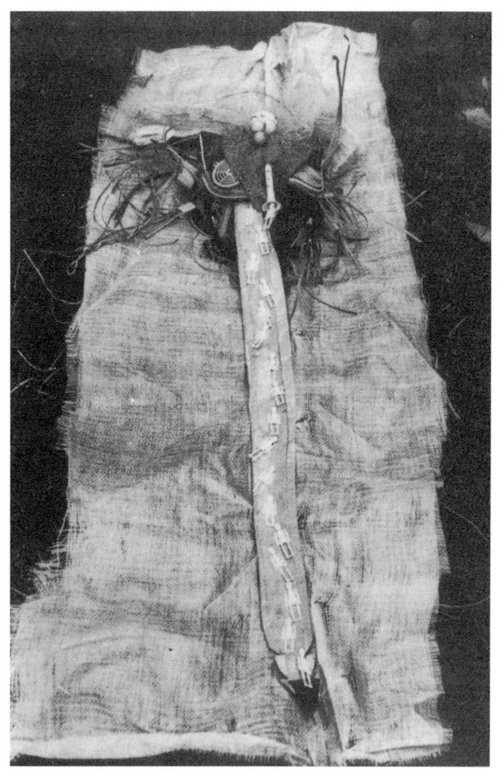

Mask of 'All-Devouring Time', from **The Buddha Ballet**, Hampstead Heath, London, 1967. Collection of the artist.

the painting".[5] Her desire was first realised in her *Bichos* (Animals), 1960, articulated metal sculptures with the lucidity of a theorem and the integrity of a body, which the spectator discovered by directly manipulating them. These were the prelude to all her later experiments in spectator participation. Oiticica's early work followed a similar course, until the invention of his participatory *Penetrables* and *Parangolé*.

Both Brazilian artists saw a clear connection between Mondrian's strict 'abstractness' and his prophetic vision of an art dissolved into life itself. For them, this vision went beyond the literal notion of a formal visual language applied to the built environment (as it was being interpreted by some artists in Brazil at the time). It would be "something expressive, which would be like the 'beauty of life', something which [Mondrian] could not define because it did not yet exist", Oiticica wrote in an early text.[6] They thought of it, as they thought of their own experiments, as "a prelude to a collective state of invention".[7] Interwoven with the Mondrian vision, for the Brazilians, was the lived experience of their Euro-Afro-Amerindian grass-roots culture of the body, epitomised in the samba and the carnival which Oiticica called "the greatest public improvisation in the world".[8]

We begin to see the outlines of an extremely delicate process of cultural reciprocity. Medalla's and the Brazilians' adherence to the pioneers of abstraction led them to retain a powerful structural clarity, and allowed them to avoid a return to naturalism. At the same time they avoided a formalist interpretation of 20th century art by their sympathy with the social vision of artists like Mondrian. Thus their modernity, their pursuit of a post-Euclidian space/time, was able to link up with popular traditions in their societies of origin, traditions which, significantly, were on the verge of extinction in the highly industrialised countries. They were able to draw on a rich presence of communal art forms which unite the visual, aural, corporeal and kinaesthetic orders in a structure of mass-participation in which 'everyone is an artist'. This consciousness in turn was able to link up with the youth and 'counter-cultural' movements originating in the industrial West. It was not for the first time in the 20th century that the most modern forms, at the cutting-edge of the avant-garde, linked up with some of the most ancient.

Such links were energising because of their very paradoxes. Britain is a social–democratic country with a reasonably evenly-distributed 'high standard of living' and yet remains a remarkably stratified (or is it stultified?), and increasingly 'privatised', society. Countries like Brazil and the Philippines, divided into a small number of super-rich and huge destitute masses, ruled by almost feudal oligarchies, nevertheless possess a certain cultural fluidity in which, for example, the aesthetic is taken more naturally as part of life and behaviour by all classes. Cosmopolitan London in the 1960s became a mutual testing ground of different relative forms of 'uptightness' and freedom. If we wanted to turn the circle again, we could say that the influence of 1960s 'alternative' culture in Rio de Janeiro (to some degree imported by Oiticica himself) linked up with the inspiration he already felt from the marginal rebels and outlaws of Rio's *favelas*: two converging streams which were underground and subversive of the respectable bourgeois culture of Brazil's ruling class. This common thread of desire which seemed to surface in the 1960s, with all the widely uneven social and economic possibilities of realising it, Oiticica once summed up as: "the retaking of confidence by the individual in his/her intuitions and most precious ambitions".[9]

◆   ◆   ◆

The cool, analytical way I am writing all this makes me smile if I remember the actual

Medalla signalling to the 'head' of a giant figure made up of peoples' bodies, in 'The Questions of King Milinda', part of the **Buddha Ballet**, Hampstead Heath, London, 1967. Collection of the artist.

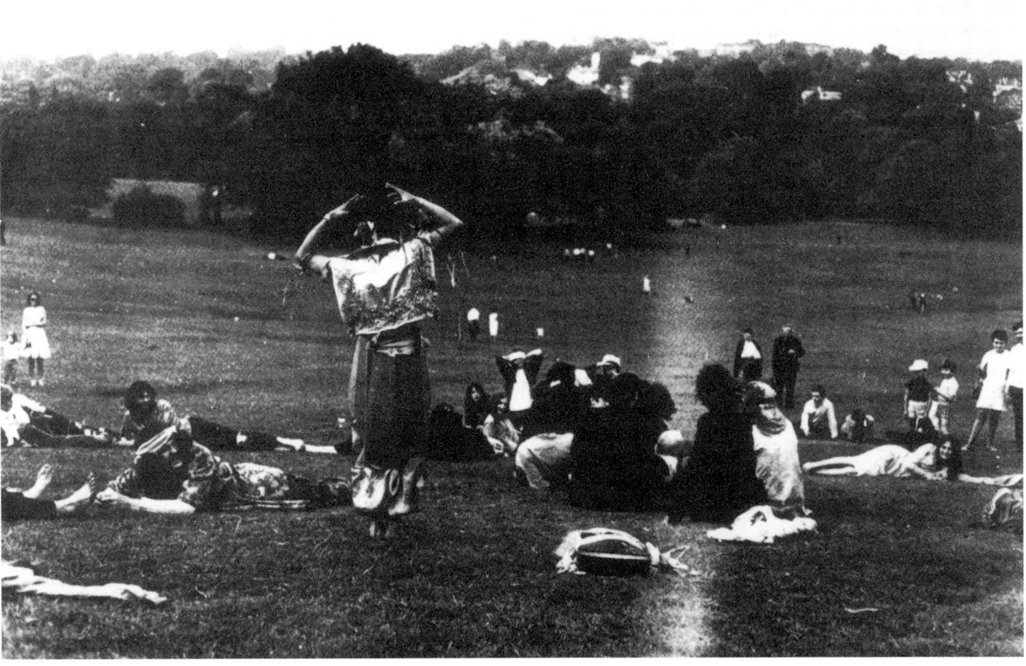

way of life of the Exploding Galaxy. Certainly it derived from no existing programme in the genres of avant-garde art. The group began to coalesce from Medalla's initiative early in 1967 and always fluctuated in numbers, although there was a constant kernel of members. The communal house at 99 Balls Pond Road, in Dalston (jointly owned by Paul Keeler and David Medalla), functioned without electricity, telephone, gas and sometimes without water. Some neighbours were sympathetic, others hostile. The Galaxy was often in the press. The tabloids attacked them in familiar terms ("FREE clothes, FREE lodging, FREE love – but you pay!": *The People*, 25th February 1968). The quality press tried to understand them (Mary Holland in *The Observer* published a sympathetic article in May 1968 entitled 'Is It The Police v. The Young?'). Galaxy members were scathing about institutionalised art, and even of the avant-garde. Derek Jarman describes in his autobiography *Dancing Ledge* attending a play by the Living Theatre of Julian Beck and Judith Malina – the acme of alternative theatre in the 1960s – at the Round House in 1967. During the play, the performers left the stage and made their way through the audience, button-holing spectators and saying things like, "I can't travel without a passport!", "I can't take my clothes off in public!", and so on. Michael Chapman of the Galaxy, a giant of a young man with curly locks, stood up in the audience and shouted, "Well I can!", and proceeded to denude himself there and then.[10] Another Exploder, Edward Pope, took a gentler view:

Every one of us became a walking justification of his own life, and honesty became a necessity for those who wished to inspire others with the creative way of life. You might see one of us on a bus, wearing clothes that could neither be called respectable nor bohemian, but you might call them bizarre were they not also full of inventive imagination and poetry. People ask: "Why do you wear that?", "What is that?", "How do you live?" and we explain, in a simple way, how, by treating things in one's life with fresh imagination, by changing their purpose, like wearing a cushion for a hat, turning an umbrella into a newspaper, or a bus into a church, one penetrates the pretence that life is humdrum, and comes to see one's own life transformed as part of the life of the imagination, the life that gives meaning and makes history...[11]

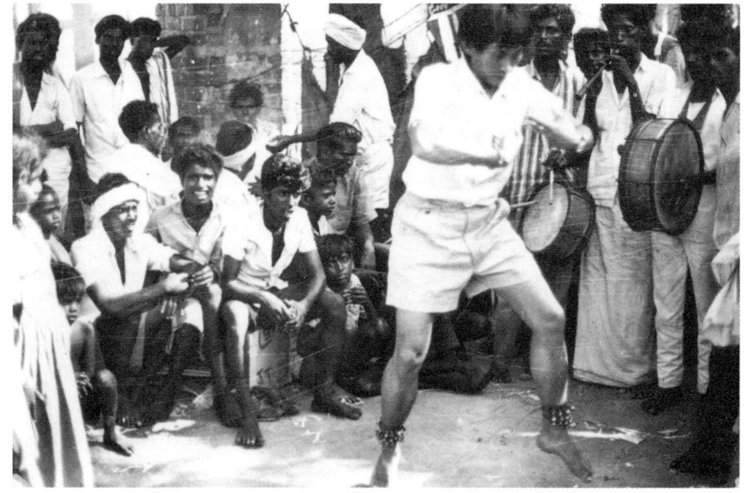
Medalla dancing in Madras, 1969.

A third description was given by Benn Levy, a

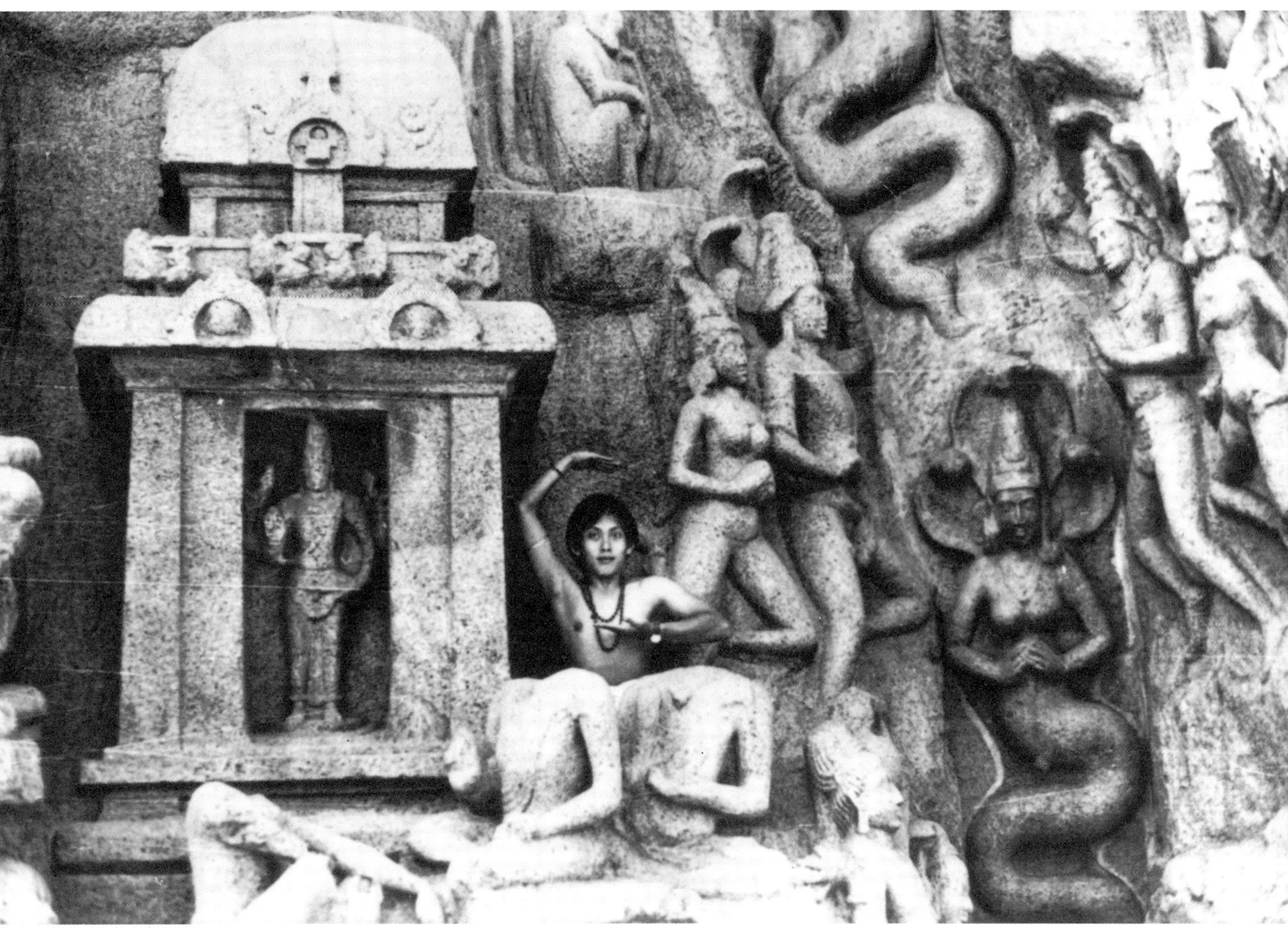

The Penance of Arjuna, impromptu at Mahabalipuram, Madras, India, 1969.

Member of Parliament, in a statement for the defence during the Galaxy's trial (see below):

There are no articles of association, no recruitment. Newcomers gravitate towards the group, find it congenial and stay or uncongenial and leave.

They are unacquisitive, as oblivious of elementary comfort as a classical religious order, unselfconsciously ascetic. Their boarding house is furnished with mattresses, sleeping-bags, packing-cases, bookshelves and little else. There they live in cheerful penury working away like beavers on projects that offer no prospect of serious remuneration, that may at best earn them a week's supply of baked potatoes, raw carrots, bread, jam, cabbage, Mars Bars and occasional eggs.

They dress and coif themselves egregiously, prompted not by fashion but by individual fancy. Their clothes are not only a proclamation of non-conformity but often an expression of surrealist humour.[12]

If the Exploding Galaxy differed from most theatre or dance companies in being of fluctuating membership, and non-professional, it differed too from most 1960s communes in trying to combine art and life according to a conscious method. Although invented by the group itself, this method had its roots in tenets of the historical avant-garde, especially those, like Dada and the Surrealists, deriving from a kinetic and transformative vision of reality. No one material or object had only a single meaning: metaphor was everywhere, even the most humble leftovers could be recycled and transfigured. Similarly, no one had a single specialised role to play. "The Galaxy makes it possible for anyone at any moment to try an infinite number of roles and functions".[13] Spectator could become actor, the world could become stage, or vice versa. It is easy today to see the naivety and idealism of such a proposal, in which the Galaxy was only one, albeit audacious, part of a much wider movement. Disillusionment has set in because of the speed and ease with which the old hierarchies, the ethos of professionalism, competitiveness and impersonality have reestablished themselves. But we are talking as much about what seemed possible as of what was possible. Eventually a rediscovery of the freshness – the 'flowerlike' quality – of that moment will inspire the next challenge to a one-dimensional existence.

Besides their improvised 'explorations' (performing and scavenging materials) all over London,[14] the Galaxy worked towards ambitious and elaborate dance-dramas. Medalla's particular contributions to these were the story of *The Bird Ballet*, a fairytale-like allegory performed at the Round House in 1967, which gave scope for thirty performers to appear in the guises of sixty-two real or invented birds, and *The Buddha Ballet*, which was held every weekend during the summer at Parliament Hill. Loosely based on Buddhist fables, these latter events were really gigantic games into which Medalla

Opposite: Drawings for **Gentle Genticles**, from a letter to Guy Brett from Manila, 19 October 1969.

Body Motion Pendulum, 1970, egg, rubber band, wood, air, suction cap, "for discovering psychic equilibrium through body movement". Bateaux Mayflower II, Paris.

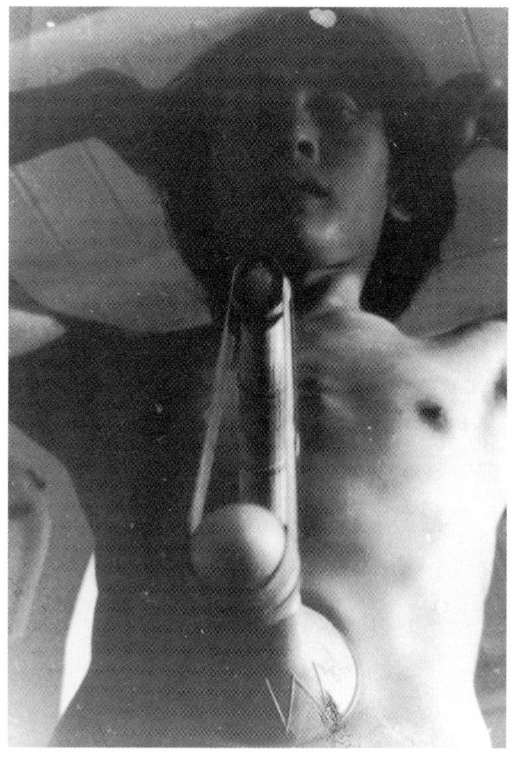

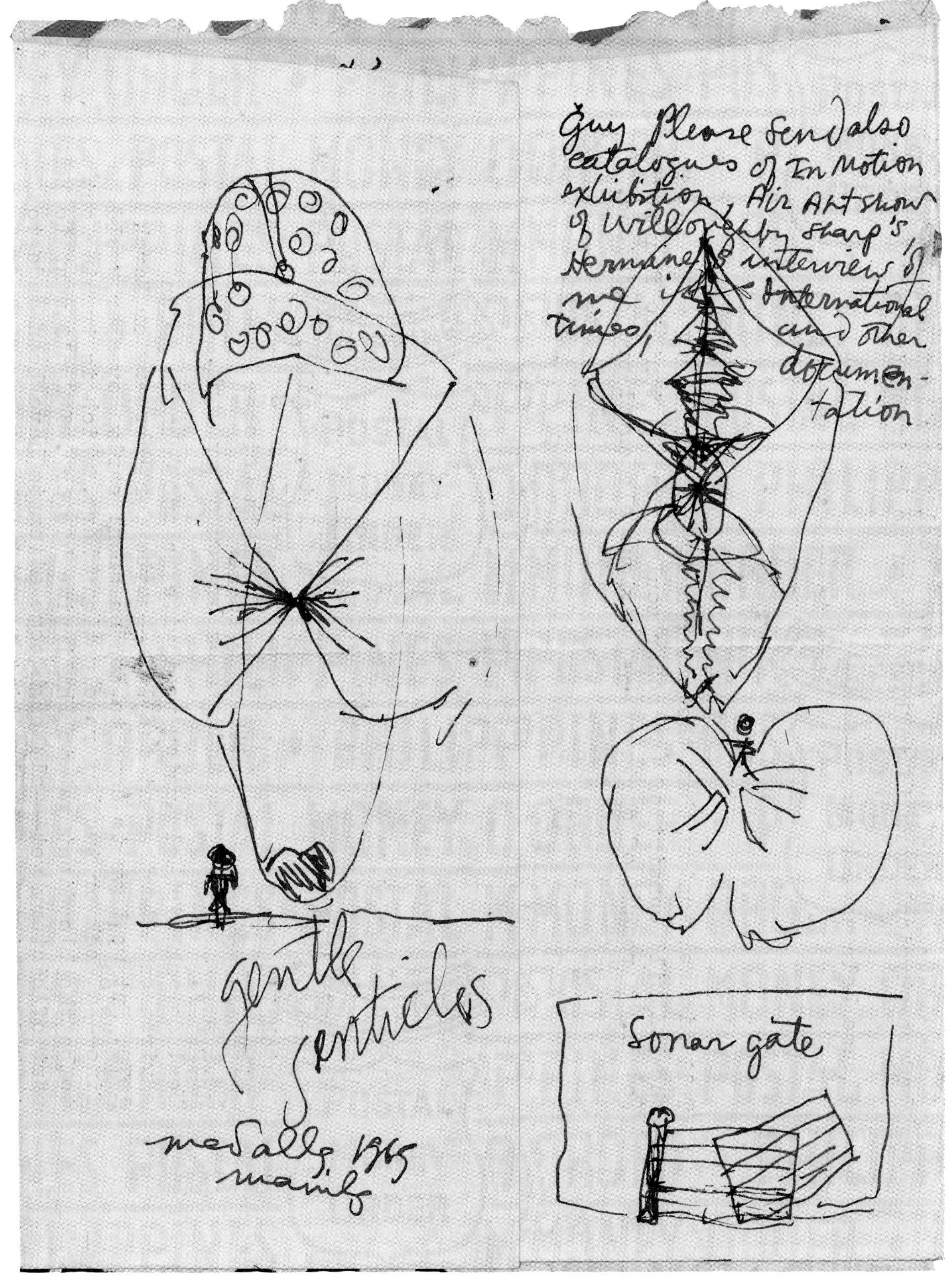
Guy please send also
catalogues of In Motion
exhibition, Air Art show
of Willoughby Sharp's,
Germano's interview of
me in International
Times, and other
documen-
tation
gentle
genticles
medalla 1965
manila
sonar gate

and a young American artist recently arrived in London, John Dugger, would endeavour to attract the passing public. Once a human body was formed out of the linked bodies of dozens of people and strode off like a ragged giant over the hill, Medalla rather romantically incorporating every anarchic or disruptive element, such as rowdy kids who were treated as fleas and expelled from the giant's hair with a massive comb.

Some admirers of Medalla's kinetic work had mixed feelings about the Exploding Galaxy. The French critic Jean Clay, for example, praised the Galaxy as a living example of an audacious break with the institutions of art, but disapproved of its 'orientalising' tendency. This was seen as a retreat into an exotic past, a failure to confront contemporary problems. For Medalla and Dugger the Buddhist stories were "of universal value".[15] I see Medalla's whole involvement with Buddhism as part of a search for another set of human relations in art. Buddhism is a religion without priests (at least in its historic beginnings in India), akin in this sense to shamanism, and Medalla occasionally referred to his preference for the image of the artist as "questioning shaman", rather than the artist as "enforcing priest". At the same time, Buddhism, Indian and Chinese art generally, gave a new impetus and depth to his kineticism. It should be remembered that ancient Indian thinkers had developed concepts of far greater expanses of space and time than had scientists in Europe at least until the 20th century. These insights had been arrived at intuitively rather than by empirical observation and measurement. The way for the mind to grasp such concepts was by means of metaphor. Metaphor made the leap of imagination between the human and the cosmic scale, as was beautifully demonstrated in the story of Buddha's image for the vastness of time, which so entranced Medalla (p. 64).

His interest in Buddhism could be seen as another instance of the ancient/modern paradox, which has been so fruitful in the development of 20th century art. In the event, there was no real contradiction between Medalla's earlier 'hylozoism' and his later Buddhism as analogies for the modern. The pre-Socratic Greek thinker Heraclitus echoed Indian interpretations of the universe as ever-living and ever-dying fire, as perpetual flux. Heraclitus's writings too have the subtlety of poetry, based on the ambiguity and paradoxes inherent in human language.

The favourite Buddhist text used in *The Buddha Ballet* was 'The Questions of King Milinda', one of the oldest texts in the Pali canon. This is in the form of dialogues between Milinda, a benevolent Greco-Bactrian king, and the Buddhist sage Nagasena: "A wonderful document of how two enlightened cultures (the ancient Greek and the early Buddhist), with their two different but complementary systems of thought, encountered and transformed one another."[16] David was to return to this source material, with a different emphasis, in his later performance *Voyages and Somersaults of the Pilgrim Monkey*. One new element added to his cosmological concerns at this time was "the depth of psychological knowledge" he discovered in the Buddhist writings.

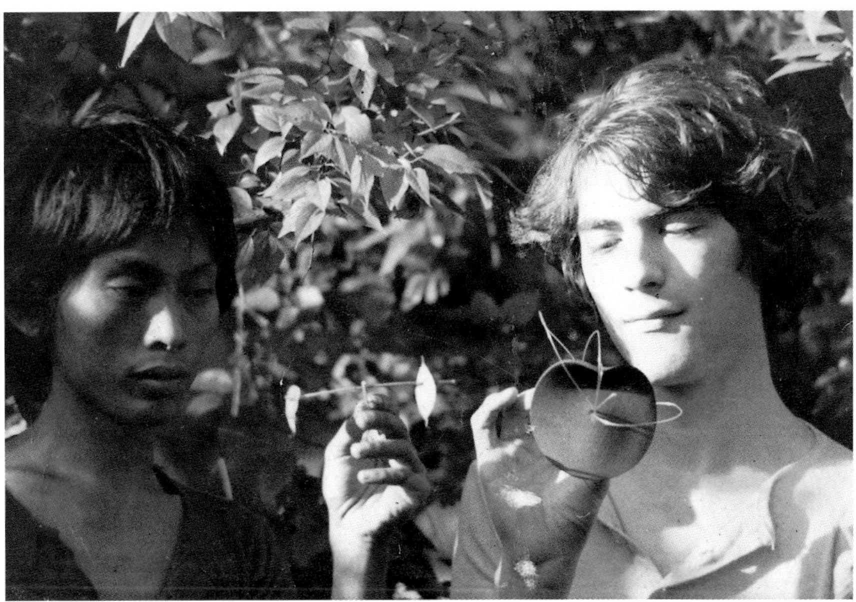

Medalla with **Leaf Balance** ("for weighing sunlight and shadow"), one of his **Ephemerals** series, and John Dugger with **Morning Glory no 2**, one of his **Perennials** series, Kew Gardens, London, 1970.

◆　　◆　　◆

Press and police harassment of the Galaxy grew to an impossible level. Eventually, in February 1968, the house in Balls Pond Road was raided and cannabis planted by plain-clothes officers (Medalla was in Holland when the raid occurred). Three Galaxy members were arrested and put on trial. Although two out of the three accused were acquitted, the raid and the trial effectively destroyed the Galaxy's peculiar kind of cohesion. It broke up, or rather exploded, its members veering away in many different directions to live very different lives. Medalla, Dugger and a number of others received an unexpected windfall from a rich admirer of the group living in Paris and set off on a journey to India. Their principal purpose was to study at source the Kathakali dance-drama of Kerala, one of the big influences on the Galaxy. Some drifted off along the way and returned to England, but Medalla and Dugger completed a journey of eighteen months. They began at Venice aboard M/V Victoria of the Lloyd Triestino line, stopped at Barcelona and visited Senegal, South Africa, Kenya, Pakistan, India, Sri Lanka, Nepal, Singapore, Thailand and the Philippines. While in Kathmandu, the two, steeped in the finer points of Buddhist iconography and aesthetics, somehow contrived to build up a remarkable collection of Tibetan *tankhas*, sculptures and ritual objects which became one of the mainstays of the pioneering and influential exhibition of Tantric Art curated by Philip Rawson and Hugh Shaw for the Arts Council of Great

Britain and held at the Hayward Gallery in London in 1971.

One result of this journey in terms of Medalla's own work was an elaboration of many of the preoccupations of the Galaxy period, combined with the lightness of the traveller. While in the Philippines he began an erotic and playful series called *Gentle Genticles*, 1969. It was broadly based on the penis sheathes and g-strings he remembered from the time as a teenager when he lived with indigenous tribes in the north of the island of Luzon and in the southern Philippines, assisting in the anthropological studies of Dr H. Otley Beyer. John Dugger wrote in a letter:

As a small boy he was impressed by the g-strings worn by all male members of the tribes and the different shapes and sizes of those small pieces of clothing, and of the various materials, and how one g-string looked funny, another virile, another domestic, another daring, another gentle... This set of works are to be fitted onto the human body. They consist of materials to serve as a g-string and mirrors which are set about the hips...[17]

Maximum in terms of the body, minimum in terms of material, incongruous, yet containing every possible nuance: a typical Medalla proposal! The related researches of Hélio Oiticica and Lygia Clark (Clark herself had said, "I use clothes to denude the body"), his own libido, combined with the Galaxy's assault on respectable convention conducted by the most peaceable strategies, combined with the Buddhist use of metaphor (the most everyday, least laboured, and elegantly paradoxical way of expressing an insight), and with a continuing influence of kinetic sculptures, such as those of Gabo and Vantongerloo – all these seem to be humorously present in *Gentle Genticles*. They come together to imply an ironic critique of the pretentious institutions surrounding art and the artist. They suggest a movement towards a more democratic form of culture by means of games anyone can play. This synthesis gave Medalla a remarkable freedom and flexibility when he came to enter into some of the debates then exercising the art world.

In 1970 the Whitechapel Gallery in London held a large exhibition of artists' multiples. It was both a testimony and a testing of the claim that multiples – mass-produced and fairly cheap examples of an artist's work in more or less unlimited editions – represented a democratisation of art, making art available in an authentic form to more people than ever before. The huge anthology (more than seven hundred items) quickly brought to a head, in a very concrete way, the issue of whether multiples simply meant an extension of the 'art object' into a flood of bibelots and knick-knacks, or a sensitising of people's psyches on a mass scale. For the catalogue Medalla sent photos of one of his *Ephemerals* (*Leaf Balance*), and John Dugger's *Perennials*, and he also sent *Parabola*, an example from the *Ephemeral* series, for the exhibition. Rather than an object you can buy, Medalla cast the notion of the 'multiple' in the form of a

Study for **The Bee Ballet**, a project for The Exploding Galaxy, London, 1967. Pencil and crayon on paper. Collection Guy Brett.

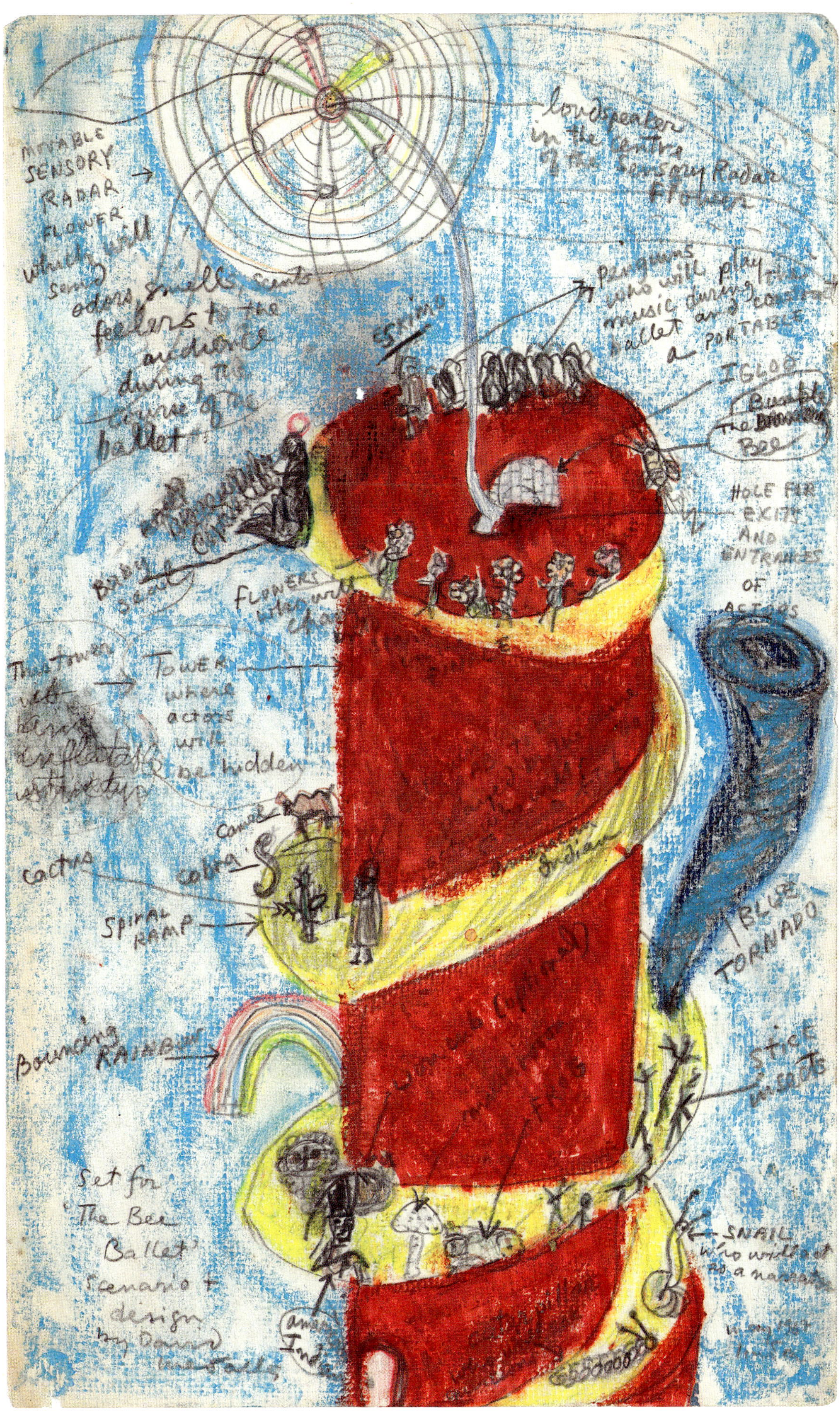

MOVABLE SENSORY RADAR FLOWER which will send odors smells scents feelers to the audience during the course of the ballet
loudspeaker in the centre of the Sensory Radar Flower
Penguins who will play music during the ballet in a portable IGLOO
Bumble the Bee
SWING
HOLE FOR EXIT AND ENTRANCE OF ACTORS
BUBBLE Bead
FLOWERS
The Tower
TOWER where actors will be hidden
cactus
cobra
Camel
Indian
SPIRAL RAMP
Bouncing RAINBOW
BLUE TORNADO
STICK INSECTS
SNAIL who will
Set for "The Bee Ballet" scenario + design by Donna

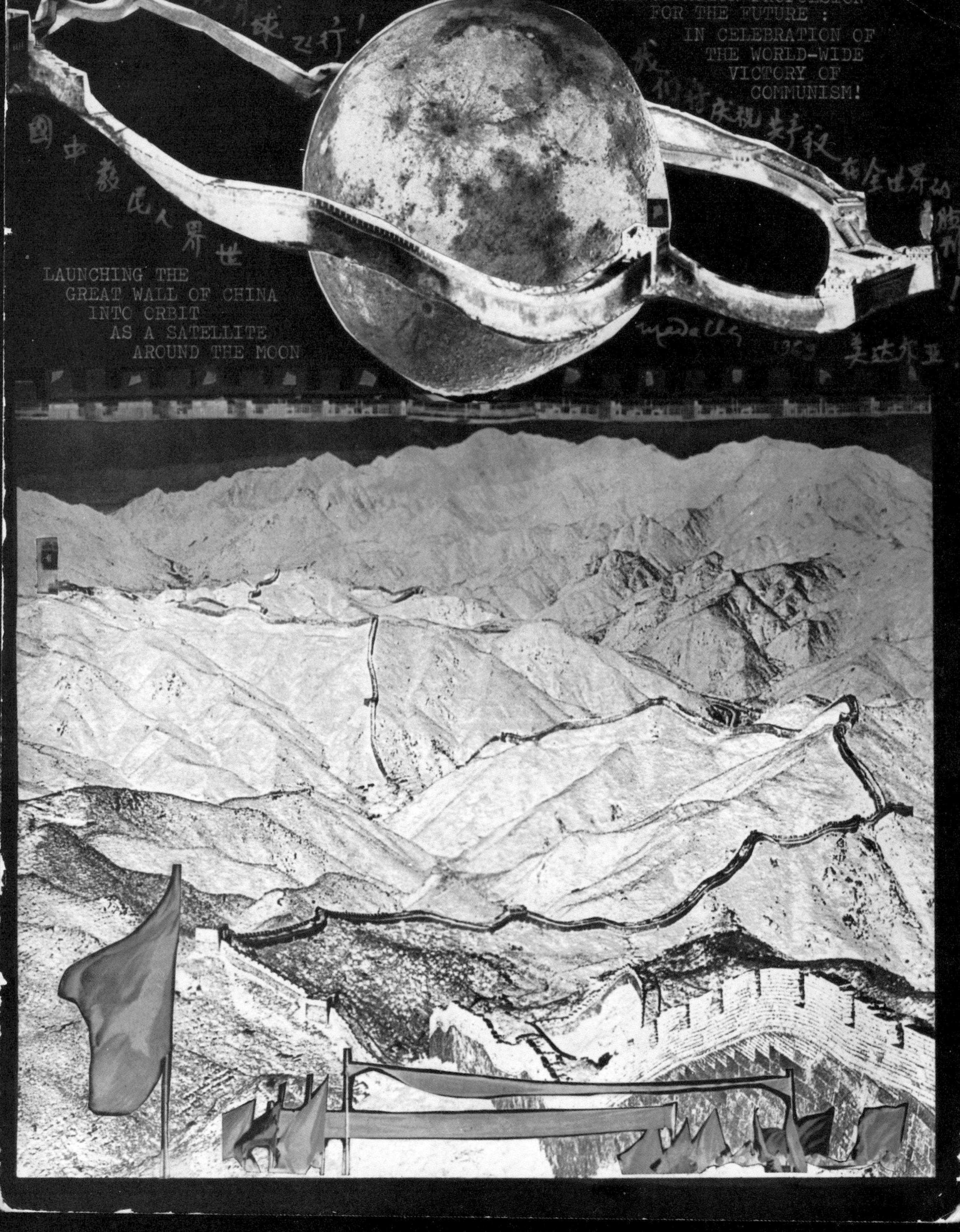
PARTICIPATION PROPULSION
FOR THE FUTURE :
IN CELEBRATION OF
THE WORLD-WIDE
VICTORY OF
COMMUNISM!
LAUNCHING THE
GREAT WALL OF CHINA
INTO ORBIT
AS A SATELLITE
AROUND THE MOON

'thought' – to be realised by anyone, anywhere, out of materials in common abundance:

> The purpose of an *Ephemeral* is to illuminate for an instant a transitory experience. It is for the maker of an *Ephemeral* (who is everyone) to realise for himself or herself the nature of that experience which naturally will always be unique, spontaneous, random and, hopefully, will reveal something of the mysterious structure and processes of the microcosmos.
>
> To create an *Ephemeral* one simply has to find the invisible relation between and amongst the most disparate objects and things...
>
> *Ephemerals* are... miniature metaphors of the Void - not monuments, or objets d'art for speculation, consumption or self-aggrandisement.
>
> The best *Ephemerals* are kinetic *kasinas* or mobile and transitory objects for meditation...
>
> *"If a process is fully attended to, the boundaries between life and art become hard to distinguish..."*
> (Rasa Gustaitis, *Turning On*, Weidenfeld and Nicolson, London, 1969, p 285)[18]

Another outcome of Medalla's African and Asian journey was a radical politicisation. At least the process began in a first-hand encounter with the huge social contradictions which are so overt in the Third World. In Europe, the Galaxy had been rather contemptuous of the young militants of 'May '68', finding them "unevolved" expressively. But Medalla returned from Asia a political radical and began devouring Marxist texts as avidly as he had Buddhist scriptures. Only the Marxist method and insights seemed capable of explaining the reasons for poverty and exploitation, and providing a framework for effective action. He found the Philippines under the Marcos dictatorship a gun-happy country in a state of "nerve-wracking fragmentation".[19] While in Manila he initiated a demonstration against the policy of the newly-built Cultural Center of the Philippines, a symbol of the Marcos's brand of nationalism, during an opening ceremony whose guest of honour was Ronald Reagan, then governor of California.[20]

Medalla's Buddhism gradually ceded to his Marxism, and later Maoism. He and Dugger lived for a time in Paris after returning from Asia, occupying a houseboat, Bateau Mayflower II, moored at the Quai des Tuileries by the Place de la Concorde. The *Megha Sutta* Bubble Machine was constructed there. Again, I believe Medalla's Marxism was an expansion and broadening of his thought, based essentially in a dynamic view of reality, rather than the linear replacement of

Opposite: **Launching the Great Wall of China into Orbit as a Satellite around the Moon**, a "cosmic propulsion for the future", 1969. Photo collage. Collection of the artist.

At Buttes-Chaumont, Paris, 1977.

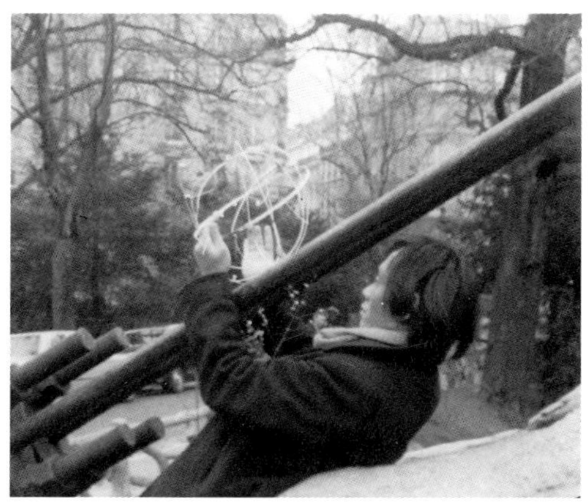

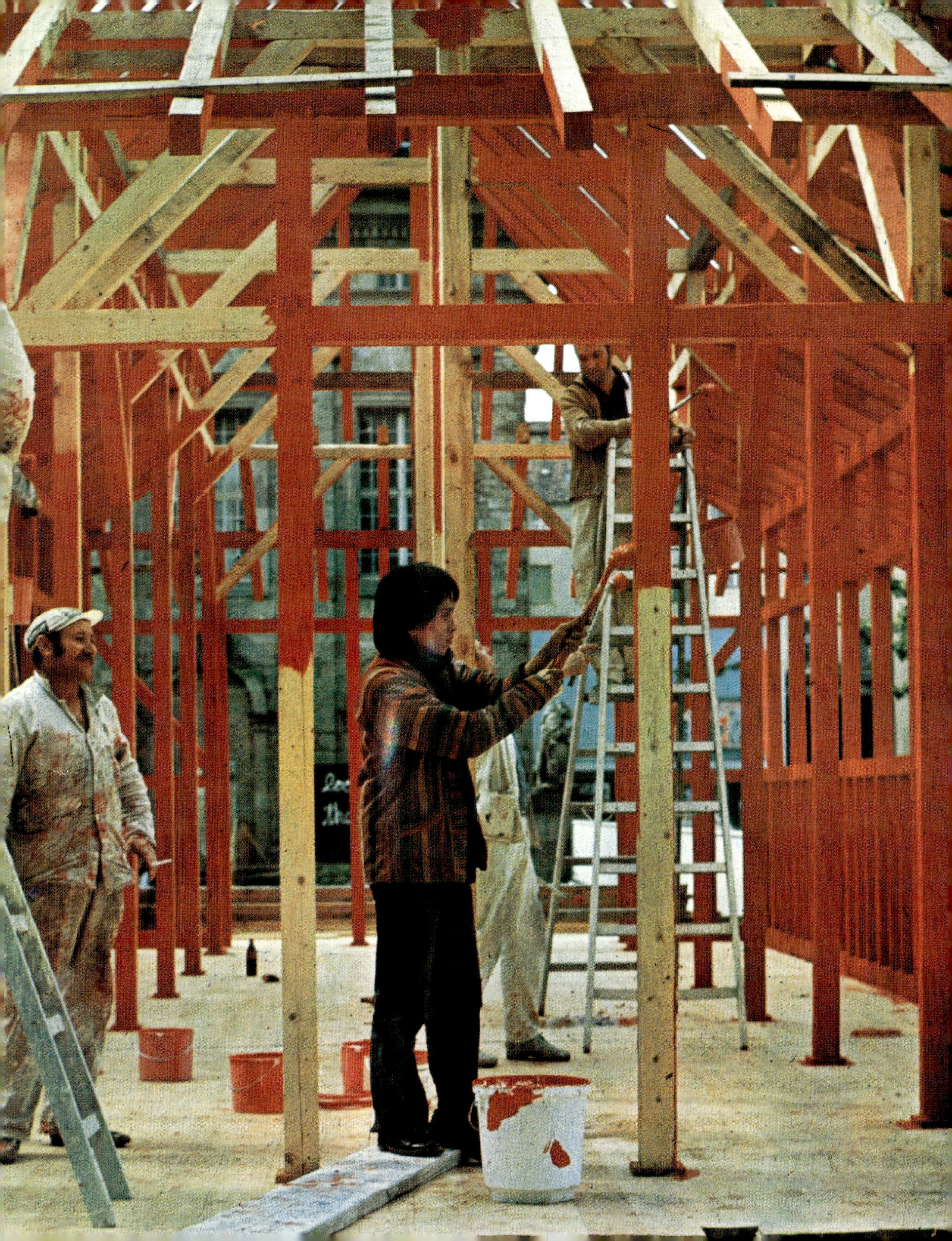

one set of ideas by another. Even after starting, with John Dugger, the Artists' Liberation Front, a group of artists and activists, in London in 1974, Medalla continued to add to his collection of oriental art. Early Ming pottery became the vehicle of a mingling of Buddhist and Marxist insights in a piece called *Ming Blue and White* which he was working on in the early 1970s.

The mid-1990s may not be the best moment to look again dispassionately at a movement in the 1970s in which many people were caught up (myself included). The photos of Medalla and Dugger in their Mao jackets, and the rhetoric of Medalla's polemics, which imitated Marxist–Leninist state discourse down to the smallest mannerisms and turns of phrase (although his analysis was usually sane and intelligent), give a dated air to an incontestable conviction: that the legacy of colonialism in the Third World could only be effectively challenged by the national liberation movements. Many sensed a common outlook uniting these movements in the Third World with the criticism of capitalist alienation in the industrialised countries. They shared a common ethos which gave greater value to human potential and imagination than to mere material and technical might, a feeling caught perfectly in a couplet by Bertolt Brecht written several years before:

From the new transmitters came the old stupidities
Wisdom was passed on from mouth to mouth[21]

Subsequent challenges to Eurocentrism, sexism and racism in culture, including the art world, had their first impetus in the revolutionary turbulence of the late 1960s. David Medalla was active early in the movement of the growing politicisation of art. Sensing his personal identity in its political and historical dimension, he became mainly concerned with struggles in the great hinterlands of the world, and the activities of solidarity and publicity so important in the metropolis. But again, while in relation to the institutional art world his political stand was uncompromisingly radical (to the risk of his professional career), to the public who came in contact with his work, his attitude was gentle, exploratory and undogmatic. A good example of this was his participation, with John Dugger, in Documenta 5 at Kassel in 1972.

Documenta 5, considered by many the best of these giant quadrennial exhibitions so far, was organised by the brilliant and unconventional Swiss curator Harald Szeemann. Szeemann had long had an interest in Medalla's work, having invited him to exhibit his Bubble Machines in 'White on White', an exhibition organised by Szeemann at the Kunsthalle in Bern in 1966, and to participate in 'When Attitudes Become Form', 1969, the first major international survey of conceptual art.[22] Seeing that Documenta was "a conglomeration of mainly Western art",[23] Medalla and Dugger decided to make some kind of break between their space and the rest of the

Painting the interior of the **Peoples' Participation Pavilion,** Medalla and Dugger's contribution to Documenta 5, Kassel, 1972.

exhibition. When they arrived in Kassel they found that most spaces had already been allotted to other artists and, rather than accept a corridor, they decided to take over a corner in the garden of the Museum Fredericianum, which was being used as a dump for the debris of the previous Documenta. The debris were cleared away and they constructed, with the help of students and workers from Kassel, a large red-painted wooden building resembling an Asian or Oceanian communal house. It measured 22 metres long, 6 metres wide and 8 metres high and they called it Peoples' Participation Pavilion.

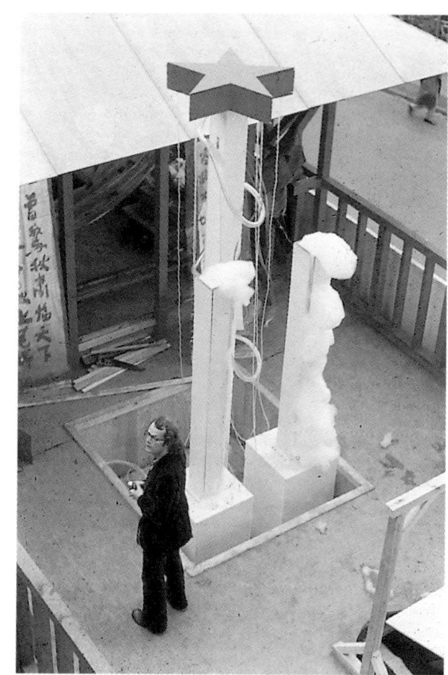

Cloud Towers: Homage to Lu Xun, bubble machines, installed at the Peoples' Participation Pavillion, Documenta 5, Kassel, 1972. Collection of the artist.

Troughs of water at the entrance acted as a 'filter'. Only those prepared to take off their shoes and wade through were able to enter (a device which dissuaded the snobbier art bureaucrats and officials). Another reason for the water was to filter out the "sensations of the other works, because seeing 200 artists together is like reading 200 books in a week".[24] The metaphor of a threshold was very apt. Inside there were straw mats, grass matting, installations including John Dugger's *Snake Pit and Gold Bars* (with live python) and Medalla's *Stitch in Time*, posters, information on liberation and independence struggles, and a prominent 'Open Letter' by Medalla denouncing the Director and Trustees of the Tate Gallery.[25]

Though highly visible and well attended, the Peoples' Participation Pavilion was mostly ignored by the art press. As the critic Benjamin Buchloh wrote some years later, Medalla's work "remained largely 'unseen' since it constituted... a contestation of the credibility of Western, hegemonic culture by an artist from a Third World country".[26] It could not easily be assimilated to the normal terms of discussion of a large international art event: it either had to be condemned or ignored.

At this period, too, there was a linked development between Medalla's own work and the formation of an artists' group. The closed cell of Artists' Liberation Front expanded to become a broad organisation with the formation of Artists for Democracy. AFD was born during a conversation early in 1974 between Medalla, Dugger, the Chilean artist Cecilia Vicuña and myself in Medalla's and Dugger's small room at Newport Place, Soho. The immediate pretext was the Chilean military coup of September 1973 against the socialist government of Salvador Allende, and the desire to mobilise artists in support of the resistance. If the Exploding Galaxy had aimed to affect the public through their appearance and behaviour – person-to-person in the routine of a big city – the members of AFD were inspired by the idea that their artistic work could actually have an effect on historical events by providing support for liberation movements worldwide. AFD organised an Arts Festival for Democracy in Chile at the Royal College of Art in London in September 1974, and then opened a 'cultural centre' in a squat at 143 Whitfield Street, which remained active until 1977.

A notable example of AFD's public role was the organisation of an exhibition by the American Indian Movement in 1976, documenting the political, legal and community struggles of Native Americans in the USA. It also featured poems, paintings and other art work. It was planned to coincide with the Hayward Gallery's prestigious 'Sacred Circles', in which a collection of some of the finest Native American traditional artefacts belonging to museums and collectors were used, with wholly unconscious but bitter irony, to boost the celebrations of the Bicentennial of the establishment of the USA. At the time, AFD was the only artists' group in London to rise above the national context to concern itself with the relationship between First and Third Worlds, and to show the indivisibility of culture and politics in that relationship.

Artistically, AFD's policy was to favour experiment but otherwise to have no stylistic bias. This was considered an inseparable part of being effective outside the narrow confines of the art world. Medalla's own works during this period were, as before, multivalent: a concept, or 'propulsion', provided a kind of root-metaphor, or

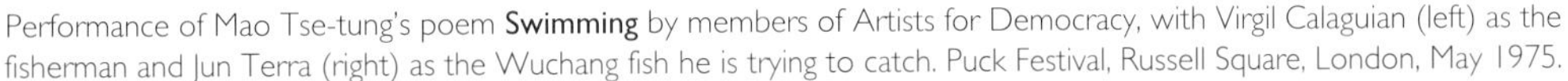

Performance of Mao Tse-tung's poem **Swimming** by members of Artists for Democracy, with Virgil Calaguian (left) as the fisherman and Jun Terra (right) as the Wuchang fish he is trying to catch. Puck Festival, Russell Square, London, May 1975.

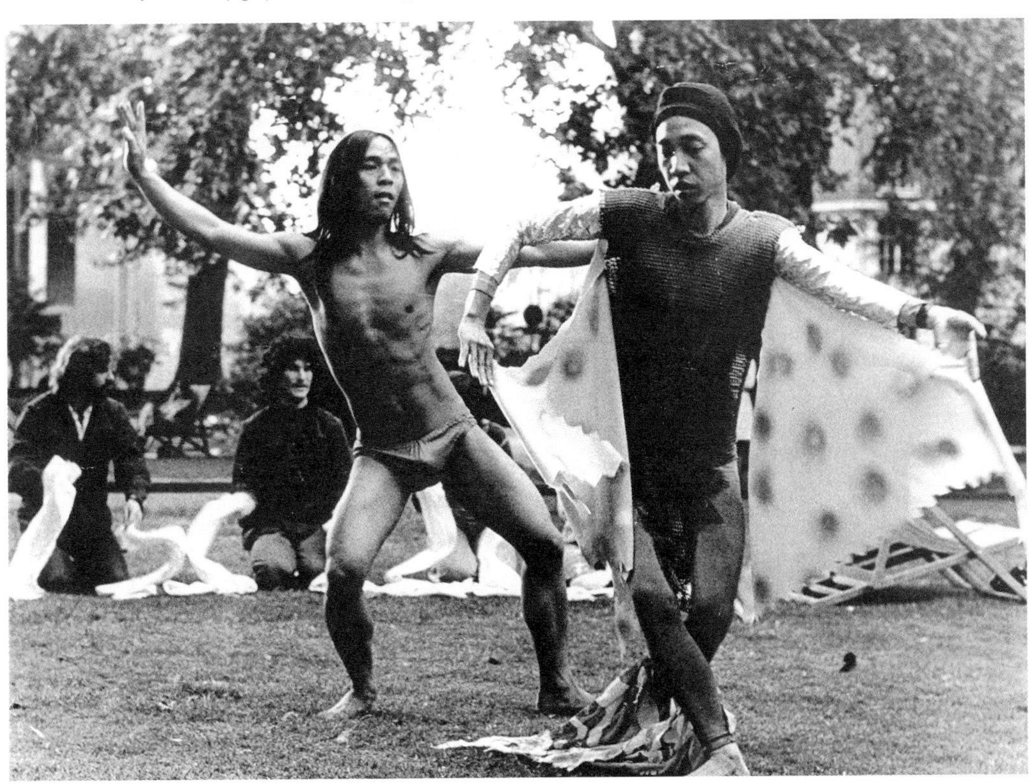

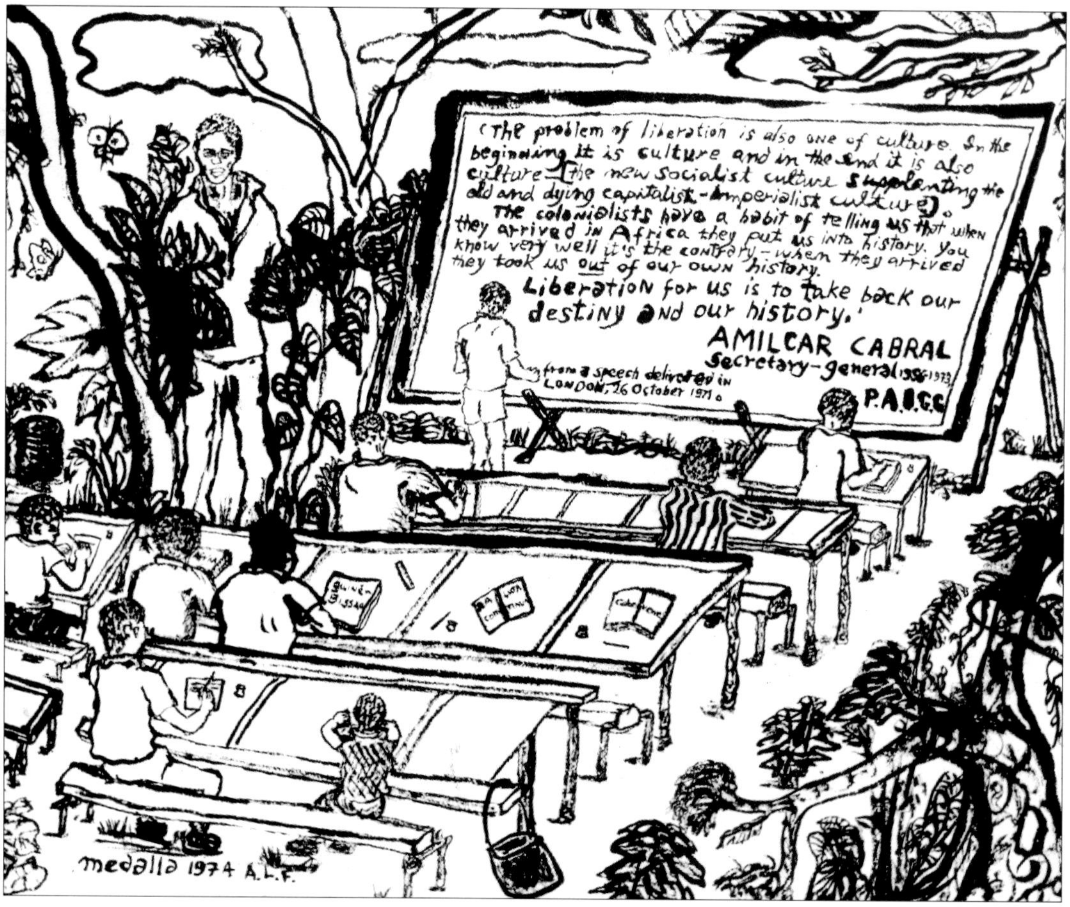

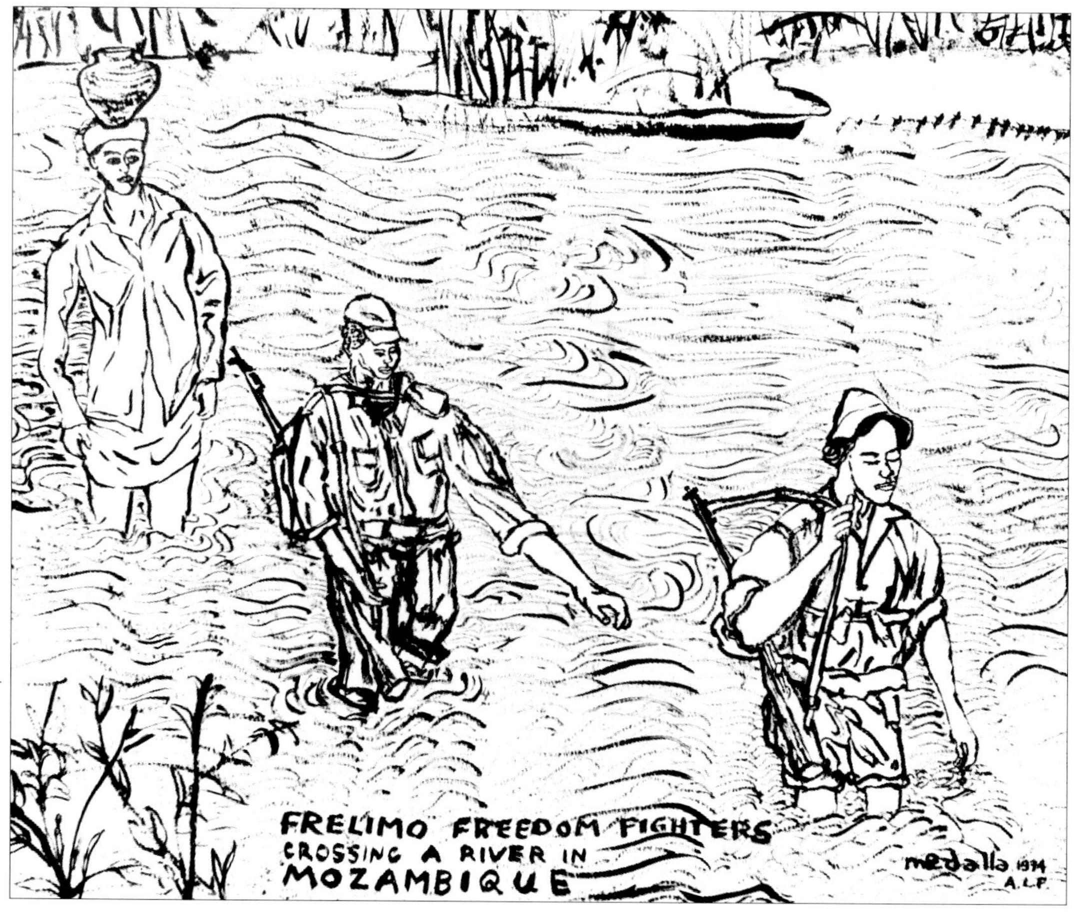

'The problem of liberation is also one of culture. In the beginning it is culture and in the end it is also culture — the new socialist culture supplanting the old and dying capitalist-imperialist culture).
The colonialists have a habit of telling us that when they arrived in Africa they put us into history. You know very well it's the contrary — when they arrived they took us out of our own history.
Liberation for us is to take back our destiny and our history.'
AMILCAR CABRAL
Secretary-general 1956-1973
from a speech delivered in LONDON, 26 October 1971.
P.A.I.G.C
medalla 1974 A.L.F.
FRELIMO FREEDOM FIGHTERS CROSSING A RIVER IN MOZAMBIQUE
medalla 1974 A.L.F.

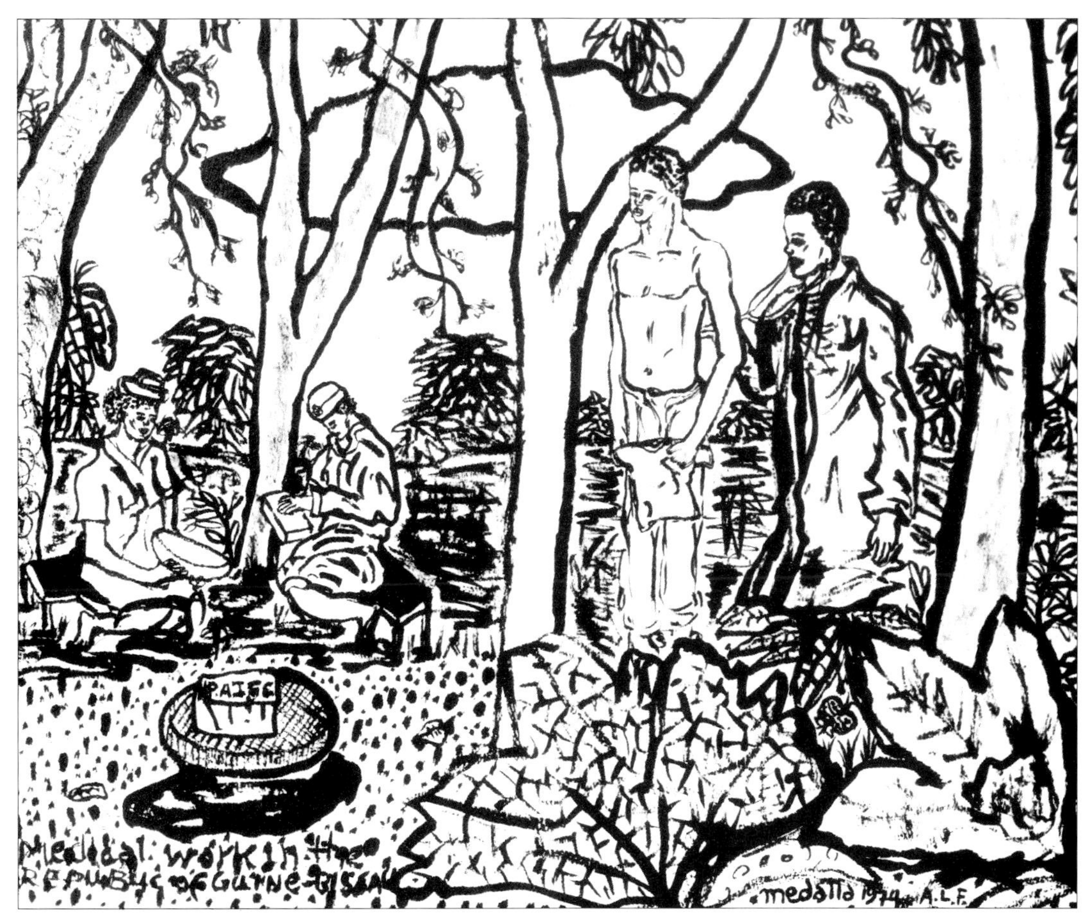

PAIGC
Medical work in the Republic of Guiné-Bissau
medalla 1974 A.L.F.

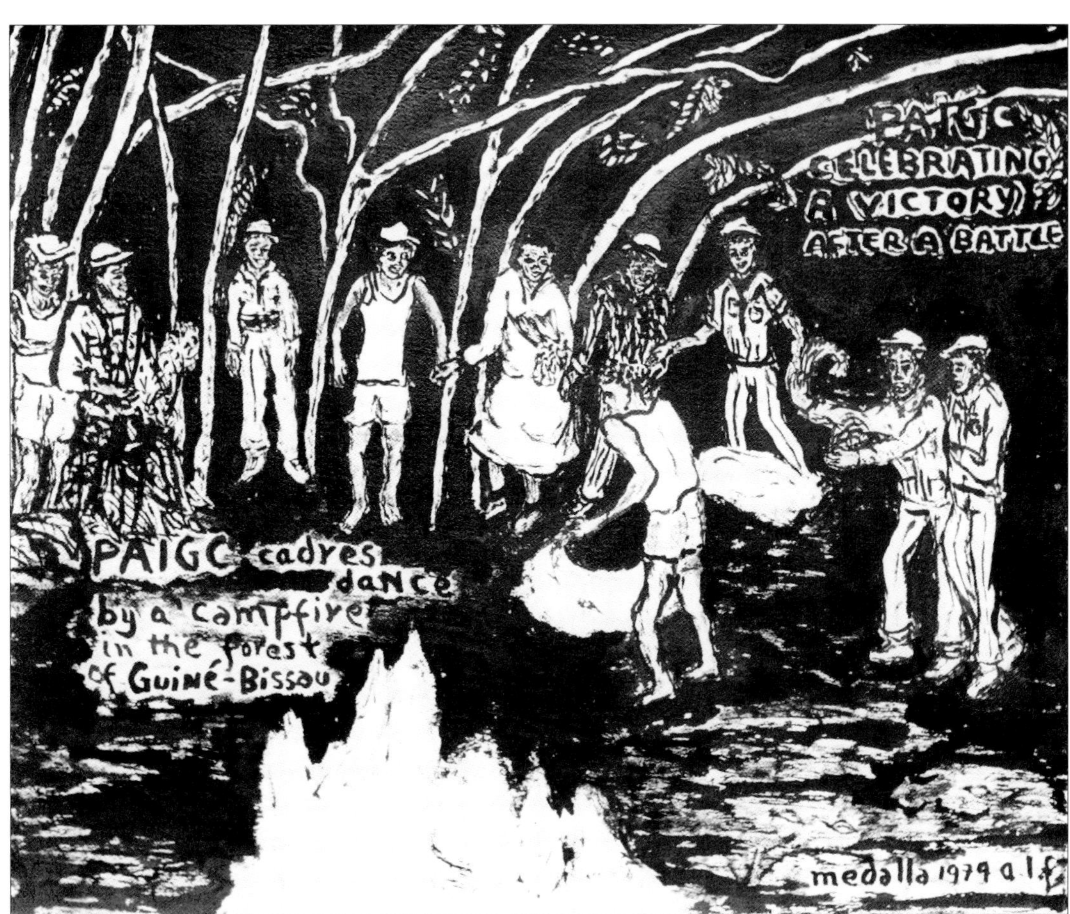

PAIGC CELEBRATING A (VICTORY) AFTER A BATTLE
PAIGC cadres dance by a campfire in the forest of Guiné-Bissau
medalla 1974 a l f

'mother-cell' (a phrase Oiticica used about his own work), which could emerge in several different media or modes. Many works contained a topical or quasi-documentary component. But overall they continued the evolutionary process he had been working on from earlier times. Marxism, for example, enriched both the kinetic and the participatory structures he had been developing since the 1960s, in ways which will become apparent in the next chapter. The most plainly agitational of Medalla's works were the series of *Africa Liberation Drawings*, 1974.[27]

He had been inspired by the struggles for independence in the Portuguese colonies of Angola, Mozambique and Guiné-Bissau. He was moved by the intelligence and imagination of the movements' leaders – Agostinho Neto, Eduardo Mondlane and Amilcar Cabral – and by the integrated way of life being built up out of the most scanty resources in the liberated areas. Cabral, leader of the PAIGC, the independence movement in Guiné-Bissau, spoke at a big public meeting in London in October 1971 at which I was present with Medalla. Cabral's reasoned condemnation of colonialism, his quiet humour, his magnanimity towards the enemy, his faith in his people without ethnic chauvinism or obfuscation, impressed us deeply, and seemed to promise real change in Africa. Medalla's drawings were based on photographs borrowed from the solidarity organisations in London but freely interpreted. The human figures are interwoven with songs, speeches, and with the land, the forest, in which and for which the struggle was being carried on. The drawings are neither facile nor folkloric. They seem to empathise stylistically with their subject in an unusual way. They have the same 'awakening', new-beginning quality as the political movement they celebrate, like a kind of poetic literacy manual.

David Medalla's series of participation 'propulsions', produced in the period between the last year of the Galaxy and the last year of AFD, including *A Stitch in Time*, from 1968, *Down with the Slave Trade!*, 1971, *The International Dust Market*, 1972, *Games of the Sea and Tides*, 1972, *Porcelain Wedding*, 1973 and *Eskimo Carver*, 1977, were not in any very overt sense political. They were not 'issue-oriented', and their mode of functioning was not the opinion-forming, the propagandistic. Ideas originating in the Galaxy period, when a group of people lived and created works of art together, here become focused through physical structures erected in a public space and open for any passer-by to enter. They simply grew and expanded by welcoming any number of contributions from any number of people. For me they are the most brilliant works of avant-garde art of the period in Britain.

Previous pages: **Africa Liberation Drawings**, London, 1974, ink on paper. Collection of the artist.
'School in the Forest'.
'Frelimo Freedom Fighters Crossing a River'.
'Medical Workers in the Republic of Guiné-Bissau'.
'PAIGC Celebrating a Victory after a Battle'.

Opposite: 'Making Soap with Palm Oil in the Liberated areas of Guiné-Bissau and Cape Verde'.

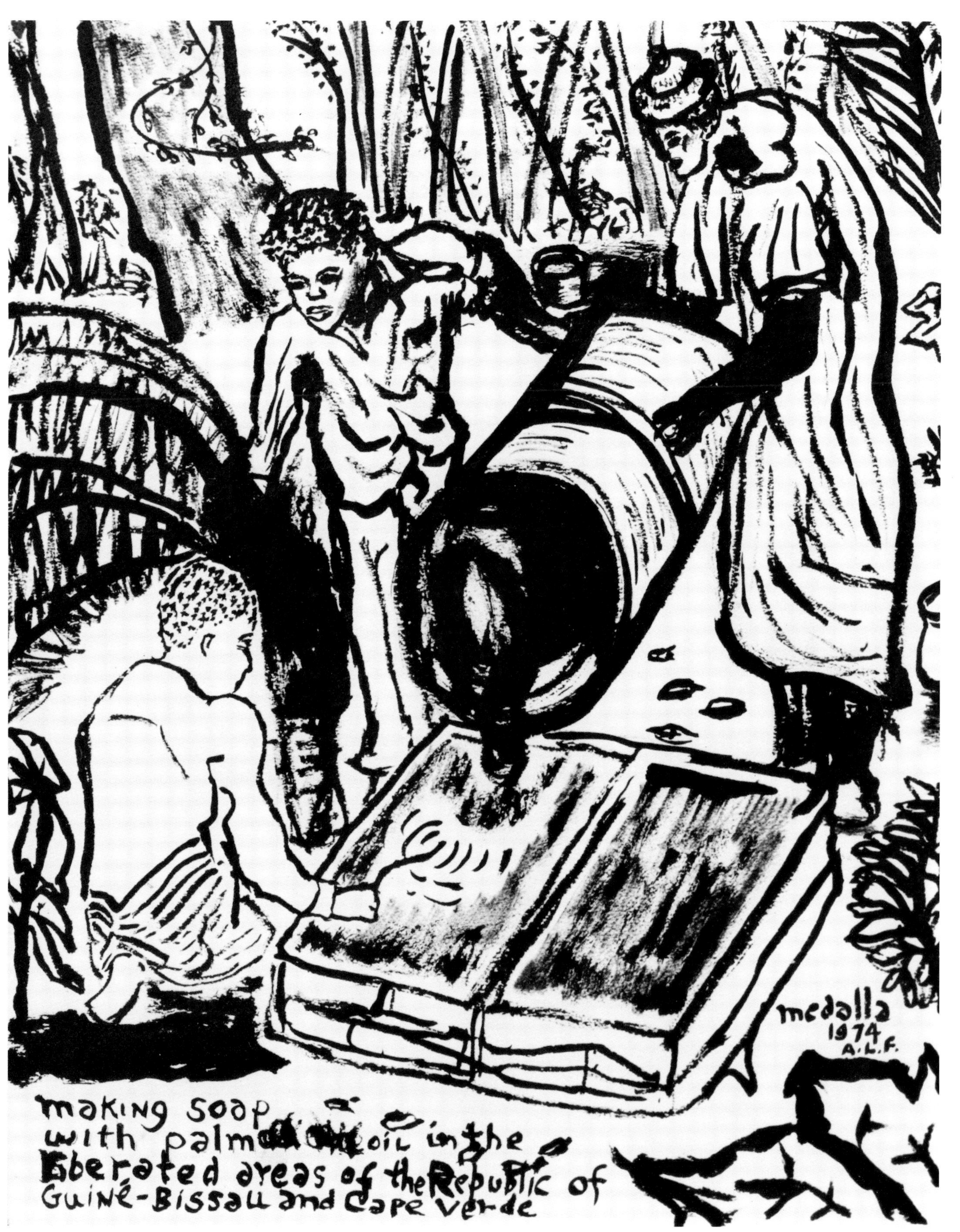

making soap
with palm oil in the
liberated areas of the Republic of
Guiné-Bissau and Cape Verde

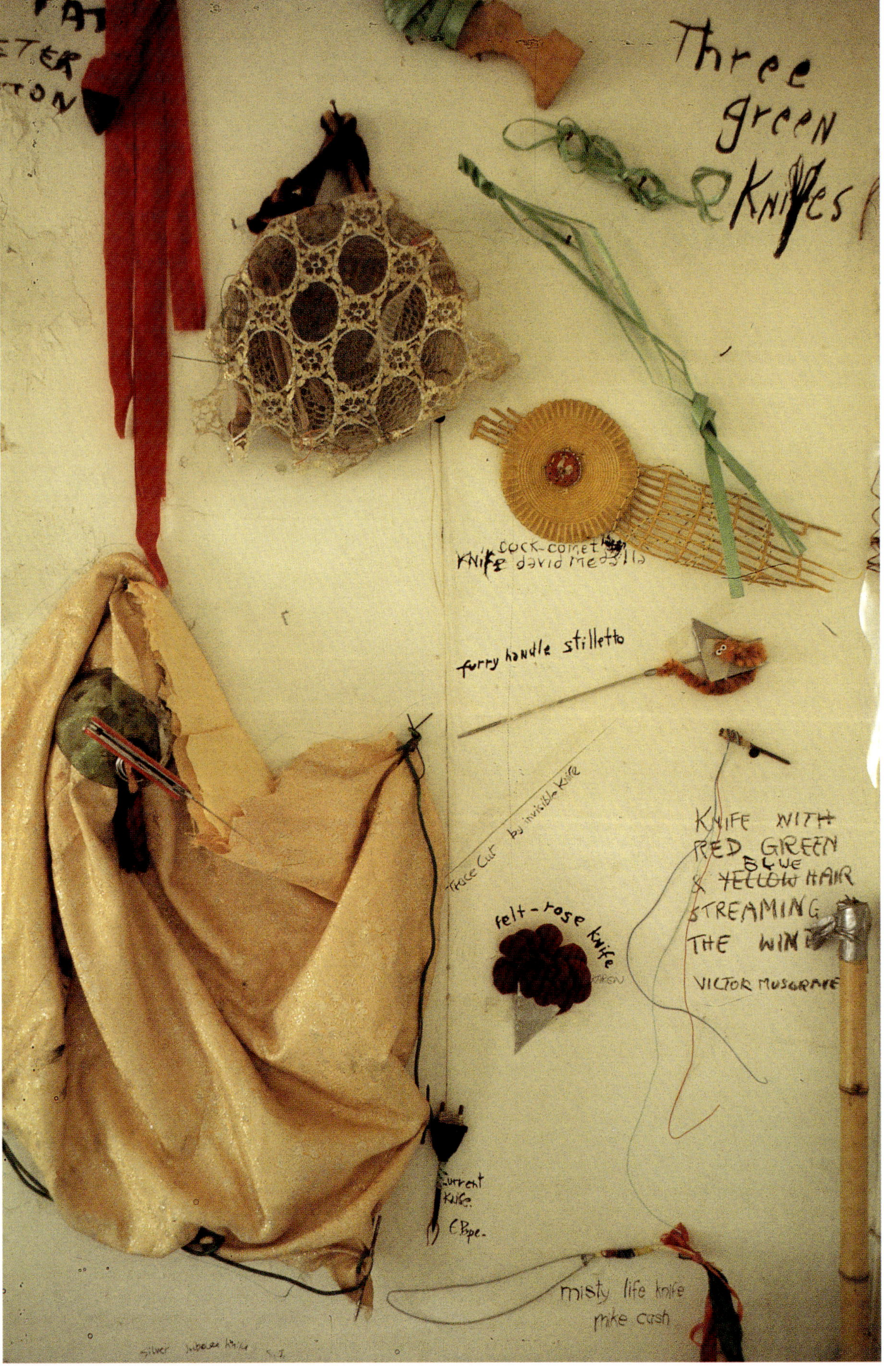
Three green Knives
COCK-COMET KNIFE david medalla
furry handle stilletto
Face Cut by invisible Knife
felt-rose knife
KNIFE WITH RED GREEN BLUE & YELLOW HAIR STREAMING THE WIND VICTOR MUSGRAVE
Current Knife C.Pope.
misty life knife mike cash
silver jubilee knife

Four

Any Number of People

The more one knows about, and thinks about, Medalla's participation works of the 1970s, the more audacious, subtle and many-layered do they seem to be. That their significance was not properly understood by many at the time they were introduced is itself probably due to a paradox. While to those taking part they were experienced as something accessible and unpretentious, playful in fact, to mainstream artistic circles they were unclassifiable. For what Medalla was clearly attempting to do was to bring together an emancipatory social and political consciousness with an emancipatory notion of artistic structure, into a kind of reciprocal relationship. He tested the possibility of this fusion in experimental situations which would be both topical and poetic, collective and individual. He was not content for art to be subservient to politics, and merely illustrate political concepts, nor for art to be so concerned with the semantics of its own discipline that it had no critical sense of the uses to which its innovations might be put. In these works he grappled with what later came to be identified as the contradiction between the 'representation of politics' and the 'politics of representation'. A number of factors influenced Medalla's experimental interweaving of artistic and social structures. Among them were:

o His discovery of auto-creative and auto-destructive forms during the kinetic period, forms which would develop and change outside the control of the artist. As we have seen, this discovery could be translated from an analogy with physical nature, to the interaction of people and social relationships.

o A corresponding transition from the machine as the source of energy to the hand. This move was paralleled in participatory experiments such as those of Lygia Clark and Hélio Oiticica – a kineticism of the body. The Brazilians proposed a form of self-knowledge in the moment of manipulating, or 'wearing', the work.

o The Exploding Galaxy's challenge to hierarchy and narrow specialisation, and the group's belief that everyone has the capacity to be creative. Following on from this, Medalla's African and Asian travels were in one sense a re-immersion in communal forms of culture. He had always maintained these were characteristic of Filipino society, even if not recognised as such by many of the country's

Eskimo Carver, a 'participation-production-propulsion', Artists for Democracy, Fitzrovia Cultural Centre, London, 1977. Details of knives made and titled by visitors.

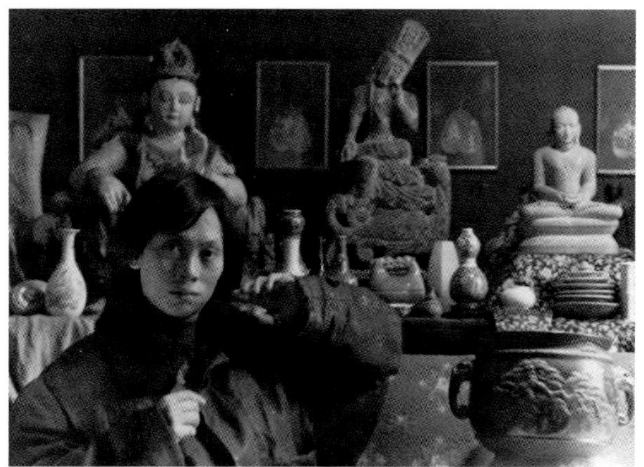
With part of his collection of Indian, Chinese and Tibetan art, Newport Place, Soho, London, 1972.

leaders. Allied to this was a sense of a connection, or interplay, between the most humble objects and great artistic forms, as well as between the everyday and the cosmic (one example, for Medalla, was the story of the origin of the shape of the Buddhist *stupa* – temple, shrine – in the forms of Buddha's begging-bowl inverted and placed on his folded robes).

○ The insights of the writings of Marx and Engels which had given Medalla a new take on his earlier experiments. What he had seen as elemental processes of material transformation (as in his Bubble Machines), he began to consider in their human dimension as part of the social history of production, and the processes of manufacture as a form of interaction with nature. Again, these processes of making see-sawed between opposites: labour and play, drudgery and hedonistic pleasure, collectivity and individuality. As a practice of interaction with the material world, manufacture ranged from the most refined forms of connoisseurship – the most minute nuances of material difference or quality apprehended by our senses, and in the process forming our senses – to the exhausting struggle with brute matter to provide the basic necessities of life. One of his favourite examples of the nature of refinement in manufacture was the great periods of Chinese porcelain. The most beautiful bowl was basically no more than a certain conjunction of earth, air, fire and water.[1]

It will be seen how these different factors came together in his new works. *The International Dust Market*, 1972 (p. 96-7), was one of several 'games'. The duration of the piece was fixed by David Medalla and John Dugger passing a piece of coal between them until it was completely worn away into dust. An act of exchange, reminiscent of Lygia Clark's *Body Nostalgia: Dialogue*, 1968, where a stone is passed from the palm of one person's hand to another's by means of pressure, was combined with an image of toil deriving perhaps from the Buddha's metaphorical image of the endlessness of time, involving a rock and a fine piece of Benares muslin.

Down with the Slave Trade!, 1968-71 (p. 100-1), was a much more ambitious 'mass participation propulsion', which Medalla tried out once or twice with the public but left at a fairly rudimentary stage before moving on to something else. The concept was extraordinary. It was again a great game: people were invited to insert themselves into a complex network of chains, plastic tubing and small colour penants, like a huge harness covering a city square. It would permit them certain movements and restrict others, in a constantly changing pattern of "reciprocal mobility" (the artist claimed to have invented a system of linkages which would never become entangled). The work's title deliberately used the most graphic and universally graspable term for oppression to draw attention to its continued existence in perhaps more subtle modern forms, and the work itself used the most hackneyed symbol of enslavement to suggest the nature of freedom. "By seizing the traditional symbol of slavery (chains) and discarding its conventional connotations, I found its paradoxical transformation", Medalla wrote.[2] The structure of the web was based on the plastic concepts of certain pioneers of abstraction, notably Vantongerloo and Mondrian.

"Mondrian's effort was to develop a new conceptual structure of the twentieth century which would be liberated, flexible and equilibriated", Charmion von Weigand had written of the artist's researches in asymmetrical harmony which culminated in the Boogie-Woogie series painted in New York in the early 1940s. Medalla's aim was to bring these discoveries forward into the present and into an active relationship to the problems of the world. He wanted people to experience the transformation of the chains from their associations with oppression to a new structure which, theoretically, would "link all the people of the world together" in a non-repressive way:

It is a collective expression of variable, random and volitional movements initiated by the individual participants acting as a whole; the work exists only as a living complex of these instantaneous and momentary movements, and therefore it cannot be consumed in isolation (by a solitary individual), or exploited and speculated upon like the majority of art objects.

By a method of freely linking one person with another, and by linking people together to form a united and mobile whole, I seek to increase the awareness of voluntary cooperation between one person and another, and cooperation between the individual and the group, without either the individual or the group dominating, without the possibility of one individual dominating another: for the links in this work are so distributed that each link contributes to the articulation of the whole.[3]

Form would become content, and content form. In the 1960s, Medalla had said that, in the movements of his biokinetic constructions, he had been searching for "continuous melodic structures" which would arouse by inference "tenderness and love" in the body and psyche of the spectator.[4] Now these melodic structures were to be brought about by the motions of the participants in and amongst themselves.

A Stitch in Time (p. 102-5), initiated in 1968, with various subsequent versions, took a slightly different direction and inaugurated a series of participation works which were based on 'production'. If this suggests something heavy, regulated and rooted, we can again enjoy a typical paradox because David has given an account of the origins of *A Stitch in Time* which emphasises travel, mobility, love and chance encounters:

One autumn day in 1968, two of my ex-lovers (until then, unknown to one another), by sheer coincidence passed by London and stayed a couple of weeks with me. One, from Paris, was on the way to California; the other, from New York, was on the way to India. When both left on the same

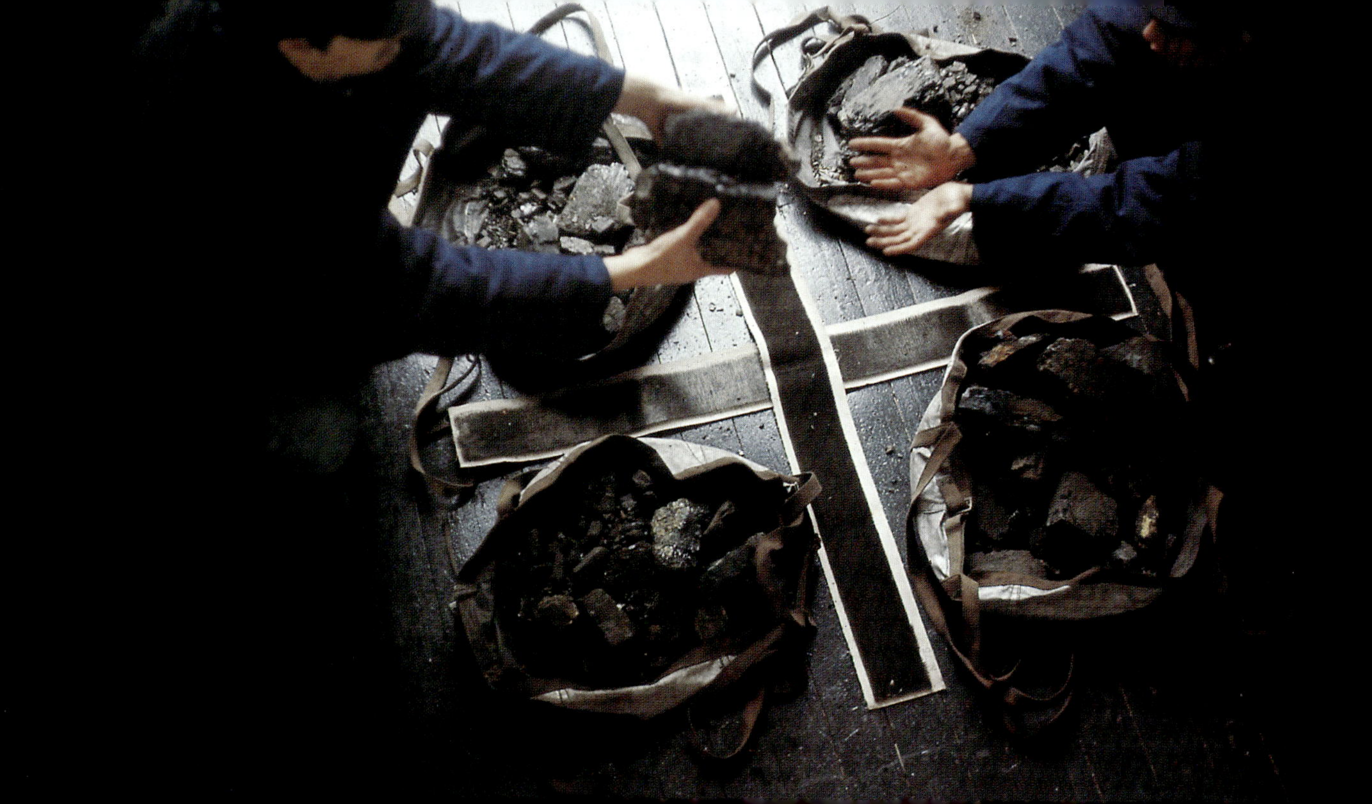

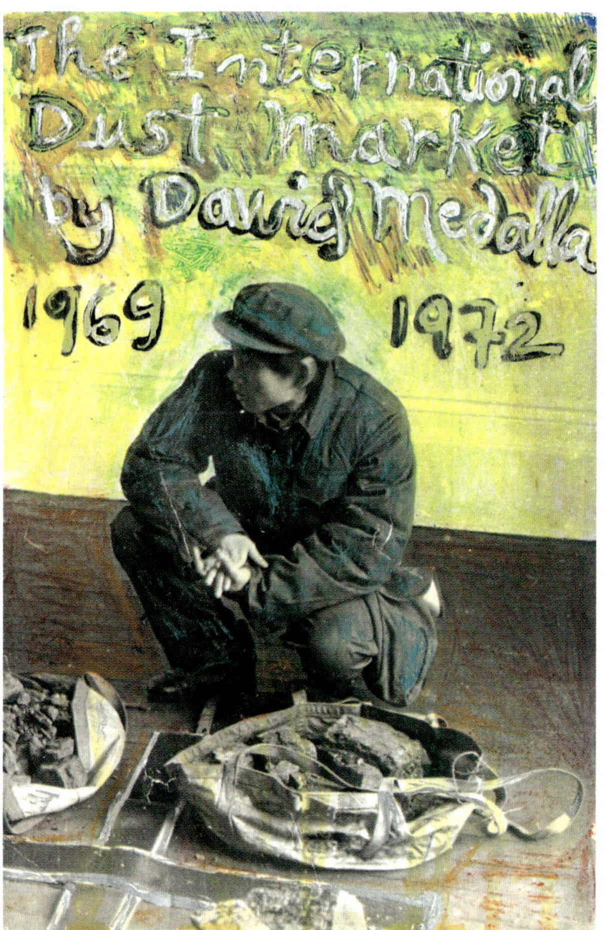

The International Dust Market, a participatory event, 1969-72. 'A Survey of the Avant-garde in Britain, Part 1, Gallery House, London, 1972.

day to go their separate ways, I gave them each a handkerchief (one black, one white), a spool of thread each, and each a packet of needles. I told them to stitch anything they liked on the handkerchiefs; it would be, I added, a pleasant and relaxing way of passing the time whenever they were waiting for airplanes, boats, trains or buses. I also said that they could pass on the handkerchiefs to others on their travels. Nine years later, while waiting for an airplane at Schiphol airport in Amsterdam, I met a young Australian with a curious-looking squarish column of materials strapped to his backpack. I asked him what it was, and he told me it was a participation artwork someone gave him in Bali, whereby various people had stitched all sorts of things – embroidery, as well as objects such as tiny bits of textiles, fragments of jeans, shells, seeds, old-style Chinese coins with holes in them, pieces of mirror-like metal, and even remnants of micro-transistors from old portable radios. I looked at the bottom of the column and I recognised the handkerchief I had given one of my ex-lovers, for on it I had stitched a simple message of love.[5]

97

This was a work, therefore, which took shape while travelling. In between these two sets of meetings, separated by a fair period of time, Medalla had constructed several stabilised, or 'localised', versions of *A Stitch in Time* in galleries and other venues. These incorporated long sheets of cotton on which visitors were invited to sew anything they like. *A Stitch in Time* always kept the quality of a light, flexible structure capable of graceful adaptation to any space or situation. The basic elements – sets of bobbins of coloured threads, needles, and white sheets – were always the same but the form of the work varied considerably. One version (Documenta 5, Kassel, 1972), inspired by the work of Kasimir Malevich, had the bobbins "suspended in simple geometric ranks so that they floated like points of colour in space above two white sheets suspended like a horizontal cross".[6] Another version ('Survey of the AvantGarde in Britain', Gallery House, London, 1972) had a line of large bobbins suspended from a ropeladder, the shadows they cast on the sheets resembled the X-ray of a vertebral column. In a third version (submitted to the Hayward Annual in 1979 but rejected), the sheet was made of white satin overprinted with designs by the artist related to aspects of time (fossils, bubble-chamber photography, etc) and featured a pin-cushion sewn to the centre of the sheet containing a thousand needles. Yet another version, at South Hill Park, Bracknell, in 1982, was "inspired by clusters of forget-me-nots" seen in the Arts Centre garden. As people gathered to sew on the sheets, *A Stitch in Time* conjured up many associations: a suspension bridge, a scroll, a surgical operation, a production line, a hammock, the long table of a collective feast. The context of the stitching was delicately suspended between collective memories both of labour and leisure.

Although at one level an open invitation to make graffiti, *A Stitch in Time*, by aspects of its form and conception, exerted subtle psychological expectations. The experience of participation was guided in certain unobtrusive ways – what David would probably call his "melodic structures" – to become a potential means of insight to those taking part. Medalla always stressed that his propositions were easy to enter. Any number of people could take part in them and they required no special initiation or knowledge of art. "People can walk in and out of my situations... they are dependent on each person falling back on his or her own resources... [their aim is] to infuse people with a certain kind of enthusiasm, to trust their own capacities to be creators."[7] Yet the conditions were not anarchic:

Each one in his or her own time could be involved in a very simple activity, which is stitching, which anybody can do, and in the process of stitching, in the rhythm of the stitching, you'll find that the material will determine its half of the entire rhythm. Take a person who is very extrovert and rather nervy. He cannot be just nervy and extrovert vis-à-vis this work, he has to thread the needle... There's a real relation between the material and the person and the actual process is purely contemplative because it is a minimal function. That's why stitching, like all forms of needlework, has a very therapeutic value, because you have to concentrate, not only in threading the needle, but in making your statement, whatever it is.[8]

Some of the cotton sheets embroidered by many hands in those years have been kept, and they are curious objects that can be seen on several levels. From a distance they look like abstract paintings. From closer-to, words and images begin to appear, giving a sociology of the public and private opinions of the kinds of people who visited avant-garde exhibitions in European cities at that time. Then, at another level, come the non-overt meanings: the crabbed or expansive design, the painstaking or insouciant, the appetite for colour, conventionality or experiment, humour or solemnity, are revealed inescapably in each contribution. Having entered the work, each person had to decide what they would do, how much time they would give, what they would leave behind of themselves. Each person's statement was inevitably influenced by those of others. It was a dialogic, kinetic, transformative structure for exploring the relationship of public and private, individual and collective, normally thought of in static and schematic categories.

The same orientation can be seen mischievously infusing *Porcelain Wedding*, 1973 (p. 106-9). The first enactment of this work took place, with uncanny appropriateness, in an art school.[9] Plaster casts of antique statuary stood around as the couple – a young man and woman – were encased in clay over their naked bodies by the other participants. The clay was decorated with linear designs and then cut into small squares with holes to be baked and threaded together to form suits (similar to the jade burial suits of the Western Han dynasty prince and princess which had recently been unearthed in China). For the Edinburgh showing a pie was baked for the wedding breakfast with the patterns of the constellations as its decoration: "For the poor man, Sky in the Pie!". At Arts Meeting Place in London, as a prelude to the symbolic wedding, visitors were invited to make small clay sculptures alluding to the seven days of creation: a form of 'offering'.

In the art school setting *Porcelain Wedding* could be interpreted at one level as a flamboyant parody of the Life Class (so named!). The relationship between 'artist' and 'model' was revitalised in a hands-on collective game of moulding the art material directly to the body, obliterating the element of cold detachment and surveillance, which, over the years, had congealed in this artist/model relationship, and at the same time becoming fused with the metaphor of the loving union of the couple in the marriage. The death suits in turn changed into vehicles of life. Paradoxically, however, Medalla himself maintained that *Porcelain Wedding* was "a very intellectual work". He wanted, he said, to analyse the relation between the Marxist theory of the historical stages by which production came into being and the Jewish creation myth, recasting

Pages 100-101: **Down with the Slave Trade!**, a 'mass-participation propulsion', 1969-72. At three different venues. Page 100: At Jans Kirkhof, Utrecht, Holland, March 1972. Clockwise, page 101: Drawings for structures of flexible connections. Pencil and crayon on paper. Collection of the artist. At Bateaux Mayflower II, Quai de Tuileries, Paris, 1970. At Camden Arts Centre, Hampstead, London, 1971.

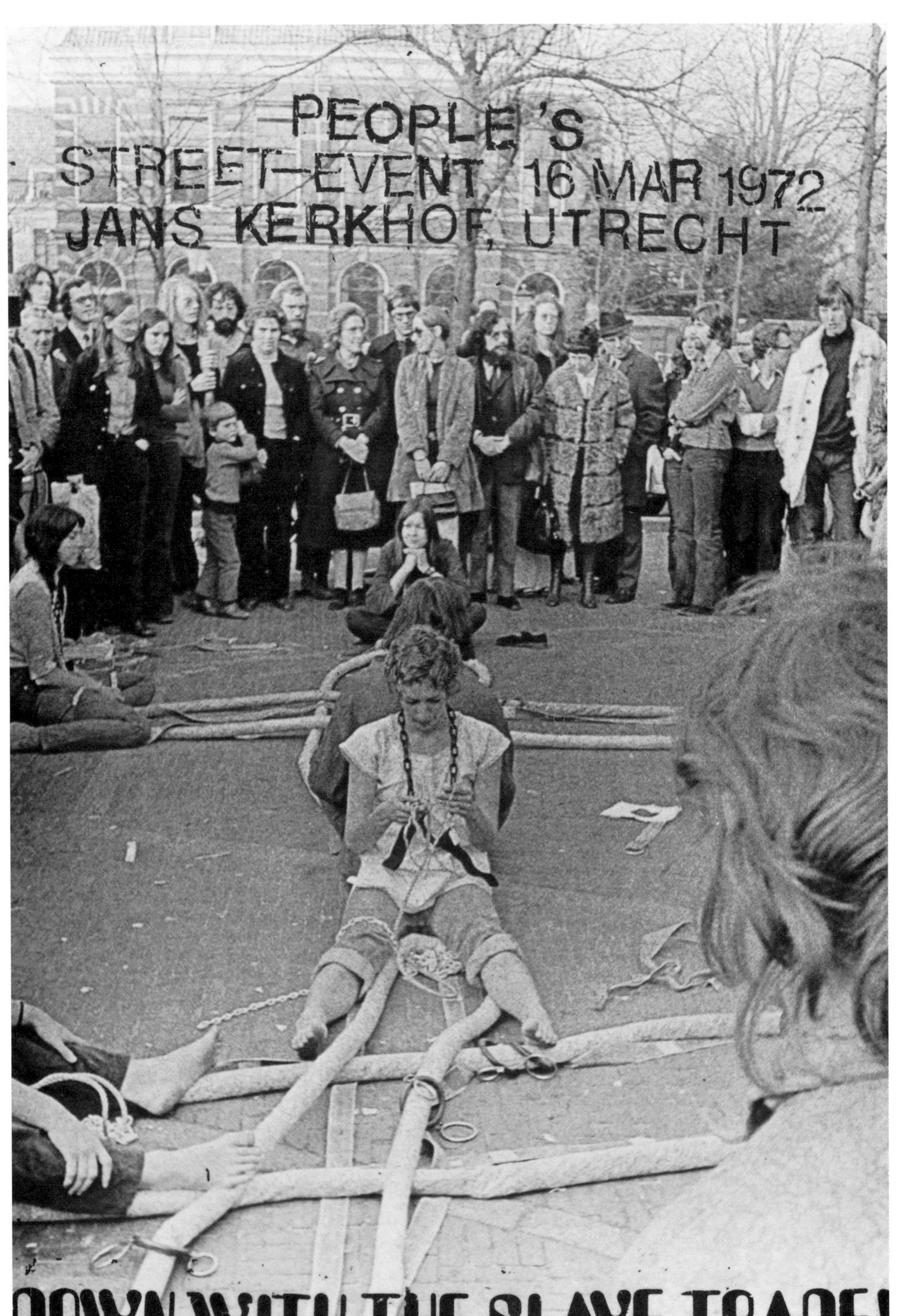
PEOPLE'S
STREET-EVENT 16 MAR 1972
JANS KERKHOF, UTRECHT
DOWN WITH THE SLAVE TRADE!
mass-participation propulsion 1968-72
by DAVID MEDALLA A.L.F.

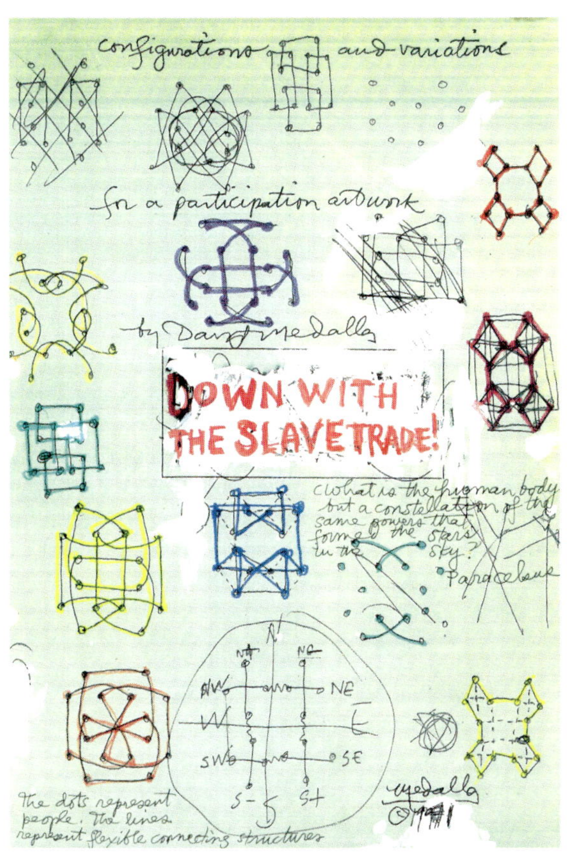

configurations and variations
for a participation artwork
by David Medalla
DOWN WITH THE SLAVE TRADE!
"What is the human body but a constellation of the same powers that formed the stars in the sky?" — Paracelsus
NW N NE
W E
SW S SE
The dots represent people. The lines represent flexible connecting structures
Medalla 1971

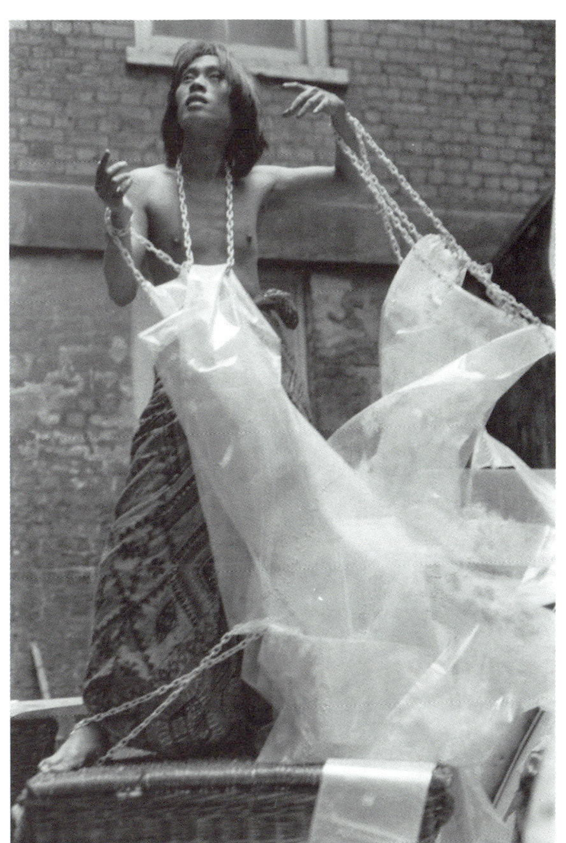

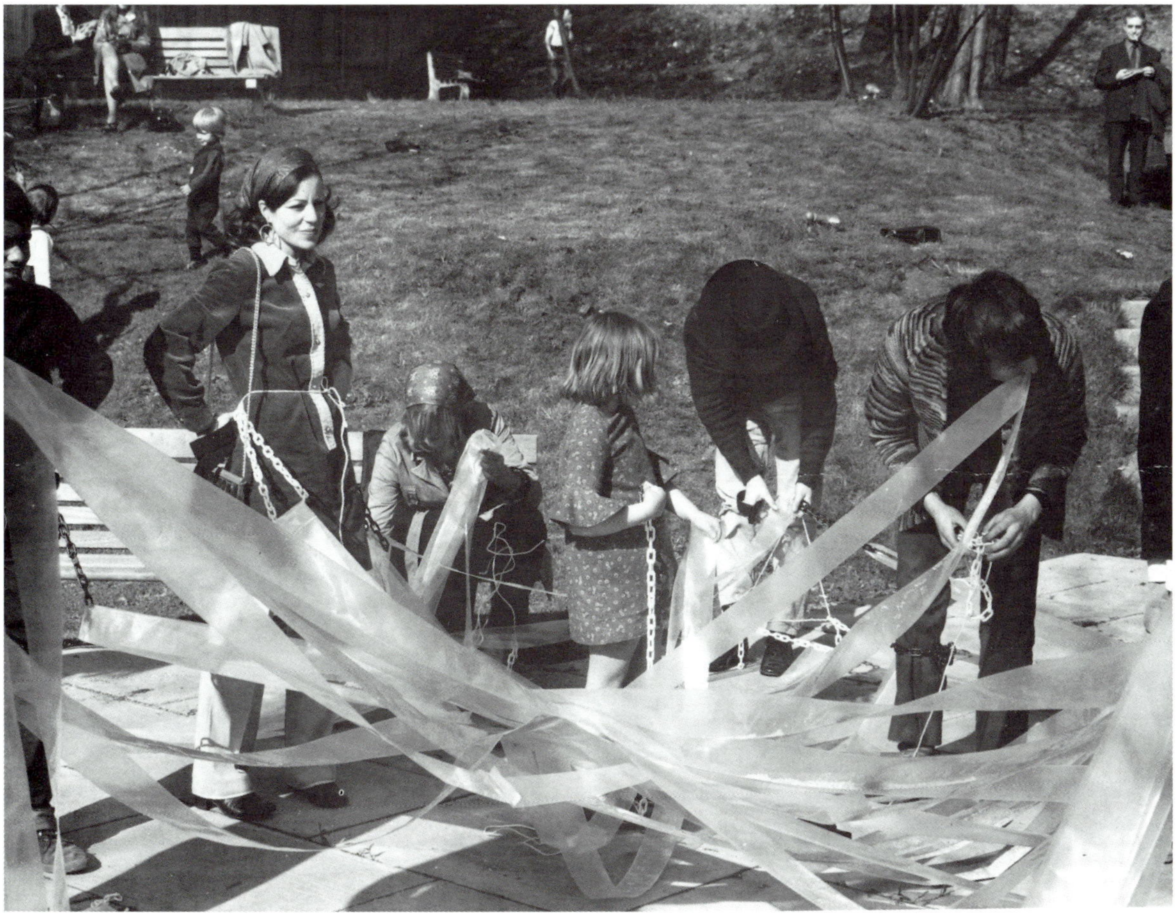

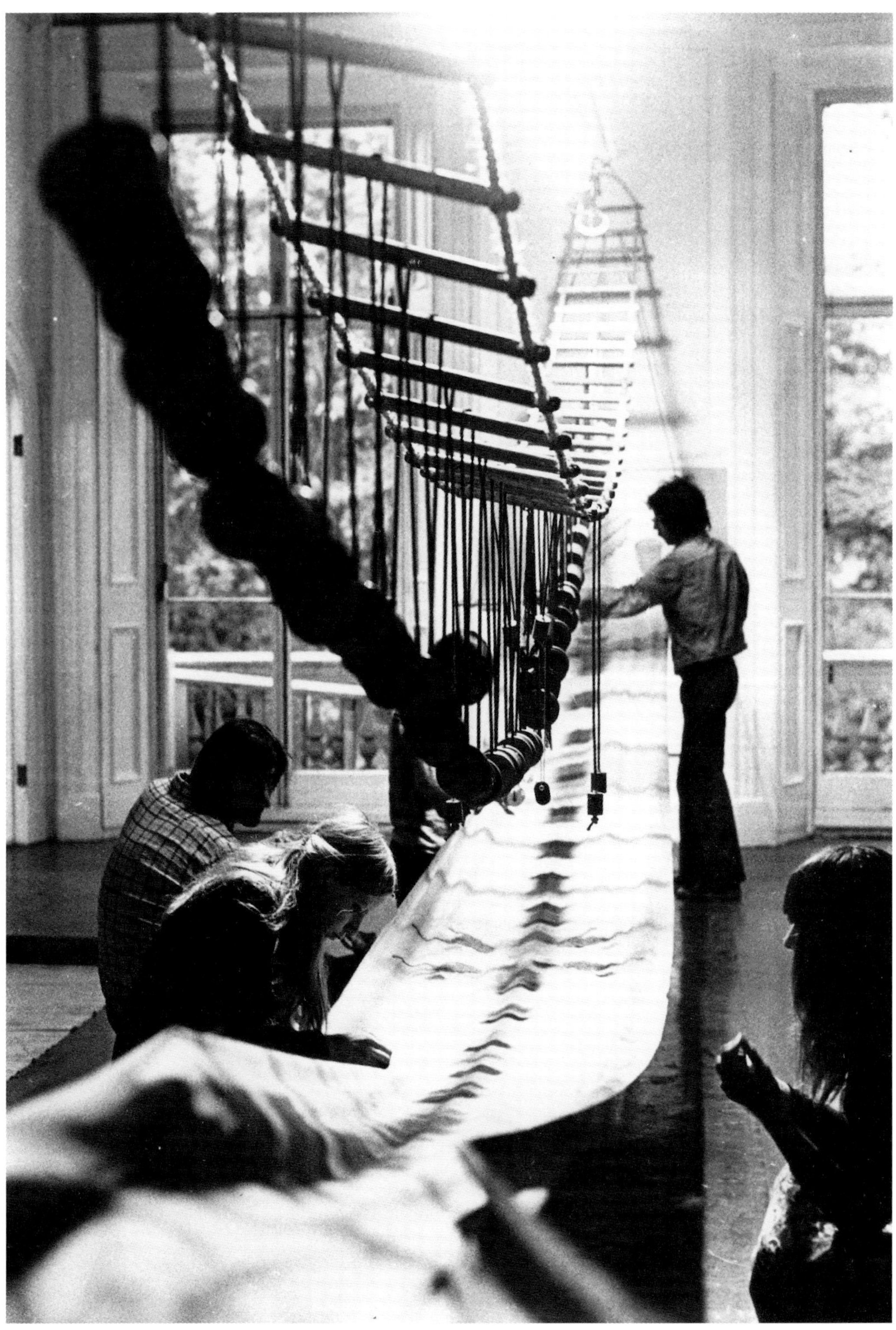

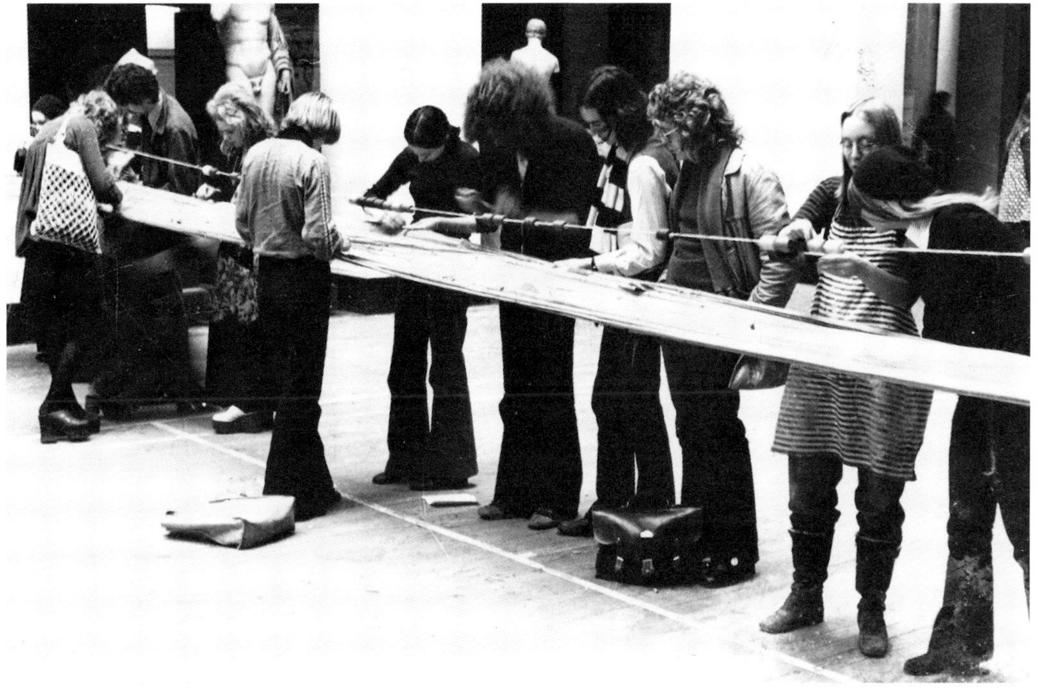

Opposite, above, and pages 104 -105: **A Stitch in Time**, a 'participation-production-propulsion', 1968-72. Four different versions. Opposite: 'A Survey of the Avant-garde in Britain, Part 1', Gallery House, London, 1972. Collection of the Arts Council of Great Britain. Above: at Edinburgh College of Art, 1973.

both in the present. "I believe in genetic memory, that prehistory is in us. Making images out of clay was shared by all of us at some moment of historical evolution. 'Preceding' is paradoxically combined here with the beginning – with creation."[10] The little clay sculptures made by visitors ranged from amorphous blobs or molecular chains to realistic models and topical slogans.

Eskimo Carver, 1977 (p. 112-15, 117), was the last event held at Artists for Democracy before the centre closed. It was possibly an even simpler proposition in terms of its central concept and even more revealing of the psychology of people taking part, and of the enigmas in the relationship between 'production' and 'art'.

Eskimo Carver came together from several inspirational sources encountered fortuitously in the stream of life. Medalla was considering a performance in which the periods of human history, from the caves to the 20th century, would each be represented by a knife singing its own song. While walking near the Centre Pompidou in Paris his eye was caught by a tourist brochure thrown away in a dustbin which contained some unpretentious photographs of Eskimos, including one of a man carving a small ivory statuette with a bow-drill. This image immediately brought to mind Robert Flaherty's documentary *Nanook of the North*, especially the scene where Nanook builds an igloo by cutting the snow into cubes with a knife and trimming them

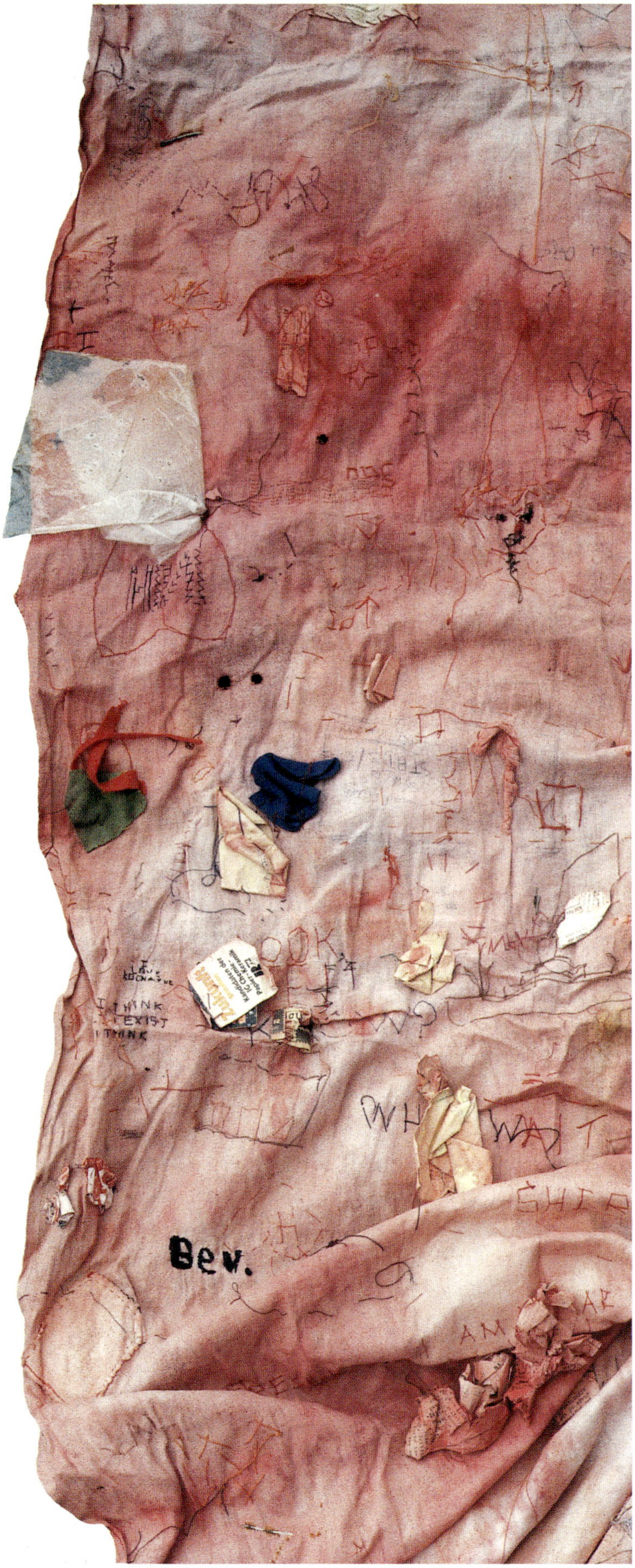

VIKKI

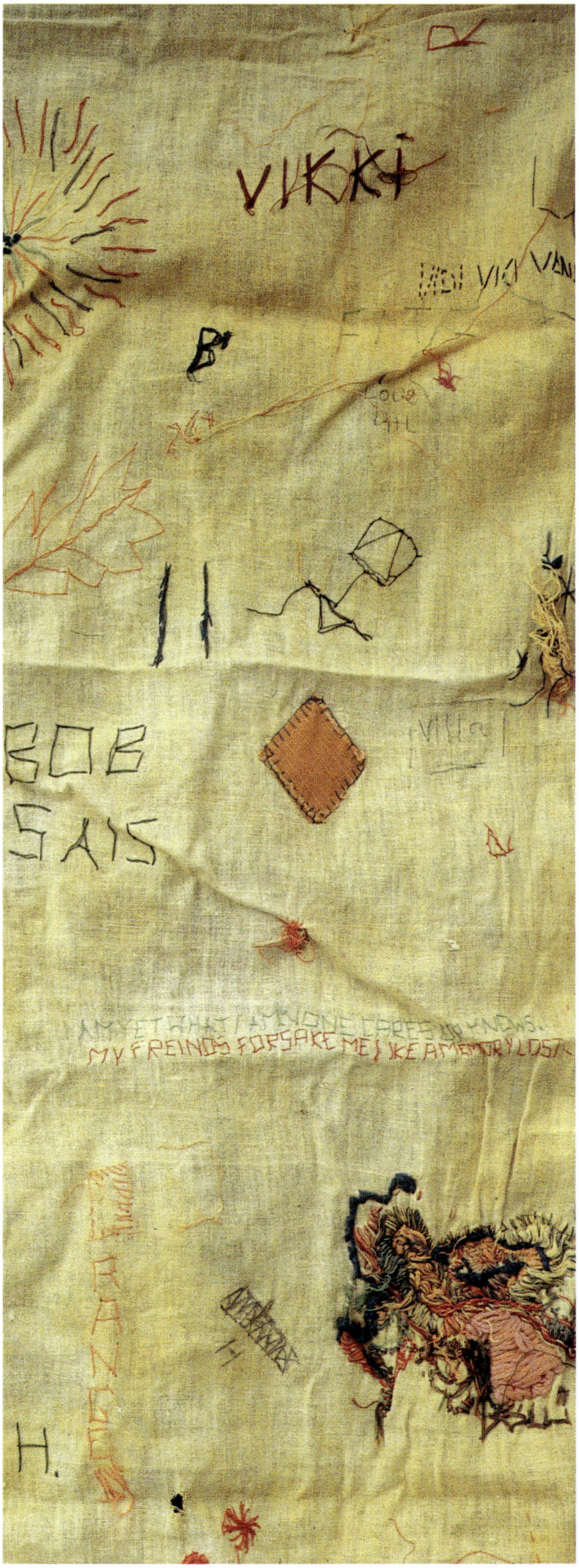

BOB
SAIS

I THINK
I EXIST
I THINK

Bev.

MY FREINDS FORSAKE ME LIKE A MEMORY LOST

H.

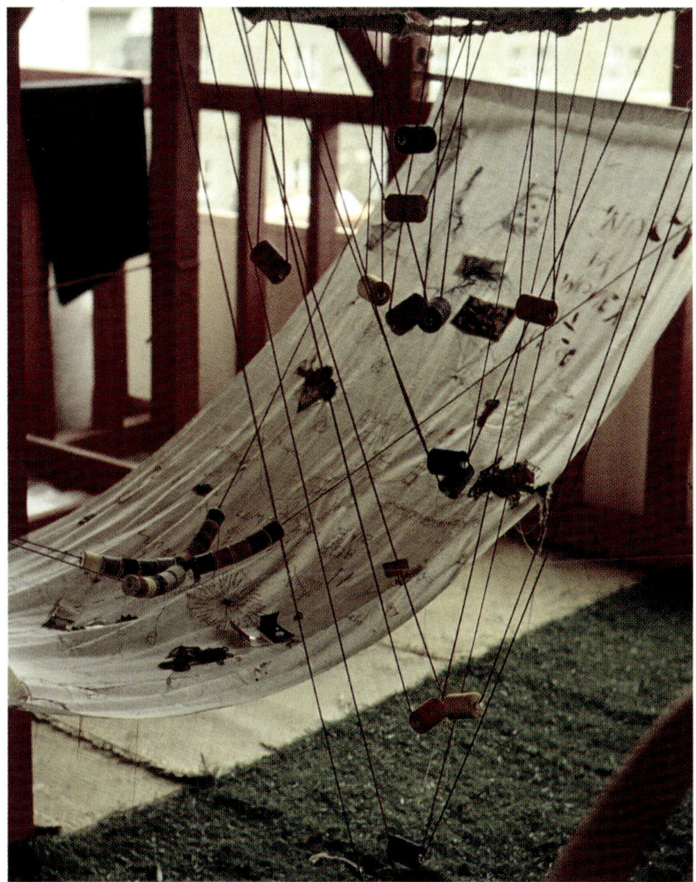

A Stitch in Time, a 'participation-production-propulsion', 1968-72.

Right: at the Peoples' Participation Pavilion, Documenta 5, Kassel, 1972.

Below: at Art meeting Place, Covent Garden, London, 1974.

Opposite page: details of the cotton sheets embroidered by visitors.

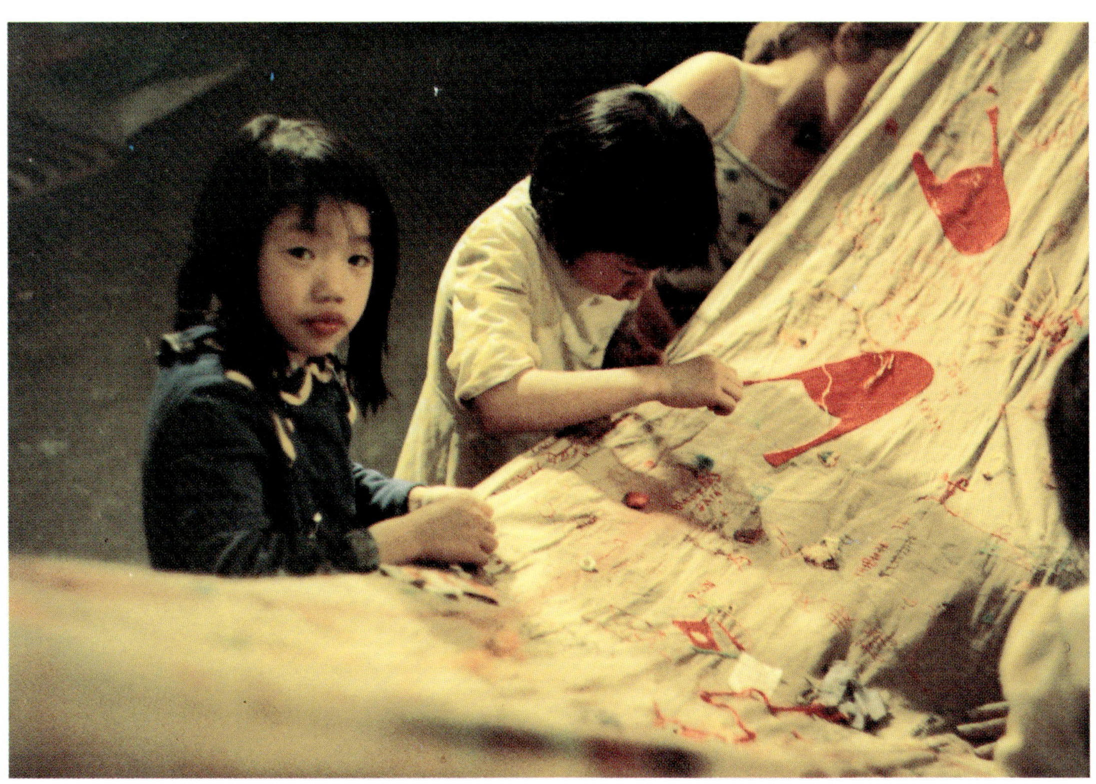

A Stitch in Time, a 'participation-production-propulsion', 1968-72.

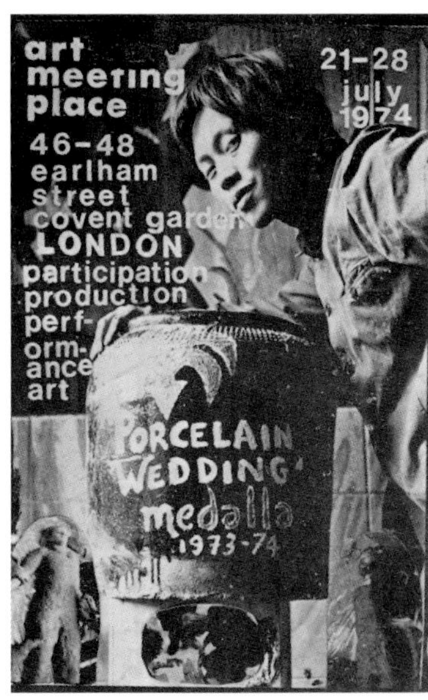

art
meeting
place
21-28
july
1974
46-48
earlham
street
covent garden
LONDON
participation
production
perf-
orm-
ance
art
'PORCELAIN
WEDDING'
medalla
1973-74

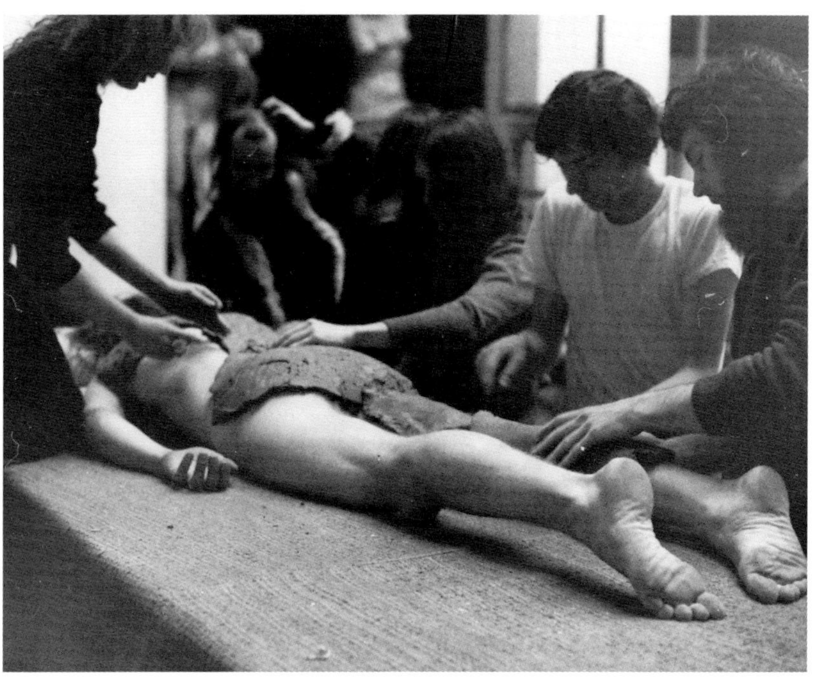
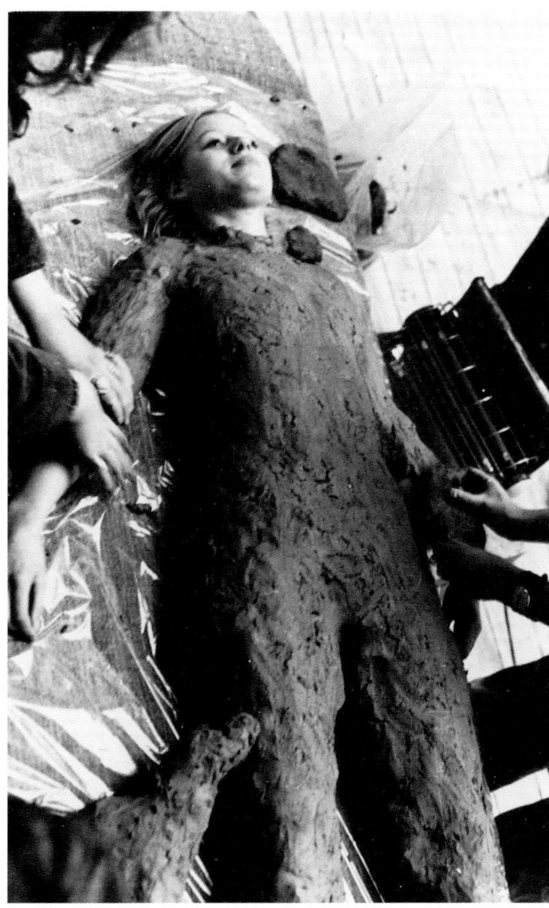
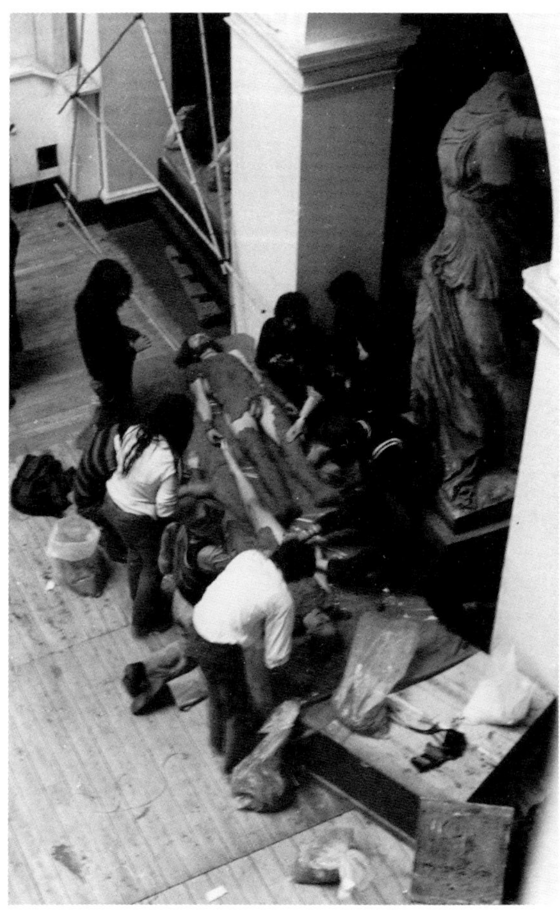

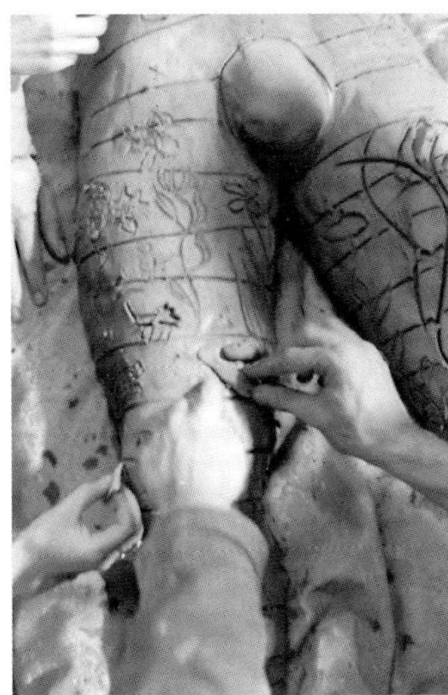

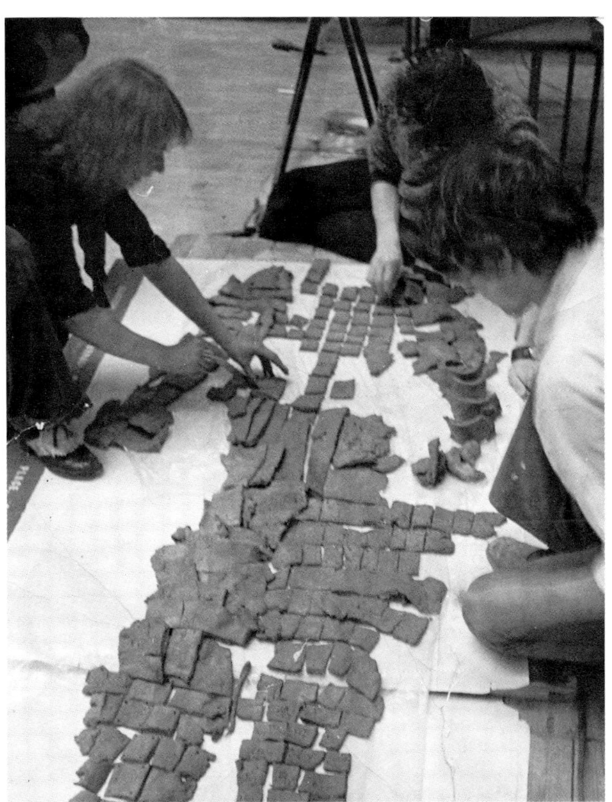

Porcelain Wedding, a 'participation-production-performance', 1974. All photos, with the exception of invitation card, opposite, and top left, this page, were taken during the performance of the work by students, under the artist's direction, at Edinburgh College of Art. Photo top left and invitation card were taken during another enactment of the work at Arts Meeting Place, London.

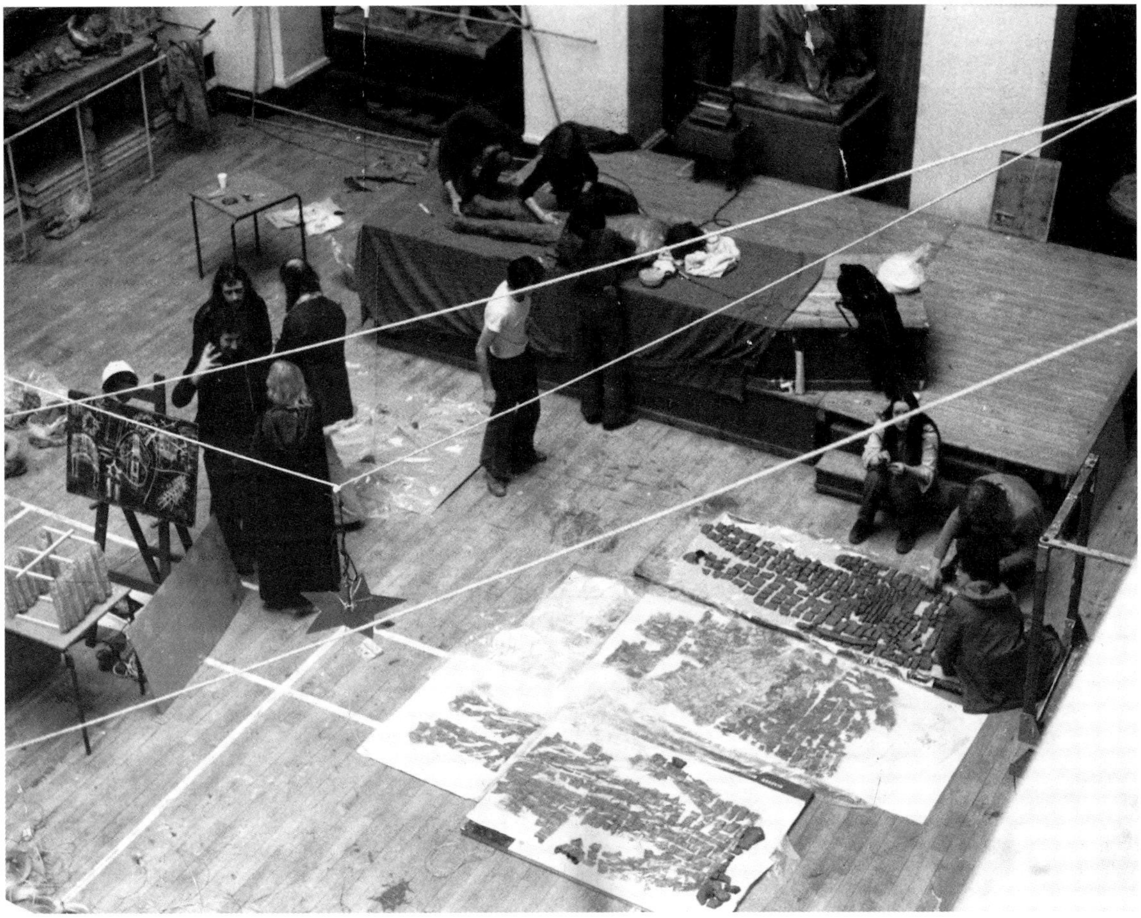

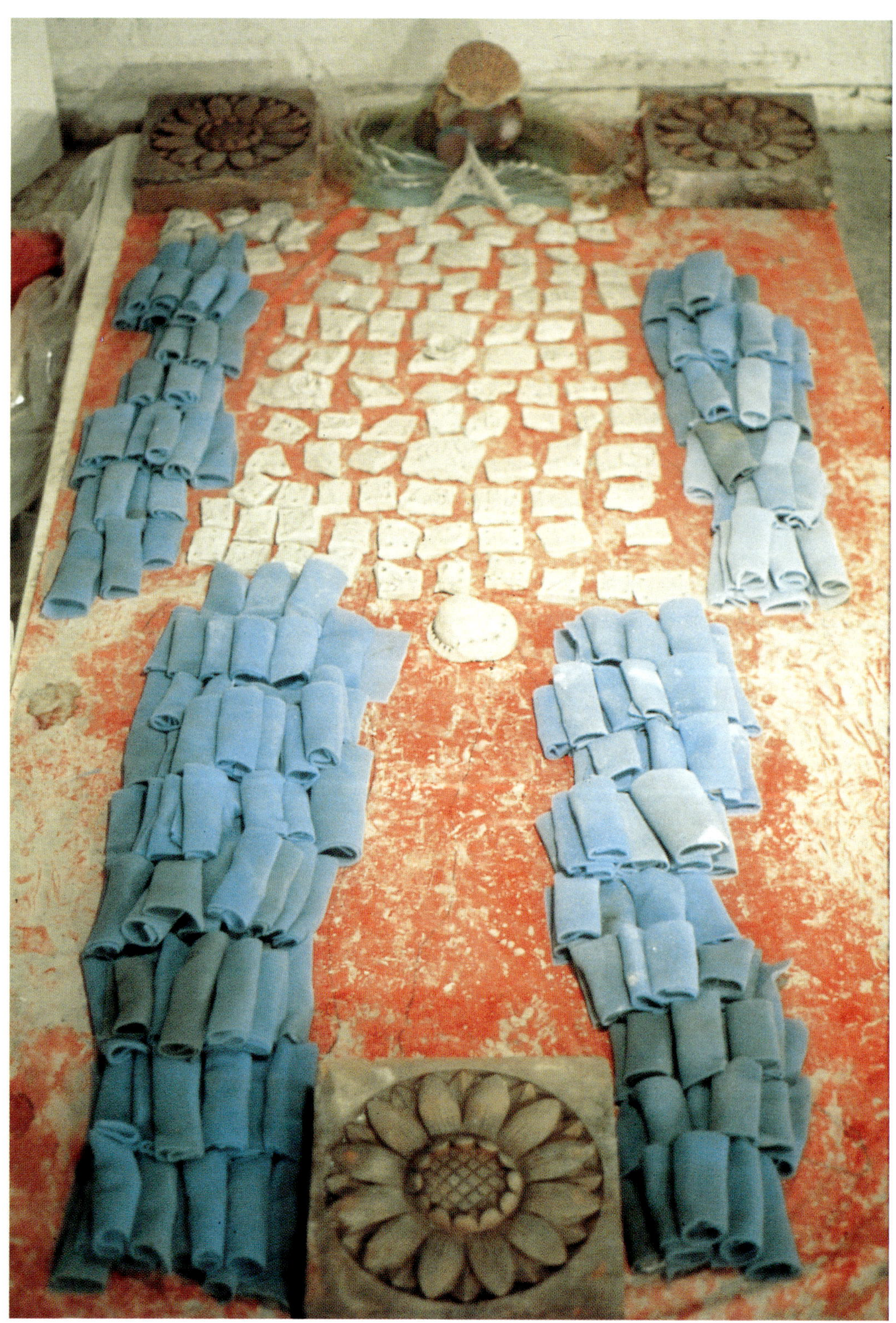

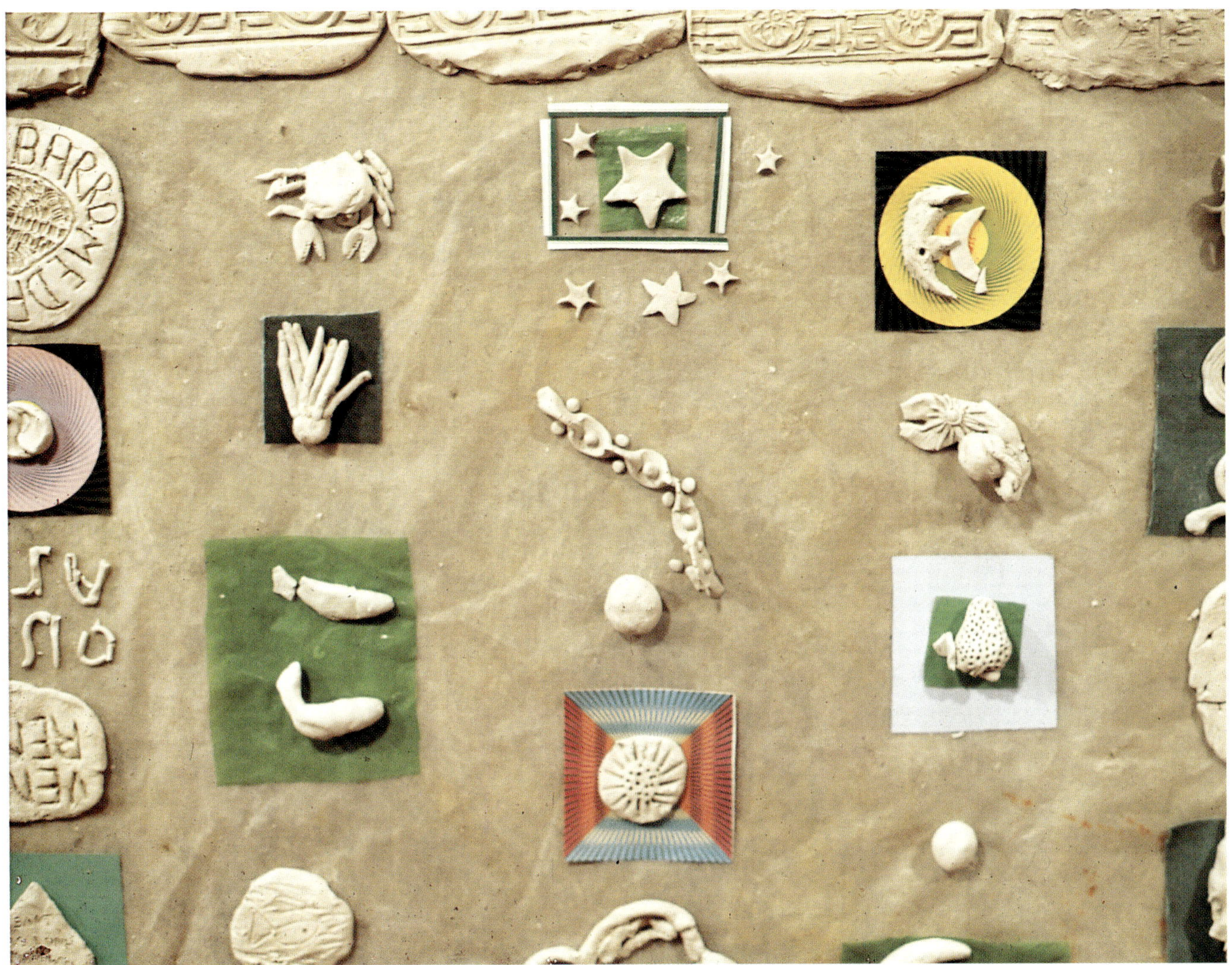

Porcelain Wedding, a 'participation- production-performance', 1974, Arts Meeting Place, London. Opposite: one of the clay suits laid out prior to firing.
Above: some of the clay models made by visitors, inspired by the '7 days of creation'.

until they fit together. Later, in London, David bought a book in a second-hand bookshop of Tom Lowenstein's retranslations of the Danish anthropologist Knud Rasmussen's transcriptions of Eskimo oral poems made originally in the 1930s. And about the same time, English newspapers were featuring stories about the building by trans-national companies of a pipeline to extract oil from Alaska, at that period the most expensive of such projects undertaken in modern times.

Medalla's event consisted of several elements. There was an exhibition of his drawings and transcriptions of Eskimo poetry, and a performance, *Alaska Pipeline*, which allowed the British tabloid newspapers' glorification of pioneering pipelayers set against a racist denigration of Eskimos, effectively to condemn itself. The third part was an invitation to visitors to make knives (or drums) out of non-perishable garbage which had been collected in the neighbourhood and piled in a corner. Over a period of four weeks each knife and drum (there were very few drums as it turned out) was signed, titled by its author, and added to the collection on the walls in a playful parody of ethnographic museum displays.

The ambience opened people's minds in a certain way. The Inuit people have given some of the most succinct and eloquent descriptions that exist of the mixture of desire/anxiety/pleasure which is present in the human urge to compose poems and songs. They traditionally have a democratic, non-professional practice of creating them:

The Eskimos hardly ever sing or perform the songs of others. Every man and woman, and sometimes even children, has his own poems; and this despite the fact that it is justifiably regarded as a large-scale and difficult task to create a good new song.[11]

As the collection of knives built up, everyone, including the artist, was astonished by the variety of peoples' contributions. Medalla observed:

You cannot say that one knife is better than another... It is really a show – or a concept if you like – that effectively destroys the idea of the unique art object. Each of the knives is unique and every single one has a quality of its own and yet what is interesting is the aggregate. If you put such a proposition in a public place, literally it's an endless proposition, there is no end to people coming in and making knives. I could easily inundate, say, the Tate Gallery...

The second thing that is fascinating about it for me is the kind of significations that occur: because each of the objects, by being given the specific concept of KNIFE – we know what knives are and how they are used - and the people, being given a range of materials which they did not make any decision in the choosing of, in the process certain things are revealed, about, I think, the psychology of people... because they range from very functional-looking knives to an amazing kind of fantasy...[12]

Although the objects retained the semblance of knives, some explicitly, some very faintly, they were linked with every possible knife fantasy or desire: 'love knife', 'invisible knife', 'knife by chance', 'vanity knife', 'misused knife', 'gay young blade', etc. Sometimes a knife was indicated only in the most schematic way (a point, or angled cut) in what was otherwise a spontaneous collage made from the waste. The result was a marvellously witty and tangible way of exhibiting the relationship between the practical and fantastic sides of the human psyche. Use-value or instrumentality became the direct means of letting loose the polymorphousness of imagination. And imagination in turn worked upon materials – 'garbage' – which are the instrumental objects of our civilisation reduced to purposelessness and disorder.

This reciprocity of mind and matter was given a unique form in the contribution of each individual. And yet occasionally there seemed to be an involuntary process of 'rhyming' taking place too. Why did so many knives take on the appearance of fishes? Was it because the carver in the big drawing was himself carving a fish? Or was it an unconscious connection with one of the staples sustaining Inuit life? For this was a mass exploration of metaphor too, of transferable meanings. Medalla himself suggested that the garbage could both be seen as something 'cosmic' – "the formless chaos being given specific form by individuals" – and as something 'topical': the turning of the Arctic by heedless exploitation into a vast garbage dump.

The artist was intrigued by what he had set in motion. While made up of hundreds of highly personal and individual contributions, the whole or aggregate exceeded the bounds of any individual personality, including the artist's.[13] He began to think of new extensions of the work developing out of its participatory, its improvisatory, its hand-made stage. These projects involved the use of new technology, up to then irrelevant to the work. One scheme was to use computers to make a morphological study of the knives. He would analyse their forms and colours, and the resulting statistical data would then be coded and reconstituted and projected by means of lasers into the night sky "as the continuous projection of one continually changing image of a cosmic knife".[14] Another notion was to preserve the individual knives by packing them together and setting them in a plastic matrix which would itself be in the shape of a giant knife, like insects in amber.

◆   ◆   ◆

Medalla's participation works were from the beginning a means of breaking with certain ingrained taboos and restrictions governing the artistic scene. As Petti Benitez has pointed out, the 'London' that David invited or gathered around him in his groups of the 1960s and 1970s (from Signals through to Artists for Democracy) constituted a "cacophony of voices": voices of people of many cultural backgrounds, and of many artists or potential artists not represented in the British art system. His 'participation production propulsions' were seismographs of the same heterogeneous metropolis. Through them he put forward the startling idea of invading the monocultural,

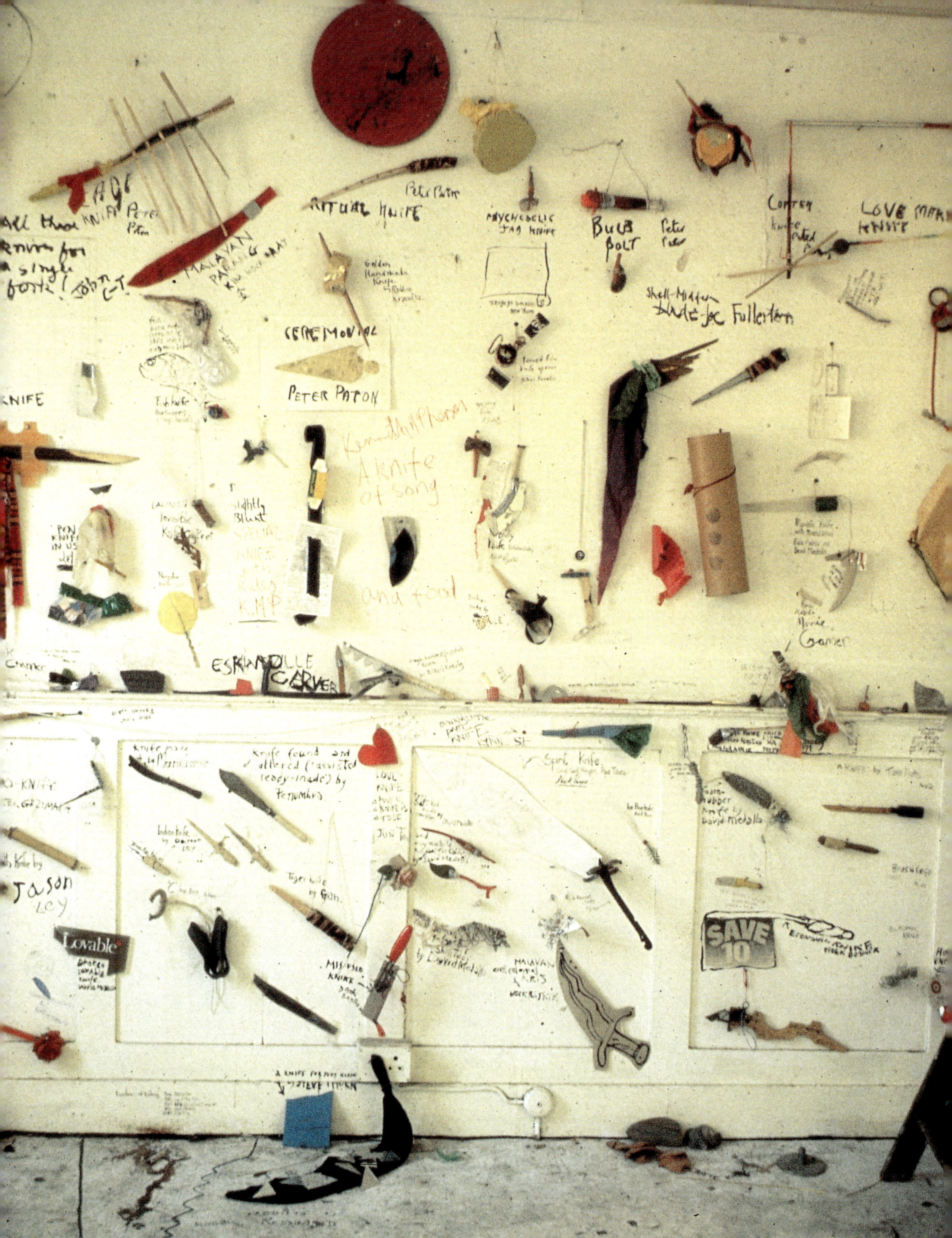
RITUAL KNIFE
PSYCHEDELIC TAG KNIFE
BULB BOLT
LOVE
MALAYAN PARANG KNIFE
CEREMONIAL
PETER PATON
A knife of song
and food
ESKIMOLLE CARVER
Knife found and altered ('assisted ready-made') by Penumbra
Spork Knife
Lovable
SAVE 10
JASON LCY
MALAYAN KRIS

monological and monolithic institutions of the art world like the Tate Gallery by the sheer pressure of a latent creativity.

In *Eskimo Carver* the challenge to forms of alienation in the system of culture was extremely subtle. The knives, by their spontaneous poetry and wit, often put to shame collages sold for large sums in West End galleries, or preserved in self-important isolation in modern art museums. Both recognised artists and 'ordinary people' took part in *Eskimo Carver* but one really "could not say that one knife was better than another". At the same time this work linked one part of the system – the context of contemporary art – with another part, the context of ethnographic art, and the image made by ethnographic museums of 'other cultures'.

Ethnographic museums embody a disturbing paradox. They present objects as evidence of cultures as communities, as seamless systems of shared beliefs and communal practices, which we consume individually and privately, almost as voyeurs. It becomes hard to make any bridge between these assumed poles of individuality and collectivity. At one level *Eskimo Carver* was a kinetic experiment in overcoming this form of alienation. The device of mass participation, the element of giving something of oneself in return rather than merely taking, was the key to this experiment. Since it was not pedagogical but unrestrained in its subjectivity, this collaboration was

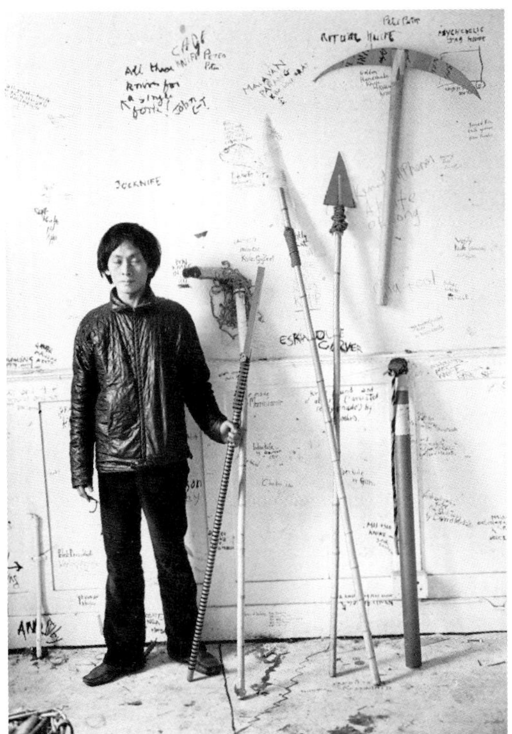

Opposite and left: **Eskimo Carver**, a 'participation-production-propulsion', 1977, Artists for Democracy, Fitzrovia Cultural Centre, London.

Pages 114,115,117 - **Eskimo Carver**, 1977. Some of the knives made and titled by visitors.

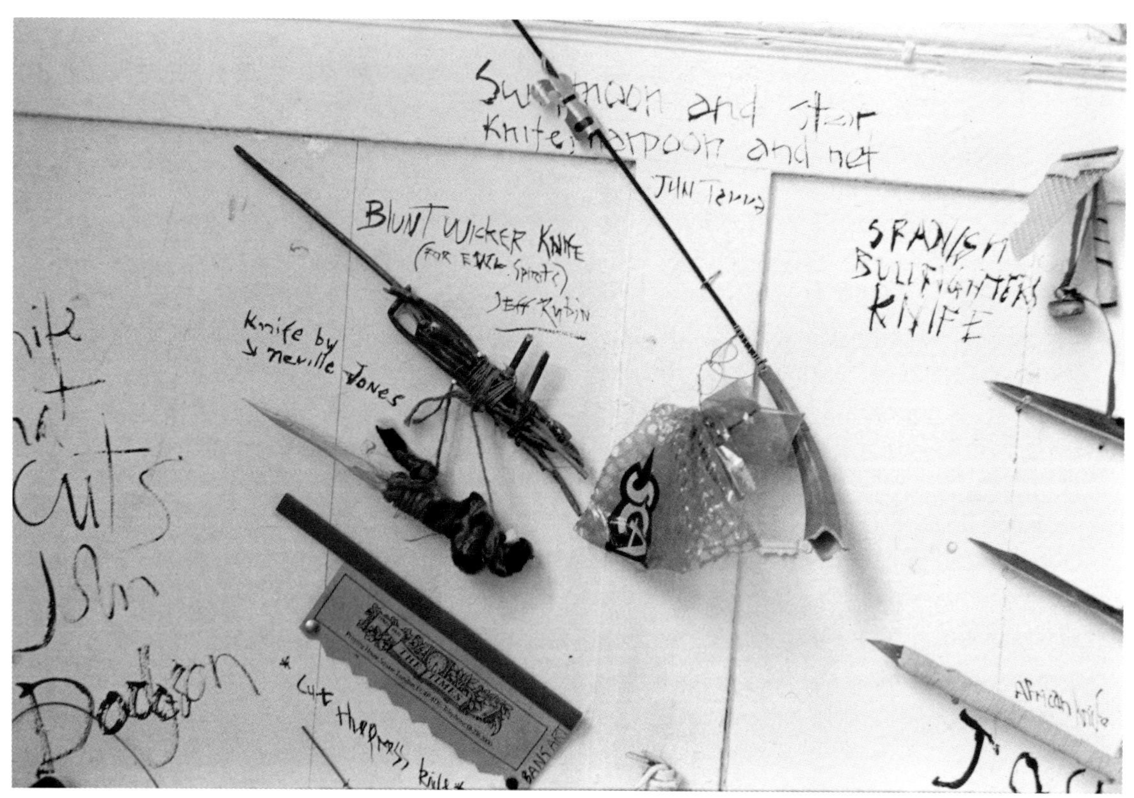
Sun moon and star
Knife harpoon and net
John Terry
BLUNT WICKER KNIFE
(FOR EVIL Spirits)
Jeff Rubin
Knife by
Neville Jones
SPANISH
BULLFIGHTERS
KNIFE
African knife
cuts
John
Dodgson
Lux Hugnss Knife
BANS ART

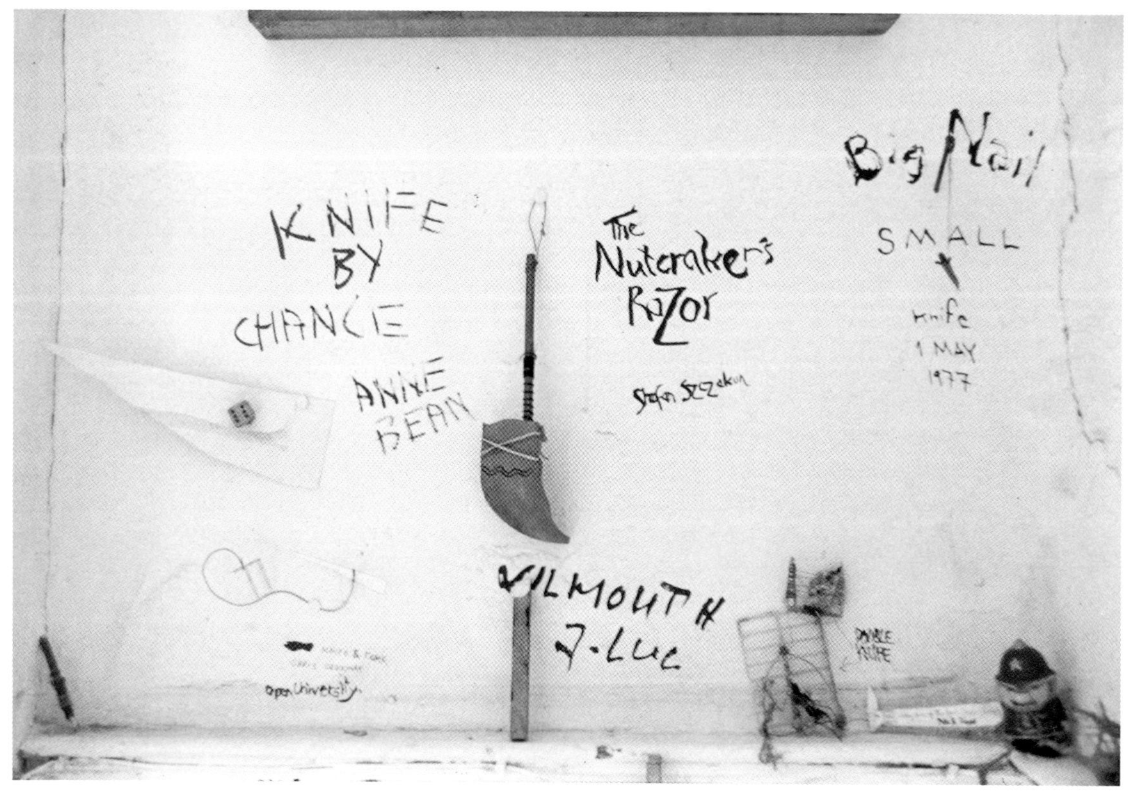
Big Nail
KNIFE
BY
CHANCE
The
Nutcrakers
Razor
SMALL
knife
1 MAY
1977
ANNE
BEAN
Stefan Szczelkun
KILMOUTH
J-LUC
knife & fork
Chris Crickmay
open University
DOUBLE
KNIFE

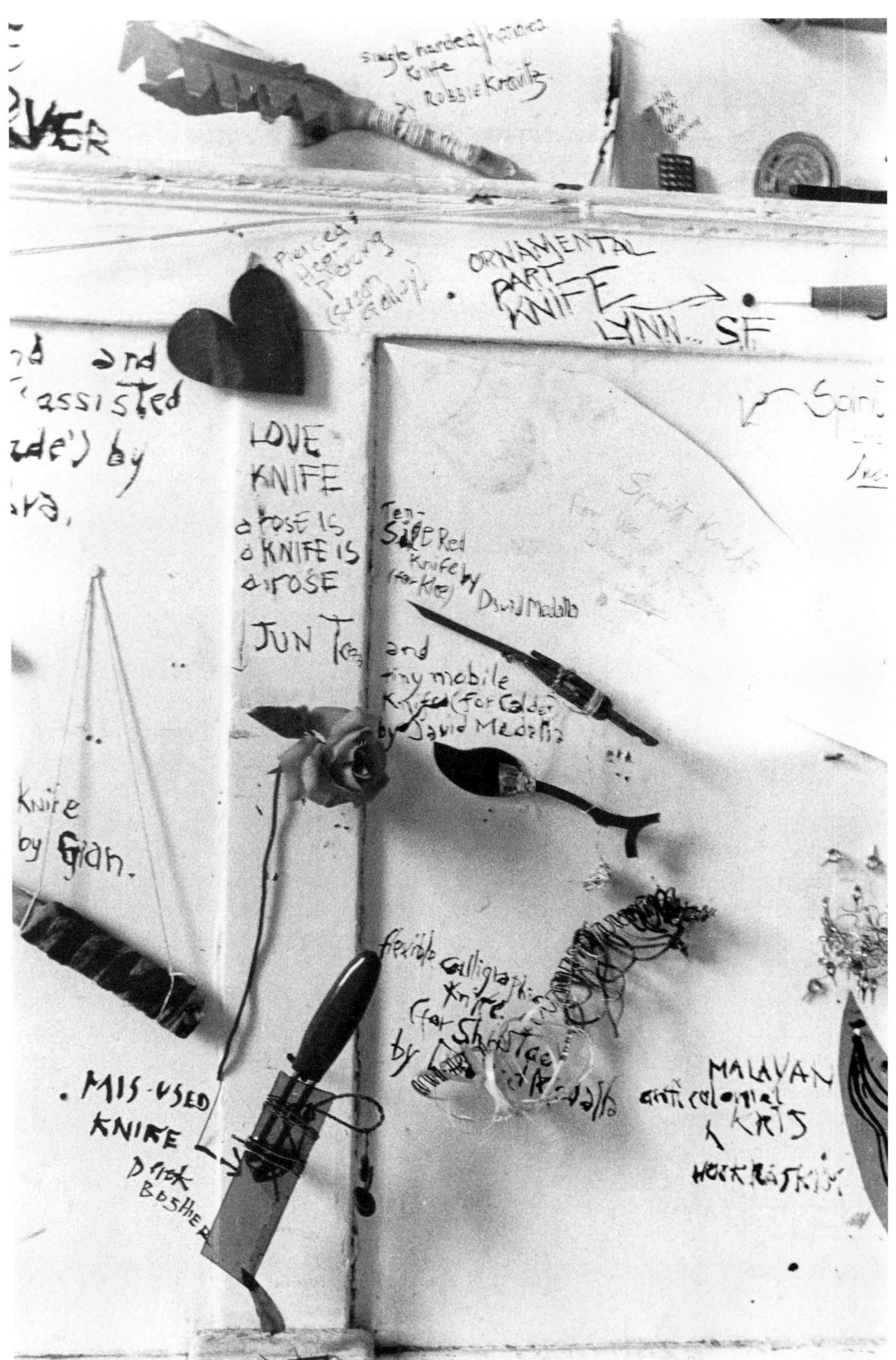
single handled/handled
Knife
ROBBIE Kravitz
Pierced
Heart Piercing
(Susan Gallo?)
ORNAMENTAL
PART
KNIFE
LYNN... SF
Spirit
and and
("assisted
ade") by
LOVE
KNIFE
a rose is
a KNIFE is
a rose
JUN Tea
Ten-
SIDE Red
Knife by
(for Klee) David Medalla
and
tiny mobile
Knife (for Calder)
by David Medalla
Knife
by Gian.
flexible calligraphic
Knife
(for Shantael)
by David Medalla
MALAYAN
anti colonial
KRIS
HERK RASKIN
. MIS-USED
KNIFE
Dick
Bosther

potentially a way of receiving information about another culture, and of another people's historical predicament, without objectifying it in order to alienate and control it. This rebounds in turn upon the nature of the contemporary artist/spectator relationship.

Medalla's participation works of the 1970s, like his earlier kinetic machines, epitomised the gap existing between the experimental and official art streams of the time. Taking only the British context, we can see a cultural ferment going on, and a wealth of questioning, which was simply not reflected in the mainstream art world. Whatever the art institutions may have gained in efficiency and the polish of their presentations, they lost in relaying the breadth and depth of the issues being raised among the most imaginative and audacious artists and groupings of the time. This was probably inevitable since the process of 'grooming' artists for official acceptance became synonymous with a product-oriented concentration on the formalistic aspects of art.

Examples from Medalla's work again make this clear. The non-rigid, softly-hanging, temporary structure of *A Stitch in Time* could be seen in formal terms as a proposition within sculpture. Similar structures have been seen since in other artists' work, even up to today. But to have interpreted it in that way would have meant denying all the other modes of 'non-rigidity' present in the concept, beginning with its multiple authorship and unlimited growth. Similarly *Eskimo Carver* could be said to have anticipated the wave of sculpture made from the scavenging and re-presentation of waste during the early 1980s by a younger generation of ecologically-minded artists. Their installations and objects using dumped plastic bottles, old washing-machines and so on, quickly became a central feature of some of the sculpture of the 1980s. The process of recycling was seen by the more radical critics at the time as implying a critique of capitalist society. For Medalla, however, the problems of consumerism and commodity production could not be illuminated by the mere creation by the artist of a new object, since they were bound up in the relationship between artist and spectator.

A situation where many people are alienated by the business of gaining a livelihood from discovering their capacities as artists is paralleled by one in which the work of art becomes a super-fetish. The two phenomena are intimately connected. That was why Medalla's proposition for taking the waste objects and materials from the flux of everyday life into complex imaginative realms involved an invitation to the passers-by to work this transformation themselves.

Accessible and playful though they are, the forms of participation art pioneered by Medalla, Oiticica, Clark and a few of their contemporaries, reveal deep-seated contradictions in the presentation of art which no museum or institution has been able properly to come to terms with, even up to today. Although museums may find it easier today to assimilate the novelty of such works at certain levels, notions of material transformation, fluidity of authorship, indeterminate limits of the object, and so on, are still hard to handle, and therefore convenient to forget. At heart these remain artistic problems. At one level, Medalla's participation works represented his search for something which, in contrast to the artist's tight control of forms, would open the door to an immense diversity. It may be seen what a brilliant extension this was of the concept of the Bubble Machine: translating a metaphor of endless change from a 'natural' to a 'social' field of reference. At the same time, the device of participation could not be applied in a mechanical, formulaic way. Not just any process of participation or mass authorship is interesting. The poetry of *Eskimo Carver* was not merely due to the invitation to the public to take part, but the ambience, the atmosphere of expectation, created by Medalla. He produced this ambience as an artist, not as a sociologist. In the early days of his critique of capitalist alienation, Marx wrote that if the conditions truly existed for us to produce things "as human beings..., our productions would be so many mirrors reflecting our nature".[15] Perhaps by 'produce as human beings' he meant: if the spark of artistic pleasure was in the air. As it is in the practice of Eskimo poetry, as it was in *Eskimo Carver*.

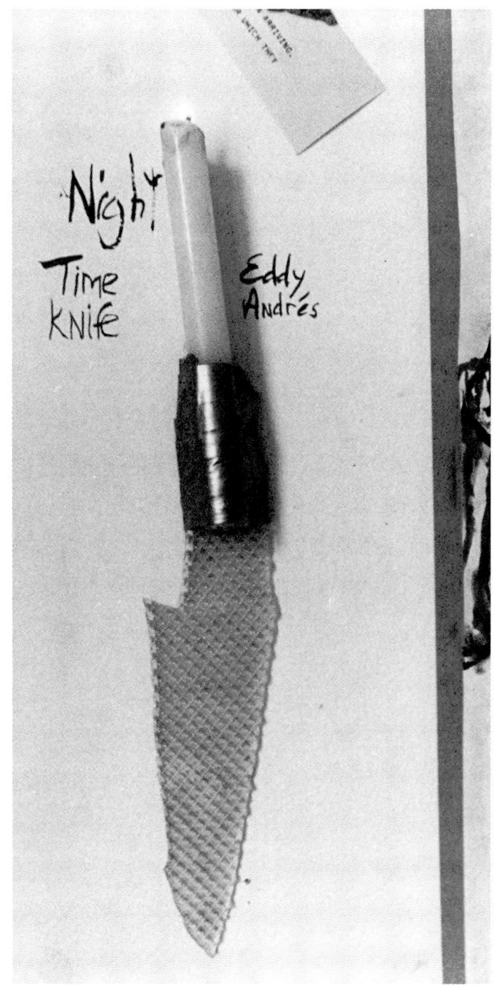

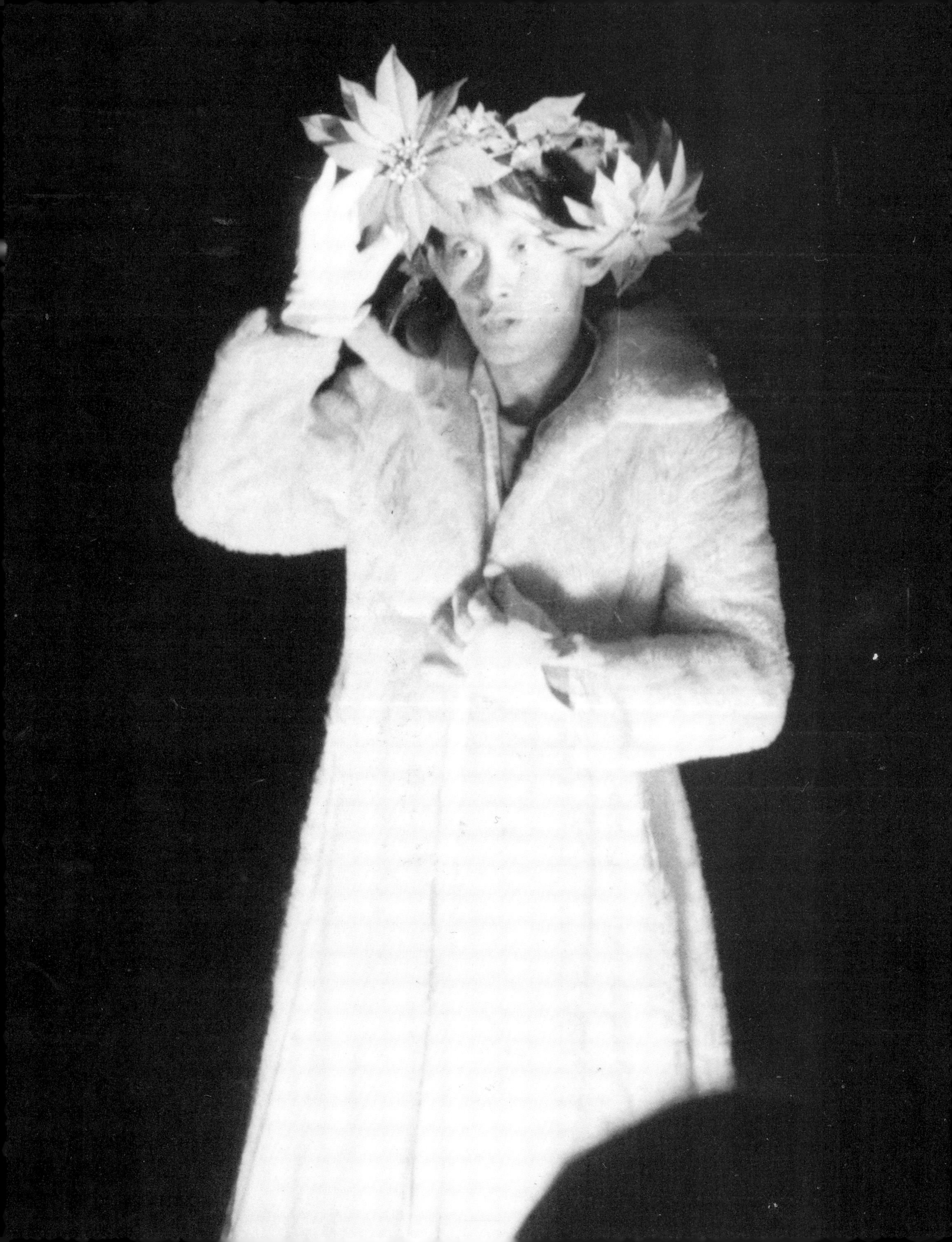

Five

Instant Stages

At this point I become acutely aware of the inadequacies of the linear and chronological order I have adopted for writing about David Medalla's work. The fact that most of the rest of this book will be a discussion of his performances and paintings should not imply that these replaced earlier genres. Medalla has continued to produce projects for new participation works which up to now it has not been possible, for various reasons, to realise. 'Participation' also remained an element in the structure of certain performances. Similarly, performance, and especially painting, was never really absent from his activities. He concentrated on and developed one or another among several modes at certain periods. The phase of performance of the 1980s actually began in 1975 with the Vermeer event at the Serpentine Gallery, two years before *Eskimo Carver*. His avant-gardism has always run side-by-side with work in traditional media, perhaps another expression of his dislike of belonging to a particular camp. Or, to put it in a more positive way, he realised that the excitement of exploring the possibilities of new genres which are just emerging, goes together with the awareness that certain old genres persist for a very long time in the history of art: a great pretext for the play of irony. Nevertheless, I believe that important changes took place in Medalla's art in the late 1970s.

No doubt many factors influenced these changes. No doubt, too, they all added up to a characteristic need to escape from structures he was beginning to find constraining. Artists for Democracy, for a start, was changing. At the cost of several splits and defections Medalla had retained effective control. A number of artists left to form a group more specifically centred on political consciousness-raising, the Poster-Film Collective. The venue in Whitfield Street changed its name to the innocuous-sounding Fitzrovia Cultural Centre. It broadened out as an experimental centre open to any progressive proposal and was not inhibited by bureaucratic procedures, 9 to 5 hours, or stylistic preferences: an attractive proposition in a city which can impose a depressing isolation on artists and their publics. The most incongruous diversity of events ensued. One night there might be a meeting of an exiled Third World opposition group which ended in furious faction-fighting. Another night, there might

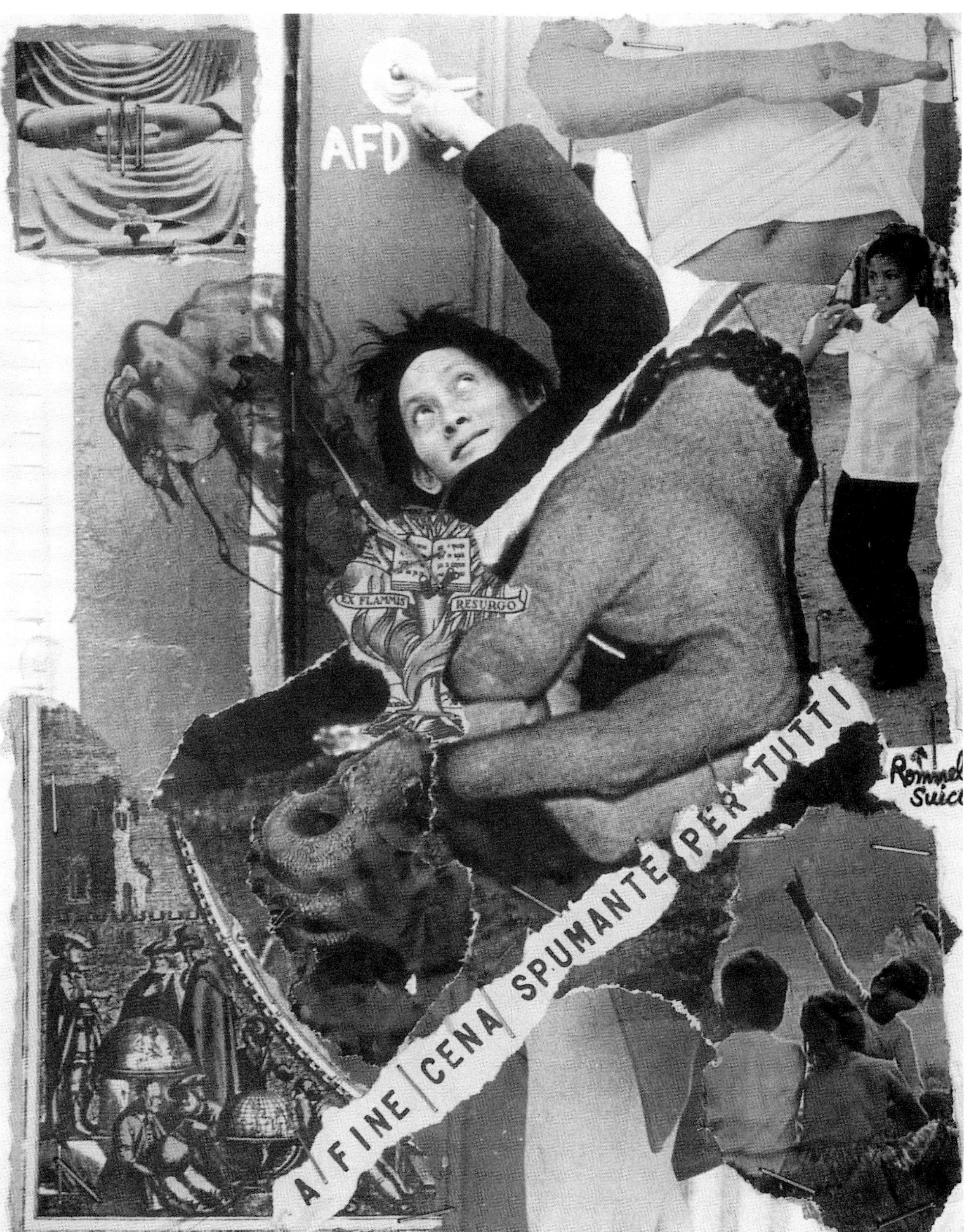

AFD
EX FLAMMIS RESURGO
A FINE CENA SPUMANTE PER TUTTI
Rommel
Suici

be a luxurious champagne opening for a young artist.[1] All this was typical of Medalla's 'cacophony of voices'. In particular, early experimenters in performance and video, in artist/audience dialogue, in the exploration of self and of identity, congregated at Whitfield Street, artists like Rasheed Araeen, Anne Bean, Paul Burwell, Virgil Calaguian, Anne Cloudesley-Thompson, Philip Cohen, Morrie Cremer, Steve Cripps, Rose English, Rose Finn-Kelcey, Rose Garrard, Nick Gordon-Smith, Susan Hiller, Bertha Husband, Charles Hustwick, George Isherwood, Caroline John, Merdelle Jordine, Tina Keane, Andrew Kim, Sonia Knox, Roberta Kravitz, Atilio Lopez, Lynne MacRitchie, Jonathan Miles, Steve Oxley, Nick Payne, Steve Pusey, Carlyle Reedy, Peter Smith, Steve Sprung, Sylvia Stevens, Rino Telaro, Jun Terra, Giles Thomas, Joshua Thomas, David Thomas, Caroline Tisdall, Anna Thew, David Toop, David Turner, Kerry Trengove, Shelagh Wakely and others. But the Fitzrovia Cultural Centre was, after all, though legally occupied, a former squat. As the agreement ran out, Medalla and Nick Payne (then the Centre's manager) found alternative premises, but it was impossible to secure enough public funding to pay the rent and AFD closed in 1977. For the next two years Medalla lived in a succession of dilapidated and insecure squats in Lambeth, Brixton, Vauxhall and Covent Garden, until, in November 1979, thoroughly disillusioned with the measly rewards of twenty years work in England, he left for the continent.

In a conversation published in *Black Phoenix* in 1979, David Medalla and Rasheed Araeen assessed the relationship which had been attempted at AFD between art and politics. Replying to Araeen, Medalla's conclusion was fairly pragmatic:

Araeen: I got interested in AFD because of its orientation towards the problems of the Third World. But I think AFD merely became a sort of support organisation and it didn't really address itself to the basic and essential ideological issues regarding the cultural relationship between the Third World and the West. Don't you think it was the failure of AFD not to deal with this question, of cultural imperialism, particularly vis-à-vis radical artistic practice?

Medalla: Yes I think in that respect it was a failure… We had many cultural workers, the artists, who would support all these struggles but had little knowledge of actual politics. On the other hand, there were the political radicals who came to AFD, but they had no desire whatsoever even to look at a drawing or painting or listen to a poem.[2]

The attempt to take art out of its ghetto of art galleries and the homes of the rich, and reconnect it with the larger world came up against another structure of denial. "I don't think politics is everything of humanity. It's like religion which is not everything of humanity. My concept is that every human being is multifaceted."[3] Medalla also gave a further analogy:

Opposite: **A Fine Cena Spumante per Tutti** ('After Dinner, Champagne for Everyone'), 1977, collage. Collection of the artist.

I was interested in politics the way Rembrandt was interested in Christianity. He was not a Protestant or a Catholic. He made sure he was not claimed by one camp or the other. He was interested in the progressive aspect of Christianity.[4]

Possibly in reaction against the pose of excessive seriousness and puritanism of left-wing groups and regimes, Medalla turned again towards the pleasures of the senses and Rabelaisian good humour. One unlikely but revealing event he attempted to organise in 1978 (jointly with the Spanish artist Oriol de Quadras and the Italian artist Rino Telaro) was the AFD Grand Artists' Banquet. The letter inviting a hundred "living international artists" to send in their favourite recipes and to come to London to prepare their dishes at a great cook-in was decorated with ancient hedonistic quotes: "*Friendship dances around the world, calling on us all to awaken to the joys of a happy life*" – Epicurus; "*He brought me to the banqueting table and his banner over me was love*" – The Song of Songs. Famous artists' banquets, from those organised by Leonardo and Titian in the Renaissance to Picasso's and Apollinaire's for the Douanier Rousseau, were invoked, and even Ho Chi Minh's presence in London in the 1920s as a young assistant to the great chef Escoffier was mentioned.

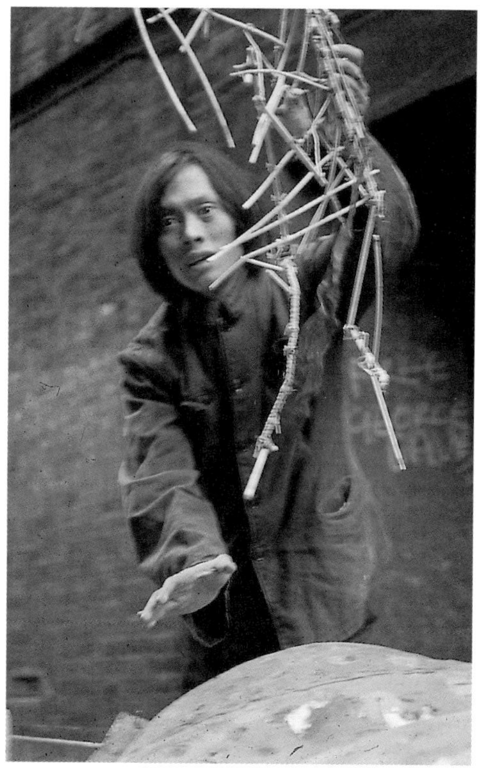

Performing **Tatlin at the Funeral of Malevich** in a skip, Covent Garden, London, 1974.

Without wanting to become excessively serious myself, it seems to me that this light-hearted proposal signified two things: first the suggestion of the banquet – "where every heart was generous and all wines flowed", to quote Rimbaud – as a model for international gatherings of artists to set against the portentous 'international conferences', mainly attended by arts administrators, which were beginning to become fashionable, and second, the characterisation of the banquet as "a polemic against the degradation of taste in modern life".[5] On the one hand it can be seen as part of a growing disgust on Medalla's part with some negative aspects of British culture, and on the other as an indication of a new direction in the investigation of art, the artist and the imagination, which he was about to undertake.

Clearly, Medalla's long sojourn in England has given him plenty of opportunity to observe the English with the eye of an outsider. Paradoxically, he has never felt the need to become an 'insider' in order to feel at home. It may be his own cherished notion of independence that preserves him from the anxiety of wanting to 'belong', while prompting him to open up a conversation with almost every stranger that crosses his path. At the risk of falling into stereotypes, one can say that his openness and garrulity is the opposite of the prevailing English habit (at least in the middle class) of reserve and fear of contact. I have often had the impression that Medalla finds out more about the other in a few minutes than the average English person could do in months – and even then we would be not sure we had it clear, because of what has been left half-vague, half-surmised, skated around. It seemed in the 1960s as if this climate was beginning to change, and that David's natural inclinations fell in line with some mysterious unplanned cultural metamorphosis. The lifestyle of the Exploding Galaxy and the structure of Medalla's participatory art works – like the be-ins, love-ins, think-ins, and other gatherings of the time – were open and inclusive and 'all could join'. For a while it seemed that a Marxist, for example, could also be a hedonist or a dandy, and, without appearing wild or fanciful, an artist could describe her work as an attempt to "release the general creativity of everyone without any psychological or social limits".[6] Such was the large vision of the time, which we can only view today from the perspective of a drastic subsequent narrowing-down. The larger vision and the inclusive structure gradually gave way to a proliferation of cults, clubs and subcultures, exclusive and often mutually hostile. In Britain, deepening economic crisis and social polarisation, cuts in public spending and social

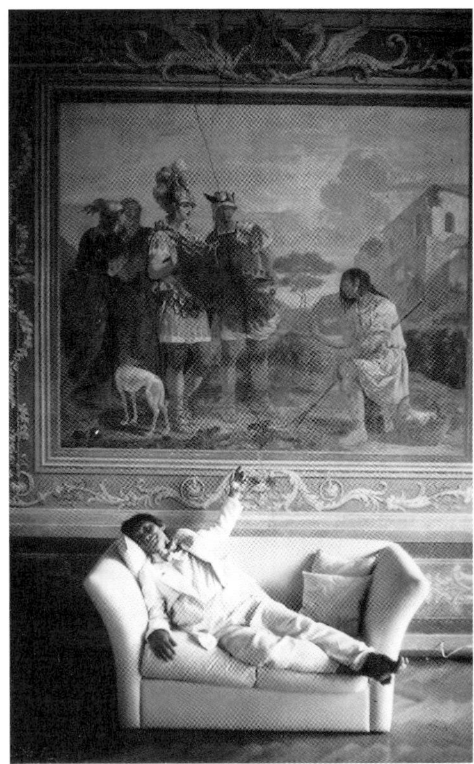

Il Re Pastore ('The Shepherd King'), impromptu below a fresco possibly by Fontebasso, Villa Bice, Treviso, Italy, 1986.

welfare, the prioritising of private interest, only exacerbated, if they did not cause, this phenomenon of 'tribalism'. They brought to the fore again a latent violence in English life which has always been there, that reciprocal psychological condition that Geoffrey Gorer, writing in the 1950s, called "the fear of what one may do to the stranger, or what the stranger may do to one".[7]

These seem to me to be some of the circumstances which lie behind a small group of 'English' works Medalla produced in the late 1970s, such as *Boys of England* and *The Rhapsody of the Dagger and Ammonia Boy*. At the same time he was aware of

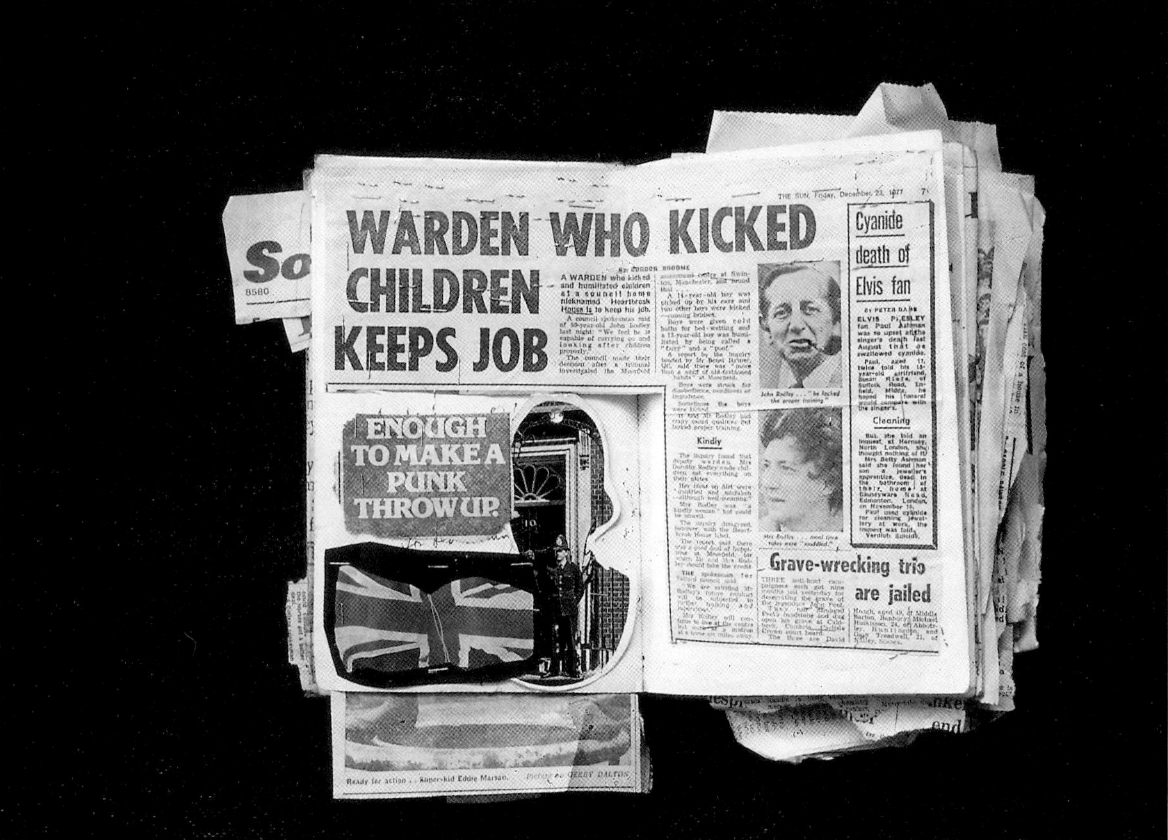
THE SUN, Today, December 23, 1977
So
B580
WARDEN WHO KICKED CHILDREN KEEPS JOB
Cyanide death of Elvis fan
ENOUGH TO MAKE A PUNK THROW UP
Grave-wrecking trio are jailed
Ready for action ... Superskid Eddie Marsan.   Picture by GERRY DALTON.

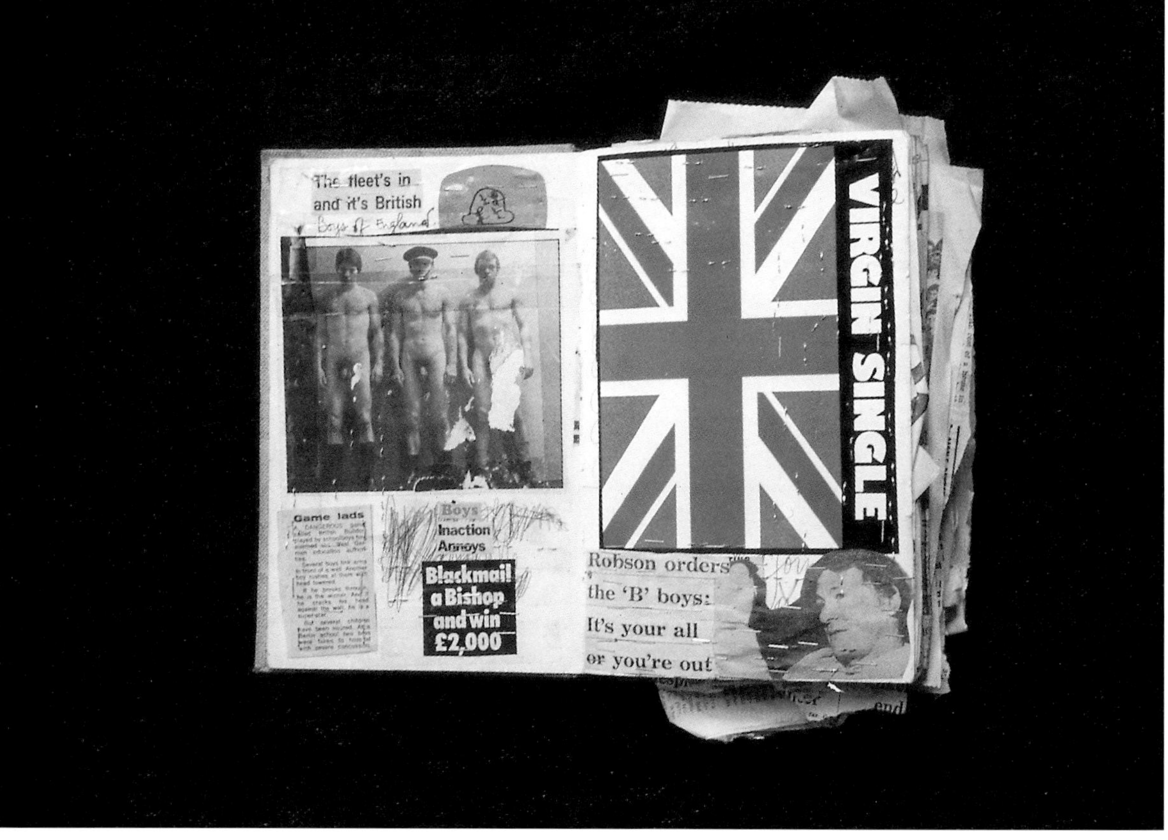
The fleet's in and it's British
Boys of England
VIRGIN SINGLE
Game lads
Boys Inaction Annoys
Blackmail a Bishop and win £2,000
Robson orders
the 'B' boys:
It's your all
or you're out

these changes in a more than merely local sense. It was a general problem of culture which, in a shrinking world, had simultaneously the ambivalent tendency of uniting people and tearing them apart.

Boys of England: A Feverish Triumph exists as a collage book (it appears to have begun as the text for a performance sequence). *The Rhapsody of the Dagger and Ammonia Boy* series consists of two long, narrow, horizontal paintings on board and a number of small narrative pictures. Both are elaborated from ballad-like texts written by Medalla, evocations of misery and urban squalor of a particularly English kind. *Boys of England* resembles an over-stuffed press-cuttings book, but is actually a kind of palimpsest since the newspaper cuttings are stuck onto, or repeatedly stapled down over a handwritten text. The impression is of bizarre excess, an excess of brutal misdirected energy and an excess of tabloid sensationalism and fanning fear. The two are in a kind of symbiosis. Most of the cuttings were taken from the *South London Press*, a local newspaper for the parts of London where the artist was temporally living. One of these, a story about a youth who victimised people in the streets of Kennington by throwing ammonia in their faces and lunging at them with a knife also formed the basis for the series of paintings. Incongruously, David adopted a jewel-like scale and colour for his treatment of scenes of environmental dilapidation, in some cases he painted on scavenged wooden panels already containing stuck-on frames for some forgotten purpose which he incorporated as window-like devices.

These works are not a simple condemnation. David described his aim dispassionately as a wish "to examine the various ways in which boys in England expressed themselves through costumes (gear), speech, body language, dances, games, sexual fantasies, rituals, rites, etc".[8] An obvious erotic interest vies with the fear of being attacked (while working on the pictures in a small abandoned launderette in Lambeth Walk, David himself was taunted and verbally abused by quite young children, egged on, he felt, by racist parents). The 'dagger and ammonia boy' himself is pictured as vigorous and beautiful, even if all around him is in decay, as if his crime was a desperate attempt to bridge a gulf with the other. The childlike style of the painting seems to represent also the persona of the boy, hinting at some repressed sensuality and hidden tenderness. I think David's real target was "the environment which produced such a juvenile monster", an environment which is the product of outmoded capitalism, certainly, but also of a cultural poverty which he saw operating at all levels of British society.[9] In making this street-level investigation of the boys of England, perhaps there was an unconscious desire to separate the gross categories and stereotyping purveyed by the media from a genuine bubbling of creativity, which is always there, and in this case seemed to revive the old higgledy-piggledy English tradition in the irreverent cacophony of Punk fanzines, appearing widely at the time, made by putting together snippets of newspaper headlines and pictures, which David

Opposite: **Boys of England: A Feverish Triumph**, 1977-78, collage book. Collection of the artist.

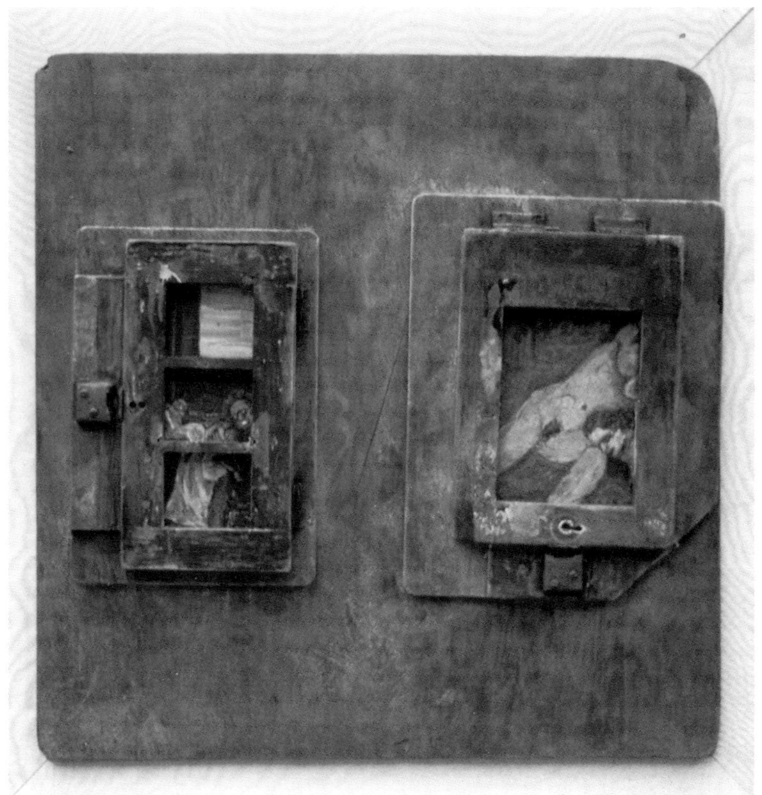

Rhapsody of the Dagger and Ammonia Boy: Rape, 1981, oil on wood, 66 x 65 cms.
Collection of the Arts Council of Great Britain.

himself adopted in a series of spoof identity documents.

The mixture of the objective and subjective in these works was probably important too: a quasi-sociological investigation of the boys of England, on one level, combined with an imaginary projection into the world of one individual. The unpredictable experiment of the participation works had revealed many things, as Medalla himself said, "about the psychology of people". The growing aggregate of stitchings and sewings, or improvised knives, was immediate evidence of the chaotic ragbag of images and ideas we all carry around in our heads. These, it seemed, could either issue as a mouthing of *idées reçues*, or as an amazing kind of poetry. Or perhaps both in strange new combinations! There were the most incongruous meetings between materials, references, cultural allusions, desires and dreams. By a curious and fruitful paradox, the participation works, with their proposition for releasing a creativity which is present in everyone, caused the artist to reflect upon another and equally true fact: the existence of the exceptional personality, the outstanding

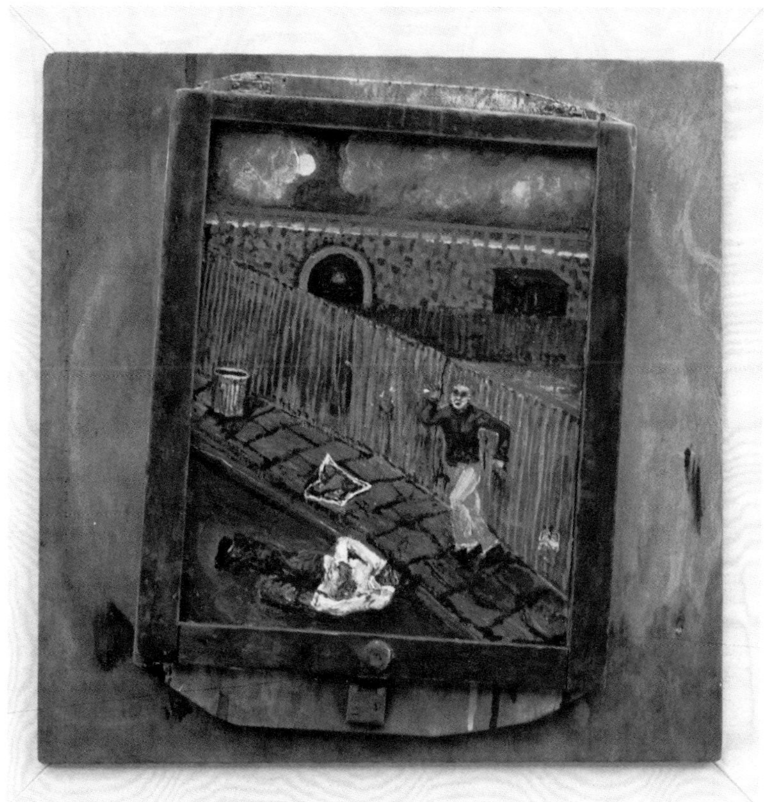

Rhapsody of the Dagger and Ammonia Boy: Assault, 1981, oil on wood, 66 x 65 cms.
Collection of the artist.

imagination. Not that an interest in communal creativity excludes an interest in the outstanding individual, because it may very well be that the content of the exceptional project is, once again, what is common and shared by all (or, "what we don't know that we know", in Susan Hiller's succinct phrase).[10]

Medalla had already set off in this direction with the *Vermeer* performance staged at the Serpentine Gallery in 1975, and with a performance cycle called *Tatlin at the Funeral of Malevich* which he presented in London around the same time as *Eskimo Carver*. Other artists' work, and the examples and lives of others, have always been enormously important for Medalla. He has often presented works in the form of homages. Now, he began to develop this relationship consciously and much more elaborately to entwine his own experience in the present with what he knew, or imagined, of the lives of particular people in the past. He seemed to want to gain a new understanding of what imagination is, what imagination can do – not in the abstract but in intimate relation with the possibilities and limitations of life at particular

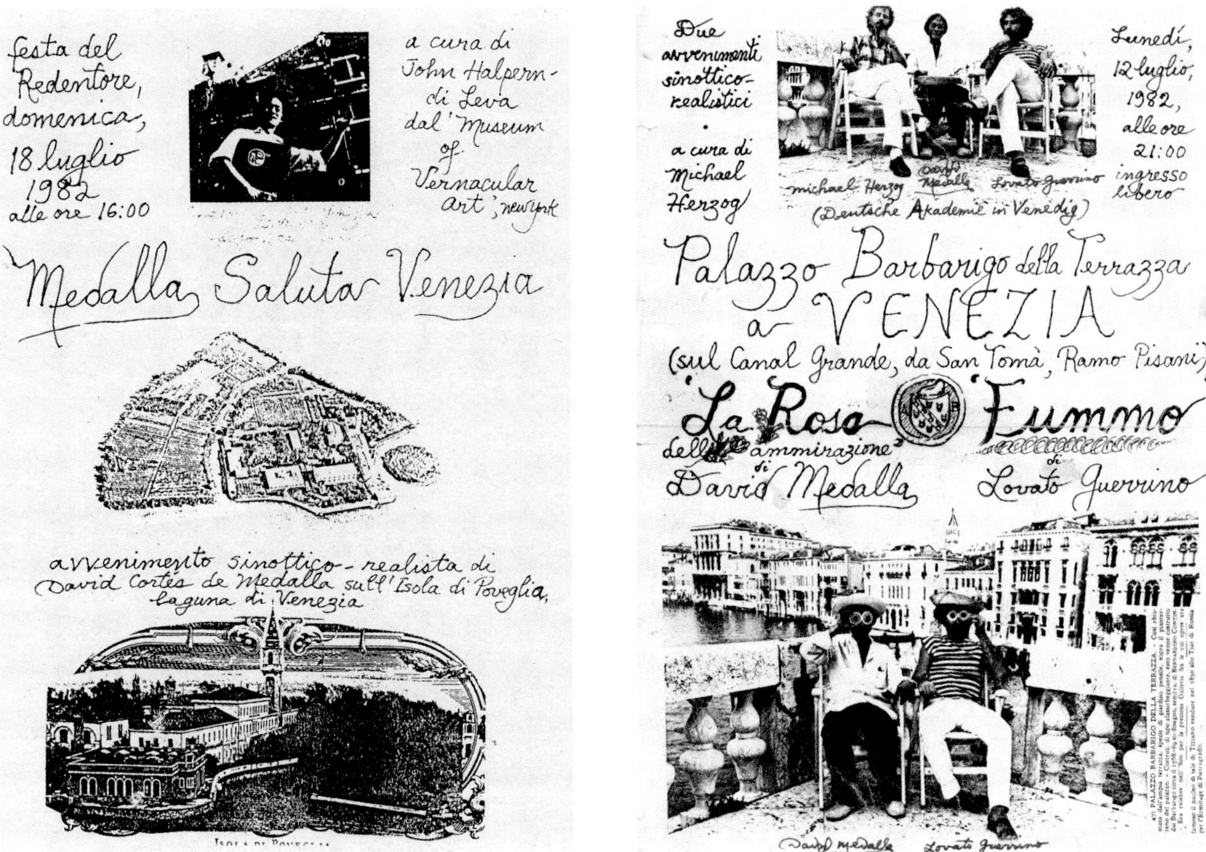

Above and opposite: Posters for performances, 1982.

pages 130-31: Part of the audience at **The Heist Man Cometh**, the first in the performance series **A Shot in the Dark**, in collaboration with Brian Morgan, Finborough Theatre, Earls Court, London, 1983. People were invited to bring cameras of all kinds to film the performance and one another, intending to contradict the idea that photography is a disturbance. The resulting documentation was collected for exhibition.

moments of history, and in relation to the nurturing effects of particular cultures. David's way of presenting the workings of imagination have been paradoxical and laced with ironic humour. For one thing, the historical figures he has concentrated on have been very varied. Many have been artists, poets or musicians (for example Leonardo da Vinci, Tatlin, Brancusi, Malevich, Mondrian, Rembrandt, Piranesi, Vermeer, Mozart, Rimbaud, Hart Crane, Marianne Moore). But there have also been figures like Magellan, Giordano Bruno, Marie Curie, Alexander the Great, Claudia Muzio, Sojourner Truth, Victor Segalen, Augustin Barrios, Casanova and Beau Brummel. For another thing, they have been engineered into imaginary meetings and dialogues, incongruous milieux and time-travel, and they may be evoked or 'represented' by anything from an original work to a tenth-hand kitsch derivative or other metaphor. In each of these incarnations Medalla imagined intensely, and identified personally, with the hardships and exaltations of a historical figure who had undertaken an exceptional project.

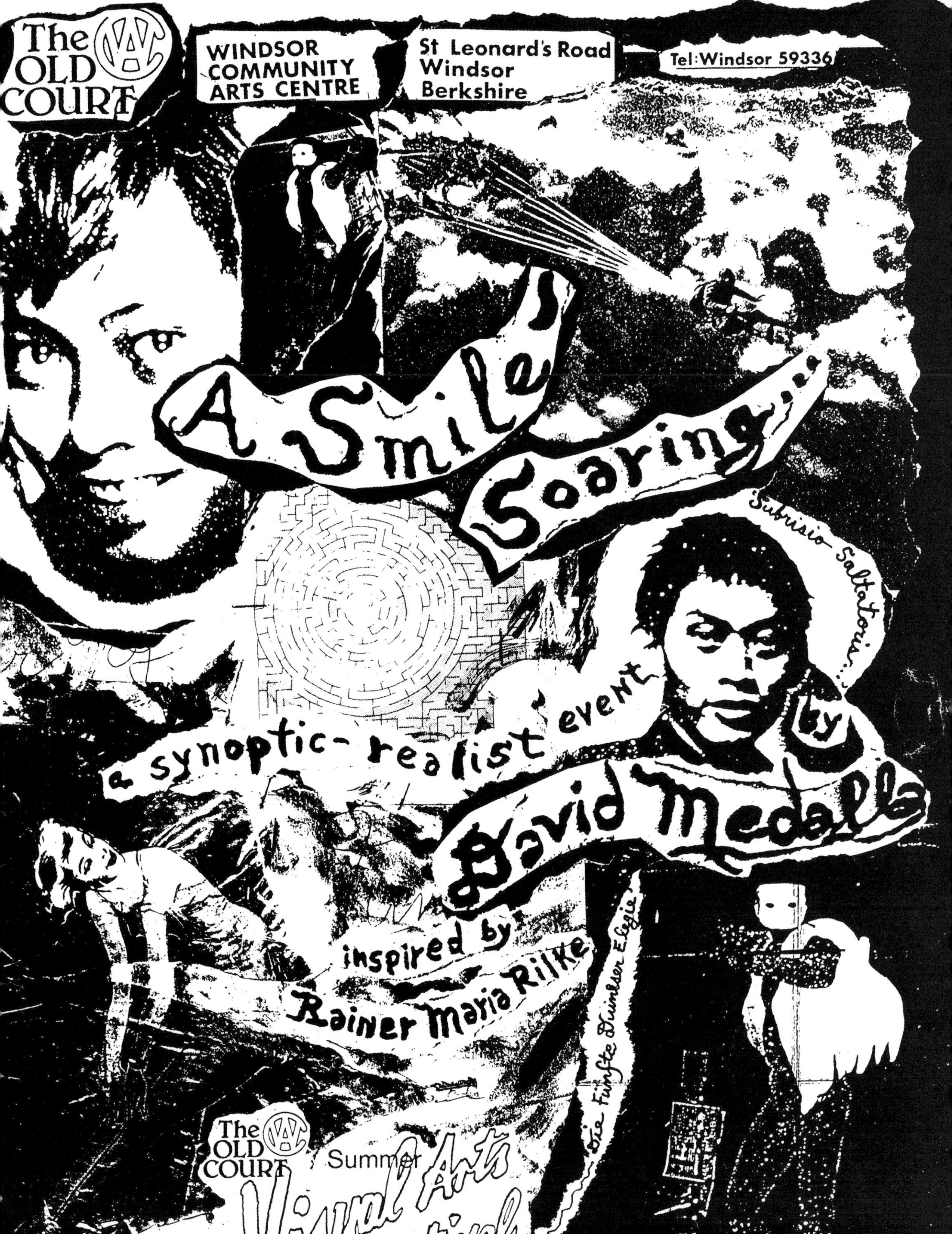

The OLD COURT
WINDSOR COMMUNITY ARTS CENTRE
St Leonard's Road
Windsor
Berkshire
Tel: Windsor 59336
A Smile Soaring...
Subrisio Saltatoris...
a synoptic-realist event
by
David Medalla
inspired by
Rainer Maria Rilke
Die Fünfte Duineser Elegie
The OLD COURT
Summer Visual Arts

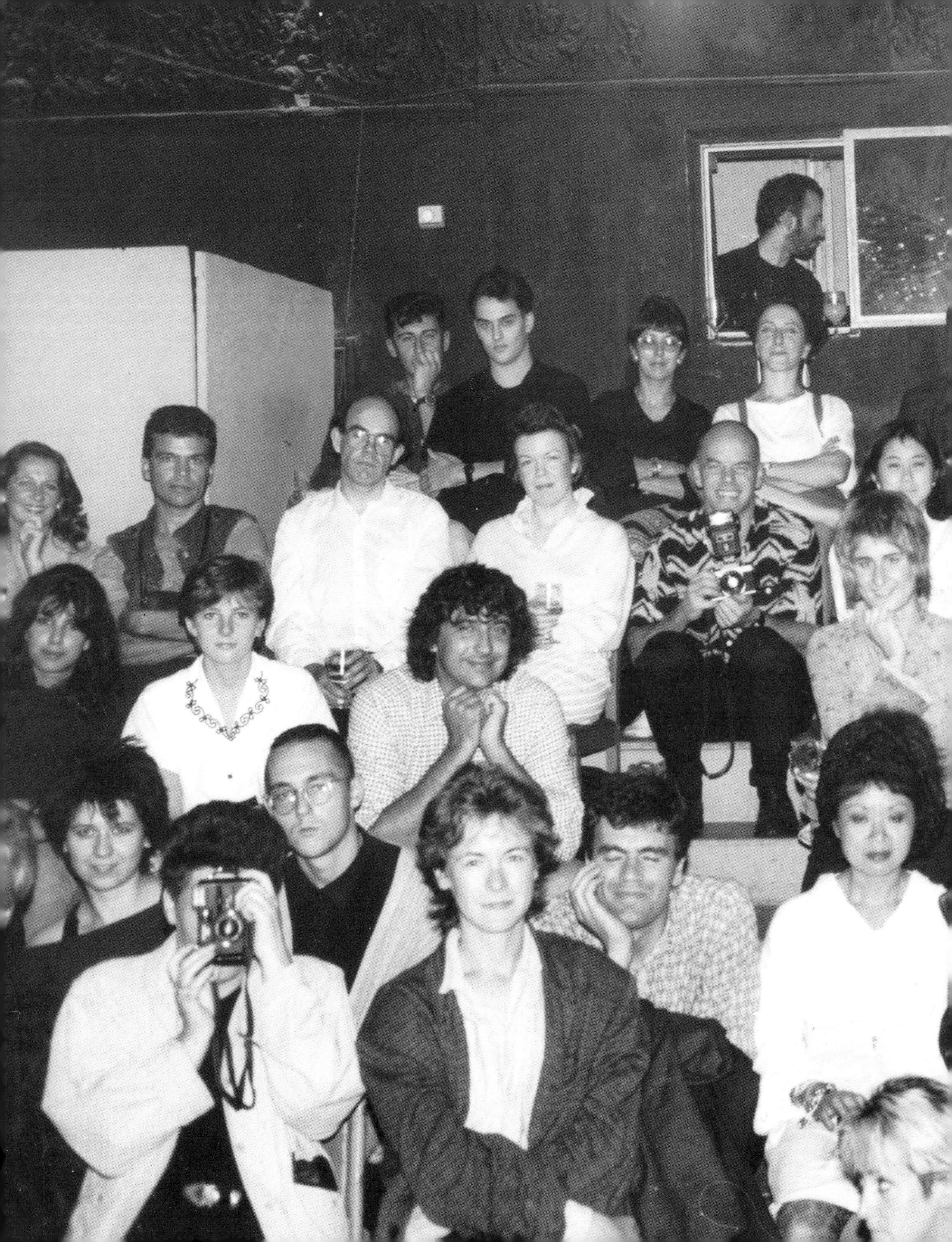

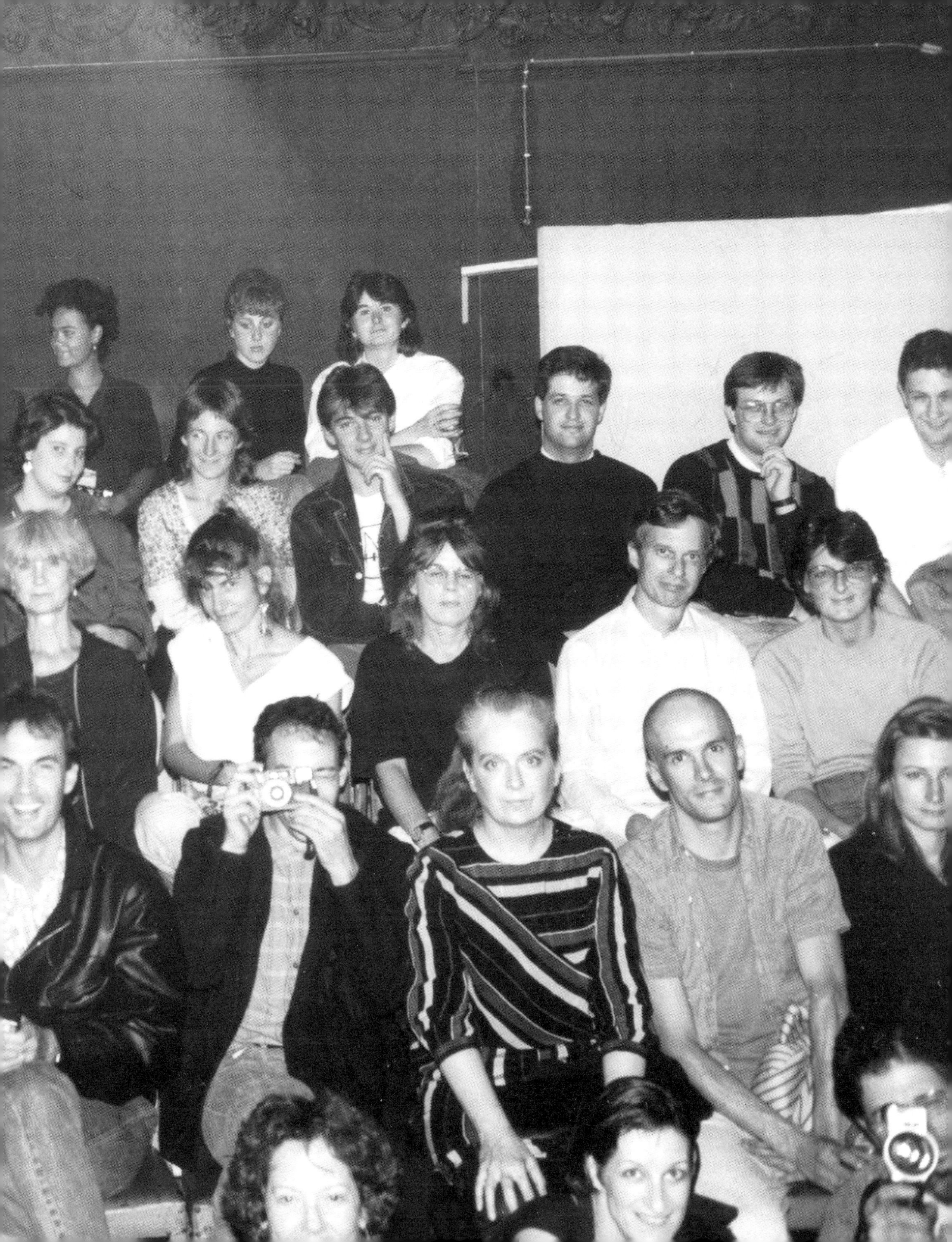

It all became part of an exceptional project of his own. First he set himself a goal of physical mobility. Despite few financial resources, and determined to experience for himself, through actual people and places, the reality of different cultures, he began to wander over Europe. Between 1980 and 1985 he stayed in Italy, Germany, Holland, Belgium, France and Spain, depending almost entirely on friendships and chance encounters for food and shelter. Second, as concerns artistic method, he set out to expand the 'realism', the investigation or representation of reality the artist makes, so that it might become more all-inclusive, multi-focal, multi-temporal. The perception of life as flux and perpetual change now took a new form for which Medalla coined the term Synoptic Realism (he first used it in reference to *The Rhapsody of the Dagger and Ammonia Boy*). This 'realism' would ideally incorporate the visual, understood in its contemporary form as a complex mosaic spanning everything from optical sensation to paravisual phenomena and dreams, together with the level of subjective sensations, volitions, desires, aspirations, memories, in their complex interactions with the conditions (historical, economic, cultural, linguistic) in which people live. Medalla's third determination was not to divide such 'objective' investigations from his own subjectivity. From centring around the spectator, his work moved sharply towards himself, his own life and place in the world, and the links between himself and others, both those he knew and those he could not know. Great historical events and changes were conjured up, not with academic detachment, but in terms of affective feelings, like those of friendship, empathy, emulation, compassion, camaraderie which, in a curious and largely unexplored way, do cross the linear boundaries of time and space. Synoptic Realism was a general term he applied to his paintings and writings as well as performances and 'impromptus', or perhaps it was the sum of all of them. In the nomadic existence he led in Europe in the early 1980s, performances and impromptus, "guerrilla tactics" as he called them, necessarily became his preferred vehicle.

This choice was influenced by more than just necessity, however. It was the result of a positive enthusiasm. The genre of performance art, which grew from scattered beginnings in the late 1960s to become a widespread practice through the 1970s and early 1980s, before starting to die away or become diffused in other modes during the late 1980s, is a piquant phenomenon in contemporary art. It could be described as one of those occasions in which modernity expresses itself by a paradoxical reversal within the overall drift of social trends. For, in an age of mass reproduction – of art books, music cassettes, videos, repeatable ad nauseam – here was a genuinely ephemeral form. Performances were so many and varied, so dispersed in time and space and so rarely repeated, that it was impossible for one person to know more than a fraction of the whole phenomenon. There were photographs, and the occasional video of course, but these tended only to emphasise the uniqueness of the actual experience (this was independent of the fact that modern media were often used within the performance). Performance is a genre which is irretrievable and escapes the data bank, the new 'information order' (even the inventory of over 150 of Medalla's performances listed in Appendix 1 evokes something that cannot exactly be verified, or fully documented, perhaps adding to its suggestiveness!). Again, because performance art was a new genre and had no established conventions of its own (at least at the beginning: conventions quickly began to develop), 'readings' of what happened, even memories of what happened, varied wildly from person to person. One remembered parts of performances, rarely the whole. Therefore the experience became one of true ephemerality, of the memory of 'magical moments', as in life. This may have been the artists' intention, certainly it was part of Medalla's.

If performance art of the 1970s was a new genre, however, it was also a reminder that performance in a broad sense has played an essential role in the history of 20th century visual art. Again, this is a fact which is difficult to record in museums. Along with the experimentation they may have conducted in the solitude of their studios, artists gathered socially in places which often became centres of experimentation too, of a collective kind. At the beginning of the century there were the Cabaret Voltaire in Zurich (birthplace of Dada), Le Lapin Agile and Le Chat Noir

Mark Greaves filming **'The Hand of Marie Curie'**, study for **Parables of Friendship**, 1983, ink on paper. Private Collection.

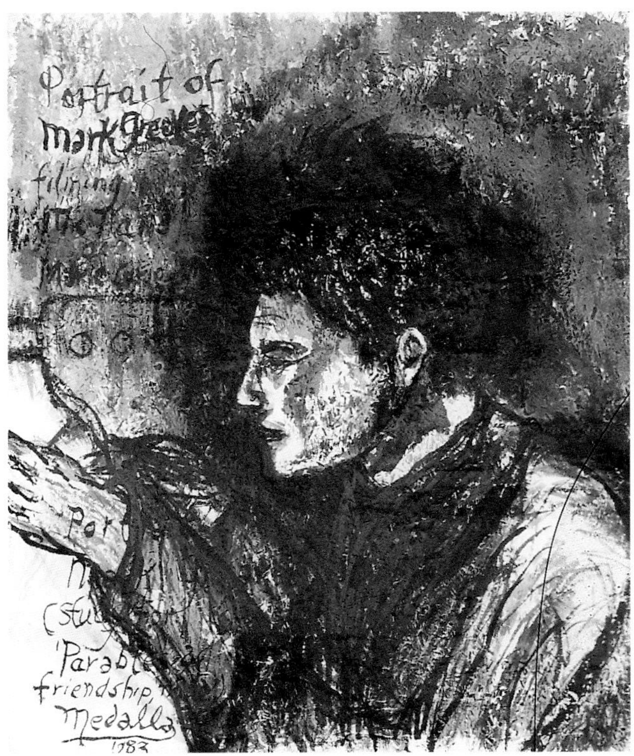

in Paris, Els Quatre Gats in Barcelona, the Café Pittoresque in Moscow, the 'futurist evenings' on various theatrical stages around Europe, and others. Performance, theatre and dance were an important part of Bauhaus activities, and performance reappeared in the 1950s and 1960s in happenings which emerged across a range of 'isms' from Nouveau Realisme (Yves Klein), Kinetic Art (Takis, Tinguely, Aubertin), to Pop Art (Allan Kaprow, Robert Rauschenberg), Fluxus (George Maciunas, Carolee Schneemann, Charlotte Moorman, Yoko Ono, Joseph Beuys, Nam June Paik), Minimal, Conceptual and participatory Art (Yvonne Rainer, Robert Morris, Leopoldo Maler, Susan Hiller, Vito Acconci and others), Pop Art (Claes Oldenburg, Jim Dine, Marta Minujin and others), Autobiographical and Body Art (Anna Mendieta, Stuart Brisley, Gina Pane, Carlyle Reedy, Michel Journiac). In fact, what is here called performance art probably denotes a broader and deeper phenomenon; it is one indicator of those vital edges and borders of modern art where painting and sculpture mingle with theatre, music, film, poetry, dance and even architecture. The aims described for the Cabaret Voltaire by its guiding spirit, the poet Hugo Ball in 1916, reveal three aspirations which seem to have remained constant in trying to create something other than an institutional destiny for art:

The Hand of Marie Curie, Theatre de Lantaren, Rotterdam, during 'Perfotijd I' 1983.

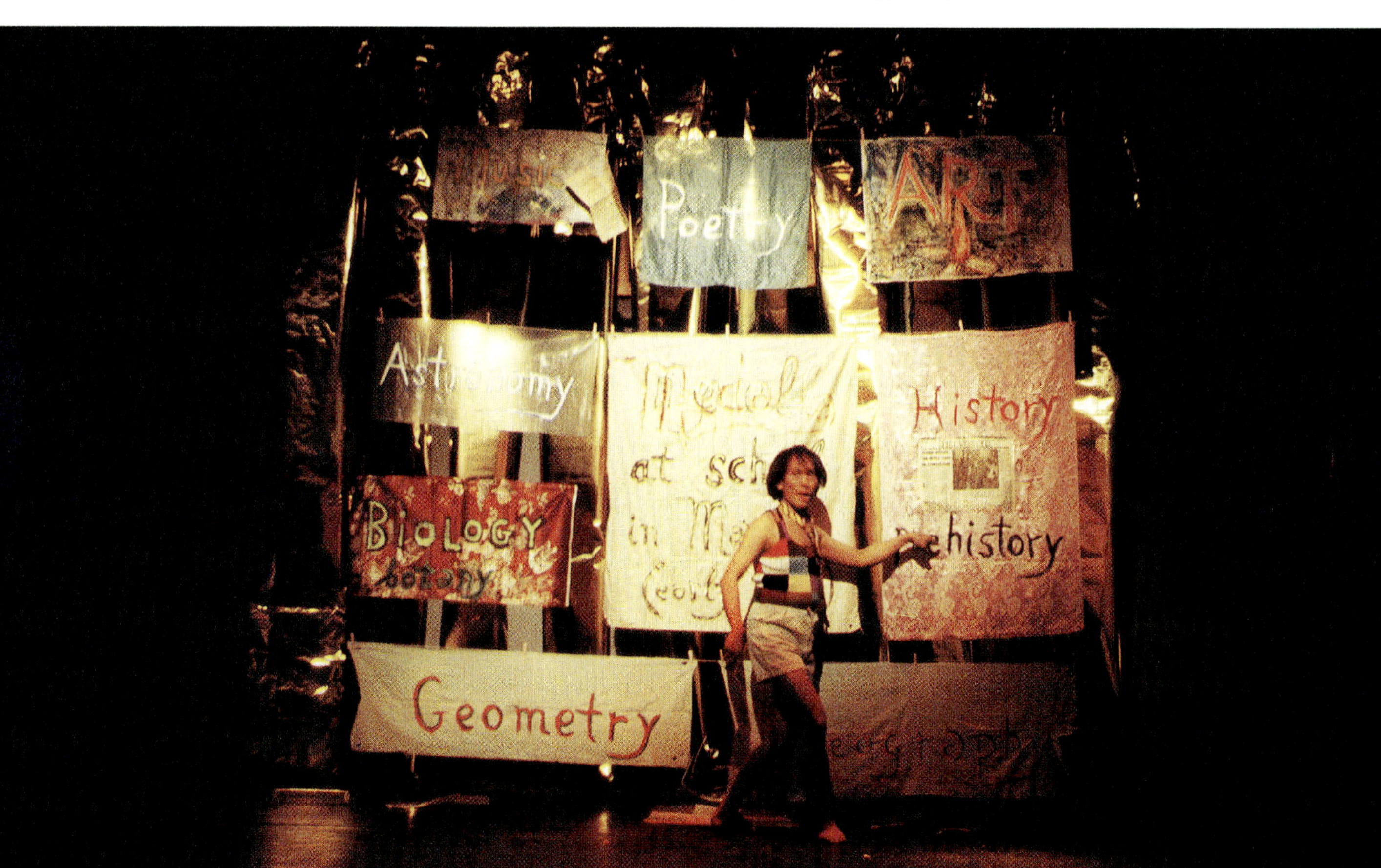

Cabaret Voltaire. Under this name a group of young artists and writers has formed with the object of becoming a centre for artistic entertainment. The Cabaret Voltaire will be run on the principle of daily meetings where visiting artists will perform their music and poetry. The young artists of Zurich are invited to bring along their ideas and contributions.[11]

In other words: 1) entertainment, 2) the interrelationship of the arts, 3) participation.

The revival of performance in the late 1960s and early 1970s no doubt had many causes, and served a great many motives and forms of sensibility. But I believe one can say it arose in answer to a number of definable needs. One very simple reason was to overcome the isolation in which the artist often works: David Medalla himself

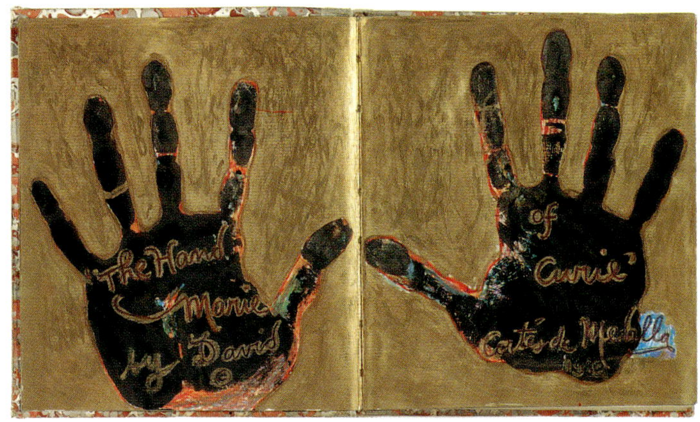
From the script-book of **The Hand of Marie Curie**. Collection of the artist.

put this almost touchingly by saying: "Often, when travelling, in order to survive, and get to know people in a 'foreign' place, I approach nightclub managers and the like to allow me to give performances."[12] Artists tend to be isolated from each other and from their audiences too by the superstructure and professional apparatus that every art form supports. In a way the antithesis of all this apparatus, but in the last analysis actually supporting it, is the artist himself or herself, with his or her body. Therefore the artist's person, or body, became the focus in performance. This was true whatever discipline the artist originally came from: painting, sculpture, theatre, music, poetry, film, or other, leading to fascinating plays of nuance, inflection and crossover.

This focus produced the extraordinarily fruitful paradox on which performance art was based: that the artists (protagonists) were simultaneously 'being themselves' and 'acting a role'. They were simultaneously 'real' and 'metaphorical'. Adam Nankervis, Medalla's collaborator in his New York performances in the early

1990s, referred to this ambiguity by asking the question: "Were we playing a role or simply playing with each other?"[13] In performance art the subjective, the unrehearsed, the vulnerable, met on equal ground with the objective, the rhythmic, patterned and formed. For all these reasons performance answered another powerful need. It was attractive to artists who felt they had an identity, or were constructing a new sort of identity, outside the given and approved social norms, whether for cultural, sexual, ethnic, political, artistic, or other reasons (or a combination of all of these). Most of the early performances which took place at AFD – for example by Rasheed Araeen, Paul Burwell, Virgil Calaguian, Rose English, Tina Keane, Sonia Knox, Robbie Kravitz, David Medalla, Nick Payne, Carlyle Reedy, Gennaro Telaro, Jun Terra, Anna Thew – explored these questions of identity by interweaving a testimony of subjective experience with the objective and historical.

We have already mentioned Medalla's production, at around this time, of a number of collages in the form of spoof identity documents for himself (p. 35). They were an allusion to the mental world of the person so identified, whose efflorescence in time and space contradict the bureaucratic reduction of the human psyche. Medalla's performances, or the great majority of them, were an investigation/celebration/reverie on the nature of art, the creative process and the imagination. One of their structuring devices, a device which the artist proved to be of enormous elasticity, was that of the 'meeting'.

Besides its implications of sociability and dialogue, the motif of the meeting contains two elements always dear to David Medalla: the random and the incongruous. In discussing the use of the motif of the meeting in the structure of novels, Mikhail Bakhtin identified the meeting on the open road as alluding to the random ("The road is especially appropriate for portraying events governed by chance").[14] And in his famous image challenging rational and routine associations, Lautréamont described the chance meeting of an umbrella and a sewing machine on an operating table. Meetings of people in the world at large, complemented by meetings of objects in an interior or still–

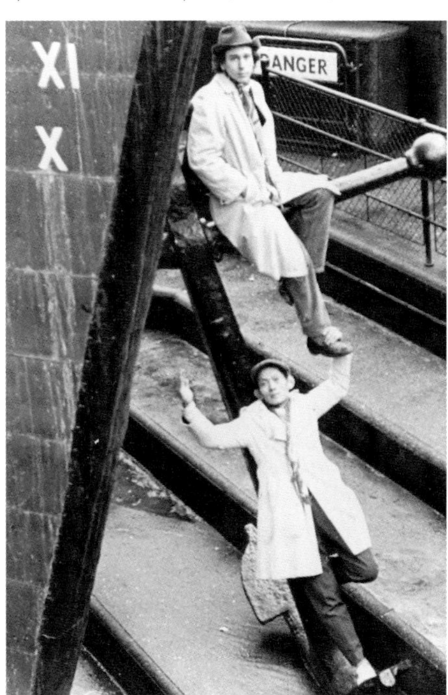

Opposite: a 'Conversation Bi-langue', a floor collage used in **The Beachcomber's Dream-Tree,** an episode of **Magellan and the Circumnavigation of the World,** "Mayfair Illuminations", Hill House, Berkeley Square, London, 1978. Collection of the artist.

With Oriol de Quadras in **Magellan and the Circumnavigation of the World,** a performance cycle. 1978. The Cutty Sark, Greenwich, London.

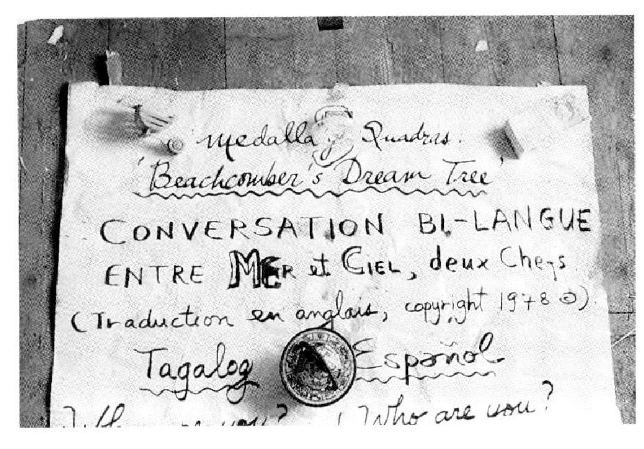
© Medalla & Quadras:
'Beachcomber's Dream Tree'
CONVERSATION BI-LANGUE
ENTRE MER et CIEL, deux Chefs
(Traduction en anglais, copyright 1978 ©)
Tagalog   Español
Who are you?

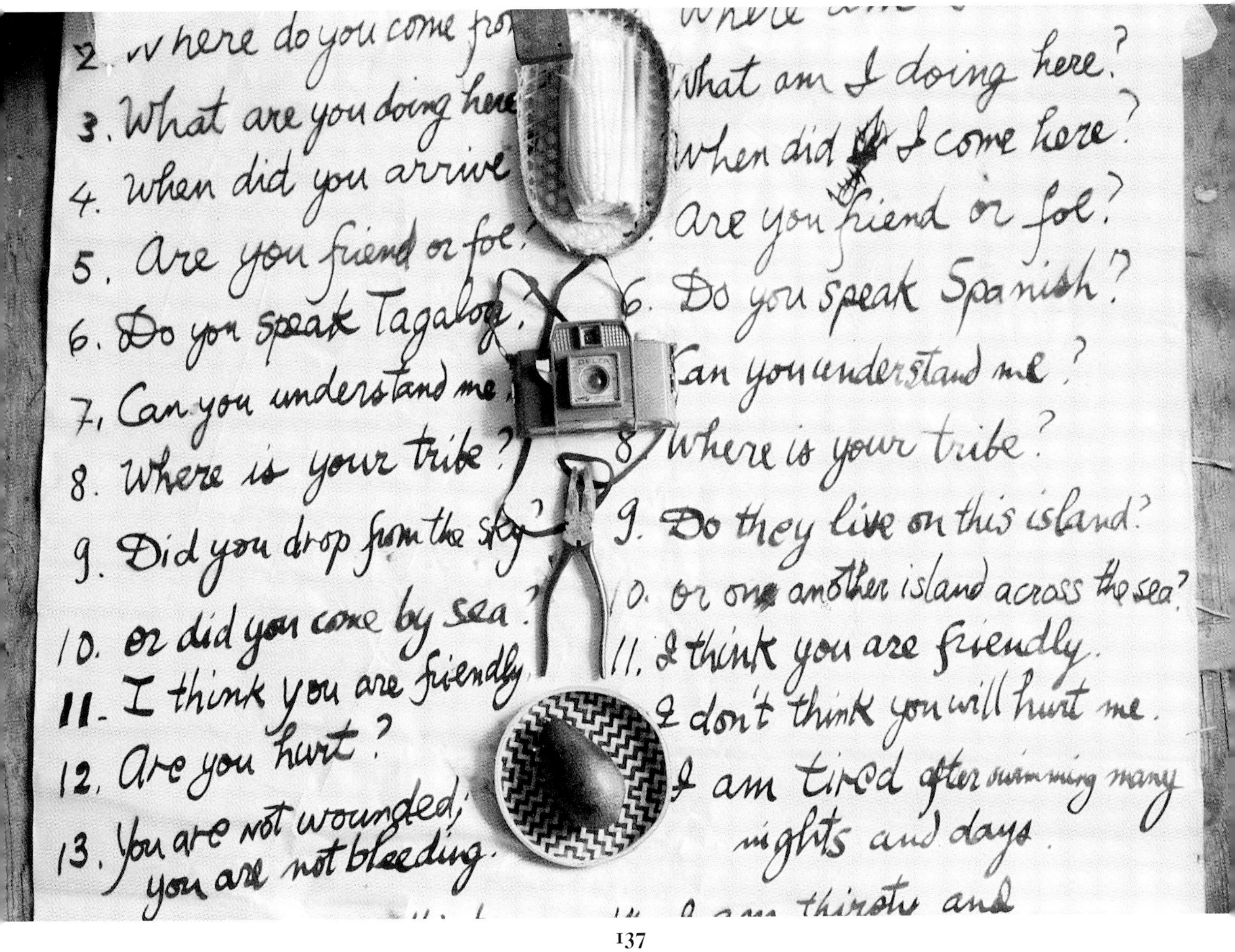

2. Where do you come from?
3. What are you doing here
4. When did you arrive
5. Are you friend or foe?
6. Do you speak Tagalog?
7. Can you understand me?
8. Where is your tribe?
9. Did you drop from the sky?
10. Or did you come by sea?
11. I think you are friendly.
12. Are you hurt?
13. You are not wounded, you are not bleeding.

Where
What am I doing here?
When did I come here?
Are you friend or foe?
6. Do you speak Spanish?
Can you understand me?
8. Where is your tribe?
9. Do they live on this island?
10. Or on another island across the sea?
11. I think you are friendly.
I don't think you will hurt me.
I am tired after swimming many nights and days.
I am thirsty and

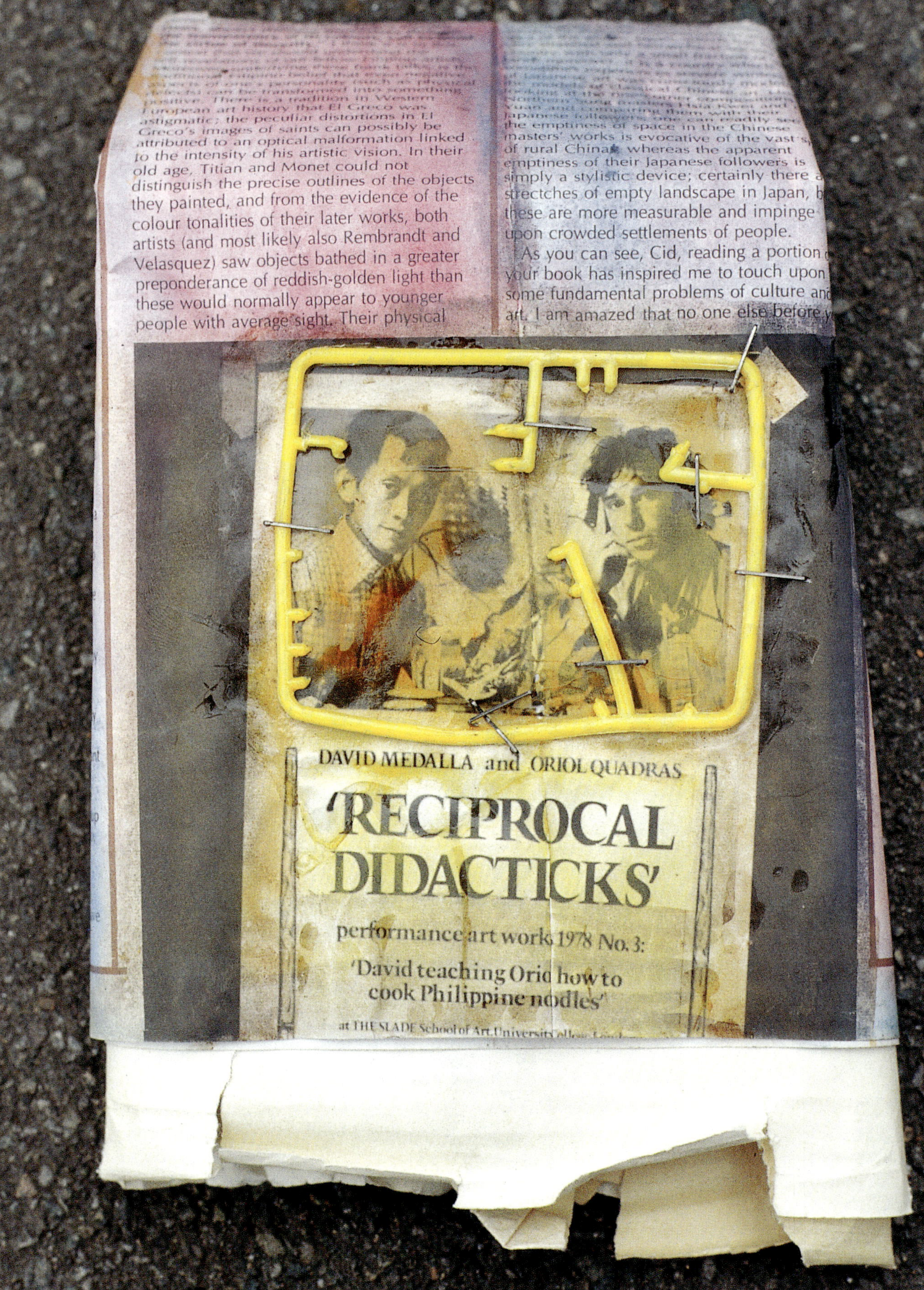
astigmatic; the peculiar distortions in El
Greco's images of saints can possibly be
attributed to an optical malformation linked
to the intensity of his artistic vision. In their
old age, Titian and Monet could not
distinguish the precise outlines of the objects
they painted, and from the evidence of the
colour tonalities of their later works, both
artists (and most likely also Rembrandt and
Velasquez) saw objects bathed in a greater
preponderance of reddish-golden light than
these would normally appear to younger
people with average sight. Their physical
As you can see, Cid, reading a portion
your book has inspired me to touch upon
some fundamental problems of culture and
art. I am amazed that no one else before y
DAVID MEDALLA and ORIOL QUADRAS
'RECIPROCAL
DIDACTICKS'
performance art work 1978 No. 3:
'David teaching Oriol how to
cook Philippine noodles'
at THE SLADE School of Art, University

life mode, both governed by chance and the incongruous, and with one context suggestively interchangeable with the other: this would be an apt analogy for the performances of David Medalla.

One level of meetings in these performances is between artists, or other historical figures, who may or may not have met in reality. In the performance their paths cross, perhaps only briefly and they converse, or they meet only indirectly, producing pairs (eg., Malevich/Tatlin, Brancusi/Tatlin, Mozart/Medalla, Rimbaud/Barrios).[15] There are also the meetings between factual and fictional figures and the meetings of contemporaries with immortals. A second level is the meeting of the performers with one another, and with the historical figures they are impersonating or alluding to. Most of Medalla's performances have been evolved in cycles with a particular male collaborator he was close to at the time (for example, the *Buddha Ballet* sequences of the late 1960s with John Dugger; the *Magellan* series, 1978, touching on the global concept and on colonialism, with the Catalan artist Oriol de Quadras; *The Hand of Marie Curie*, a film made with Mark Greaves, 1983; *The Signs and Wonders of David and Kai* and the *Gay Galaxy*, 1984-85, with the German artist Kai Hilgemann; *A Shot in the Dark*, 1987, with the English writer Brian Morgan; and recent Manhattan performances with the Australian artist Adam Nankervis). Allusions to the past were always made inseparable from the performers' relationship with one another in the present (for example, they would discuss on stage how their own divergent origins affected their interest in a particular historical figure, and so on). *Reciprocal Didacticks*, 1978, was the title of a series with Oriol de Quadras which specifically explored the widely different 'know-hows' they happened to have as individuals with different backgrounds.

A third level of meeting is between artist and audience. This has always had, in Medalla's performances, a special quality. It can only be said to be a combination of a certain graciousness and his aesthetic convictions. Early Dada and Futurist performers were out to shock their audiences (who were assumed to be respectable bourgeois). Often success was measured in terms of insults which rained down on the stage. David has described his attitude to the audience in the following way:

Part of the fun of giving a live performance is the possibility of things going wrong, especially if one is using technological devices. Adrenalin starts flowing when the audience responds during the course of a performance. Even a 'hostile' audience can be activated positively by a performer, as long as the performer is concentrated on putting across his/her ideas, vision, feelings, with imagination and an instinctive way of improvising in all kinds of unforeseen situations and events. The important thing, for me, is not to insult the audience, whoever that audience may be, sympathetic or not to the performance artist.[16]

Opposite: **Reciprocal Didacticks**, 1978. Collage, Collection of the artist.

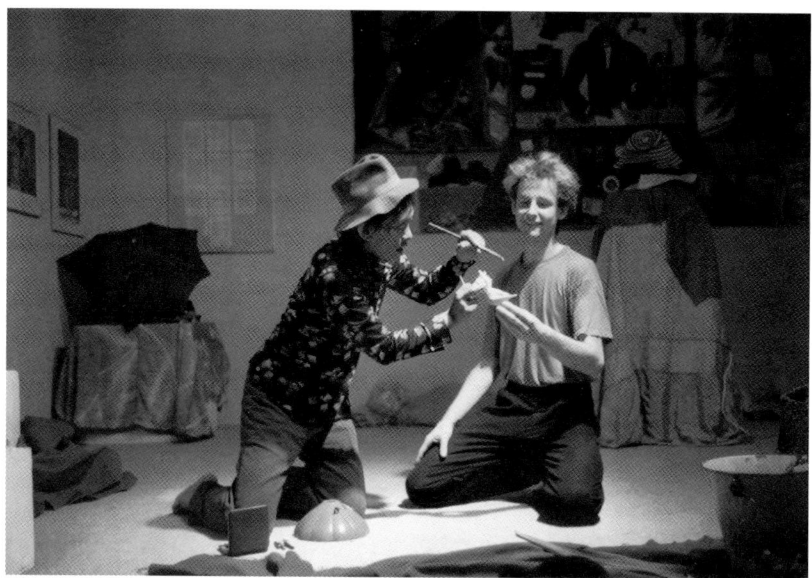

With Kai Hilgemann ('The Signs and Wonders of David and Kai') in **A Dream of Fillippo de Pisis in Venice**, Camden Arts Centre, London, 1985.

Some performers, I suppose, who are unhappy with themselves or their art, become abusive, but I don't have that in my psychic makeup, I like being a good guest. In a performance you are both the host and the guest. I admire Marianne Moore's attitude to being a proper host and a correct guest.[17]

He will sometimes break off to explain what he is doing to the audience, which will then develop into an impromptu speech on some aspect of art with plenty of digressions. I remember him once interrupting a performance at South Hill Park, in Bracknell, to give presents to the family of the artistic director Alistair Snow who was shortly to move to another job.

The structure of meetings is a device for crossing temporal barriers, spatial barriers, and barriers created by convention and taboo. It can also cross the barriers between waking and dreaming life. The dream is a frequent figure in Medalla's performances and impromptus, indeed in his entire body of work. It could be said that the paradoxical unity, and ambivalence, between the states of sleeping and waking, between the unconscious and conscious, between the fictive and real, is an essential part of a kinetic view of reality. In the writings of Heraclitus, this phenomenon is linked with other unities of opposites, especially the unity of the living and the dead. Heraclitus's thinking is expressed in a series of beautiful aphorisms which have a remarkable affinity to the kind of insights offered by David Medalla's performance art works. There are three especially:

Men asleep are labourers and co-workers in what takes place in the world.

Immortals are mortal, mortals immortal, living the other's death, dead in the other's life.

The same... living and dead, and the waking and the sleeping, and young and old. For these transposed are those, and those transposed again are these.[18]

These various forms of the meeting of people are complemented by the meetings of objects. Objects here would include the almost endless assortment of props used by Medalla and friends in their events, as well as fragments of costume, masks, slides and pieces of music: all the elements of a 'kinetic collage' which makes up the performance. Although most of these objects and pieces of material have been found, salvaged or scavenged in the course of David's peripatetic existence, in amongst them are some rather rare things that may have cost him a lot of money. However, he might use these casually and treat some thrown-away leftover as if it was infinitely precious. In the performances, luxury, or beauty, flows in an unpredictable flux between worthless and valuable items and can't be pinned down to either because so often this aesthetic quality is the result of the inspired conjunction, or weaving together in a rhythmic sequence, of apparently unrelated things. The whole recourse to found objects is laced

The Elixir of Immortality, with Simon Parish, South Hill Park, Bracknell, 1987.

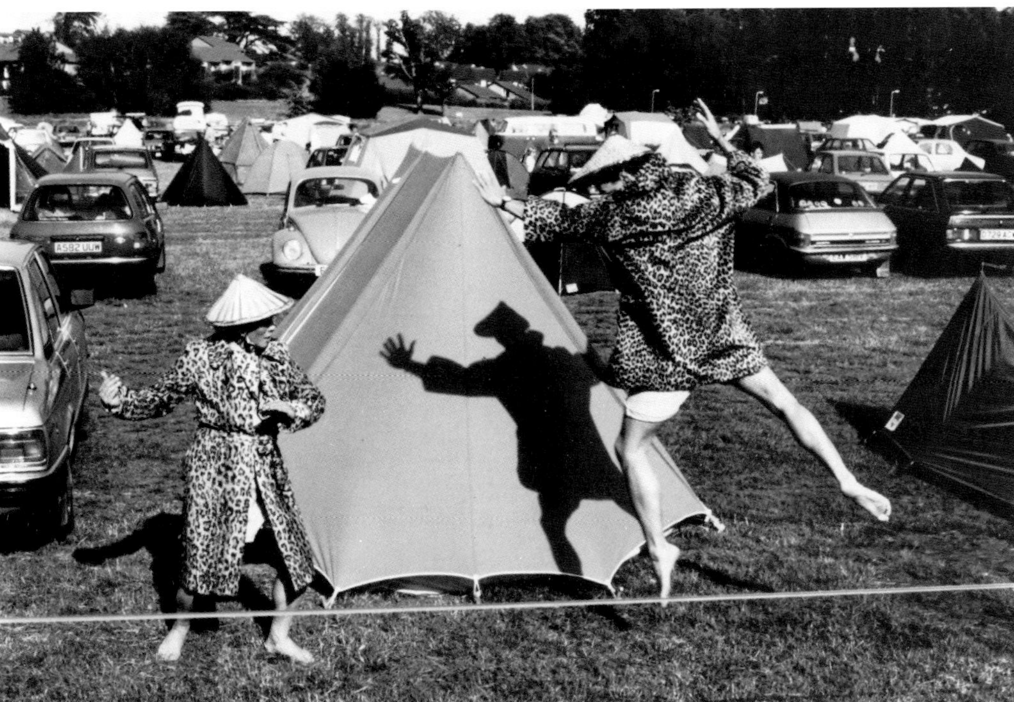

with an ironic perception of the relationship between material hardship and the attribution of value in the world, its topsy-turvy reversals of wisdom and folly.

Random memories come to mind. The artist picks up and opens in front of the audience an old black suitcase. It is opulently lined with red chiffon. Out of the chiffon are emerging ranks of naked, pink baby dolls. The artist tilts the case towards the audience and all the dolls cry in unison. The dolls are hoisted up in a libidinal dance at the climax of the performance, *The Desire and Pursuit of the Whole*. Another time, in a piece called *Subrisio Saltat*, performed at South Hill Park Arts Centre, at a moment when the text refers to hoops in the poem by Rilke which inspired the work, Medalla leaves the performance area and takes a coin from his pocket to get some 'Hula-Hoop' snacks from a dispensing machine, which he then puts on his fingers as rings. The artist once planned to exhibit all his props and costumes and remnants of past performances as part of a show of his work, all jumbled together in a 'chaos' room. Many are toys or pieces of kitsch. A central irony of Medalla's performances is to approach great art by means of its apparent antithesis – vulgar kitsch – and serious ideas or profound emotions by means of toys. This in itself is perhaps a disguise: to use the 'vulgar' to dispel vulgarity, or, as Sir Roland Penrose said of the raison d'être of the artist, "to create beauty in the most miserable circumstances".[19] Many of his found objects wittily suggest a longing-for, or a recapturing through the cheapest means, of beauty, nature, expansive largesse, pleasure, etc. He might recreate the plenitude of a Titian with a jumble-sale hat and a piece of curtain, or a gorgeous tropicalism by appearing dressed in several superimposed layers of cheap floral frocks and a swimming cap. The use of kitsch by artists is a sort of litmus test of imagination. Kitsch can simply look like kitsch, or a mere sign of the artist's attempt at populism. But if a subtlety of nuance and an energy is produced out of what is supposed to be cheap sentiment or debased great art, then we have a restatement, through the artist's irony, of the cosmic belief that 'all things are one'.

An element of paradoxical poetry here is to take the vulgarisation or trivialisation of a great artist – say, Mondrian napkins or cigarette-lighters – and use them to return to the artist in a way which is more witty and piquant, more in the spirit of the artist, than forms of academic dryness and reverence.[20]

In fact an amusing reversal could be made of the traditional notion of bathos in relation to Medalla's use of found objects. If bathos is "a lapse into the ridiculous by a poet aiming at elevated expression",[21] Medalla's performances could be described as a leap into the elevated by a poet apparently aiming at the ridiculous. It is a deliberate effect of course, not unintended as bathos is, but this only points up the attendant dangers of any pretension to 'high art'. The reversal can be pursued further still, because, whereas traditionally poets invoked gods, figures of myth, etc, and suddenly found they had become entangled in the mundane details of everyday life, Medalla tries

Opposite: **The Desire and Pursuit of the Whole**, Diorama, Regents Park, London, 1986.

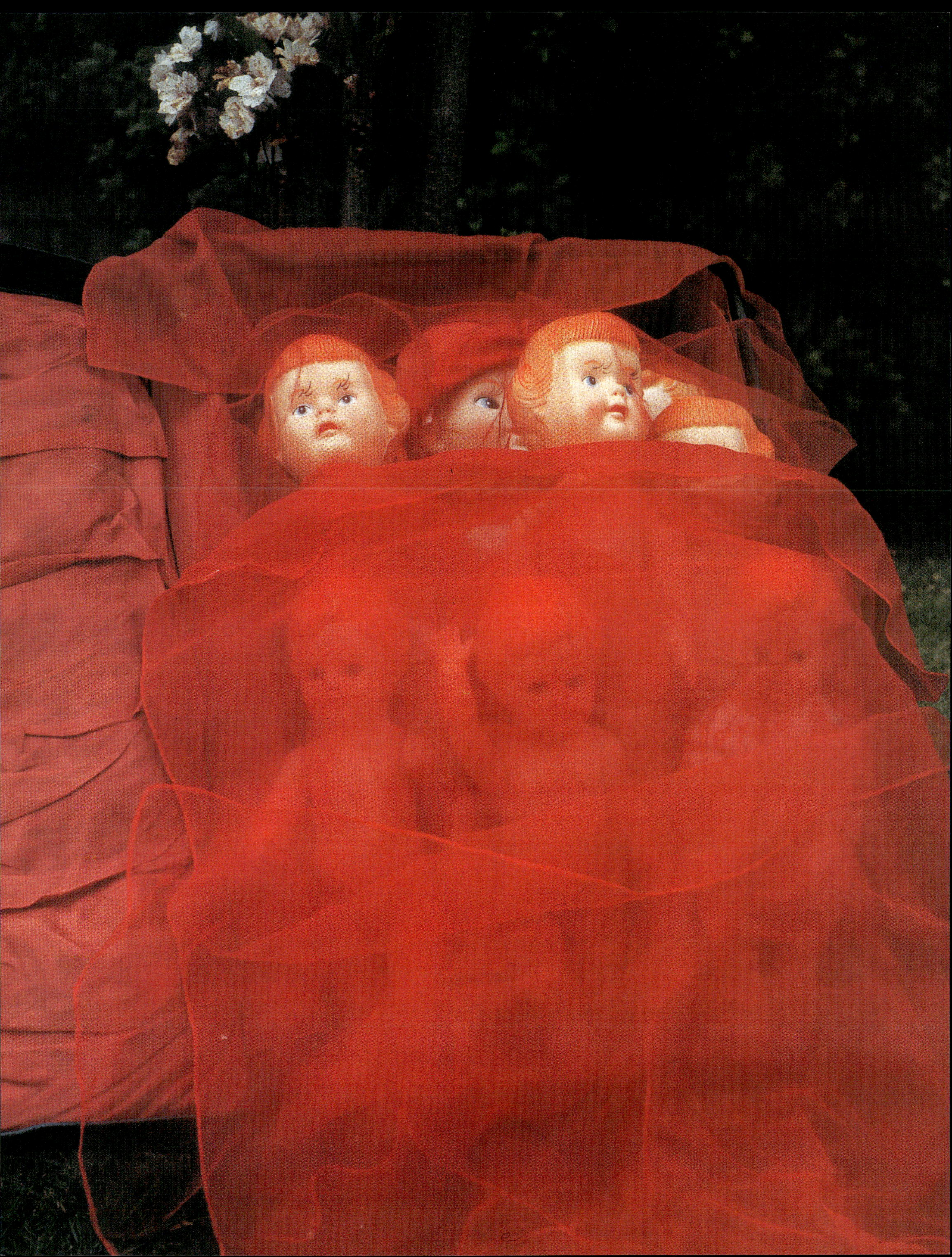

to move from an absolute entanglement in the constraints of everyday life to invoke in a new sense the figures of myth. He often explores the paradoxical nature of the grand and trivial in his investigation of imagination. Compared, for example, with Magellan's circumnavigation of the world (which Medalla claims is a voyage of errors), which was alluded to in the performance with Oriol de Quadras in London, the passion of Beau Brummel for a perfectly-tied cravat, which featured in Medalla's solo piece *Bonjour Beau, Bonsoir Brummel / Bongo Bo, Bonsai Brahma*, 1980, given in Nice, might appear laughable:

It is easy to moralise and condemn the dandy as a useless human being. I think that dandyism, of which Beau Brummel was an example, is one expression of man's dream of freedom, at a time when the cities were beginning to grow into vast metropolises under the impact of the first industrial revolution. Perhaps, in the last analysis, this dream of freedom is an illusion. Nevertheless it gives dignity to human beings in the face of their existence... Every manifestation of this dream in history interests me.[22]

Medalla has described his performances as "clusters of micro-dramas and poetic plays".[23] They are usually complex in construction and carefully-planned. Nevertheless he makes almost a virtue of fallibility. Things sometimes go wrong. The tape recorder does not always work. His costumes fall apart with such regularity that I had to accept his explanation that this was a deliberate ploy.[24] His performances are the very opposite of a slick product or a perfectly crafted routine. Most audiences usually remember his pieces as either a truly magical experience or an embarrassing failure (they can fail, but not for reasons of a malfunctioning taperecorder). In both success and failure, in the taking of risk, the audience feels implicated, for Medalla seems to make an ethic and an aesthetic of rejecting the slick. It is as if he wanted to evoke the small-scale beginnings, the improvised, spontaneous, inventor-like atmosphere of the origins of great art forms (the birth of opera – at first a rudimentary unity of painting, declamation and music – or the birth of cinema: both inspirations for Medalla's performances), and at the same time to evoke the beauty of certain great art works by means of the most rejected materials and in the most unpromising conditions. When David shared the bill, as happened sometimes, with a heavy-metal rock group, and the atmosphere had been somehow brutalised in advance by the installation of the enormous black cubes of the rock group's sound equipment, the most startling contrast was set up as David Medalla took the stage. In general his performances evoke a tender atmosphere, the light tone of a kind of urban *fête-galante*, covering a deeper purpose:

Situations tend to be very ephemeral, but I think one can relate many things: history, music, literature and mythology, and poetry in a very intimate and entertaining way, in a humanising way, especially in urban situations...[25]

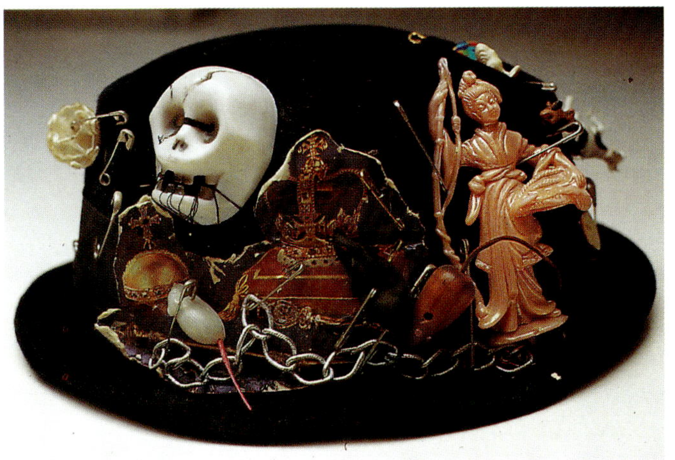

'Three Blind Mice Hat', used in **Boys of England** performances, 1977.
Collection of the artist.

◆　　　◆　　　◆

Medalla explored the enigmas of art in his earliest post-Galaxy performance (*Johannes Vermeer of Delft*, 1975) and in many subsequent works. The immediate occasion of the Vermeer performance was a video 'investigation piece' conducted by the Paris-based, Argentinian-born artist Lea Lublin, which itself was part of a video festival at the Serpentine Gallery in London. Lublin was interviewing visitors according to a long list of questions: "Is Art a Sublimation? Is Art a Sexual Problem? Is Art a Religious Phenomenon? Is Art an Enigma?"..., and so on. Instead of replying in words, Medalla staged a performance. It was done with the help of AFD members, somewhat rough and ready, based on Vermeer's art. His friends enacted a series of *tableaux vivants* based on the compositions of several of Vermeer's most famous works, such as *The Lace-Maker*, *Woman Reading a Letter* and *Woman Entertaining a Cavalier*. As they did so, Medalla stood aside, drawing back a heavy curtain to reveal each scene and reading from a little novella he had written about the life of the painter.

As a paradoxical counter to the prevailing view of Vermeer as a painter of serene light, Medalla interpreted his paintings as intrigues. What was happening at the 'decisive moment' at which, in the Baroque convention, time was arrested in the picture? Medalla's novella speculated on this in worldly terms, drawing on socio-economic determinants of Vermeer's day. Rather than resolving the enigma of the paintings, such worldly wisdom only heightened it. The 'intrigue' obviously involves the relationship between the artist (Vermeer) looking in at the sitters, and the sitters sometimes looking out at the artist, given that the picture, for all its luminous naturalness, is an artificial construct. Are the sitters fictions enacting roles dreamed by the artist, while nevertheless looking at him as a real protagonist in their lives? Vermeer not only painted himself painting (once), but also included many paintings within the painting. They are part of the story, but then so are the apparently storyless or merely decorative furnishings. For once we see the pictures as allegorical; everything, every object and its placement, becomes a metaphor.

Medalla extended this contradiction between nature and artifice, compounded in the freezing of time, by having living people reproduce the natural/stylised world of Vermeer's interiors. Living bodies posing in the compositions of famous paintings always produces a *frisson*. Although it has probably been a stock device of striptease shows for years, Medalla anticipated its later use in a fine-art context by filmmakers like Jean-Luc Godard and Derek Jarman, and by the Mexican theatre director Jesusa Rodríguez. In David's case this departure built on experiments he made in performances in Paris and London in the early 1960s, which he called *Body Ideograms* ("abstracted body movements... rather like a fluid succession of *tableaux vivants*).[26]

One of Medalla's most characteristic vehicles of the early and mid 1980s was his performance *Voyages and Somersaults of the Pilgrim Monkey*, first given in the Great Hall of the Academy of Venice in 1981, following an event entitled *In Veritá* by Lovato Guerrino. The monkey was his alter-ego. The monkey seated on a pillar in Veronese's great painting *The Family of Darius Before Alexander* in the National Gallery, London, was one of his inspirations; *Monkey's Journey to the West*, the novel by Wu Ch'eng-en, was another. In the Veronese, the monkey's presence is supposedly peripheral but somehow central (in Renaissance painting the monkey symbolised intuition). The theme of Wu Ch'eng-en's book fitted his own wandering existence at the time.

Sylvia Stevens and Steve Oxley in **Johannes Vermeer of Delft**, Serpentine Gallery, London, 1975. The performance was devised by Medalla in response to **Is Art an Enigma?**, a video investigation work by Lea Lublin which was part of a video festival at the Serpentine Gallery.

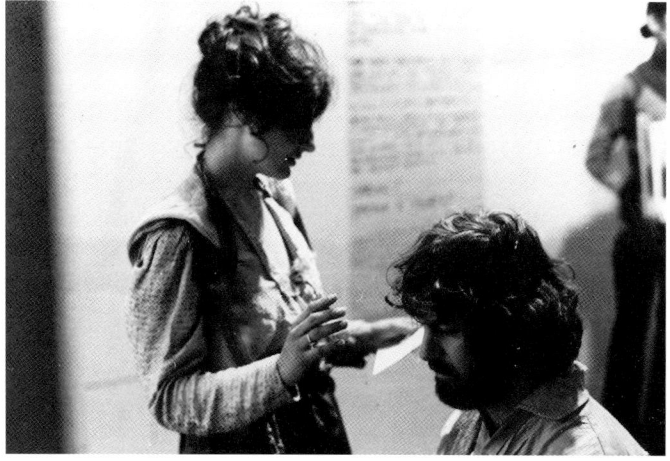

The monkey, too, embodied the light, graceful tone of the narrative and the ability to "somersault through space and time". There was an elastic series of episodes in which monkey would arrive in a succession of historical moments:

I made the monkey go forward in time from ancient Greece to 20th century France where he meets a boxing kangaroo which was brought to France by Australian soldiers fighting in the First World War. This kangaroo was bought by a circus - they had a circus in Montmartre and this kangaroo was an attraction, along with Chocolat, who was painted by Toulouse-Lautrec. So every somersault involves a meeting with another animal and each refers to an artistic problem. Then at another time the monkey goes to 17th century Venice and meets the rhinoceros painted by Pietro Longhi and he also goes to New York in the mid-Fifties at the height of the Abstract Expressionist movement. I use hundreds of masks... In the New York sequence monkey enters a cinema. It is the first time he has been in a movie house. I examine the problem of moving pictures. And the film being shown is *King Kong*. So I wear a King Kong mask. That piece is performed with operatic music. I used a device for starting the music by making an actual sandwich of slices of fresh bread in which I inserted an audio casette tape. When I began to munch the music started... sometimes the music came out of portable speakers concealed behind my ears. Very incongruous...[27]

These episodes were woven around a central core of a story which cast the problem of art in the form of a dialogue between different cultures. In the Exploding Galaxy period, Medalla had worked extensively with the early Buddhist text, *The Questions of King Milinda*, representing a dialogue between Milinda or Menander, a Greco-Bactrian king, and the Indian Buddhist sage Nagasena. *Voyages and Somersaults's* central story was loosely based on a fable by the Persian poet Firdausi which tells how Alexander the Great, during the course of his conquests, encountered a large, empty, domed building in the Persian desert. Alexander invited two painters, one Greek and the other Chinese, to decorate the interior of the dome. They were to paint one half of the dome each and neither was to see the other's work until the task was finished. The Greek painted a magnificent scene of the wonders of creation, encyclopaedic and precise down to the smallest details. When the Chinese painter's work was unveiled it was revealed that he had simply polished his half of the dome. He made it as smooth and shining as a mirror, thus reflecting the half painted by the Greek artist.

It gave me an insight into two different cultures. One believing in the realistic enumeration of reality in the Aristotelian sense, the other was interested in the Taoist cosmic whole, both really rather important. One cannot have one without the other...[28] One was about the ego-based (Greek) and the other the non-ego-based (Buddhist) concepts of 'identity' and the 'self'...[29] [I wanted to show] how two divergent cultures can have real unity if each culture understood what was important to the other.[30]

Voyages and Somersaults of the Pilgrim Monkey was first performed in the Great Hall of

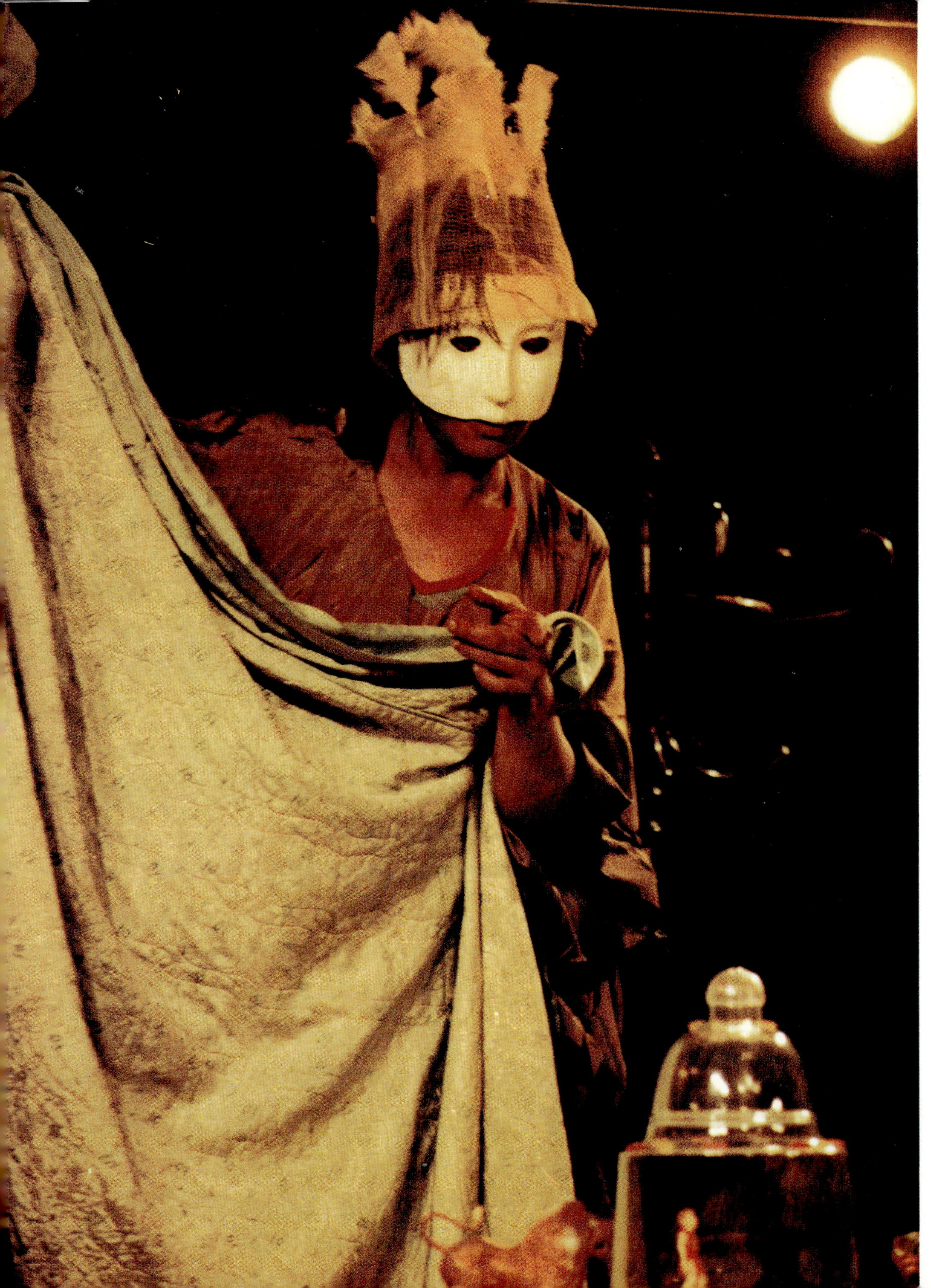

the Academy in Venice on 16th March 1981. Paolo Rosetti, an architectural student, played the part of Eros (in jeans). Enrico Oliviero and Gianni Sandri, two young artists from Creazzo (Vicenza), provided the music; the Brazilian actor Atilio Lopez and the English mime artist Lindsay Kemp lent costumes; Lovato Guerrino, the Venetian artist, made the Pilgrim Monkey's mask. Manuel Cristaldi, a young photographer from Milan, helped in constructing Medalla's minimal stage set of two Greek pillars made from two white columns of ribbed crêpe paper. The Greek painter's mask was made by David from a takeaway pizza. After the event the veteran Venetian painter Emilio Vedova, who had been in the audience, was moved to stand up and deliver an impromptu speech of appreciation which lasted almost as long as the performance itself.

It is interesting to compare a large-scale format in David Medalla's performances with a miniature one. He devised a performance for fingers and toes during the Exploding Galaxy period, *Tar Pot Eb Ot Woh*, and he presented another miniature piece in 1983 at Bracknell, *Next! Tantalizers*. This featured a passage in which Medalla illustrated the words of a post-war song, 'Black Mischief', sung by Marlene Dietrich, with small objects (a toy camera, a toy ring, a tin of Spam, a paper fan, a Rembrandt reproduction rolled inside a black silk stocking, a porcelain doll, a Michelangelo's David key-ring, and a cigarette-lighter bearing the emblem of the American Embassy) dangling from David's fingers. Fingers became "signifying termini" for thoughts and feelings.

What is unknowable from photographs or verbal descriptions is the role music has played in Medalla's performances. This element of the collage revived a particular passion of the artist since childhood. Parallel to the performances themselves he was making an exhaustive study of the history of opera, singing and the voice. The "musical potpourri"[31] of each work was taken from a fantastic collection of (mostly) secondhand LPs amassed in a matter of months of assiduous searching in Britain's record stores, charity shops and car-boot sales, and filling David's rooms almost to the

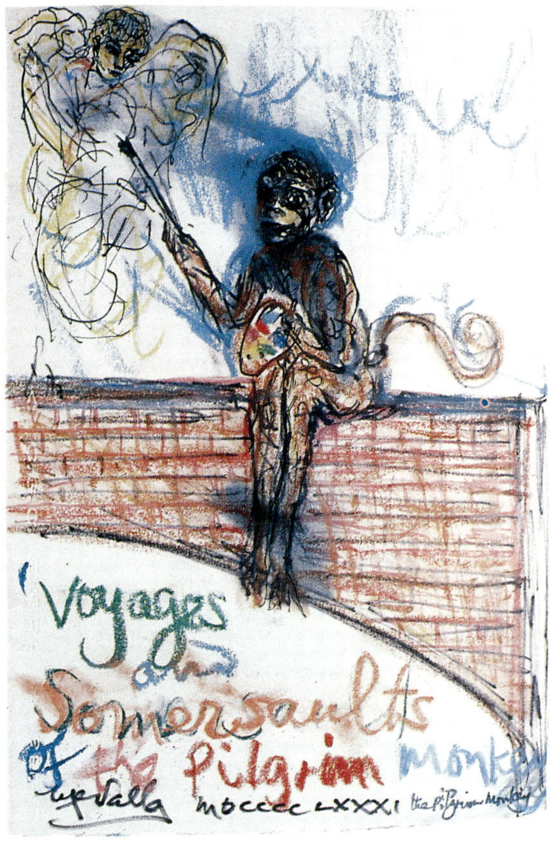

Title page of the script of **Voyages and Somersaults of the Pilgrim Monkey**, 1981. Crayon and watercolour. Collection of the artist.

Opposite: Medalla in **Voyages and Somersaults of the Pilgrim Monkey**, a 'synoptic-realist performance', first performed in Venice, 1981, here at South Hill Park, Bracknell, 1982.

ceiling. At this time (c.1986) he compiled and sent round to friends a History of Opera on cassette, fastidiously selected and execrably recorded on his jumble-sale equipment. As always, his enthusiasm, his sense of discovery, was highly infectious. The great voice, the great singer, was a most enigmatic and exacting paradigm of artistic creation. It was a phenomenon full of incongruities. To begin with, the voice is the most elementary, unaided aural medium: a part of the body. The great singer could emerge anywhere, in any class ("You can't fake it as you can in art").[32] At the same time this art is precarious ("even great singers can boob").[33] At one moment a singer may be adored, at another cursed. The profundity of singing has no obvious relationship with a particular lifestyle: one singer can live an extravagant and turbulent life, another the most humdrum existence. One may have a smooth path through life, another continual trials, and so on. Finally, great singing pinpoints a problem of aesthetics:

The argument for sheer 'beauty' of voice is reduced to a mere matter of lyrical hedonism unless the voice transcends its 'beauty' and becomes something more. A singer like Franco Corelli, conscious of his own vocal powers and at the same time aware that this gift must be purified in sympathy with inner emotion, is thus able to attain a higher aesthetic sphere than mere 'natural beauty'.[34]

◆   ◆   ◆

David gave the name 'Impromptus' to a whole array of works over the past fifteen years that require no funds, no art world approval, no elaborate planning: an epitome of the spontaneous and ephemeral. Sometimes they have been short performances, sometimes no more than a 'pause' in his peregrinations through the streets and buildings of countless cities, captured by camera. An activity descending from that of the *flâneur* (Baudelaire's "wanderer in great cities") but less passive, since David reconstructs what was seen as sign or as metaphor. While the element of fun, absurdity and *jeu d'esprit* is very obvious in Medalla's impromptus – and to make pompous interpretations of them would be obnoxious – nevertheless they have a deeper sense and cover a complex variety of emotions and issues in the form of a 'poetics' of the flux of life itself.[35]

The wanderer in Rome formed a close, if ironic, relationship with the huge population of statues inhabiting every corner of the city, some noble, some ignoble, many worn and weathered and scarred with graffiti. They spoke in Medalla's *Annals of the Talking Statues of Rome*, or *Statuamachia Romana*, 1979 (p.154-5). Not satirical comments on Rome's political life as they have done in vernacular tradition down through Roman history,[36] but as raconteurs of events and meetings they may have witnessed and are still there to tell of. An incongruous 20th century counterpart to Roman statuary are the mannikins in shop windows, a similarly vast and this time cosmopolitan population which Medalla posed with in his series *Mr Casanova International*, 1985 (p.160). The title was inspired by a tabloid newspaper competition

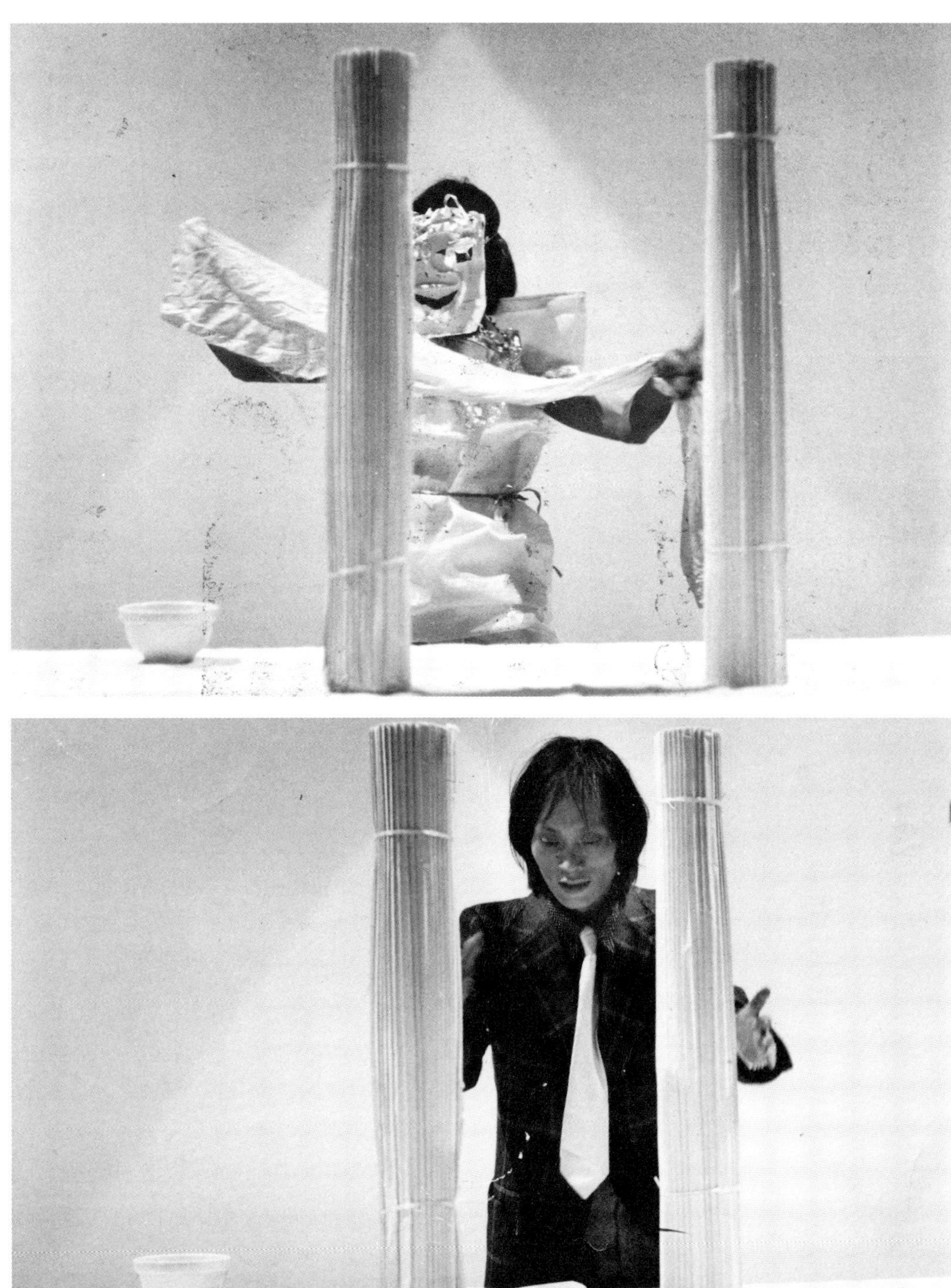

David Medalla performing **'Voyages & Somersaults of the Pilgrim Monkey'** in the Great Hall of the Academy in Venice, 1980.

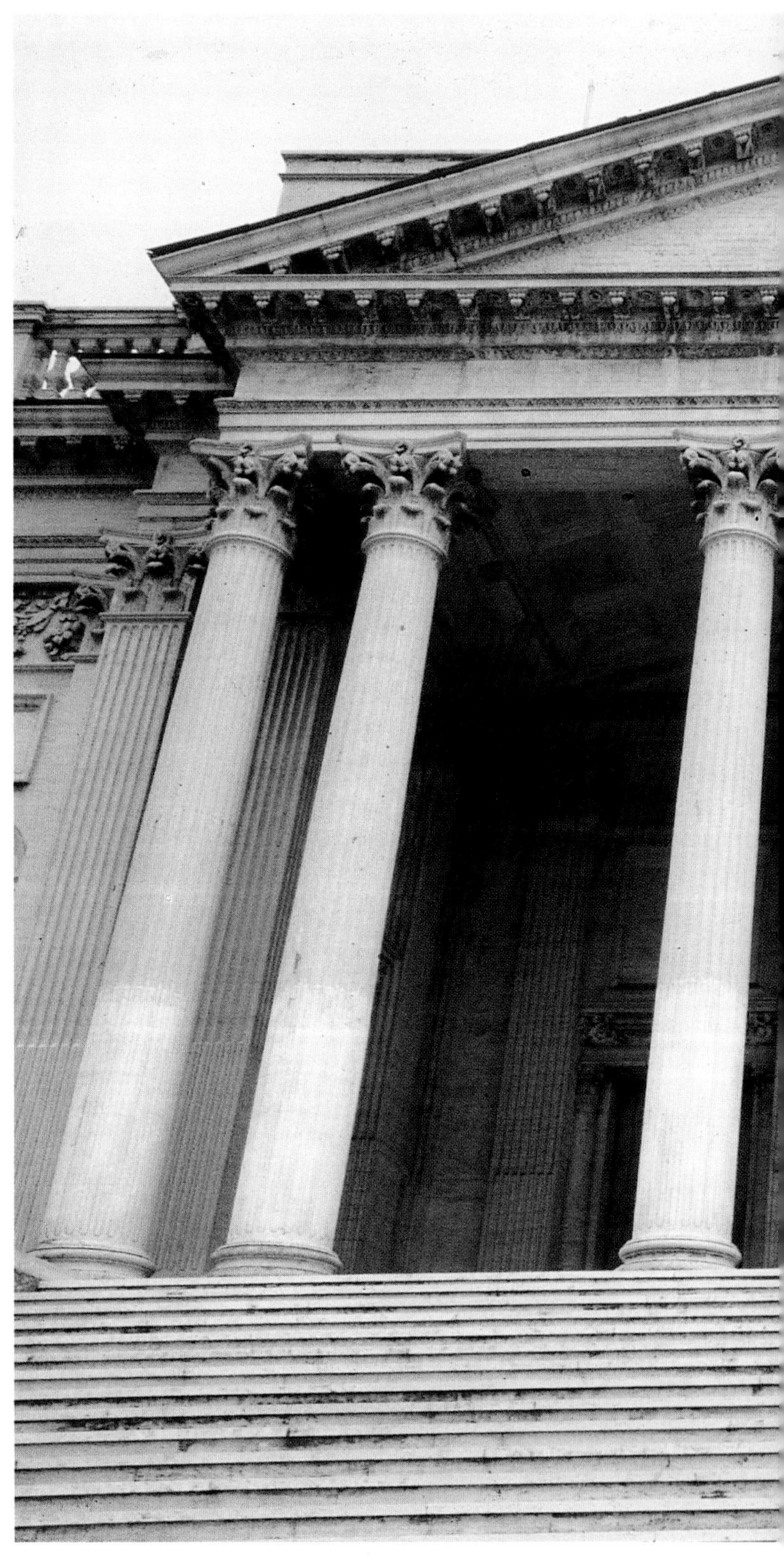

Medalla Saluta Roma, impromptu at the British School in Rome, 1980. Collection of the artist.

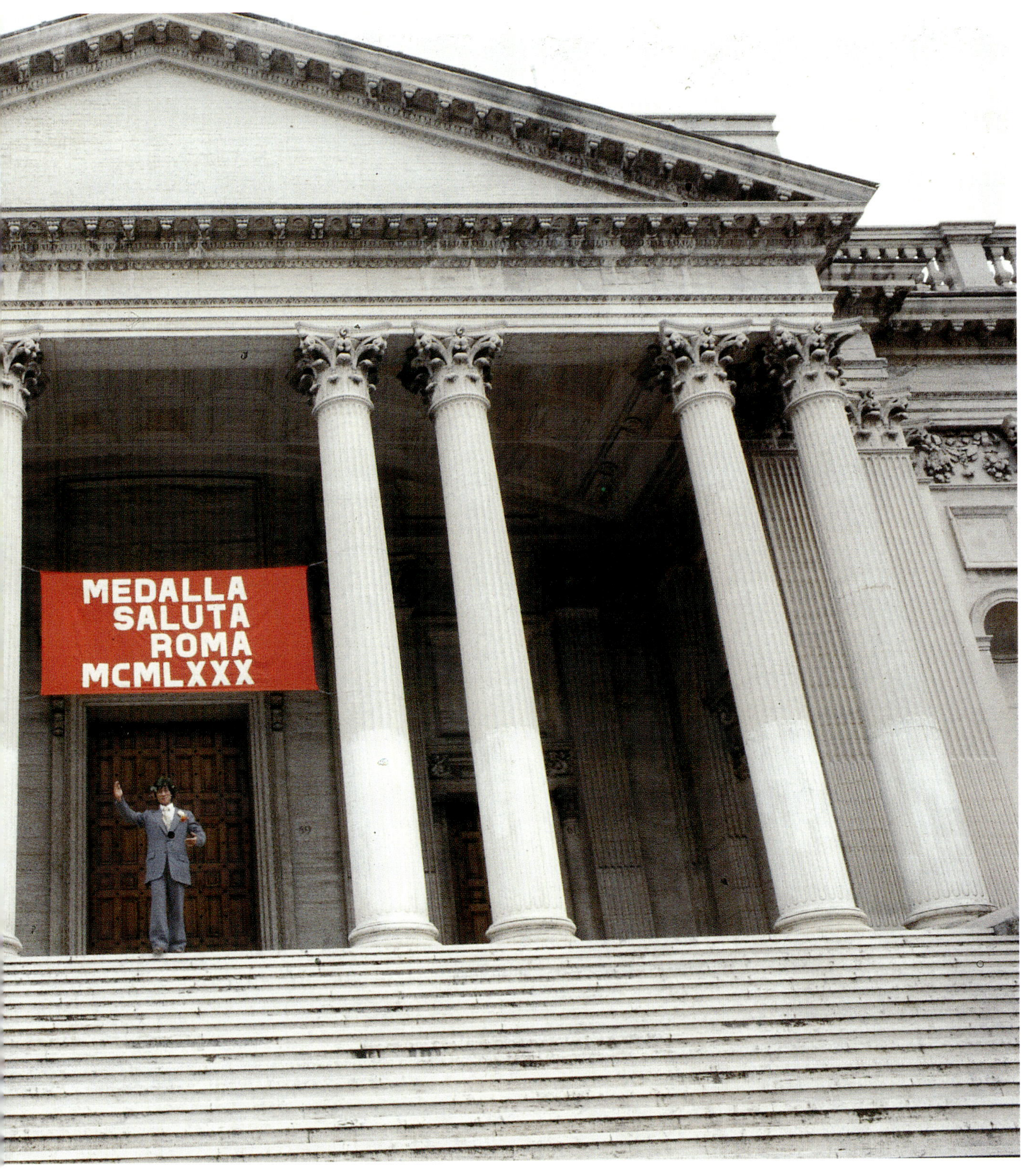
MEDALLA
SALUTA
ROMA
MCMLXXX

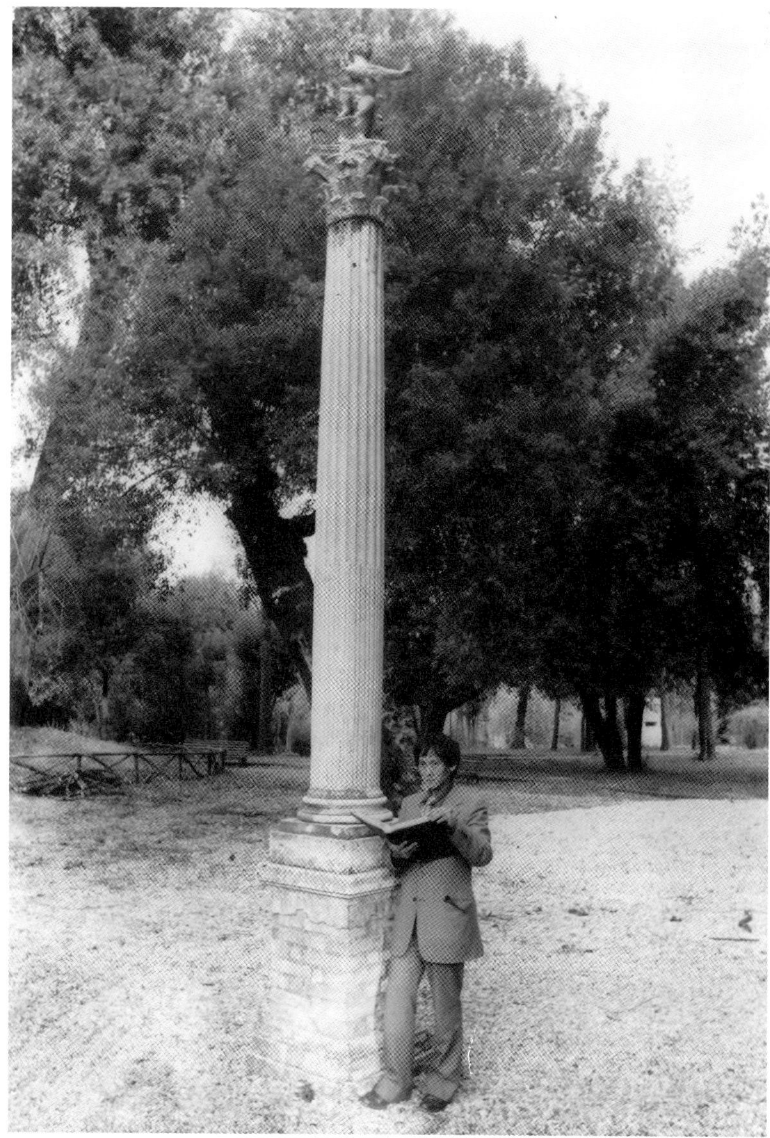

Above and opposite: **Statuamacchia Romana, or Annals of the Talking Statues of Rome,**
impromptu at the Villa Borghese, Rome, 1980. Collection of the artist.

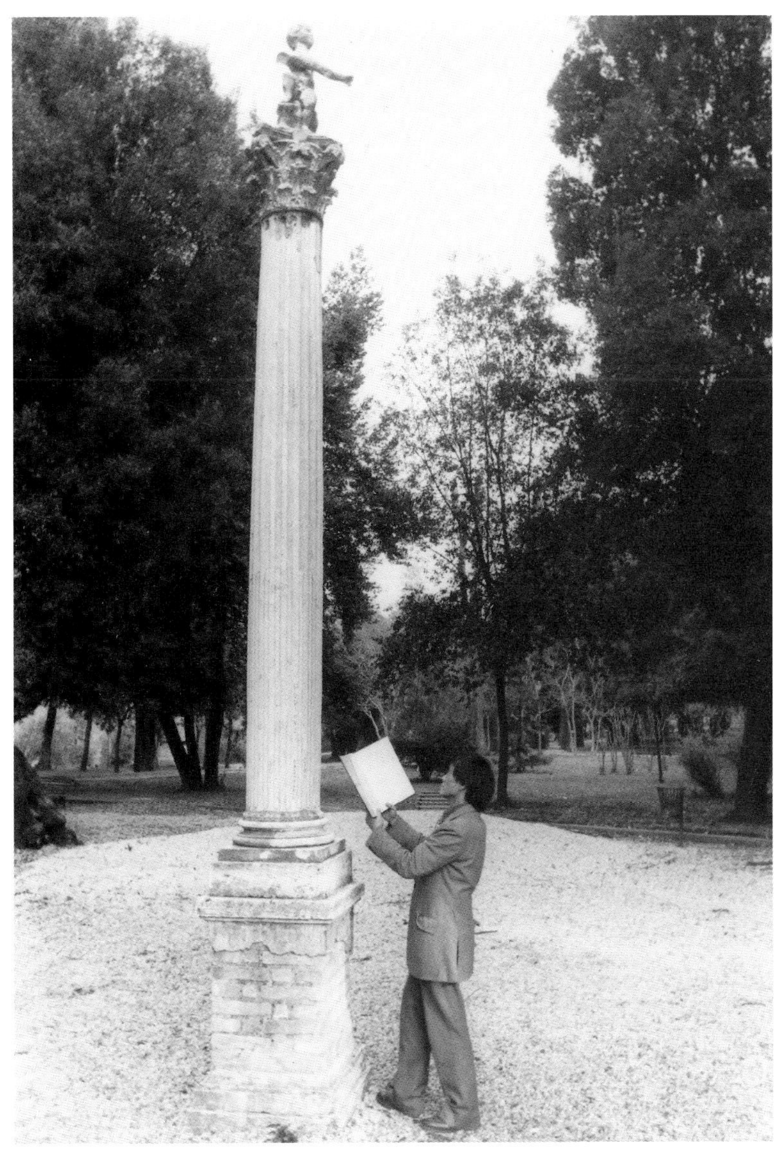

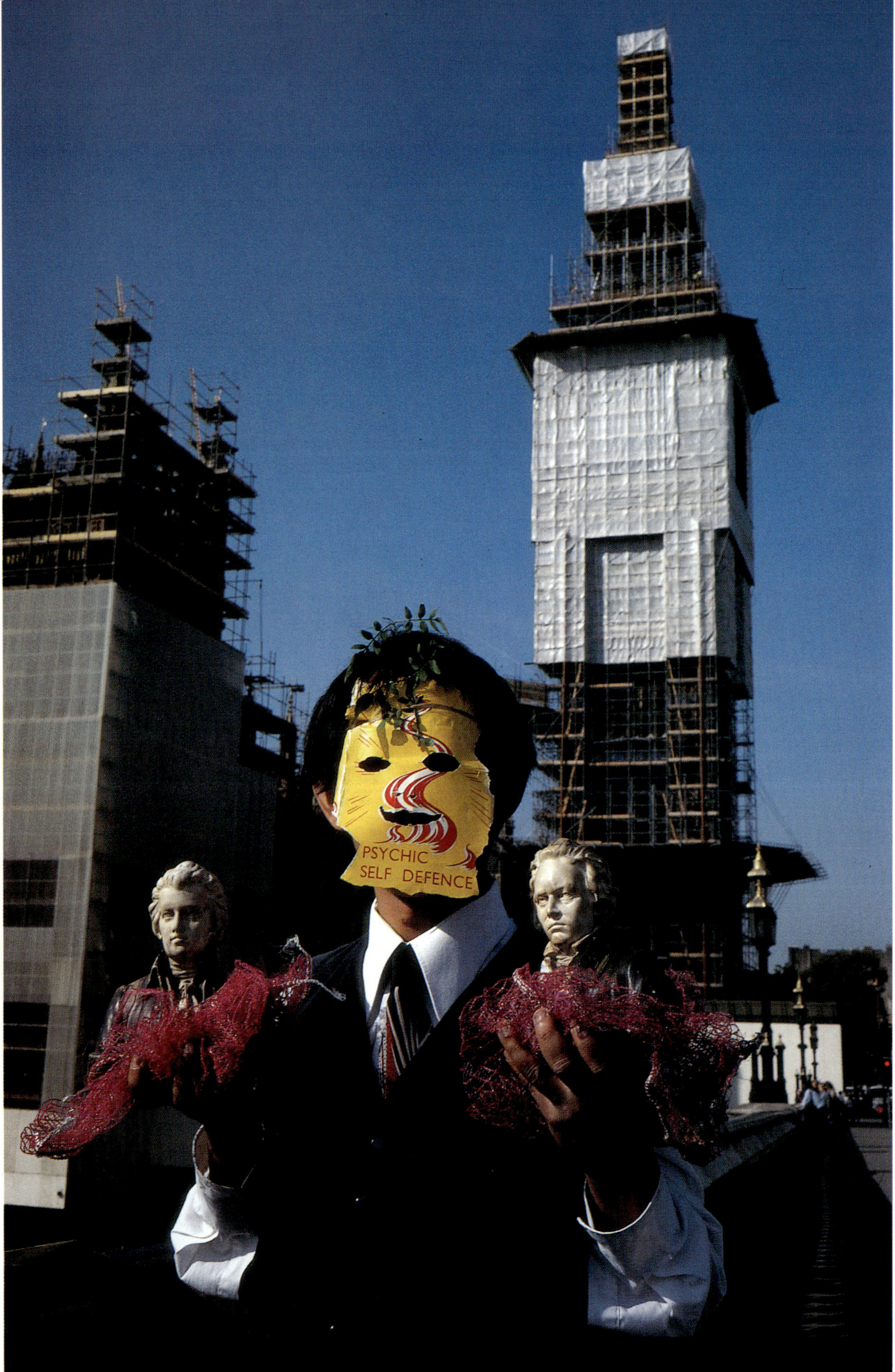

PSYCHIC
SELF DEFENCE

to find the best lover, and by its stereotypical reference to a historical figure the artist admires as "a very experimental man and revolutionary for his time".[37]

Before following up some other threads in Medalla's on-going sequence of impromptus we could look at one in more detail. *Psychic Self-Defence*, an impromptu at Westminster, was made in 1983, at a time when he was leading a precarious existence in a succession of dilapidated squats in various parts of London:

I was in a constant state of paranoia. As a squatter I felt the threat of wrecker-squads with crow-bars, sent by landlords, who were often delirious in brutally vandalising often beautiful property which had remained vacant for years. Going to jumble-sales was one of my few luxuries. I found Mozart in Dalston and Beethoven in south London; they were both hand-painted and must have belonged to a set... I could only think of psychic survival in terms of the arts. I wanted Mozart and Beethoven to be like gloves, boxing gloves. Big Ben wrapped up reminded me of the *stupas*, or *dagobas*, of Kathmandu. I wanted the sprig to be like a laurel wreath, reminiscent of Apollo, god of the arts. The book-jacket was yellow with a flame-like design. Making it into a mask with the flame coming from the mouth reminded me of oracles, and the representations of prophetic speech, secret speech.[38]

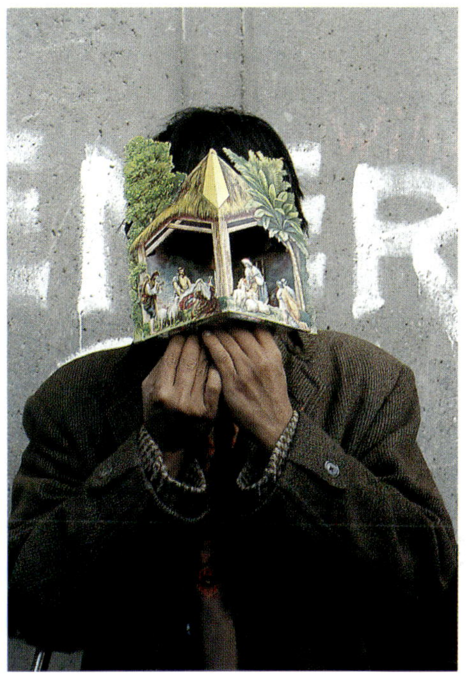

A Celebration of World Mythologies in Rotterdam, impromptu at the Blaak flea-market, Rotterdam, 1984. Collection of the artist.

Opposite: **Psychic Self-Defence**, impromptu at Westminster, London, 1983. Collection of the artist.

The artist has placed himself at the centre of London as an expression of his desire to survive psychically in a hostile environment. The symbol of London, and a symbol of the western concept of time, has been temporally transformed into the semblance of an opposing philosophical concept of a Buddhist model of an atemporal cosmos (the *stupa*) that centres around the egg/seed/womb. Both the person and the environment are wearing masks which cement their secret, momentary conjunction in a new image. In an instant the environment is changed and can be read in another way, and a purely pragmatic and technical circumstance (the covering of Big Ben for cleaning) becomes a metaphor for a spiritual reality. This would be typical of the graceful wit of Medalla's guerrilla poetics. With a Zen-like economy of energy, the environment unwittingly, ephemerally, becomes the prophetic sign of another possible

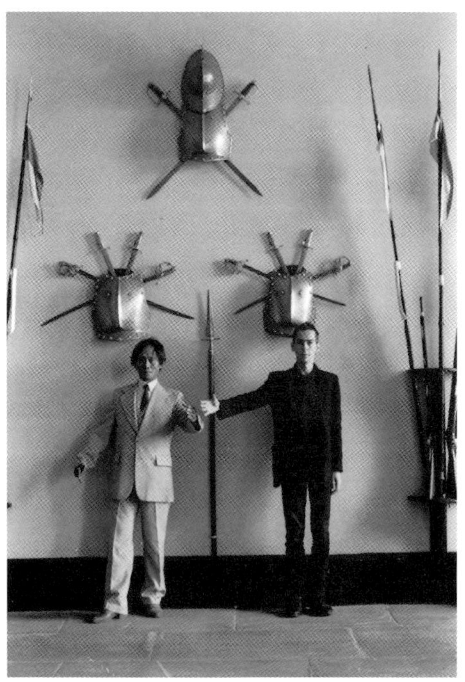

David Medalla and Brian Morgan, impromptu in the **Indian Trophy Room of the Duke of Wellington**, the Royal Military Academy, Sandhurst, 1988. Collection of the artist.

future and the artist exercises a power he does not possess. By means of photography, the capturing of a moment out of the flux of time can take on a surprisingly dense resonance. The momentary can become monumental, while retaining the insubstantiality of a dream. No more, no less, than an inspired intervention in the daily manufacture of images.

'The dream' would be as good a starting-point as any to thread a way through the capriccios of Medalla's impromptus. *Dreaming of Filippo de Pisis Dreaming in Venice*, 1985: David found some young men sleeping or sunbathing on the Zattere and climbed onto an upturned boat fully clothed to "share their dreams".[39] When he woke up they had gone. Are they dreaming him or he dreaming them? Filippo de Pisis was a painter from Ferrara who lived in Venice between the wars, "a kind of late impressionist, a friend of Bonnard and Tzara, a member of the *scuola metafisica* which included Carra and di Chirico, a minor but delicate painter. He was an eccentric homosexual who painted young men, landscapes and still-lives... The random elements have a kind of harmony. Venice is a city which is very difficult to incorporate into any kind of artistic statement."[40] Rome, by contrast, prompted a parody of the Baroque, *Medalla Saluta Roma*, 1980, a sort of grandiloquent fantasy gesture by an ordinary besuited visitor or tourist. Irony and inspiration were both part of the impact Italian art made on Medalla during his travels of the early 1980s, and these extended to other contexts too. Nowhere could the two responses combine more fruitfully than in the ocean of junk, secondhand goods and kitsch characteristic of every big city. A tour through the Rotterdam Blaak, the fleamarket, became *A Celebration of World Mythologies in Rotterdam*, 1988 (p.157). In a momentary impulse he lifted a nativity Christmas-card to his face. "The strange symmetry of the whole thing was like transforming myself into an African, or maybe New Guinean, mask. A conflation of cultures is produced: incongruous and rather magical."[41]

There was a way in which the hedonism and sensuality in Italian or French painting could be reintroduced or rediscovered in the most unpromising circumstances. This would be a way to "penetrate the pretence that life is humdrum", to return to Edward Pope's description of the Exploding Galaxy's philosophy. I

A Dream of Fillippo de Pisis Dreaming, impromptu at the Zattere, Venice, 1984. Collection of the artist.

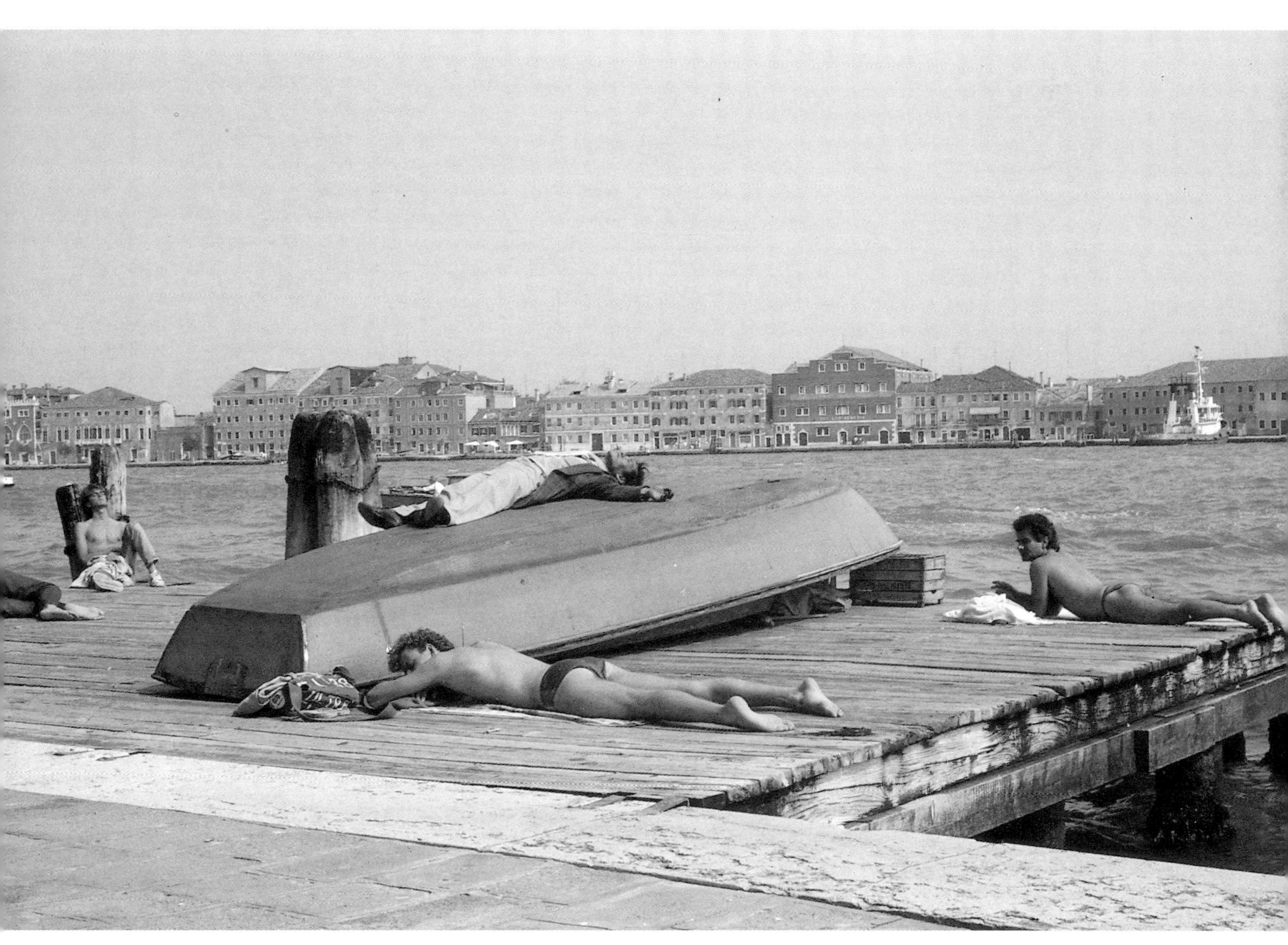

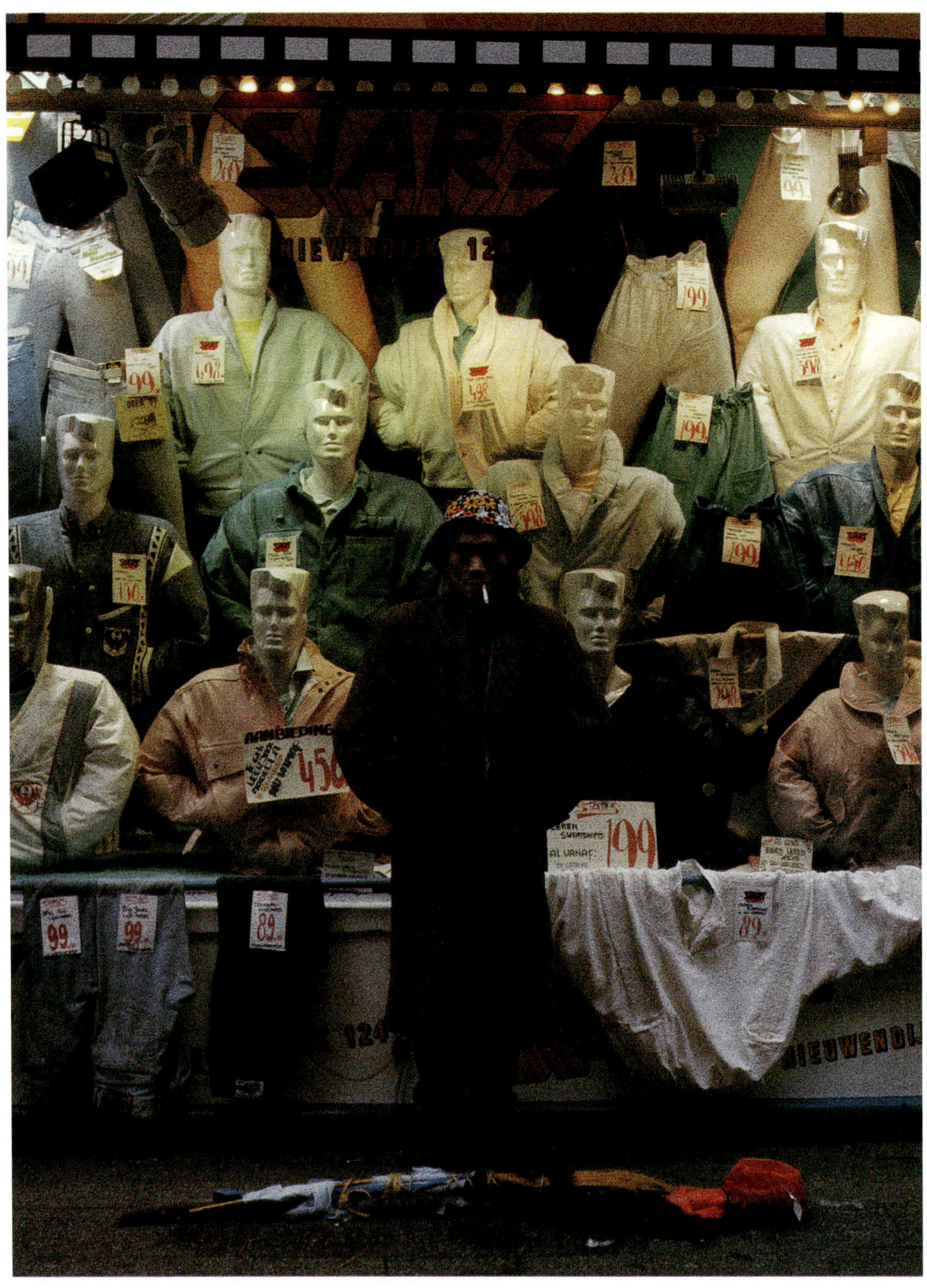

Mr Casanova International, impromptu at Frankfurt, 1985. Collection of the artist.

photographed *David Smelling Forget-me-nots and Black Tulips*, 1986, (p. 4) lying in a flowerbed in the middle of Finsbury Square in the City of London one morning with office-workers streaming past. While living in New York in the past few years David has had a project, *Les Parfums Excelsior*, to travel to every state in the USA and to sniff the perfume of its official state flower! A sort of Polynesian performance version of a work Marcel Duchamp made in collaboration with Man Ray in New York in 1921, *Belle haleine, eau de voilette* ('Sweet breath, veil water'), a scent bottle with a label incorporating a photo of Duchamp dressed as a woman. Medalla's version is environmental: certain symbols of civic pride are returned to the pleasure of the senses, to which, in spite of themselves and rather primly, they do still refer.[42]

Related to this was a more dangerous, perhaps quixotic venture. In New York in the early 1990s Medalla conducted a special performance every time he went to see someone off or meet someone at the Port Authority Terminal. Rebelling against the fate of this public space, viewed by the New York homeless necessarily as a place of refuge and shelter, by potential muggers as a killing-ground, and by travellers as somewhere to hurry through as quickly as possible without looking to right or left, David would linger incongruously on the escalators impersonating the figures from Watteau's wistful departure-painting *The Embarkation for Cythera*. His theory was that a reminder of Watteau's graceful and gallant gestures would "withdraw poison and fear from the atmosphere" because, as he would say, quoting Thomas Mann, "laughter comes from the heart".[43]

"The instant props and stages for our ironic performances."[44] Often, in my own case, a telephone message from David would announce the discovery of a new site for a photocall: the flotsam-filled corner of a canal in Camden Town, garage doors painted Barnett Newman-like with monochrome colours, a preserved foetus in an antique shop in Crystal Palace, Sir Richard Burton's mildewing stone bedouin tent funerary monument in an obscure south London graveyard, a field of poppies, the goldfish pond in the Butterfly House at Syon Park (instant japonaiserie), a mosaic pavement – 'Arthur & Co' – the remnant of a vanished *fin-de-siècle* shop in Notting Hill (p. 29). All became stages, monumental or miniature. An unsuccessful job application for the post of archivist at Sandhurst Military Academy provided the scene for a mock heroic impromptu with Brian Morgan in front of a wall patterned with the rusty weapons of an imperialist past – another junk shop! And so on, far and wide. *Immoderato Incantabile* shows Medalla sitting at the organ of San Agustin Church, Manila, Philippines on New Year's Eve, 1985. He was on a rare visit. Marcos was still in power, and the popular movement against his dictatorship was growing daily. "I had to be careful but I felt I had to do some action which would in some way contribute to the change. As I was playing the organ I mouthed a series of maledictions and curses (normally in church you give benedictions, blessings). I tried to use all the languages I know, including some of the Philippine languages. The organ of course drowned my words... 'immoderate, unsingable'."[45]

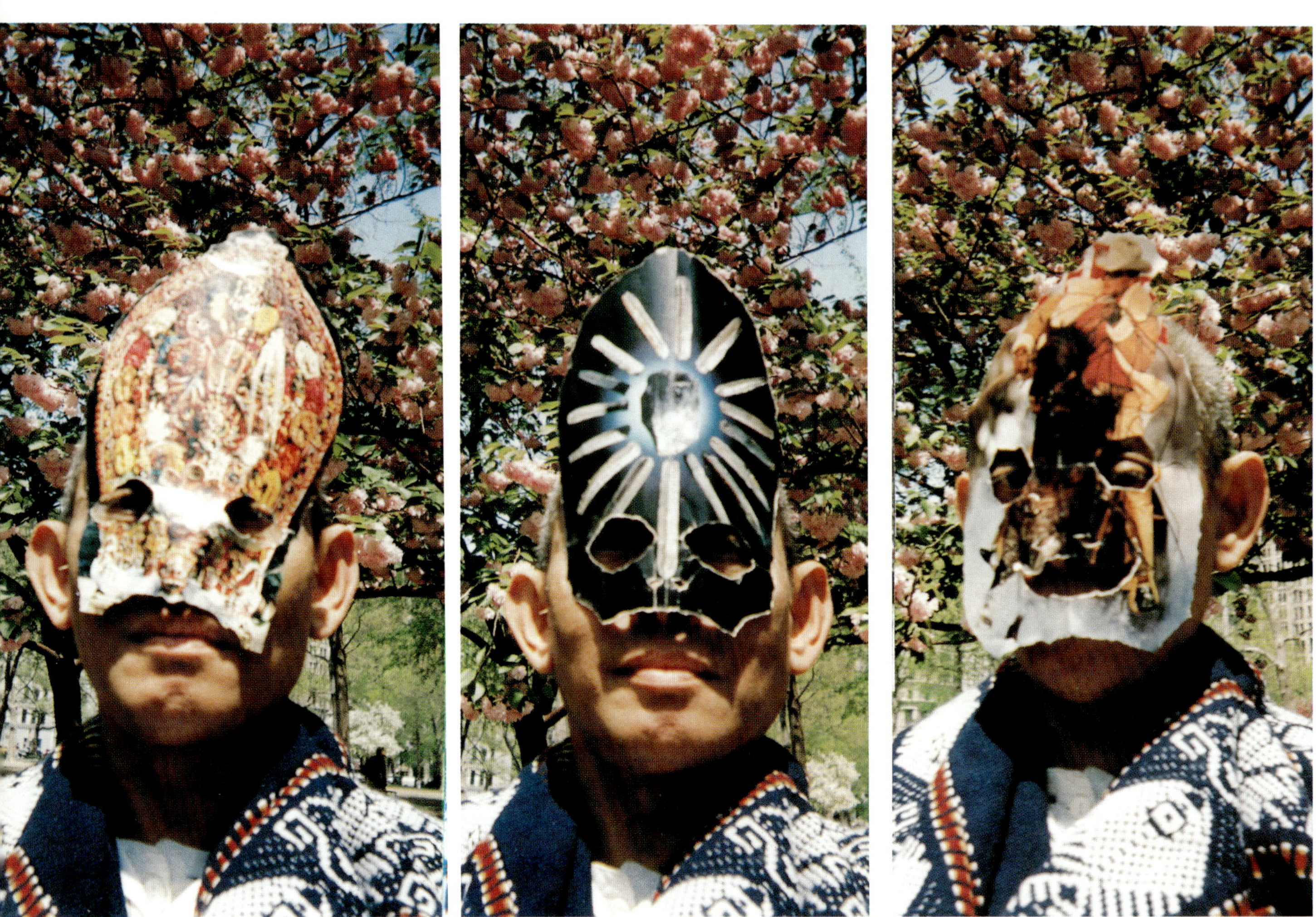

Impromptus with torn-paper masks, Madison Square Park, New York, 1991. Collection of the artist.

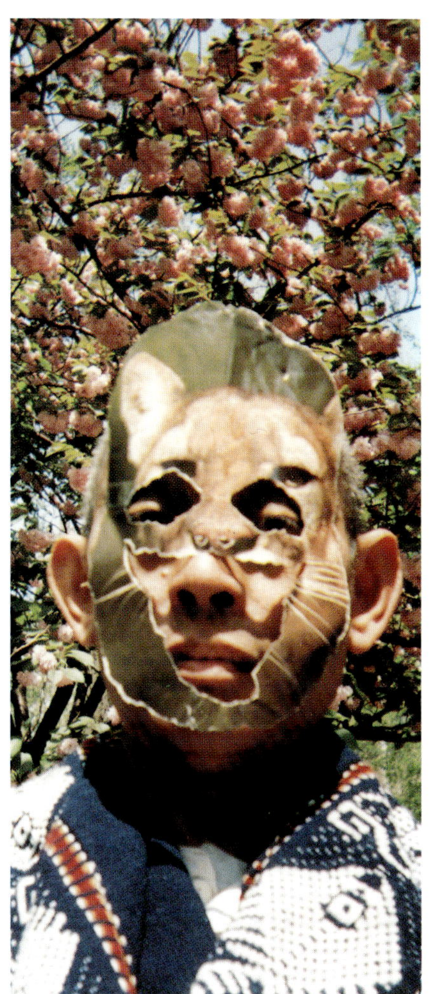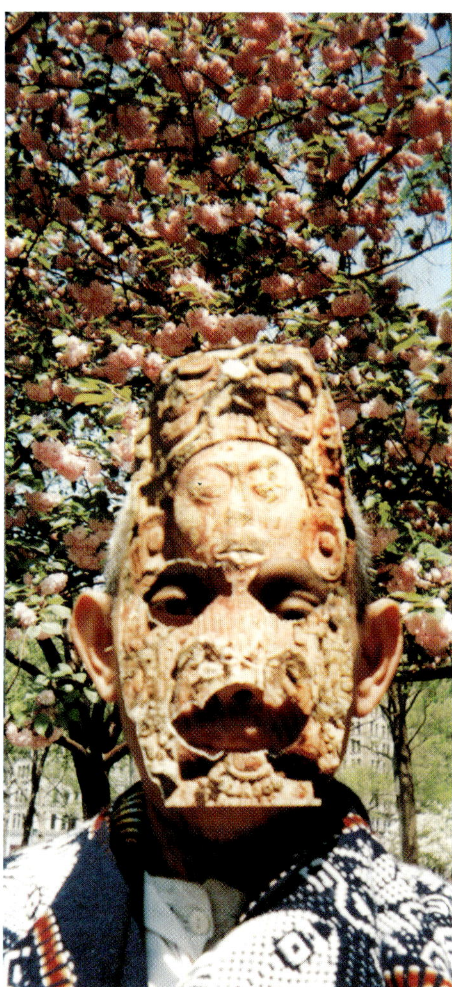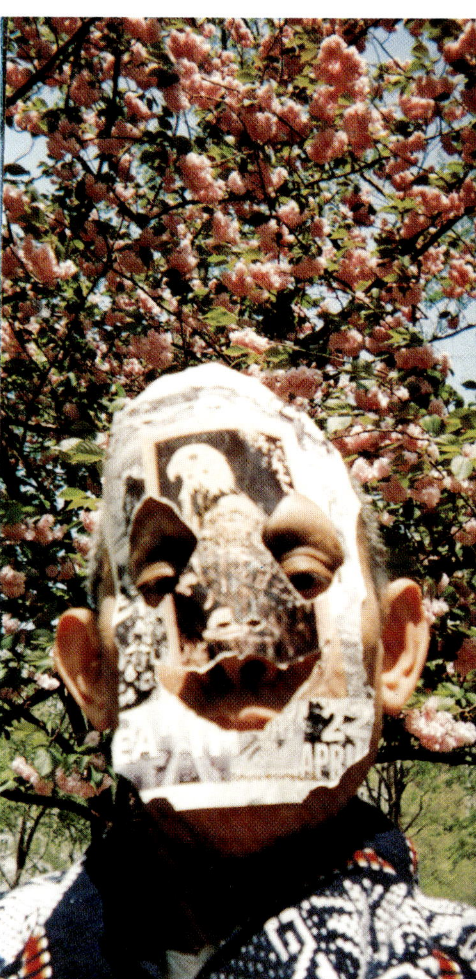

Here music functioned as a sort of mask (through which the truth could be spoken). In a sense all Medalla's performances and impromptus can be seen as a reinvention of the masquerade. All masking is also unmasking – *viz*, Lygia Clark's paradoxical "I use clothes to denude the body", or Oscar Wilde's neat reversal: "Man is seldom himself when he speaks in his own person. Give him a mask and he will tell you the truth." Or again, Rose English's witty and ironic remark, during her performance *Walks on Water* at the Hackney Empire in 1989, when dressed in flimsy stripper's briefs with an elaborate headress of feathers surmounting her head, she said: "I have this strange feeling I am over-dressed and under-dressed at the same time." Medalla's performances belong to the genre of the selfportrait too, of course, but not in the sense of projecting the image of a single, uniform self. In this respect they are very different from the strategy in recent art of putting oneself on exhibition as an unchanging trademark persona. For Medalla, identity is kinetic, shared, a complex amalgam. His work constructs new identities out of worn-out fragments of the old. A feature of his masquerade is its ceaseless variability. It can take place anywhere. Anything can be made into a mask, as 'masking' can present anything from a critical insight to a

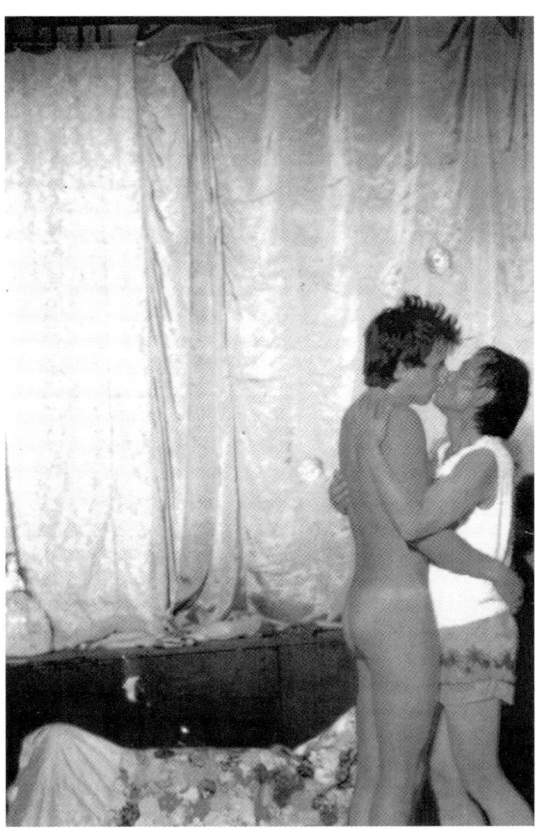

With Alessandro Fiorella in **The Desire and Pursuit of the Whole,** a synoptic-realist performance at the Diorama, Regents Park, London, 1986.

ravishing dream. The masking and unmasking of the person is presented inseparably from that of the surroundings, the world. In *Psychic Self-Defence*, Big Ben was inadvertently wearing a mask of tarpaulin and scaffolding. In today's conditions, Medalla's strikes one as a deeply humanistic response. The mask stands for a particular notion of value because, as Bakhtin says so beautifully, "even in modern life, the mask is enveloped in a peculiar atmosphere and is seen as a particle of some other world. The mask never becomes just an object among other objects".[46]

Nowhere is Bakhtin's insight confirmed in a more fascinating way than in a series of torn-paper masks which Medalla made in the early 1990s from the pages of magazines and brochures. As in *Eskimo Carver*, there is no end to the making of these masks. There are already thousands of them, as there are of the thrown-away advertisements and features whose content is transformed by the tearing of two eyeholes and a mouth. Significations of business, industry, science, leisure, culture, tourism, change into benign, fierce, baroque, satirical, contemplative and cosmic masks of an inexhaustible carnival of metaphor. Here the ideal in performance of a meeting between the body, imagination, the everyday and the ephemeral is superbly realised.

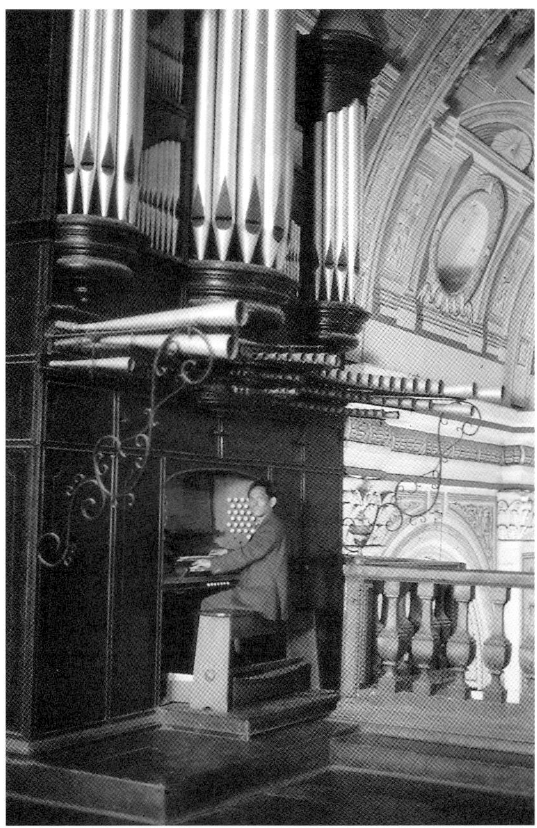

Immoderato Incantabile, impromptu at the organ of San Agustin Church, Manila, New Year's Eve, 1984. Collection of the artist.

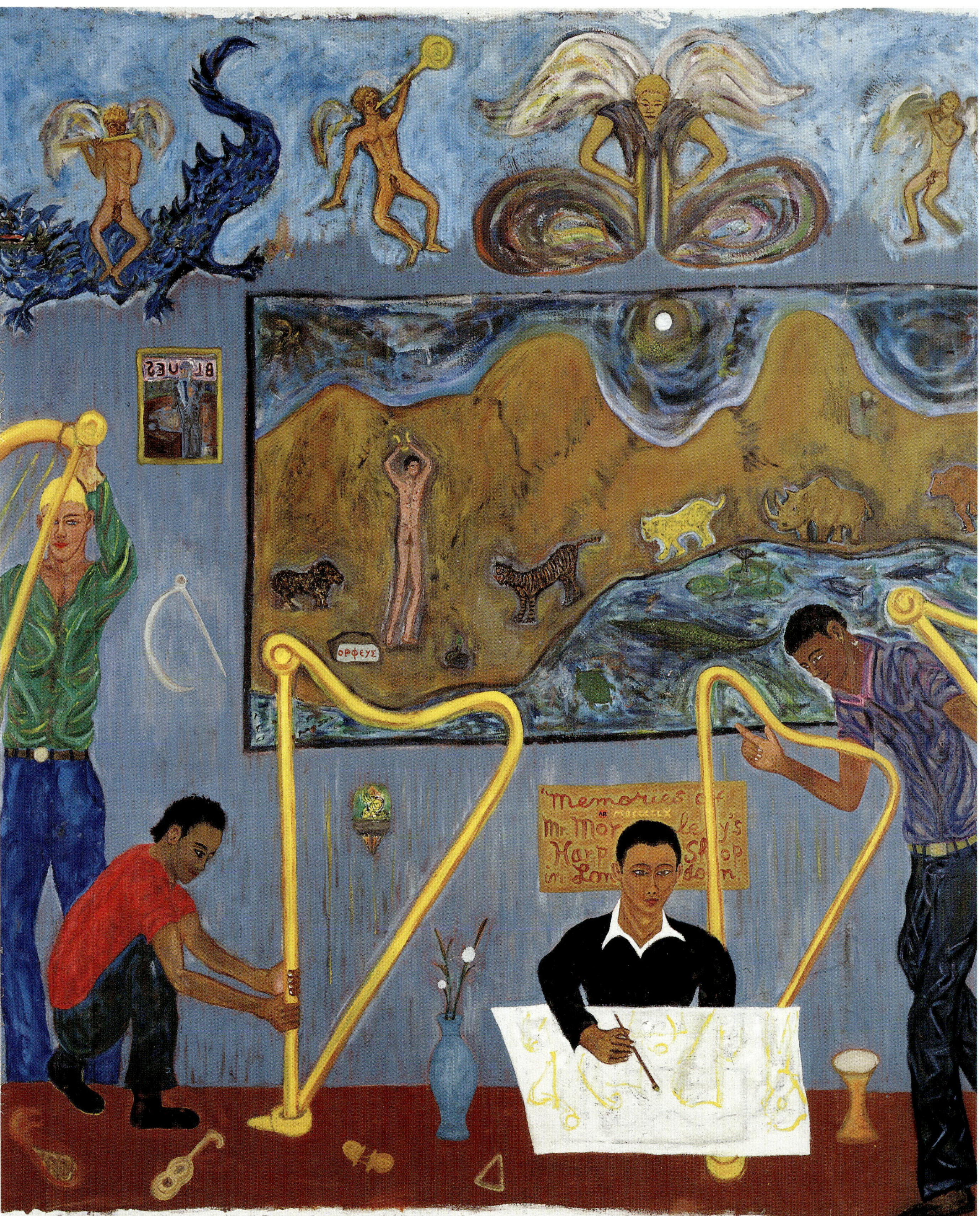
BLUES
ΟΡΦΕΥΣ
'memories of
Mr Mor   ley's
Harp   Shop
in Lon   don.

Six

Painting Against the Grain

A separate chapter on Medalla's paintings rather pulls them out of the flow of his work. He has always produced paintings, drawings and collages, and they have usually been 'figurative'. Even during his kinetic period he produced figurative alongside abstract work. He likes to explore an overall concept or theme, like *The Mohole Flower, A Stitch in Time*, or *Tatlin at the Funeral of Malevich*, in several media simultaneously. I do not believe he has ever felt that 'painting' was at issue in a polemical sense. His attitude has little in common either with the ultra-radical view that avant-garde experiment and modern technology have created the conditions where painting would go out of date and cease to exist, or with the conservative view that experiment has been a temporary aberration or deflection away from a tradition which should be returned to. He went on his independent way. He continued to experiment without becoming the victim of the constant turnovers of style in modern art, which have given every style, in his words, "an auto-obsolescent element". "I am trying to go against that grain [because] I think it is stupid to destroy what was discovered from Manet onwards..."[1] And he continued to look back at the past for discoveries that could help us understand the contemporary world.

In fact, looking at Medalla's work as a whole, I think the dynamic which has always propelled it forward has not been one where new modes like kinetics, or performance, would supersede painting or sculpture. Rather his interest has lain in the reciprocal and paradoxical relationships between the new and traditional modes, especially as regards his underlying conviction that "all is motion and change".

"I think in all my work there has been a desire to provide visual/tactile models of the transformation of matter into energy."[2] If so, this would give us a key to the *raison d'être* of his painting. If the effect of his kinetic sculpture is to make all that is solid insubstantial and changeable, and if his performances and impromptus explore a poetics of the ephemeral, the paradox of his painting, of painting generally, would be to fix what is fleeting. The history of painting as a language and a craft is the history, not only of the production of pure colours from nature, but also the production of substances which would stabilise and fix the colours to last a long time.

The sun-pictures of P.K. Hoenich, contemporary with Medalla's kinetic work, and mentioned in the second chapter, are an apt reference for both sides of the

Opposite: **Memories of Mr Morley's Harp Shop in South Kensington,** 1988, oil on canvas (detail). Collection of the Artist.

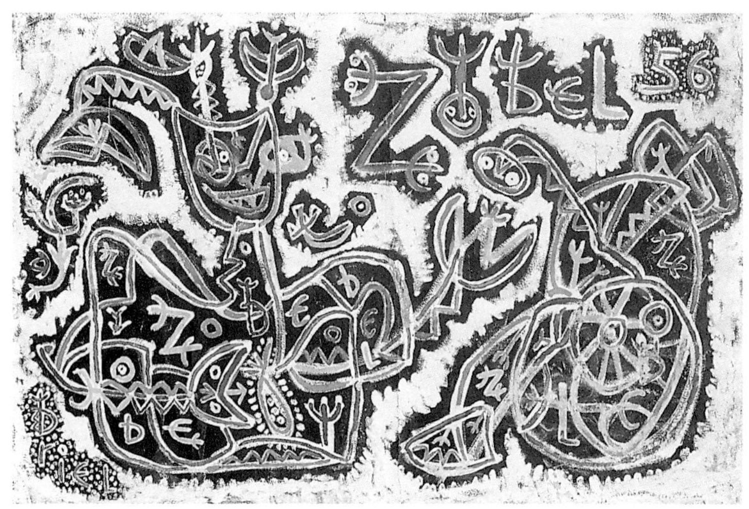

Imaginary Portrait of don Fernando Zobel de Ayala, 1956, Private Collection, Manila.

contradiction. Hoenich was concerned with articulating the fleeting play of sunlight on a wall so that it became a picture without actually becoming fixed: a sort of halfway-house between nature and art (painting). Goya expressed the painter's truth when he said that "in nature there is only sunlight and shadow". The means of representing the immaterial, however, could only be material. To dematerialise the material and materialise the immaterial can be seen as equivalent. They are both part of a movement/stillness, lasting/fleeting, matter/energy dialectic.

A further paradox of painting is that, although at one level and according to one way of understanding, its subject is the momentary and fleeting, at another it is concerned with an experience of the timeless, the changeless. This is one reason for its poignant relationship to human affairs. Its colours not only describe, articulate and struggle as part of historical events, but also simply are.

Although he has never completely abandoned it, painting has been particularly important at two periods of Medalla's life. One was right at the beginning, with the work he produced as a teenager in New York and the Philippines, and the other has been recently, in the last ten years or so, up to today. The extreme separation of these two periods in terms of the artist's own life is echoed in another polar relationship they apparently make: a typically paradoxical or incongruous one. David's early paintings were considered highly avant-garde and rather shocking when they appeared in the Manila of the 1950s. Amongst most Filipino artists at the time, paint was still handled and thought of in the traditional manner, whereas David was already mixing sand with his paint and applying eggshells, bird feathers, sea shells, leaves, animal bones, bullet cases, tin cans and other objects to the canvas. He was amongst the first in the Philippines to respond to the American Abstract Expressionists whose innovations had been transmitted there by Alfonso Ossorio, a painter and collector, member of avant-garde circles in New York and friend of Jackson Pollock. And yet, for all his full-hearted immersion in the expressionist dynamics of the gesture and rude, or *brut*, figuration, Medalla was already showing an ironic self-consciousness and a taste for dandyism and the masquerade by marking his pictures with an enormous pseudonymic signature, 'Gaybriel', which was woven into the expressionist design.[3]

His second major round of paintings began in the mid-1980s and could only appear as the antithesis of avant-gardism in both its modern and post-modern guises. Indeed, it is hard to categorise Medalla's recent paintings or link them with the work of his peers. They distance themselves from the conventions of the unconventional (the artist irked some at the 1992 'Fluxattitudes' exhibition at the New Museum in New York by failing to do what was expected of a Fluxus artist and instead to use the room consecrated to him to work on a large, unfinished, allegorical oil-painting); and his paintings clashed equally with the unconventional treatment of conventions, the whole gamut of self-conscious parody, mimicry, quotation, deconstruction and fragmentation of recent painting genres. They seem to be out on a limb of their own, with a quality of their own: sincere, tender, poetic, awkward yet graceful, autobiographical, richly worked, unfinished. They are his own version of the late 20th century return to painting, his own re-engagement with tradition, his own answer to the question of how it is possible to paint today.

During the 1980s Medalla began to align himself in a provocative way with painterly traditions. On the one hand he liked to confound those who saw him as an apostle of new media by saying that his performances, in fact everything he had done, were 'paintings'. "You've all misunderstood me. I'm basically a painter. I always have been...", I heard him say. And it became possible to see his conjuring with rags and chiffons, with second-hand pyjamas, with lady's hats and frocks as a performed painting. It was a typical case of 'reciprocal mobility' – in other words, to claim for two art forms areas of interaction and identity which are conventionally denied by those with vested interests in isolating one particular form. His references to past artists flowed easily between the two genres:

In both portraits [by Lorenzo Lotto: the presumed *Self-Portrait* in the Borghese

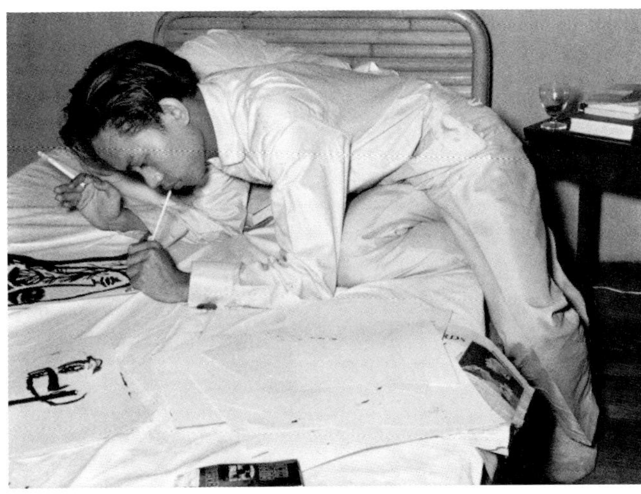
Drawing portrait studies for his painting
The Ecstatic Republic, Ermita, Manilla, 1959.

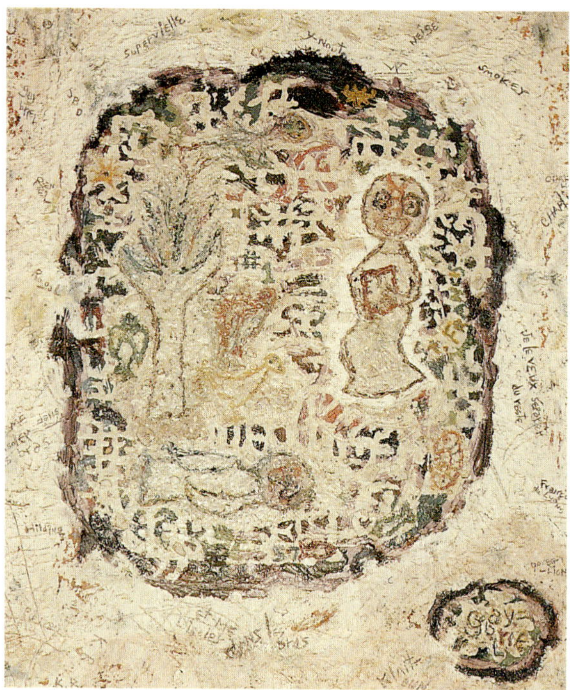

St Francis of Assisi, 1956, mixed media: oil paint, sand, shells.
Private Collection, Manila.

Gallery in Rome and the *Portrait of a Young Man* in the Venice Academy] there are petals scattered on a table; in the Venice portrait the petals are accompanied by a lizard or chameleon or salamander... in the Villa Borghese self portrait, the jasmine and rose petals surround a small skull touched by the right hand of the artist. (I used this image of the skull and flower petals in my second performance in Nice, but in quite a different context - after an execution scene!) Torn petals seem a constant motif in the works of Lorenzo Lotto. I've seen in reproduction two altarpieces by him in which torn petals are scattered on the ground. Lorenzo Lotto was the painter *par excellence* of ephemerality...[4]

On the other hand Medalla conceived for painting itself, as conventionally defined, a new programme of 'realism'. He set out on an attempt to reconnect painting with lived life, which would stretch from the minutiae of daily experience to a larger, cosmic whole. This was his concept of 'Synoptic Realism', a project so ambitious that it really has to be interpreted on two levels: the level of intention or aspiration, and the level of the body of paintings so far produced, or in progress, at the arbitrary moment at which this book is being written. Both levels have validity, if one respects the existence of different triggers, or 'propulsions', or time-scales, where the workings of the imagination are concerned. Both intention and realisation were wrapped up with a period of intense study of Renaissance and Baroque painting which Medalla made in

Italy in 1980, wandering for months from city to city, and between church, palazzo, museum and gallery. These studies joined with the powerful attraction, felt for years and absorbed mainly through books, towards Buddhist painting, especially the mural paintings of the Ajanta caves in India and the Dunhuang caves in China, and Tibetan *tankha* scrolls.

As far as aspiration was concerned, Synoptic Realism would throw its net as widely as possible: its whole aim, as mentioned in Chapter Five, was to integrate the multiple, disparate nature of visual experience, from the traditions of painting, "which are not any longer homogeneous or uni-traditional but a complex amalgam of so many styles and tendencies",[5] to the panoply of modern visual information – the visual and paravisual, microscopic and macroscopic, direct and second-hand – and, on the psychic plane, ranging from conscious and articulate utterance to the world of dreams, desires and memories. The artist summed up Synoptic Realism as:

...the depiction, in all sorts of media (painting, sculpture, video, performance, etc) of the multiple interpenetrating levels of reality (perceptual/optical, sensory/mental, mythical/historical), dream-reality as well as the reality of everyday existence.[6]

When it came to realising these ambitions in paintings, Medalla turned to a number of different structuring devices. One was loosely derived from the Renaissance idea of

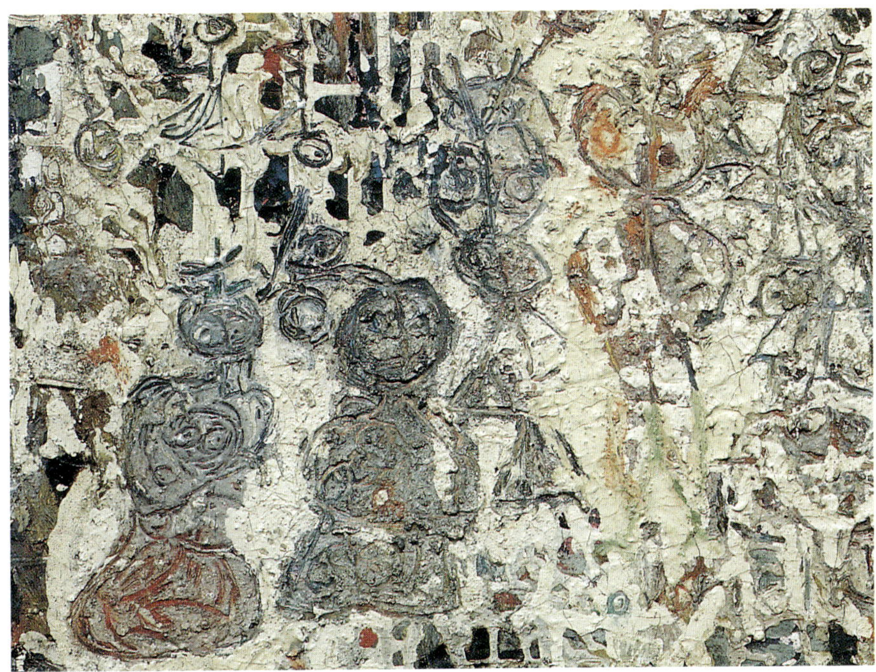

The Joyous Kingdom, 1956, casein and sand on canvas, 46 × 56 cms. Collection Ateneo Art Gallery, Manila.

programmes of paintings based on the five senses, and began with a series, *Parables of Friendship*. This scheme also evolved from the theme of meetings, reciprocity and collaborations which structured many Medalla performances. In 1985 he recounted to Jun Terra his plan for a cycle of paintings based on historical friendships, for example:

...the friendship between father and son - Paracelsus was very friendly with his son, and Rembrandt too with his son, not in a Confucian filial-piety sense, but they were really friends. Rembrandt was very poor and it was his son Titus and his second wife who organised his life so he could paint. And there was a beautiful friendship between Michelangelo and Vittoria Colonna - it survives in poems and letters where this rather misanthropic aged artist full of *terribilità* became a friend of this remarkable woman, a great poet in her own right... Then there is the friendship between Emily Dickinson and the novelist Helena Jackson who wrote *Ramona*... One of these paintings which I want to do is a very interesting group of friendships – the school of Capri it is called. In Capri, at the beginning of the century, there was a group of Russian exiles. Gorky, his publisher Pianitsky, Gorky's mistress who was an actress, the famous Russian bass Chaliapin, and Lenin. They were all friends. It was an interesting moment in time when they were not burdened with running something like the Soviet Union... Apart from that I also want to do a painting on the group of the La Solidaridad and the Indios Bravos [*pioneers of Philippine independence* – GB]: Rizal, Lopez Jaena, the Lunas, Marcelo del Pilar. And I want to include Blumentritt and his friendship with Rizal. I don't want it to be just a documentary record, but an examination. That friendship was very important for Rizal. Without Blumentritt's support Rizal would not have been able to publish his novels – but this will be much later on. I am giving myself a five-year plan...[7]

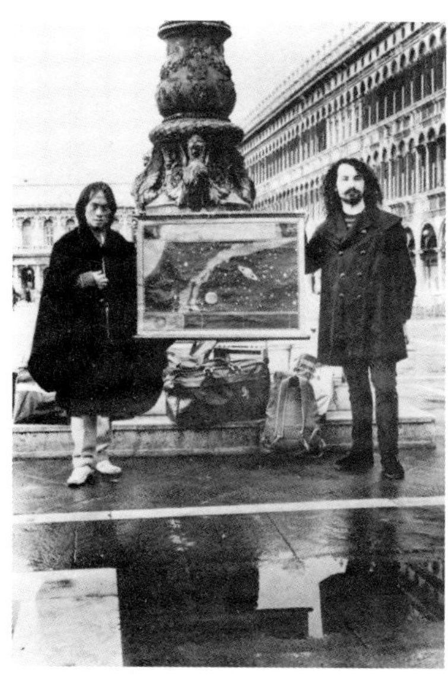

Here They Pose Together, with Lovato Guerrino at Piazza San Marco, Venice, 1981.

Examples were clearly chosen to show that friendships are unpredictable or incongruous according to the stereotypical barriers of age, family, sex, race, class, or profession. They cut across these fixed structures with an affective and kinetic logic of their own. They are themselves metaphors, or equivalents, for other modes of relationship, as David himself hinted most suggestively by linking the theme of friendship with the stylistic programme of Synoptic Realism. This comes out in his several references to Titian's early painting *Sacred and Profane Love*, now in the Villa Borghese, which he described in a letter to the Filipino critic Leo Benesa as "unquestionably the most beautiful painting in Rome".[8] Titian's painting was a model of the fusion of disparate elements in a new synthesis. In his allegorical depiction of two women, one naked symbolising sacred love, the other clothed symbolising profane love, Titian brought together, not only the abstract values of different forms of love, but also the coordinates of space and time, the genres of art (still

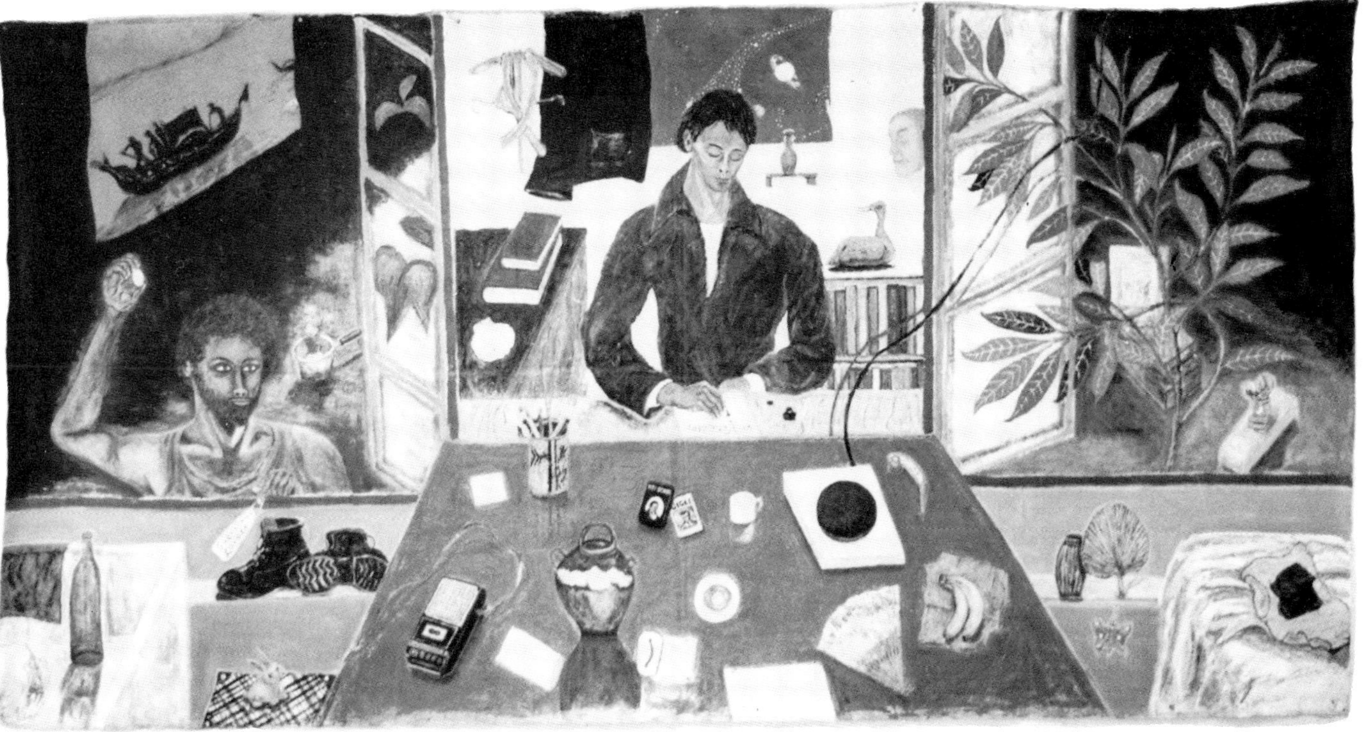

Parables of Friendship: Myself and Lovato Guerrino at Castello in Venice, 1983, Acrylic on canvas.
Collection Agnes Arellano and Michael Adams, Manila.

life, landscape, portraiture), as well as mythological and historical references, in a most subtle and enigmatic integration:

There is between these two women mutual understanding and genial reciprocity. After all, the sacred and the profane are interdependent, not in conflict or opposition as bigots mistakenly assume.[9]

Medalla paraphrased Cézanne to tell me once, with a twinkle in his eye, that Synoptic Realism was an attempt to "do Titian over again from modern culture".

Myself and Lovato Guerrino at Castello in Venice, the largest of Medalla's *Parables of Friendship* so far realised, and concerning his own, not a historical relationship, was begun in 1983 and painted from memory in the unfavourable conditions of a succession of London squats. Medalla himself has given an exhaustive description of its subject-matter, composition, colouring and so on (see Appendix 2). In this painting, a fleeting, magical moment of the kind that matters only to the individual ("Guerrino entered the room in the moonlight bringing me an egg from his

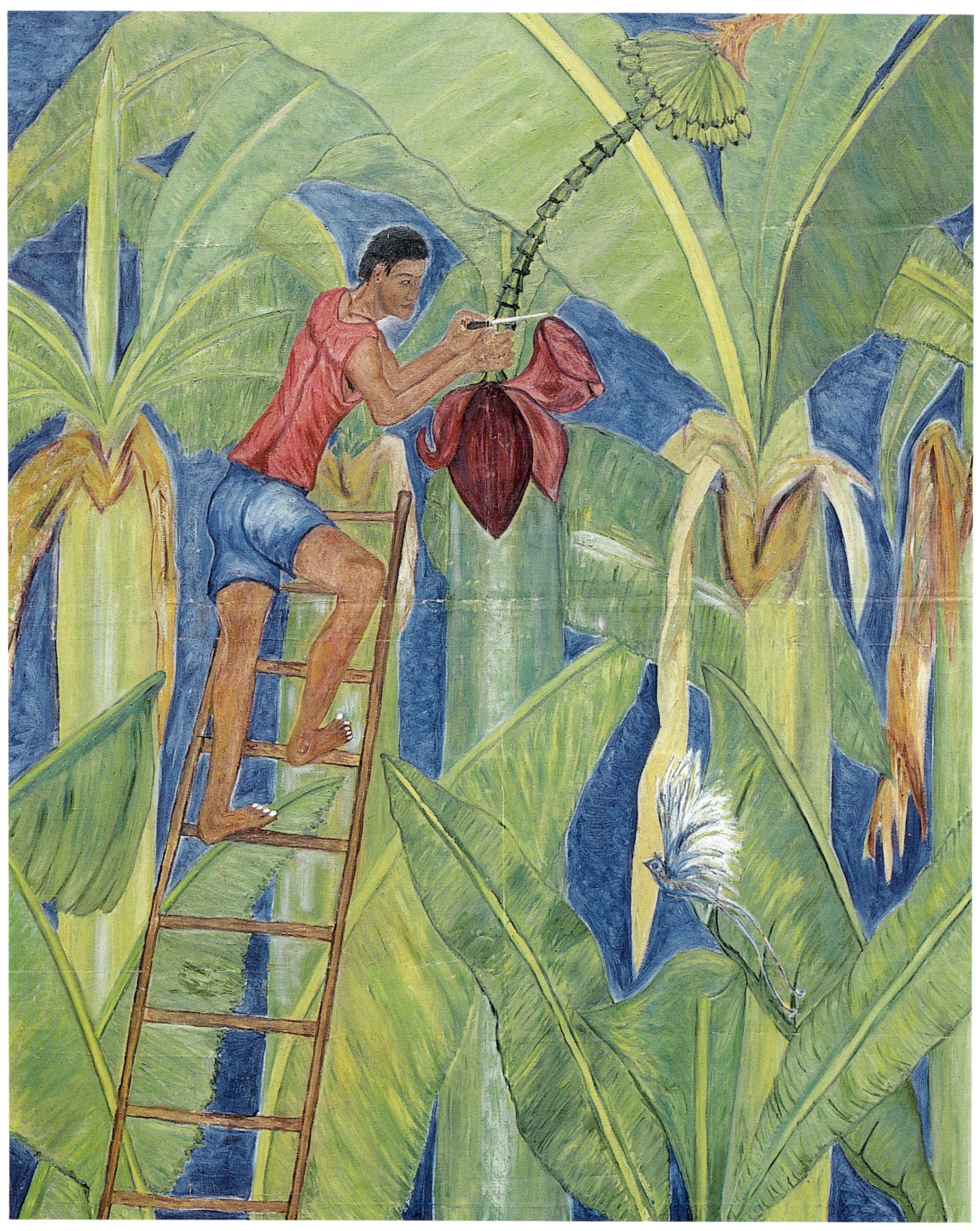

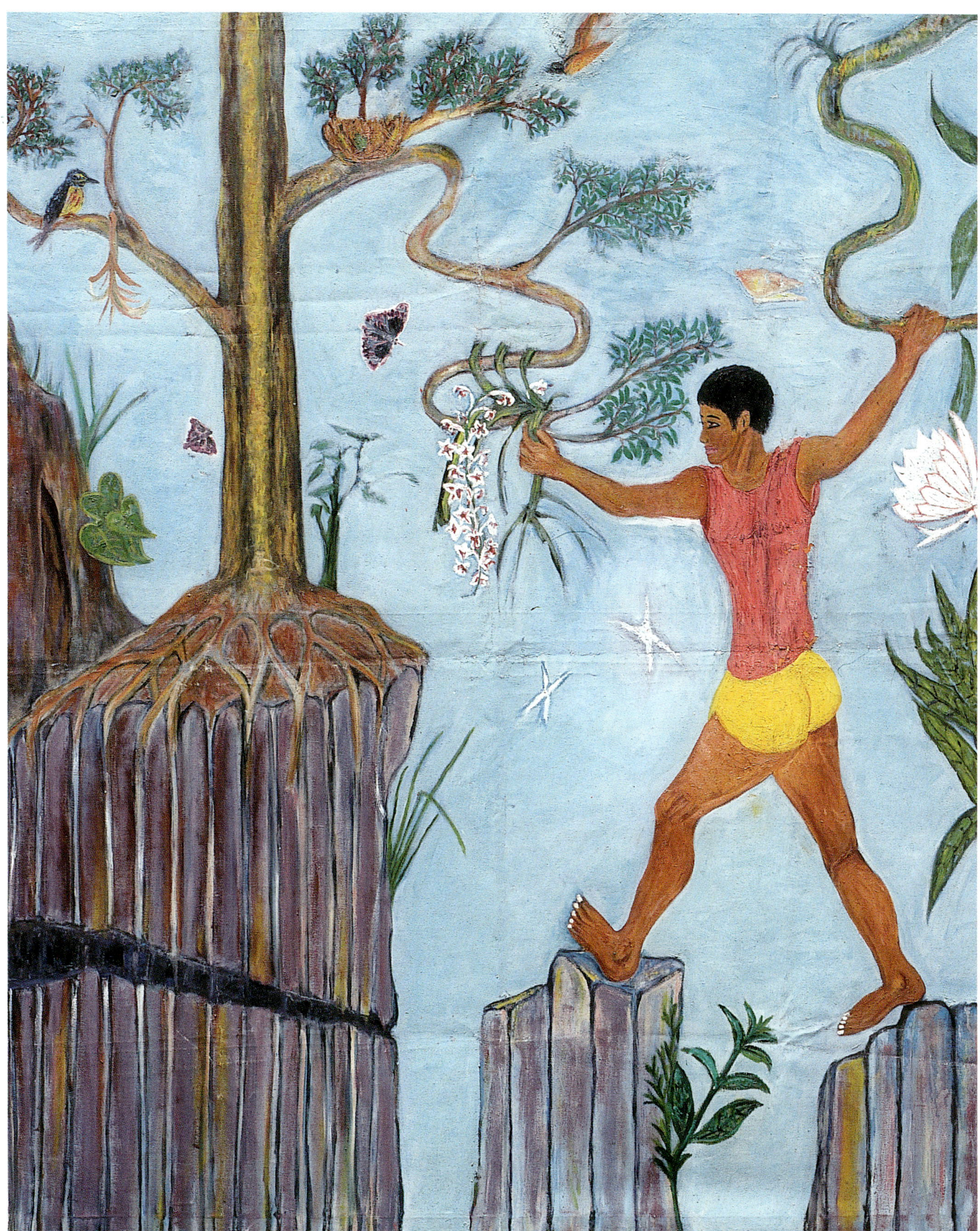

parent's farm in Vicenza"), is meshed in with an elaborate elucidation of two friends' pragmatic and imaginative worlds as revealed through an accumulation of objects and their multiple references. The painting is a fusion of landscape, interior, still-life, portrait and self-portrait conventions. Seen in relation to the parallel work Medalla was doing in performance, and to his previous kinetic and participation art, such a painting shows, beginning with the way the artist mirrors his thinking and working self in the picture, an elegant irony that, alongside the most startling formal changes, genres do persist in the history of art. The stillness of still-life continues to encompass the new.

The richness of cultural objects in *Myself and Guerrino* is echoed by a richness of natural objects in *Luz. Vi. Minda.*, or *Filipiniana*, an ecstatic and tender series of large paintings David produced after his visit to the Philippines in 1985. Each painting features the monumental figure of a young man. His hands reach to the core of some natural cornucopia: the flowing milk of the coconut palm, a vibrant fish which makes a hieroglyph of energy, a chalice-like bird's nest held up against the moon in the cave's mouth, an entanglement of blossoms in an aerial ballet. The artist was clearly deeply stirred by his re-immersion in tropical nature after his years in the northern hemisphere. Memories of childhood suffuse the young workers and the childlike wonder of the mode of depiction. Once again, the *Filipiniana* paintings were intended to be part of some huge projected cycle that never got completed, this time dealing with labour in the Philippines, from the agricultural to the industrial. The paintings that were made, however (five in all), have their own validity. Each one is centred upon the examination of a gesture of taking the gifts of nature without dominating or abusing.

A sexed monkey makes its appearance in one painting, testifying to the erotic dimension of the pictures and to the painter's mischievous subjectivity. Some of Medalla's large pictures of the 1980s and 1990s repeat the motif of the De Pisis performance (p. 159): the artist surrounded by the objects of his desire, his interlocutors, or his fantasised alter egos. His presence ties the strands together of a number of underlying and pervasive themes. Among these are the themes of language, communication and social justice in *A Prophecy*, and the myths of art in *Mr Morley's Harp Shop*.

A Prophecy in the Shadow of La Grand Arche in Paris is a kind of global allegory emerging from a typical nomadic moment. On July 14th 1989, Bastille Day, the 200th anniversary of the French Revolution, the artist had gone to attend the inauguration of La Grande Arche at La Défense in Paris. He arrived early and spoke to a group of immigrant workers from different parts of the world who were cleaning the area where the ceremonies were to take place. Some spoke English but few could speak French. Even the most intelligent person becomes helpless, awkward and easily duped outside their familiar environment, language or mode of discourse. *A Prophecy* combines an image of the artist, derived from a painting of Christ Pantocrator made by an anonymous Catalan artist in the Romanesque period, with a free rendering of a

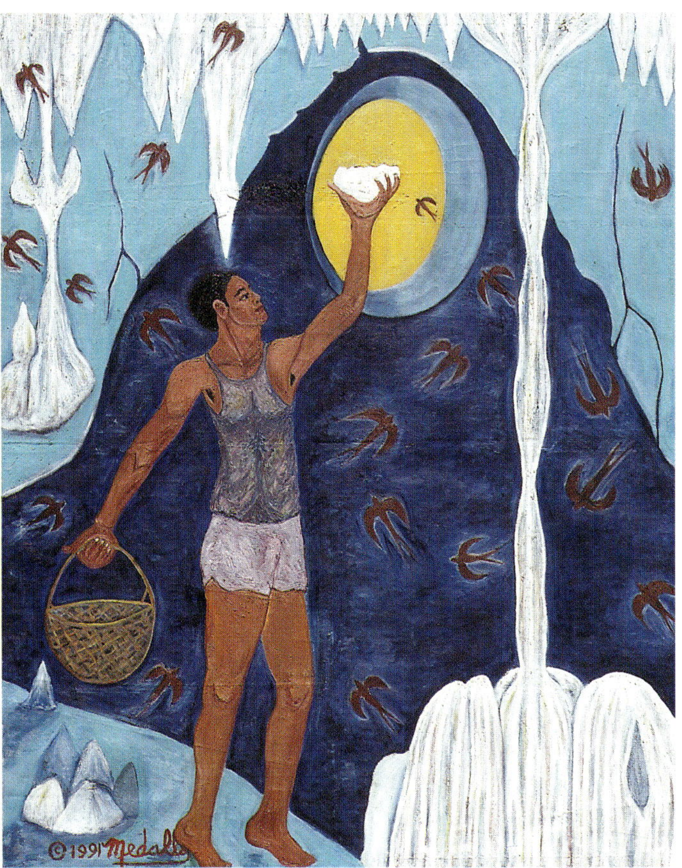 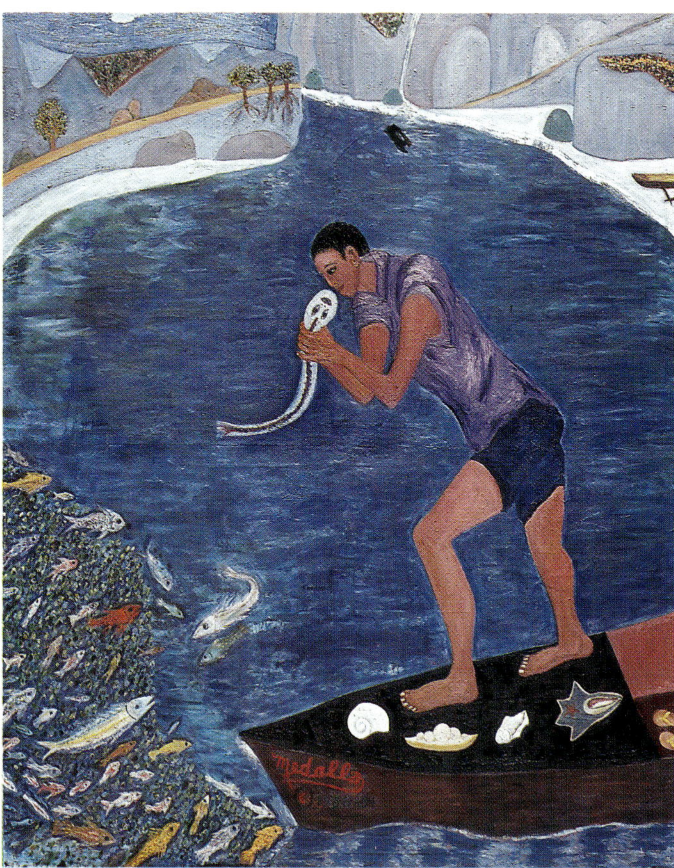

Luz. Vi. Minda. series (or **Filipiniana**), 1986, oil on canvas. Collection of the artist.
Page 174: **Puso ng Saging** ('Heart of the Banana'), 1986.
Page 175: **Binatilyong Kumukuha ng Ligaw na Bulaklak sa Isla de Kalis, Coron, Palawan** ('Young Man Gathering an Orchid on Kalis Island, Coron, Palawan'),1986. Above: **Taong Kumukuha ng Pugad ng Balinsasay** ('Man Gathering the Swift Bird's Nest'), 1986.
Above, right: **Binatang Nakahuli ng Isda** ('Young Man who has Caught a Fish'), 1986.

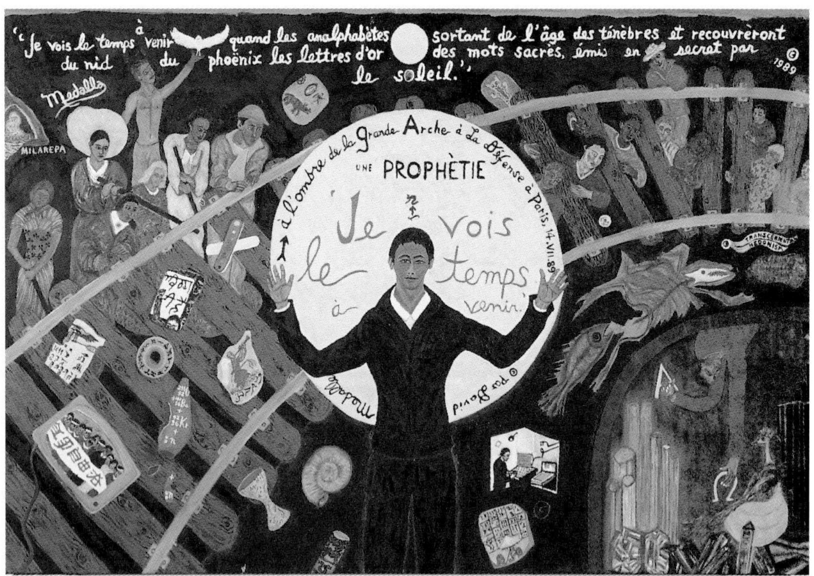

A Prophecy, 1989, oil on canvas, 210 X 310 cms. Collection of the Arts Council of Great Britain.

photograph of Chinese workers and peasants who overturned at night the railway track being used by invading Japanese during the Second World War. Overlaid on these images are fragments of the world's scripts. In the upper left hand corner is an imaginary portrait of the Tibetan poet and yogin Milarepa, who is often depicted in the gesture of listening to the echo of his singing voice. At bottom right a boy recovers from a phoenix's nest the golden letters Alpha and Omega.

A Prophecy is a multi-layered, multi-directional painting which refers to day and night, to sky, earth and subterranean depths, to past and to future, to 'objective' historical events and to subjective dreams. The dynamic motif of the overturning of the railway track of aggression and oppression supports the fragments of human communication visualised in a mode which evokes both the sedimented archaeological past and a possible liberated future. The painting refers to both extinction and renewal. The artist fuses together documentary and symbolic forms. Particularly poignant is his self-image. In this depiction, the 'prophetic' relation he appears to take to the real world and the painted world is neither simply the bystander/observer, nor the heroic protagonist and creator familiar from artistic convention, but the inviter, the open stranger, the potential friend.

Memories of Mr Morley's Harp Shop in London (p. 166) conjures with a different form of hieroglyphic. The large, linear, yellow forms of harps are being brought in and arranged rather than played. In the boys' hands they seem to double for hearts and for angels' wings. An old memory of a magical moment – the sight of harps being rearranged in the window of a shop in South Kensington in the early 60s – is combined with the frieze of an angelic orchestra and a painting-within-the-painting of Orpheus, in a nocturnal landscape, charming the animals with his lyre-playing. The group of boys is multi-racial, as the crowd is in *A Prophecy*. Is the whole painting an allegory of the powers of art to unite, to sublimate aggression and to "withdraw poison and fear from the atmosphere"? Are the men 'tamed' by the gentle musical/angelic metaphor of placing the harps in the window, complemented by the scene of Orpheus taming the wild animals in the elemental landscape, and the artist himself, reflected in the shop window, explaining the scene by painting it? Are there echoes back to *Boys of England* and forward to Medalla's New York Port Authority '*Watteau*' performances? Perhaps there are, but the painting is finely tuned in its paradoxes and contradictions. It contains the celebration and the curbing of energy, the subtle workings of enchantment, and the inevitable coercive moulding of nature symbolised in the invention of musical instruments. What attitude does the artist take up towards such phenomena? David likes to quote Rimbaud's remark: "*Tant pis pour le bois qui se trouve violon!*" (Too bad for the wood that finds itself a violin!')

In most significant recent art we see the invention of an aesthetic of the fragment. One of its *raisons d'être* has been to resist the creation of fake unities and the false homogenisation performed by the mass media. It is a testimony of the artist's independence and truth-telling. Taking on this experience of the fragmentary and disjointed, David Medalla's paintings seem to try to go further and to seek out a new kind of integrative process, to intimate a new harmony made out of the flux of the incongruous, the multi-faceted and the many-layered.

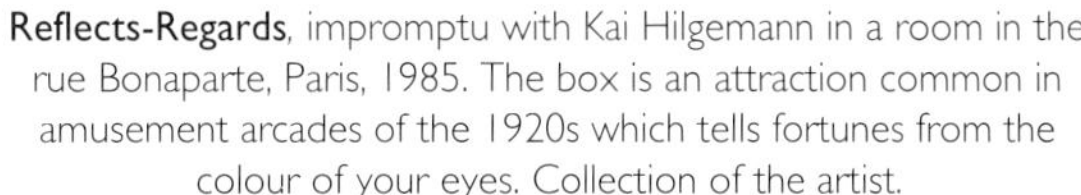

Reflects-Regards, impromptu with Kai Hilgemann in a room in the rue Bonaparte, Paris, 1985. The box is an attraction common in amusement arcades of the 1920s which tells fortunes from the colour of your eyes. Collection of the artist.

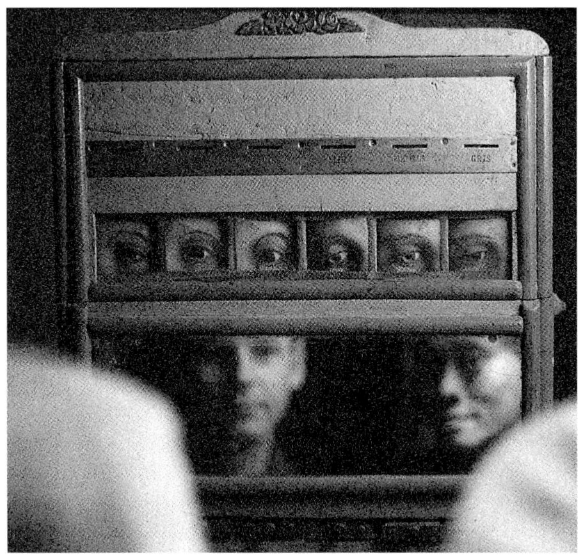

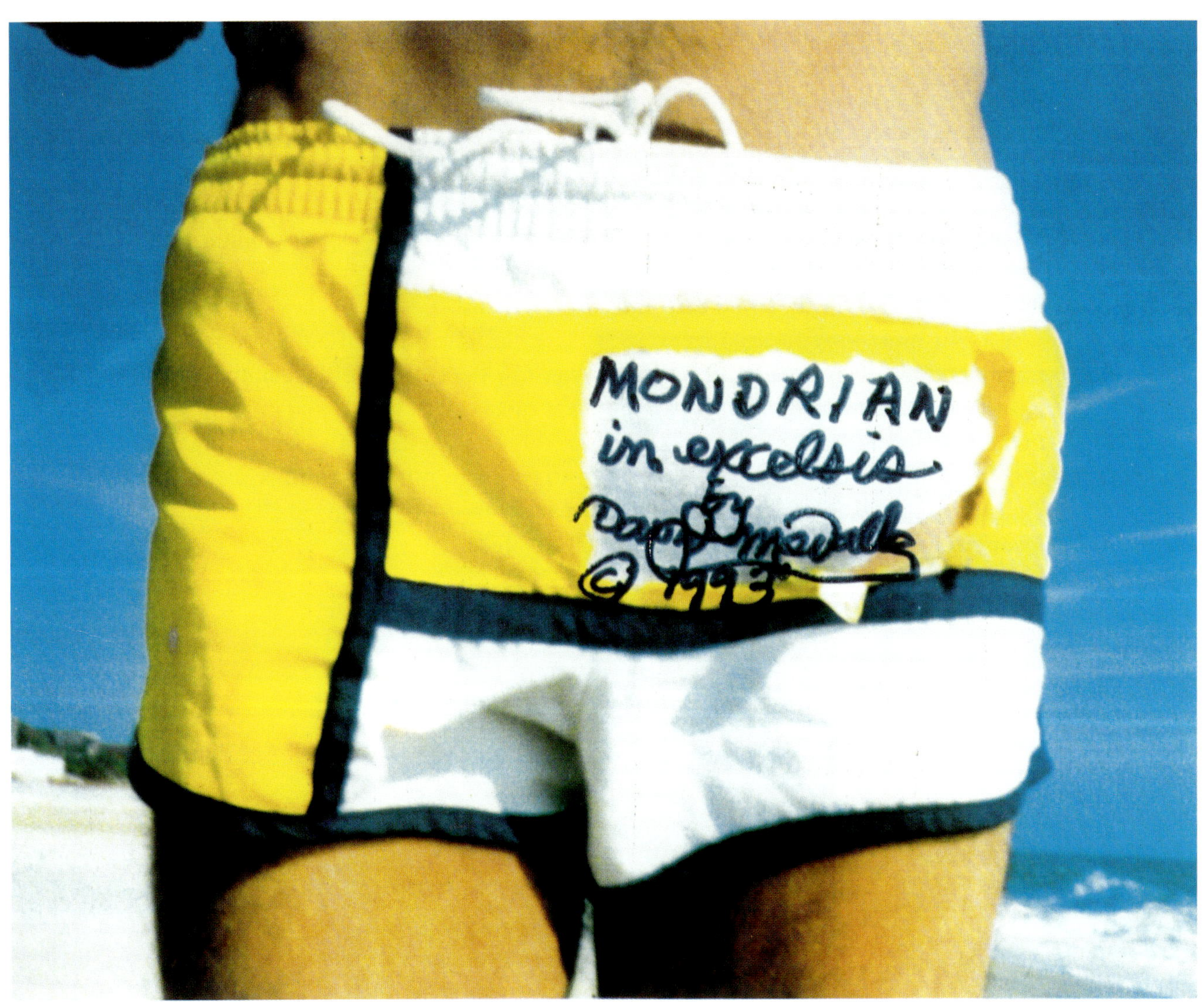

Mondrian in Excelsis, impromptu with Adam Nankervis, Fire Island, New York, 1993. Collection of the artist.

Seven

Coda: Unfinished Business

I hope that an air of finality will not hang over a final chapter. Just as it is impossible to make a 'complete' book about the work of David Medalla, or about any artist for that matter, so it is impossible to call it finished. This is, indeed, as much an aspect of the 'impossible' as are the unrealised (if not unrealisable) dreams and projects for geomorphic, aerial or interplanetary art works which Medalla has articulated throughout his career and has lately called his 'Art of the Impossible'. The enigmas surrounding art, its relationship to life (and even to death, as will become clear in this chapter), are called enigmas because they are not susceptible to a direct approach or a final solution. "Questions and answers about any artist's life and art will always be endless and therefore will only be partial".[1] Medalla's *The Secret Portrait of* ... (p. 37) conceptualises this infinity by its mass of questions, of sample questions, which may bear on the complex amalgam of transitory factors which comes to constitute 'the portrait'. 'Was this portrait painted in the city, or in the countryside?', 'Was it painted in silence, or accompanied by conversation or music?', and so on. The more direct questions there are, the more they point in every direction.

The Secret Portrait of ... is a youthful text dating from 1954 in New York, according to Medalla. He revived its enquiry, or reissued it, in 1992, during a second period when he has been living mainly in New York City. Along with a number of other earlier ideas, it came to fit a kind of double strategy he adopted in the face of an ever more rapid institutionalisation of art and its fetishisation by the art market. On the one hand he assumed a growing mood of ironic negation towards conventional and simplistic measures of success (expressed in his titles, The *Secret* Portrait, Art of the *Im*possible, University of *Failure*, Site and Sight/*Un*seen, etc). On the other his mood was one of exultation towards the possibilities of a new culture emerging which would unite the urgent demands of everyday life with the transcendent powers of art.

After taking part in the exhibition 'Here and There: Travels II', curated by Chris Dercon at the Clocktower Gallery on Broadway and Leonard Street in 1989, Medalla decided to stay on in New York. He found himself a tiny room on Lexington Avenue in midtown Manhattan, a sort of hole-in-the-wall, small crevice or perch, from which he roamed over the city in his customary form of art-life cruising. Curiously enough, about twenty years before, Hélio Oiticica had spent six years in Manhattan, occupying a room on the Lower East Side, and also roaming over the city in an activity he liked to call "the experimentalised day-to-day", a sort of fusion of thinking and

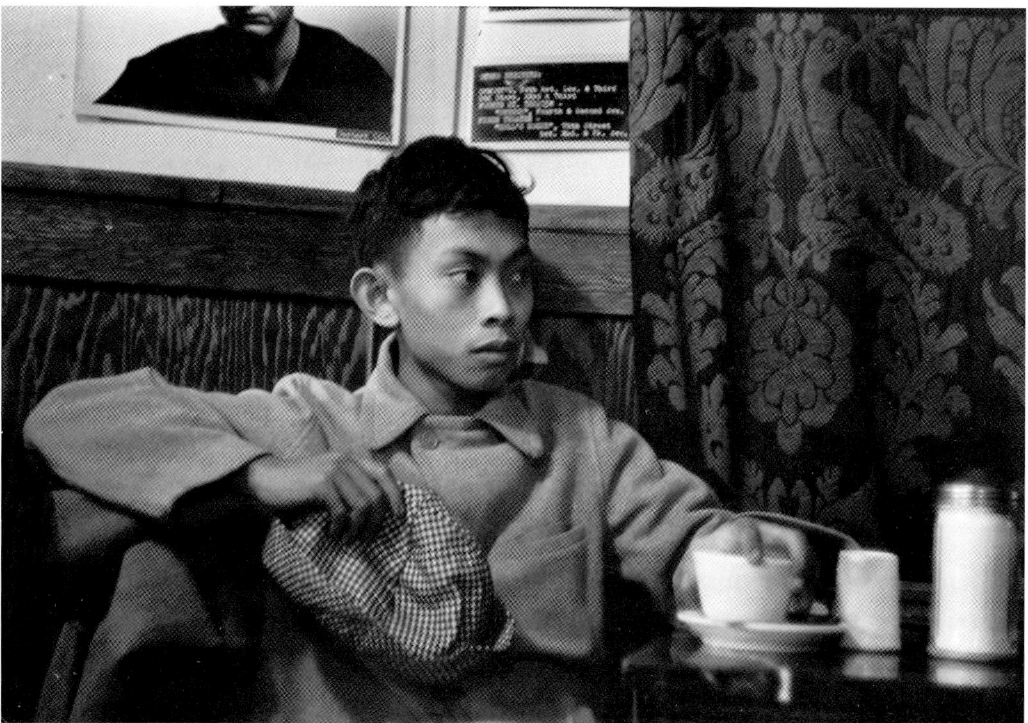

In the Café Rienzi, Greenwich Village, New York, 1955.

living processes.[2] Oiticica's activities became hard to separate into conventional artistic categories of the visual, the verbal, the performative, and so on. Similarly, the ethnic diversity and dynamic actuality of New York have in some way had the effect on Medalla of rendering his past work and past life simultaneous and present. He in New York, or New York in him, becomes an experience of the 'synoptic', and many themes are interwoven in a new mosaic.

A cross-section of 'Medalla in Manhattan' would reveal him working in several genres at the same time. In 1990 and 1991 he was writing a weekly column for the *Filipino Express*, a newspaper of New York's Filipino community. His writing there has the tone of a genial *flâneur*, weaving things seen and people encountered the length and breadth of Manhattan, into lightweight but serious reflections. At the same time he was working, in the minute space of his room, on a series of large paintings, *New York Epiphanies*, in which the city becomes the scene of imaginary encounters poeticised and fantasised as allegories of culture. The sincere mood and sustained production of his paintings contrasted again with the improvisatory and ramshackle presentation of his performances in which, by ironic paradox, he reflected on value through the medium of the valueless. A long piece he gave in the Great Hall of Cooper Union in March 1992 was called *Five Immortals at Drop-Dead Prices*.[3] In turn, the performances became the subject of literary treatment in the 'synoptic texts' of a book produced in 1990, *A Shot in the Dark*.[4] Twenty-five poems reflect back on the experience of making performances over several years as an intricate, unpredictable conjunction of props, places and people. In September 1990 Medalla gave a series of lectures at the Museum of Modern Art, entitled 'The Dream of Yadwigha', on "the sources in global cultures of modern art".[5] At the same time he was dashing off the hundreds of torn-paper masks and staging impromptus in New York and London, many with the young Australian artist Adam Nankervis.

The first of his New York Epiphanies, with its ceremonious title, *Marianne Moore on a Pangolin Welcoming to Brooklyn Mei Lan Fang from Peking*, is clearly a special way of conceiving of the "integration of the positive aspects of various cultures", which he had argued for in his MOMA lectures. 'Epiphany' suggests an ecstatic vision, a transfigured moment, occurring in the course of ordinary, everyday New York life, and the imagined 'meeting' between the American female poet and the great transvestite star of Peking opera in the 1920s – the meeting of cultures at various levels in other words – is portrayed according to an appreciation of the correct behaviour of host and guest which Medalla had always admired in the thought of Marianne Moore. Both ride fabulous beasts incongruous in the New York context and would-be anachronistic were they not themselves merely the products of metamorphosis.

It is remarkable to what extent Medalla's New York production is populated by ghosts. The poet and actor in the painting just described, the ghosts of Federico García Lorca, José Martí and Vladimir Mayakovsky in *Palimpsests of Poets' Passions*, a performance at the Clocktower Gallery; Piet Mondrian in an elaborate homage-project occupying Medalla at the present time; the *Five Immortals* in the performance at Cooper Union; Michel Foucault in the *Three*

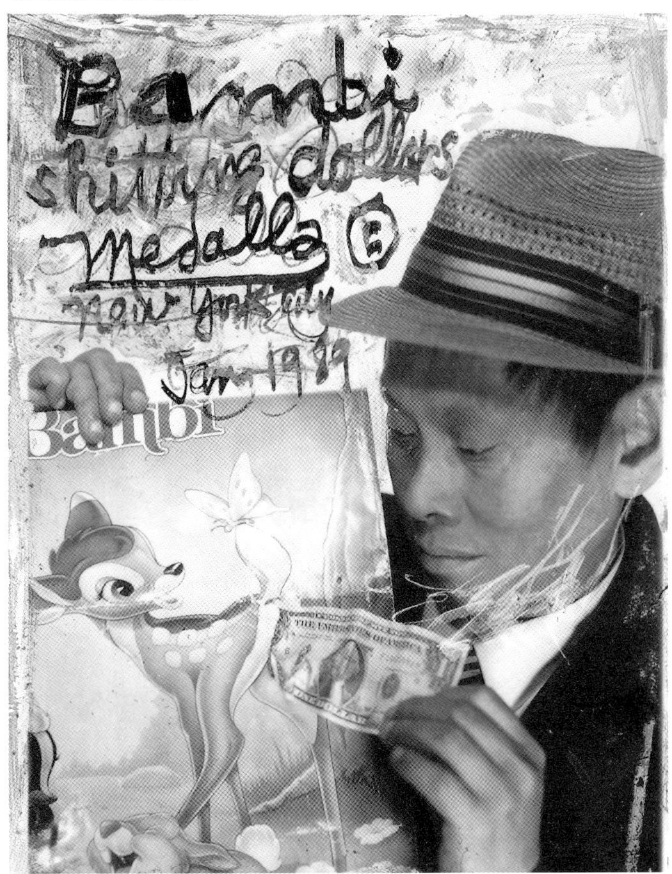

Bambi Shitting Dollars, New York, 1989, painted polaroid. Collection of the artist.

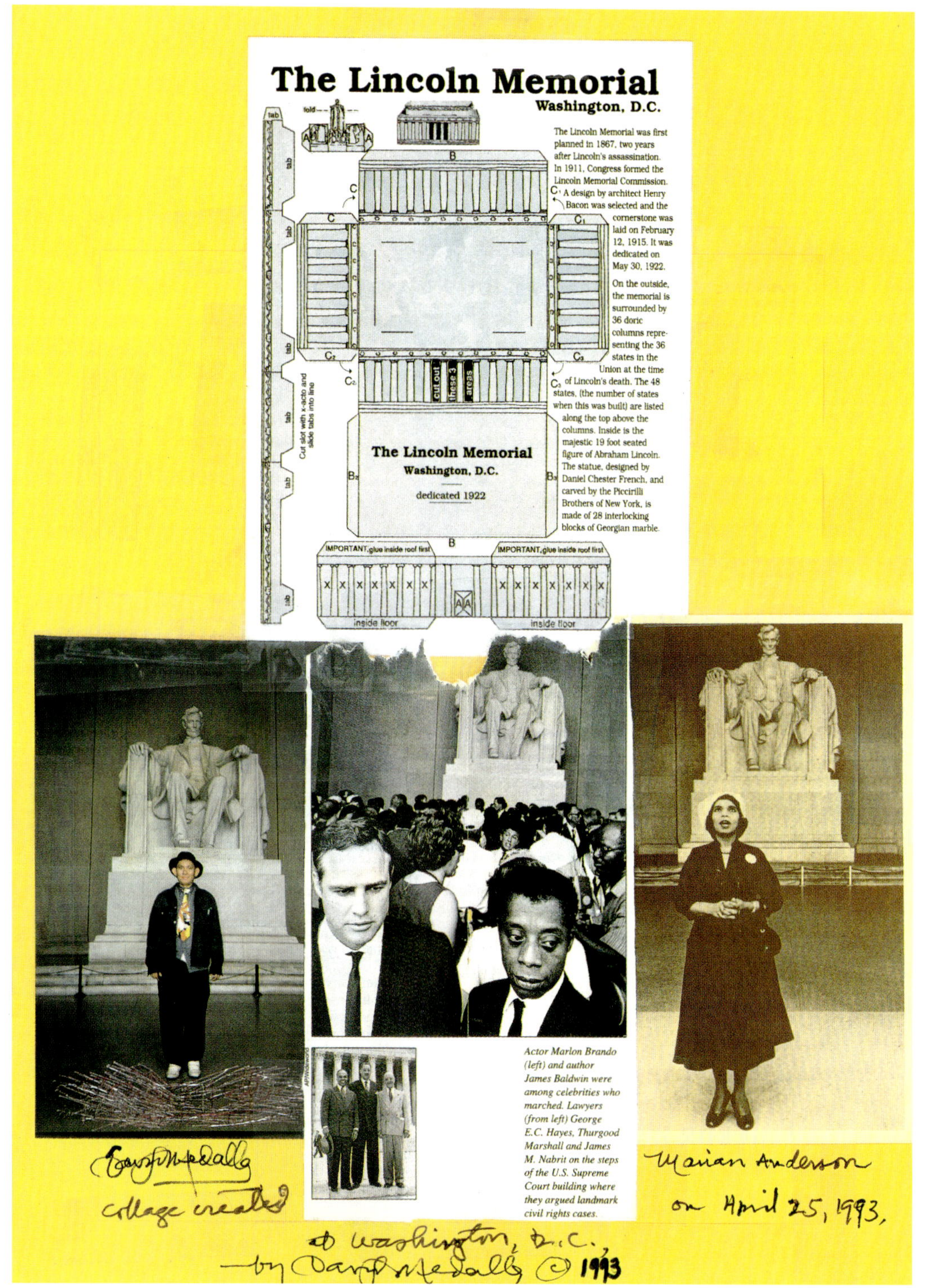

Actor Marlon Brando (left) and author James Baldwin were among celebrities who marched. Lawyers (from left) George E.C. Hayes, Thurgood Marshall and James M. Nabrit on the steps of the U.S. Supreme Court building where they argued landmark civil rights cases.

Ghost Plays about Michel Foucault, a current series of solo performances, the first of which he gave as a recitation at Café Nico in the Lower East Side, and many more. What are they doing in a city where the presence of a ghost has a piquancy, perhaps, that it would not have in London or Rome? I believe there are several ways of interpreting Medalla's preoccupation. It happened that one day, while walking on West 23rd Street, he fell down and cut his leg. The wound refused to heal and, suspecting he had AIDS, he went to have himself HIV tested. He was cleared. Perhaps it was relief at being inexplicably spared this inexplicable fate, mixed with sympathy for those not spared, that made him lighten and ironise the whole matter by compiling an index of *Incongruous Deaths*. This was a return to an old idea he had tried out in Barcelona in 1979: a performance based on people, artists and others, who had somehow copped it absurdly by a tiny shift in their customary mode of behaviour. For example there was the composer Alkan, a contemporary of Chopin, who died crushed by the bound volumes of his own musical scores which fell on him when he tried to retrieve them from his heavily-loaded bookcase; the composer Lully, who tapped his foot accidently with his baton while conducting and died of gangrene; the poet Rilke, who accidentally pricked his eye with the thorn of a rose while smelling it and succumbed to an infection; or the Catalan architect Antoní Gaudí, who stepped back to look at the progress of his building and was killed by a passing tram...[6]

If some in this throng of ghosts enable one to laugh at the fragility of life and the absurdity of death, others protest most vigorously at all those who pretend to profit from the death of another. One of the most attenuated, but nonetheless real, examples is the profit to be made out of the artist's death. "Art is a posthumous industry!" David once remarked to me bitterly, in a moment of extreme frustration with the system which feeds precisely on removing art from its transformative relationship to life. The series of current projects revolving around the figure of Mondrian explore this contradiction. They were partly inspired by reading Robert Motherwell's account of Mondrian's death, in considerable poverty, in New York in 1944.[7] In

Opposite: **Songs of Freedom: The Lincoln Memorial**, 1983, collage. Collection of the artist.

Painting the first in his cycle **New York Epiphanies**, entitled **Marianne Moore on a Pangolin Welcoming to Brooklyn Mei Lan Fang from Peking**, oil on canvas. Photo taken in Medalla's room during the 'Fluxattitudes' exhibition, The New Museum, New York, 1992.

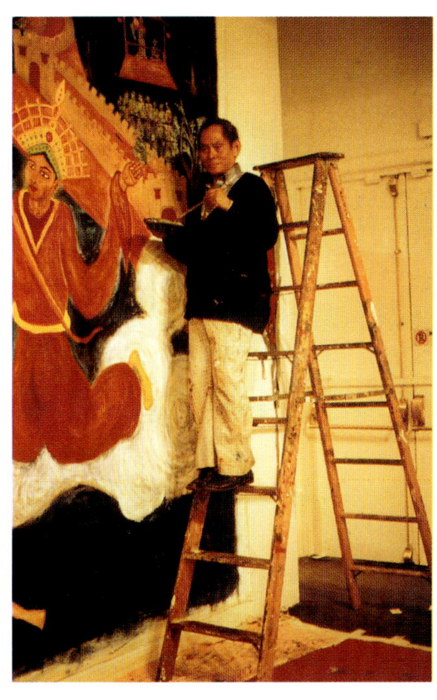

delirium on his deathbed, Mondrian, normally grave and reserved in his behaviour, "openly cursed museum officials and critics of the greatest prominence". Writing from memory in 1980, Motherwell observed that "in the days after Mondrian's funeral I became aware, for the first time, of the phenomenon that I have seen repeated too often since, viz, that when a great artist dies, the living fight over his bones".

Alfred H. Barr Jnr, the prominent critic and curator who delivered the oration over Mondrian's grave in a huge anonymous cemetery on the edge of New York City, referred to Mondrian as a sincere and devoted but minor painter. The ironies are considerable, since Barr was, even in his eulogy, dismissing Mondrian as a failure on the basis of paintings which, for Mondrian, only represented what he could afford to produce, and in no way corresponded to his dream and ambition to "do whole cities", as Motherwell wrote. Medalla's 1990s Mondrian homages involve a part called *Mondrian in Extremis*, performances based on Mondrian's last illness and delirium. In one of them, Mondrian sees a vision in the distant future of the spirit of a cleaning woman in a Dutch bonnet chasing away the HIV virus. Another part called *Mondrian in Excelsis* is a series of fantastic environmental or participatory projects, one of which is called *The Flying Mondrians*. "A small squadron of private planes will fly over the

Cloud Gates, 1994, and a plate from Stukeley's **Stonehenge**, 1740.

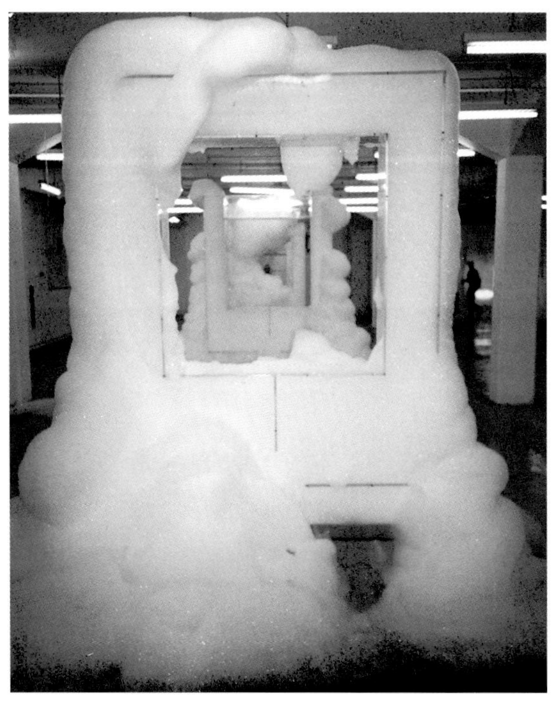
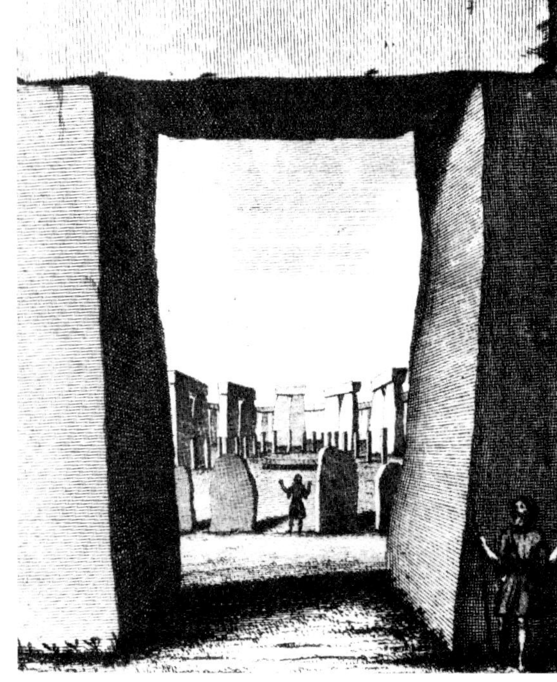

Philippine and Hawaiian islands and the Pacific at night. They will project large squares and rectangles of blue, yellow, red and white onto the dark landscape and sea, transforming them for a passing instant into a huge environmental version of a Mondrian."[8]

It is as if Medalla were trying as many ways as possible, sometimes tender, sometimes ironical, sometimes extravagant, of reconnecting with the 'living' Mondrian, who after all was a mass of contradictions himself, in an effort to overturn the ways in which the forces of commerce, museology and academic art history have rendered Mondrian 'dead'. In what way can artists be present when they are no longer present in body, when only the objects they made remain: how can they continue to exert a spiritual, a creative, an emancipatory force? It is a question which goes to the heart of our culture. An answer must in some way involve our capacity for, our sensitisation to, transformations which are incorporeal, a bridging of the physical world and the world of dreams and ideas. With all its indissoluble connection to the sensuous body, the inner life is a conceptual, imaginary space. And so, therefore, is the outer life. Simultaneously with his projects which conjure the ghosts of artists, poets, performers of the past, Medalla has been planning a new "mass participation propulsion". Called *The Dream*, it would consist of an enormous translucent plastic head lying as if asleep atop a building (or over a highway, on a river, etc). In the area of the neck would be a circular table with pads on which the public would be invited to "describe, inscribe or draw the objects in their dreams".[9] The drawings would be videotaped, stored, and projected inside the translucent head so they would glow at night. Theoretically, there could be 'dreaming heads' at various points around the world, and peoples' dreams could be transmitted from one side to the other by means of satellite.

With this further mention of dreaming (and this book's unwillingness to declare an end), I remember a favourite parable of David Medalla's (the subject of a performance he once made together with John Dugger in the fountains of Trafalgar Square, London, in 1968). It comes from the writings of the Chinese philosopher Chuang-tzu. Chuang-tzu fell asleep and dreamed he was a butterfly. When he woke up he was not sure if he was Chuang-tzu who had dreamt he was a butterfly, or a butterfly now dreaming he was Chuang-tzu...

If there is an answer to the paradox, it can only be in reciprocity. Is not the wit of Chuang-tzu's parable itself a device of the merging of incongruous opposites: the weighty human and the effervescent butterfly? Likewise, the wit in Medalla's work has always danced around antagonistic pairs of opposites, drawing them into dialogue and erasing the boundaries between them. Some, like the dichotomy between life and death, creation and destruction, microcosm and macrocosm, sensual and cerebral, durable and ephemeral, or dreaming and waking, belong to a 'timeless' mode. Others are topical and urgent, like the national, ethnic and social conflicts which threaten to

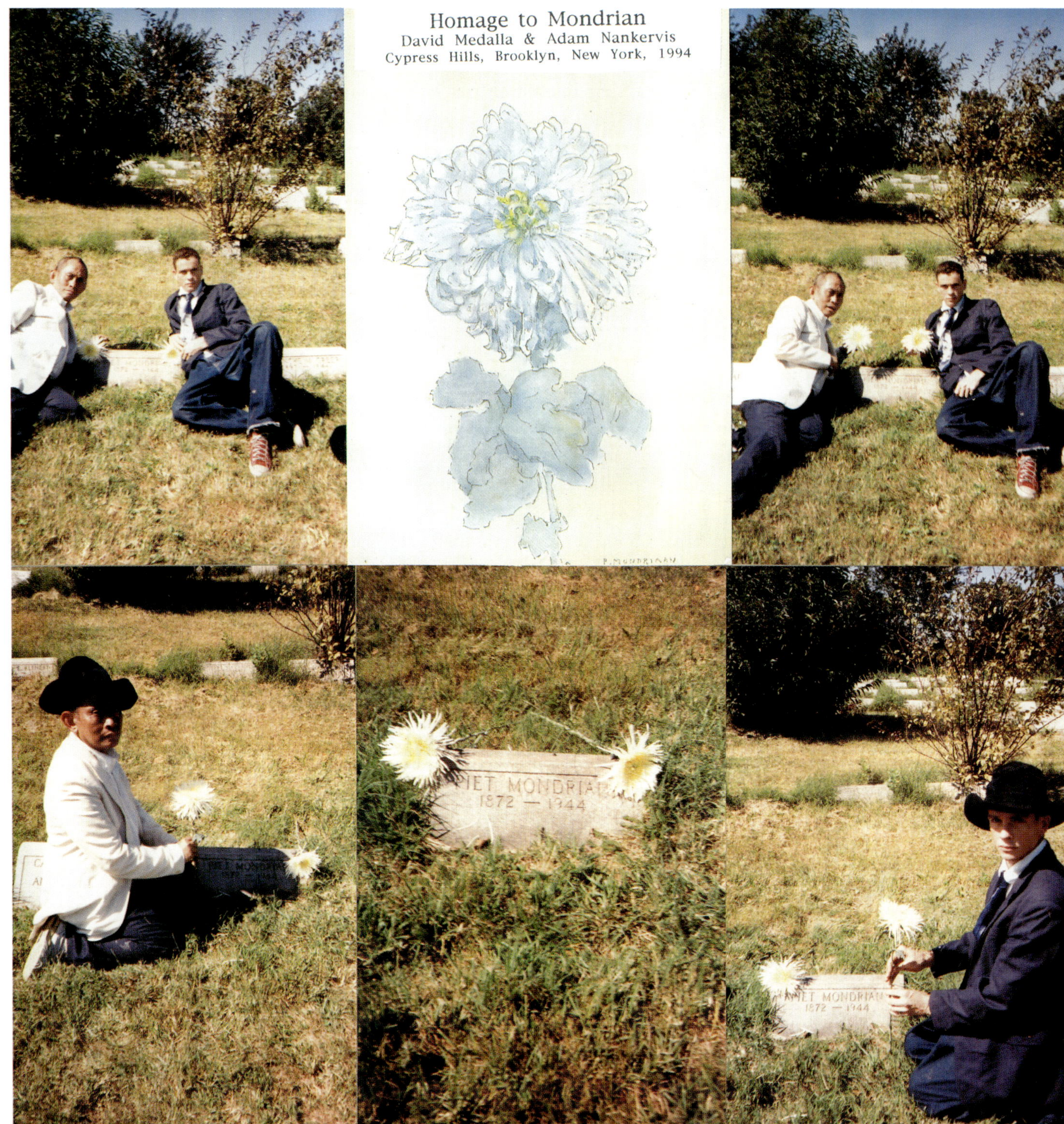

Homage to Mondrian
David Medalla & Adam Nankervis
Cypress Hills, Brooklyn, New York, 1994
P. MONDRIAN

consume our world. Or again, these poles may refer to the enigmas of the aesthetic, such as the boundary between performing and spectating, between art and life, innovation and tradition, the individual and the shared. The list is endless because each instance is itself a model of the whole.

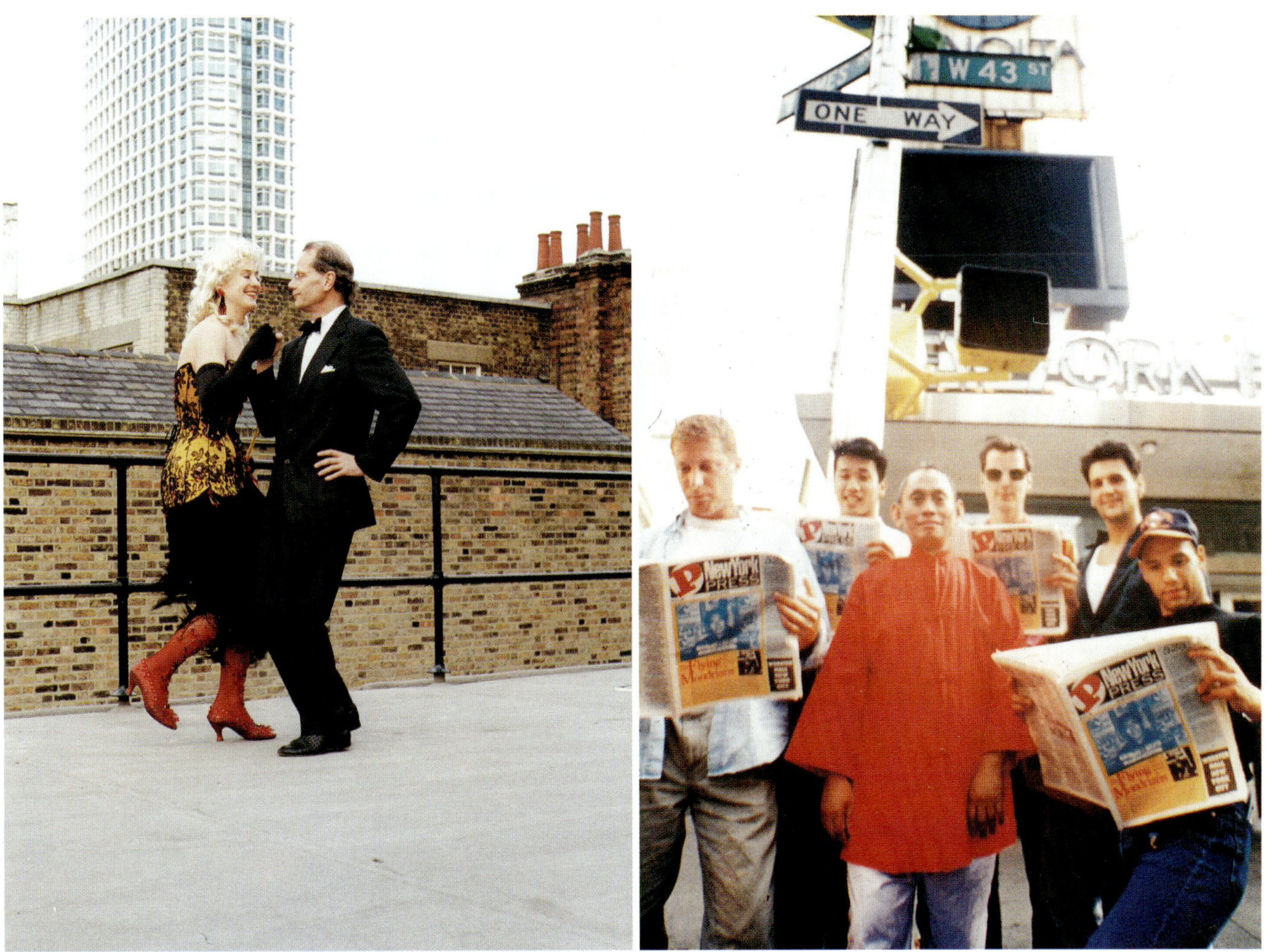

Above, left: Rose English and Guy Brett (as Piet Mondrian) dancing the boogie-woogie. Scene from a video by Tina Keane, **David teaching Rose and Guy the Boogie-Woogie**, shown at the Mondrian Fan Club, 55 Gee Street, London, New Year's Eve, 1994. Right: **Come Together Right Now!**, Mondrian Fan Club impromptu at Times Square, New York, August 1994. L to r: Andrew Reyner, Peter Ponniah, DM, Can Oral, Jens Veneman, Marcel Kahi Gonzalez. Collection of the artist.

Opposite: **Homage to Mondrian**, impromptu with Adam Nankervis at Mondrian's grave, Cypress Hills, New York, 1994. Collection of the artist.

Notes

Foreword

1. Ilya Zdanevich, poet, typographer, who took the name Iliazd when he came to France in 1921, was a friend and collaborator with Kruchenyk and the Futurists. He and the painter Mikhail Ledentu sometime around 1913 launched the shortlived movement called 'veschestvo' which means 'everythingism' which allowed artists to "use and combine all the forms of art known in the past" in response, it seems, to the exclusive futurist doctrines.

2. In his description of what he called "felicitous space" Bachelard said he sought "to determine the human value of the sorts of space that may be grasped, that may be defended against adverse forces, the space we love ... eulogized space" (*The Poetics of Space*, New York, 1964, p xxxi).

Chapter 1

1 Purissima H. Benitez, 'David Medalla: The '60s and '70s', Masters Degree thesis at the Courtauld Institute of Art, University of London, 1992, p. 33. Unpublished.

2 The totally unpredictable and surprising list of Medalla's performance venues amounts in itself to a most elastic understanding of the notion of 'a space for art' (see Appendix 1). From the Great Hall of the Academy in Venice to a bar in Brooklyn, from the Jantar Mantar environmental observatory at Jaipur to the Rotterdam fleamarket. Two of his more unexpected events involved "modern forms of secular exorcism" which he carried out in the former villa of the Nazi leader Hermann Goering at Villefranche-sur-Mer, outside Nice, with its parking space for a submarine (1979), and in the former mansion of Imelda Marcos in New York, with its tacky, mirror-lined discothèque, where he was invited to stay by officials of the new Philippine government after the Marcos's fall from power (1990).

3 Quoted in Catrina Neiman, 'Art and Anthropology: The Crossroads, An Introduction to the Notebook of Maya Deren', *October*, New York, no 14, Fall 1980, p. 15.

4 Rasheed Araeen, *The Other Story*, South Bank Centre, London, 1989, p. 56.

5 Benitez, Interview with David Medalla, op cit.

6 Ibid, pp. 2-4.

7 David Medalla, in conversation with the author, London 1976.

8 Brandon Taylor, interview with David Medalla, *Artscribe*, London, no 6, April 1977, p. 22.

9 Jun Terra, interview with David Medalla (part 2), *San Juan*, Manila, August 1985, p. 5.

10 David Medalla, 'Paris-London: Memories of the Sixties', *And*, London, no 17, 1988, p. 8.

11 David Medalla, 'Some Reflections on the Random in Life and Art', unpublished text, Rotterdam, 1985.

12 This phrase 'The Desire and Pursuit of the Whole' is the title of a book by Frederick Rolfe (Baron Corvo), who himself took it from Plato. It was also the title of a performance Medalla gave with the young Italian dancer Alessandro Fiorella at the Diorama, London, 1986.

13 Medalla wrote poetry from an early age, and he continues to use his own poems as texts for his performances. The artist-poet is central to Asian cultural traditions and has also been known in the 20th century (Klee, Arp, Schwitters).

14 David Medalla, in conversation with the author, 1987.

15 Gaston Bachelard, 'Rimbaud the Child', in *The Right to Dream*, Dallas Institute Publications, Dallas, 1988, pp. 113-114.

16 Margot J. Baterina, 'A David Among Europe's Art Goliaths', *Philippine Panorama*, Manila, 19 January 1986, p. 10.

17 Benitez, interview with Medalla, op cit, p. 5.

18 Guillermo Gómez-Peña, 'Hybrid America', *National Review of Live Art Bulletin*, UK, October 1993.

19 David Medalla, 'Tropical Stoicism', *The Filipino Express*, New York, 30 July 1990.

20 Medalla's series of five lectures at the Museum of Modern Art, New York, in 1990, 'The Dream of Yadwigha - The Sources in Global Cultures of Modern Art', was a contribution to this discussion.

21 Susan Hiller, interview in *Fuse*, Toronto, November/December 1981.

22 Quoted in Jonathan Crary, *Techniques of Observation: On Vision and Modernity in the Nineteenth Century*, MIT Press, Cambridge, Massachusetts, 1990, p 17.

23 David Medalla, informal talk with students at Chelsea College of Art, London, April 1983, quoted in Guy Brett, 'David Medalla: from Biokinetics to Synoptic Realism', *Third Text*, London, No 8/9, Autumn/Winter 1989, p 106.

Chapter 2

1 *Signals Newsbulletin*, London, vol 1 no 3/4, October/November 1965, p 18.

2 Soto wrote that he wished to discover the relationship "between the principle which governs the picture.... and a general law of the universe which governs everything". 'Statements by kinetic artists', *Studio International*, London, February 1967, p 60.

3 A pioneering survey of the new tendency in Europe had been 'Rörelse I Konsten' (Movement in Art), at the Moderna Museet, Stockholm, in 1961.

4 *Signals Newsbulletin*, vol 1 no 1, August 1964.

5 The format of *Signals Newsbulletin* was later adopted by Harald Szeemann for some of the exhibition catalogues he produced as director of the Kunsthalle, Berne.

6 One long wall on the ground floor of the Signals building was reserved for these special commissions. Artists who produced new works for this wall included Takis, Soto, Gerhard von Graevenitz, Li Yuan-chia and Mary Martin. Mary Martin's wall is now in the collection of the Tate Gallery. Medalla also commissioned works for thematic exhibitions at Signals. Works by Takis, the French artist François Morellet and the Italian artist Gianni Colombo were commissioned for 'Towards the Invisible', and for the final show at Signals Medalla invited the English artist Graham Stevens to create a large inflatable structure.

7 *Signals Newsbulletin*, vol 1 no 2, September 1964.

8 Guy Brett, *Kinetic Art: the Language of Movement*, Studio Vista/Reinholdt, London and New York, 1968, p 42.

9 Rasheed Araeen, interview with David Medalla, *Black Phoenix*, London, no 3, Spring 1979, p 11.

10 David Medalla, 'Biokinetics: a Memoir on Motion', London, 1967. Unpublished.

11 Metzger's text was written for the Belgian art magazine *Quadrum* but not published.

12 *Signals Newsbulletin*, vol 1 no 8, June/July 1965, p 18.

13 Medalla, 'Biokinetics', op cit.

14 Thematically the most complex Bubble Machine, *Megha Sutta: The Cloud Discourse* was a tubular perspex structure based on the form of the bamboo. Opaque sections alternated with transparent ones. The leads carrying electricity were encased in plastic tubing and coiled in a spiral laid inside the tray at the base of the sculpture. The lowest transparent section contained a piece of brain coral shaped by the artist into a phallus. The opaque section above it, where the electric motors were installed, had a black spherical compass attached to its outside surface. Next came a transparent section containing white swan's feathers (in ancient India the soul, *hamsa*, was thought of as a swan). These feathers stirred slightly in the air currents. Above them was a piece of white silk embroidered by the artist in gold thread with a quotation from the *Dhammapada*: "the fragrance of a good man travels even against the wind". Finally, from the topmost section of the sculpture, the foam emerged.

15 In the same exhibition Medalla also exhibited a Smoke Machine which incorporated different kinds of incense and a real lemon which was enveloped in incense smoke.

16 Hermine Demoriane, 'From Kathakali to Biokinetic Theatre', interview with David Medalla, *International Times*, London, no 42, December 1331 1968, p 8.

17 Guy Brett, interview with David Medalla, London, 1968. Unpublished.

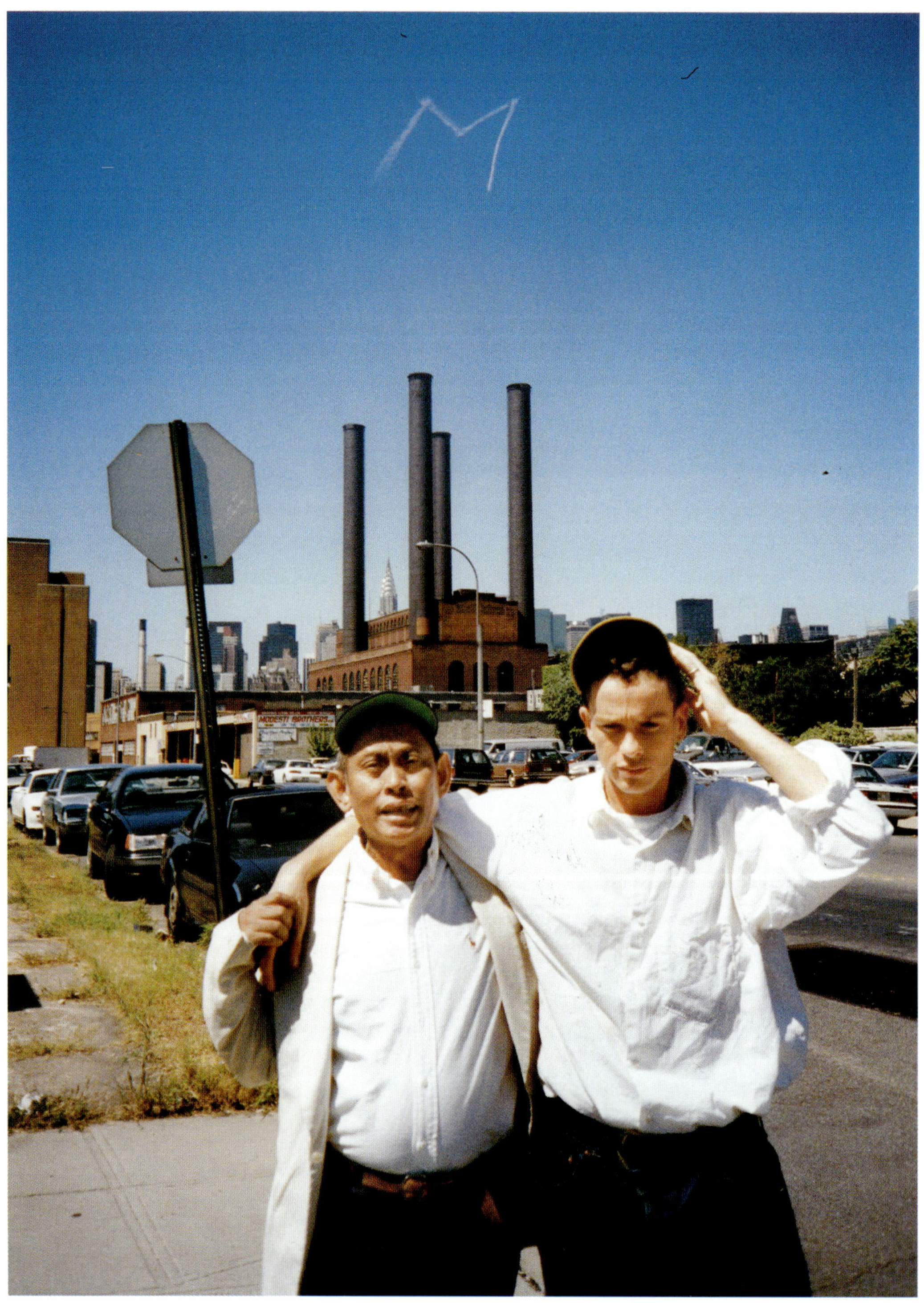

The Secret History of the Mondrian Fan Club, Medalla and Adam Nankervis beneath the letter 'M' written in smoke in the sky above Manhattan, Long Island City, New York, 1994.

18 Ibid.

19 Ibid.

20 Ibid.

21 Ibid.

22 Cid Reyes, interview with David Medalla, *Conversations on Philippine Art*, Cultural Center of the Philippines, Manila, 1989, p 150. As always, no judgement should be taken as absolute or final. Later Medalla returned to certain traditions of western Baroque art in the elaboration of his performances and paintings.

23 Ibid.

24 Demoriane, op cit.

25 David Medalla, statement in catalogue of 'In Motion', Arts Council of Great Britain, 1966.

26 Quoted in Guy Brett, 'Lygia Clark: the Borderline between Life and Art', *Third Text*, London, no 1, 1987, p. 74.

27 Demoriane, op cit.

28 Brett, interview with David Medalla, op cit.

29 *Signals Newsbulletin*, vol 1 no 7, April/May 1965, p. 11.

30 In this context it is worth noting that, in Rome, fountains provide one of the great historical examples of a unity of art and practical life. They were both the supply points of the fresh water for the city brought via aqueducts from the surrounding hills, and works of imagination with an extraordinary variety of themes into which the trickle or cascade of water was incorporated. See H.V. Morton, *The Waters of Rome*, The Connoisseur and Michael Joseph, London, 1966.

Chapter 3

1 Lewis Mumford, President of the American Academy of Arts and Letters, Ceremonial Address, New York, 19 May, 1965. Letter from Robert Lowell to President Lyndon Johnson. Both published in *Signals Newsbulletin*, vol 1 no 8, June-July 1965.

2 David Medalla, 'The Exploding Galaxy', *Paletten* 1, Stockholm, 1968.

3 Ibid.

4 Lygia Clark, letter to the author, 1966.

5 Lygia Clark, quoted in *Véja* magazine, December 1986.

6 Hélio Oiticica, Diary entry, February 1961. *Hélio Oiticica*, exhibition catalogue, Witte de With, Rotterdam, 1992, p. 42.

7 Hélio Oiticica, quoted in Catherine David, 'The Great Labyrinth', ibid, p. 259.

8 Hélio Oiticica, quoted in Guy Brett, 'The Experimental Exercise of Liberty', ibid, p. 228. A Philippine equivalent, of which David Medalla had direct experience as a boy, might be the *balagtasans*, or poetic jousts, in which poets improvised verses in front of a large audience in praise of the *lakambini*, or winner of a beauty contest.

9 Hélio Oiticica, 'Position and Program', 1966, ibid, p. 103.

10 Derek Jarman, *Dancing Ledge*, Quartet, London, 1984, p. 83.

11 *Planted*, edited, compiled and published by Paul Keeler, London, 1968.

12 Benn Levy MP, unpublished document.

13 *Paletten*, op cit.

14 "Many of our explorations took place in London streets, buses, tubes, market-places, post offices, social security offices, railway stations, museums, cafés, cinemas, lavatories, squares, everywhere....", ibid.

15 *The Buddha Ballet*, leaflet, 1968. At the time of *The Buddha Ballet*, Medalla and Dugger saw the Kerala Kalamandalam troupe of Kathakali dancers perform in London, and were profoundly impressed by it. A year later Medalla and Dugger stayed in Kerala as guests of M.K.K. Nayar, chief patron of the Kerala Kalamandalam. Kathakali sparked in Medalla the desire to study Indian dance and the aesthetics of the Kashmiri philosopher Abhinavagupta.

16 David Medalla, 'Paris - London: Memories of the Sixties', *And*, London, no 17, 1988, p. 17.

17 John Dugger, letter to the author, 25 September 1969.

18 *3>∞: new multiple art*, (ed) Hugh Shaw, Arts Council of Great Britain, London, 1970, p 54. By way of pointing out contrasting attitudes towards creativity, it might be mentioned that Joseph Beuys's contribution to the catalogue of the Multiples show was to "authorise" the

publication of two photographs of his performances "as original printed multiple works of art". In other words, he went as far as challenging the notion of the unique art object, but not of the unique author!

19 David Medalla, letter to the author, 19 October 1969.

20 The whole affair was somewhat tragicomic, at least as reported in great detail by a Raymond Chandler-style journalist, José F. Lacaba, writing in the *Philippines Free Press* of September 20, 1969. Medalla seemed equally, or even more, critical of the official Philippine *dularawan*, staged for the opening of the Cultural Center of the Philippines, as he was of the presence of Ronald Reagan. Based on a traditional art form combining *dula* (dance), *awit* (song) and *larawan* (picture), David saw the *dularawan*, fabricated to glorify Imelda Marcos, as a fake, provincial mishmash of trendy art references, and his continuous loud whispers during the performance were delightedly reported: "...if our ancestors had been as inert as these people they would never have crossed from one side of the Pasig river to the other!", and so on.

21 Bertolt Brecht, 'New Ages', *Poems 1913-1956*, (eds) John Willett and Ralph Manheim, Eyre Methuen, London, 1981, p 386.

22 Medalla was on the road in India at the time and sent only a small object in an envelope, a woven paraffin mantle to be sprinkled with blue pigment and set alight. He was the only non-western artist included in the show.

23 Alastair Mackintosh, 'Art for Whom?', interview with David Medalla, *Art and Artists*, January 1973.

24 Ibid.

25 The artist had been involved in negotiations with the Tate over the purchase of his *Megha-Sutta*. At one point, breaking confidence, the Tate's Director Sir Norman Reid secretly sent a copy of one of the Tate's letters to Medalla to Szeemann in Kassel, presumably as some kind of warning. Szeemann immediately informed the artist.

26 Benjamin H.D. Buchloh, *America Bride of the Sun*, Royal Museum of Fine Arts, Antwerp, 1992, p. 244.

27 Medalla's *Africa Liberation Drawings* were shown in various cultural centres in Britain and at the Stedelijk Museum in Amsterdam in an international exhibition organised by UMA – the United Moving Artists Collective of Holland, 1976.

Chapter 4

1 A particular stimulus for his interest in Chinese porcelain was *Early Ming Wares of Chingtechen* by A.D. Brankston (Oxford University Press, Hong Kong, 1982), an obscure but remarkable book in which the most fastidious connoisseurship and technical investigation is combined with a poetic or spiritual vision.

2 David Medalla, *Down With the Slave Trade!*, leaflet, 1971.

3 Ibid.

4 Medalla, 'In Motion', op cit.

5 David Medalla, 'A Stitch in Time', *South Hill Park Bulletin*, Bracknell, July/August 1982.

6 Ibid.

7 Steve Thorn, interview with David Medalla, Artists for Democracy, May 1977. Unpublished.

8 Ibid.

9 Edinburgh College of Art, during '123', live events and installations curated by Lynne MacRitchie, 1972.

10 In conversation with the author, Bracknell, March 1987.

11 Knud Rasmussen, quoted in *Eskimo Poems from Canada and Greenland*, (trans) Tom Lowenstein, Alison and Busby, London, 1973, p. 108.

12 Thorn, op cit.

13 Some years later, and presumably without any direct connection, the ideas behind Medalla's participatory works were put into practice on a mass scale by women protesting against nuclear weapons at Greenham Common US Air Force Missile Base in southern England. Many thousands of women decorated the perimeter chain-link fence with objects, writings, drawings, collages and photos, with a common theme capable of infinite interpretation: 'things that mean life'. Each contribution was of personal importance, but the real message and symbolic import was their sum.

14 David Medalla, 'Some Random Notes on my Cosmic Propulsion *Eskimo Carver*', London 1977. Unpublished.

15 Karl Marx, *Economic and Philosophical Manuscripts,* 1844.

Chapter 5

1 This in fact happened only once. Two tables laden with food and drink were the gift of the staff at Boodles Club to Giles Thomas, who was working in the club on a temporary job to support his painting.

2 Rasheed Araeen, interview with David Medalla, *Black Phoenix*, No 3, Spring 1979, p. 17.

3 Ibid.

4 Ibid.

5 David Medalla and Oriol de Quadras, *AFD Grand Artists' Banquet*, invitation letter, 1978.

6 Lygia Clark, quoted in Guy Brett, 'Lygia Clark: the Borderline Between Art and Life', *Third Text*, No 1, Autumn 1987, p 76.

7 Geoffrey Gorer, *Exploring English Character*, Cresset Press, London, 1955, p. 289.

8 David Medalla, 'Concerning the Rhapsody of the Dagger and Ammonia Boy', leaflet, London 1981.

9 Medalla's 1979 interview with Rasheed Araeen prompted a bitter outburst: "This is the most philistine society I've come across. The art bureaucrats and many art critics just don't have any sensitivity. They only have gross appetites, you know, the English middle class. Many of them don't feel the necessity to read a poem or hear a piece of real music or look at a work of art. They turn on the television to see the most horrific programmes; they are happy with the telly whether they are Cabinet Ministers or shopkeepers or all the way down to the bottom, the working class. They are smug and complacent with the visual diet they get from their TV sets." Op cit, p. 16.

10 Susan Hiller, 'Reflections', in *Talking about Art: Conversations with Susan Hiller* (ed. Barbara Einzig, preface by Lucy Lippard) Manchester University Press, 1995.

11 Quoted in Oriol de Quadras, 'Real Time, Real Space: A Study of Performance Art', paper prepared for Chelsea College of Art, London, 1979. Unpublished.

12 David Medalla, statement in *Live Art*, (eds) Robert Ayers and David Butler, AN Publications, Sunderland, 1991, p. 75.

13 Adam Nankervis, letter to the author, January 1994.

14 Mikhail Bakhtin, *The Dialogic Imagination*, (trans) Caryl Emerson and Michael Holquist, University of Texas Press, Austin, 1981, p. 244.

15 A propos of the Rimbaud/Barrios performance, *Eloge de l'Exotisme*, 1986, Medalla wrote: "... I have tried to locate those invisible points (metaphorical junctures) where the dynamic imaginations of those two great masters meet and touch. Those 'invisible points' meet and touch in the mind and in the heart of every individual who responds to the magic of Arthur Rimbaud's poetry and Agustín Barrios's music." Leaflet, 1986.

16 *Live Art*, op cit, p. 75.

17 Purissima H Benitez, interview with David Medalla, 'David Medalla: The '60s and '70s', Masters degree thesis at The Courtauld Institute of Art, University of London, 1992, p. 36.

18 Charles H. Kahn, *The Art and Thought of Heraclitus*, Cambridge University Press, Cambridge, 1979, p. 71.

19 Remark to the audience made by Sir Roland Penrose after seeing *A Smile Soaring* at the 'Picasso Adieu' exhibition, South Hill Park, Bracknell, 1982.

20 *The Mondrian Fan Club*, founded by Medalla in New York in 1993, is partly an attempt at such counteraction.

21 *The Concise Oxford Dictionary of Literary Terms*, compiled by Chris Baldick, Oxford University Press, Oxford, 1990.

22 David Medalla, *Bonjour Beau, Bonsoir Brummel / Bongo Bo, Bonsai Brahma*, performance leaflet, Galerie d'Art Contemporain des Musées de Nice, April 1980.

23 David Medalla, 'The Signs and Wonders of David and Kai', draft for press release. Unpublished.

24 Compare traditions of Balinese theatre. "In the middle of a wonderful shot of the masked, tailed figure squatting on the ground, someone comes up to fix his tail which has sort of fallen over. But

the dancer is not disturbed or embarrassed... [it is not] a failure, as such an event is in our culture... In Bali the theatrical is not supposed to be an illusion of reality... so it is not felt as a failure of an illusion of reality, since this is not its intent. On the contrary, the point about Balinese theatricals is that they can be done only if they are accepted as false... That is, if these 'accidents' did not happen, the thing might begin to seem too real." Maya Deren, Notebook, *October*, No 14, New York, Fall 1980, p 36.

25 Jun Terra, interview with David Medalla (part 2), *San Juan*, Manila, August 1985, p 6.

26 David Medalla, 'Recollections of Performance Art in Britain', unpublished text, 1983.

27 Terra, op cit, p 6.

28 Ibid.

29 David Medalla, *Art of Our Time*, project for a magazine, 1983, centre pages.

30 Benitez, op cit, p 28.

31 David Medalla and Brian Morgan, 'Attempts at Dancing', *A Shot in the Dark*, Medalla and Morgan Publishers, London, 1990, p 19.

32 David Medalla, in conversation with the author, 1986.

33 Ibid.

34 Mario Morini, 'A Tribute to Franco Corelli, Opera Singer'. Sleeve notes to a Saga LP of sacred songs sung by Franco Corelli.

35 Medalla treated this flux in a literary form in a series of 'synoptic texts' which reminisce on past performances and impromptus. They are published in David Medalla and Brian Morgan, *A Shot in the Dark*, op cit.

36 "The 'speaking' statues of Rome were the product of an alert and intelligent society which had no Press or any other means of self-expression... There were several of these loquacious statues: there was 'Madame Lucrezia', a battered marble at the back of the Palazzo Venezia; the 'Facchino' fountain in the Via Lata; the 'Abbate Luigi' of the Piazza della Valle; the eroded 'Babuino' in the via del Babuino; and an almost forgotten oracle, the statue of S. Ann, by Jacopo Sansovino, in the church of S. Agostino. But the most popular of all were Paquino and Marforio... ", etc. H.V. Morton, *The Waters of Rome*, p 154.

37 Benitez, op cit, p 22. Medalla went on: "His personal virtue was that everyone he made love to, except for one, became his personal friend and that's a rare virtue... [In his film *Casanova*, Fellini] wanted to show up Casanova as a horrible rake. In a way he was right, but this was only one reading. The other reading was that this man satisfied women on a sexual level and gave them an importance in his life they were never accorded. In the 18th century women took very narrow roles... from the very top to the very bottom women were really objects. With Casanova, his relationship with women may have been on a sexual level, but he actually treated them like human beings and it comes out through and through in his memoirs."

38 Guy Brett, interview with David Medalla, London 1983. Unpublished.

39 David Hirsh, interview with David Medalla, New York, October 1989. Unpublished.

40 Brett, op cit.

41 Brett, op cit.

42 *Les Parfums Excelsior* was so named partly in reference to the Duchamp/Man Ray work, partly because the official motto of New York is 'Excelsior', and partly in homage to Walt Whitman, "who loved to interject French, Italian and other non-English words in his poetry and indeed wrote a poem incorporating the word 'excelsior'". 'Les Parfums Excelsior', unpublished note, 1990.

43 In conversation with the author, 1993.

44 *A Shot in the Dark*, p 24.

45 Brett, op cit.

46 Mikhail Bakhtin, *Rabelais and His World*, (trans) Hélène Iswolsky, Indiana University Press, Bloomington, 1984, p 40.

Chapter 6

1   Jun Terra, interview with David Medalla (part 2), *San Juan*, Manila, August 1985, p 7.

2   David Medalla, letter to Leo Benesa from Rome, 8 July 1980.

3   Medalla has described the spelling of his *nom-de-peintre* as "a phonetic transcription of the name of the angel of the annunciation, and at the same time an early reference to the budding consciousness of 'gays' in America and all over the world". (In conversation with the author, September 1994).

4   Medalla, letter to Benesa.

5   David Medalla, letter to the author, 30 July 1980.

6   David Medalla, 'Performance' (part 2), *South Hill Park Bulletin*, Bracknell, No 15, July/August 1983.

7   Terra, interview, op cit, p 7.

8   Medalla, letter to Benesa.

9   David Medalla, 'Sacred and Profane Love', *Filipino Express*, New York, 19-25 November 1990.

Chapter 7

1   David Medalla, unpublished text.

2   Hélio Oiticica, 'World Shelter', New York, 1973. Unpublished.

3   The title was adapted from a flyer the artist was handed in the street advertising CDs: "Five immortal classics at dropdead prices!". The 'five immortals' were five women "representative of transcendence in moments of suffering": Sojourner Truth, one of the earliest Black women liberation fighters who helped conduct the 'underground railway' for slaves escaping to the North; Claudia Muzio, the Italian soprano of the period between the two world wars, who resisted Mussolini's attempts to use her voice for the cause of fascism; Lady Sword Mistress, a famous swordswoman in T'ang Dynasty China whose movements influenced the forms of dance and theatre; the Mexican painter Frida Kahlo, who transcended the effects of a crippling accident in her art; and Lalla Yogiswari, an eleventh-century Indian saint and yogini who also wrote poetry and was credited with miraculous powers which could save entire villages from flooding, earthquakes and drought.

4   David Medalla and Brian Morgan, *A Shot in the Dark*, Medalla and Morgan Publishers, London, 1990.

5   'Yadwigha' is the name of the woman in Douanier Rousseau's painting *The Dream*, 1910, who is lying on a sofa in the jungle. This work is in the MoMA collection, as are the others Medalla used as examples in his lectures. "I argued for a greater integration of the positive aspects of various cultures in a polymorphic new language of universal culture, thus continuing and re-invigorating the vision of the pioneers of modernism." (Letter to the author, 9 September 1993).

6   Another aspect of his response was to produce a stream of positive and life-enhancing homoerotic work in New York, especially in collages and in passages of his paintings. He participated in several group shows on the theme of AIDS, and took part in the organisation of the mighty 'Stonewall 25 Rally', commemorating 25 years of the gay liberation movement, manning the press and information office outside the United Nations building.

7   Robert Motherwell, 'Letter to Yve-Alain Bois', in *Robert Motherwell: Collected Writings*, (ed) Stephanie Terenzio, Oxford University Press, 1992, p 237.

8   John Strausbaugh, 'The Flying Mondrians: David Medalla's Impossible Art', *New York Press*, Vol 7 No 21, 25-31 May 1994. Medalla's calling-card, as founder and president of the Mondrian Fan Club, 1993, recalls a card he had printed in Paris in 1961 as 'President of the University of Failure'. At the time, in order to obtain a pass to eat cheaply in the subsidised student restaurants in Paris, one needed some form of academic registration. Medalla printed his card as a ruse to inscribe himself in an international conference of professors then taking place at the Sorbonne. He claims that many of the non-Anglophone delegates at the conference thought that Failure was a small island kingdom in the Pacific.

9   David Medalla, letter to the author, 3 January 1993.

Appendix I

A partial list of Performances and Impromptus by David Medalla between 1967-70 and 1976-94.

1967

Fuzzdeath (in collaboration with Susan Herzmark, Christian Ledoux, Malcolm Le Maistre, Edward Pope, Larry Smart, Paul Keeler and others). Part of 'The 14-hour Technicolour Dream', Alexandra Palace, London, April.

Tar Pot Eb Ot Woh, a palindromic puppet play for fingers, toes and nose, Warwick University, spring.

Mellow Yellow, with the Exploding Galaxy, UFO, London.

Krishna and Arjuna in Outer Space, with the Exploding Galaxy, UFO, London; Palais des Sports, Paris; and Magriethal, Utrecht, autumn.

The Bird Ballet, with Paul Keeler as 'eyes and ears' and the Exploding Galaxy, Roundhouse, London, autumn.

Avalokitesvara and the Monkeys, with the Exploding Galaxy, Olafsport and Pro Vadya, Amsterdam, winter.

Homage to Mondrian, dance-drama with poems, Het Anchoor, Amsterdam, winter.

1968

Lal the Idiot, dance-drama based on a Rajasthan folktale, Hampstead Heath and Arts Lab, London, spring.

Chuang-tzu and the Butterfly Dream, with John Dugger in one of the twin fountains, Trafalgar Square, during the Thang Loi Festival in support of the Vietnamese struggle against US imperialism, summer.

The Riddle of the Bird of Dharma, during the Legalise Pot Rally, Hyde Park, London, summer.

The Buddha Ballet, a series of dance-dramas with John Dugger, members of the Exploding Galaxy and the public, every Sunday between May and September at Parliament Hill, Hampstead Heath, London.

The First Mirror in China, dance-drama developed by Medalla from a story told to him by Lygia Clark, with

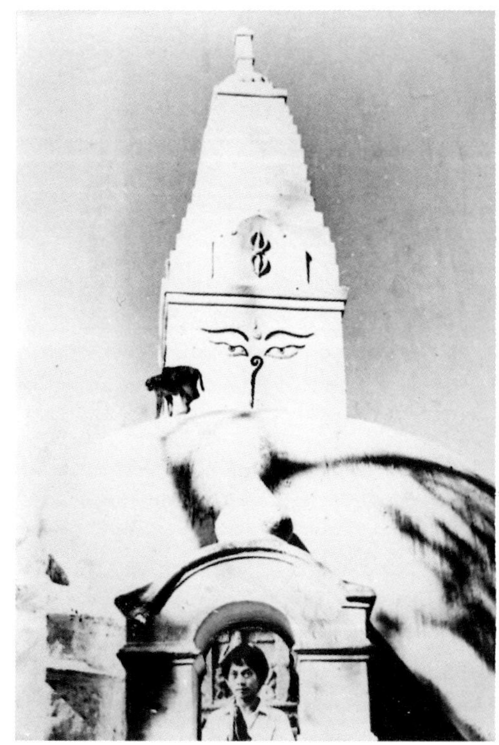

In Kathmandu, 1970.

the Exploding Galaxy, Université d'Orleans, November.

1969

Sweeping the Sounds of the Sea, events performed with John Dugger during their African and Asian voyage, 1969-70. At the Lido in Venice; port of Barcelona; Dakar; Cape Town; Mombassa; the Gateway of the East, Bombay; the coastline of Kerala, India; the shores at Galle and Matara, Sri Lanka; Manila Bay.

The Penance of Arjuna (from the Mahabharata), Impromptu at Mahabalipuram, India.

Melting the Great Wall of China, performance incorporating a wall of ice-cubes, with John Dugger and Mrs Maring Llamado, Northern Motors

198

Showroom, Manila, during Annual Exhibition of the Art Association of the Philippines, November. An event related to Medalla's 'Cosmic Propulsion', *Launching the Great Wall of China as a Satellite Around the Moon.*

Pleekabia Cinemara: A Walk, a Talk, the Sea, the Sky, an exposé of the conditions of slum-dwellers on the sea at Manila Bay (filmed for Channel 5, Manila TV).

1970

The Magic Scorpion Destroyeth the Tyrant's Palace, events inspired by the life of the Tibetan poet Milarepa, Swayambunath and Bod Nath stupa, Kathmandu, January.

The Potato-eaters: Homage to Vincent van Gogh, with John Dugger, Andrew Forrest and Jun Terra, on board 'Mayflower II', quai des Tuileries, Paris, spring.

1975

Is Art an Enigma? Johannes Vermeer of Delft, with members of Artists for Democracy on the occasion of Lea Lublin's video event, Serpentine Gallery, London.

1976

The Razor: Homage to Leonardo da Vinci, Artists for Democracy, London.

Tatlin at the Funeral of Malevich, Artists for Democracy, London, September.

Thunderous Applause – Three years work, 'London Calling', Acme Gallery, London, September.

1977

Tatlin at the Funeral of Malevich, The Food Art Show, Kettle's Yard, Cambridge.

Wooden Heart, inspired by Watteau's painting *L'Indifférent* and Elvis Presley's song 'Wooden Heart', Walworth Arts Festival and Carnival, London.

A la Récherche des Cinq Inconnus, rue des Abbesses, Montmartre, Paris, December.

1978

Fable of the Mermaid and the Drunks, inspired by a poem by Pablo Neruda, with Oriol de Quadras, Charlie Garner, Miriam Bird, Mick Morton, Giles Thomas, Charles Hustwick and Jun Terra, 'London Calling', Acme Gallery, London, January.

Reciprocal Didacticks, first of a series with Oriol de Quadras, 'London Calling', Acme Gallery; Architectural Association; Slade School of Art; Roundhouse; ICA, London.

Magellan and the Circumnavigation of the World, cycle of performances with Oriol de Quadras, inspired by Magellan's voyage which "proved that the world was round and was the first practical demonstration of the relativity of space and time". Initiated at Greenwich in front of the Meridian Line on March 23rd, performed at 'London Calling', ICA, London, May; and continued in a sequence of related performances subtitled: *Eros Anamorphico,* Roundhouse, London, June; *The Beachcomber's Dream Tree,* 'Mayfair Illuminations', Hill House, Berkeley Square, London, July; *The Education of a Renaissance Prince,* Birmingham Arts Lab, Birmingham, summer; *The Education of a Renaissance Prince (continued),* 'Mayflower Illuminations 2', Hill House, Berkeley Square, August.

1979

Proust Tropicale et Marcel Maritime, series of performances begun at Buttes Chaumont, Paris, December, and subsequently presented at Station Zoologique, Villefranche-sur-Mer, Côte d'Azur, France; the garden of the old home of Torquato Tasso, Sorrento; the Ramblas, Barcelona; Old Harbour, Genoa, 1980-81.

1980

Medalla Saluta Roma, the British School in Rome.

A Dream of Butterflies at Porta Maggiore, a 'synoptic-realist romanza' about the Pythagoreans, Rome, spring.

Truth is the Only Daughter of Time (after a proverb by Leonardo da Vinci), UMA Salon, Stedelijk Museum, Amsterdam, April.

Bonjour Beau, Bonsoir Brummel / Bongo Bo, Bonsai Brahma, two inter-related performances, Galerie d'Art Contemporain des Musées de Nice, April-May.

The Beachcomber's Dream Tree, The Razor: A Fable by Leonardo da Vinci, The Pictorial Biographies of Mozart and Medalla, programme of three performances, with the collaboration of students and resident artists, British School in Rome, April.

Statuamachia Romana: Annals of the Talking Statues of Rome, impromptu in the Gardens of the Villa Borghese, and at the American Overseas School, Rome. The following five performances formed part of *Statuamachia Romana*:

Piranesi and the Mother Scorpion, presented at the Torre dei Schiavi, via Prenestina, Rome; the Villa Adriana, Tivoli; and at the Piazza della Vittoria, Pavia, at the invitation of Italian artists Gabriele Albanesi, William Xerra and the Commune di Pavia.

Mozart and the Ghost of Palestrina, Pyramid of Cestius, Rome.

Goya and the Colossus, Circo Massimo, Rome.

The Angel of the Meridian, the encounter between Piero della Francesca and Antonello da Messina; Borgo San Sepolcro, near Arezzo; Ponte Milvio, Rome; Villa Caprarola, Lazio.

La Maga Circe, inspired by the homonymous painting by Dossi Dossi, Società Filodrammatica Piacentina, Piacenza.

Questions put to Dante beside the river Po, a monodrama, Reggio Emilia; Palazzo Ducale, Mantova.

Homage to Leon Battista Alberti, impromptu, Tempio di San Sebastiano, Mantova.

Homage to Petrarch, impromptu, library of the Casa di Petrarca, Arezzo.

Homage to Ludovico Ariosto, impromptu, Contrada del Sole, Ariosto's tomb, Ferrara.

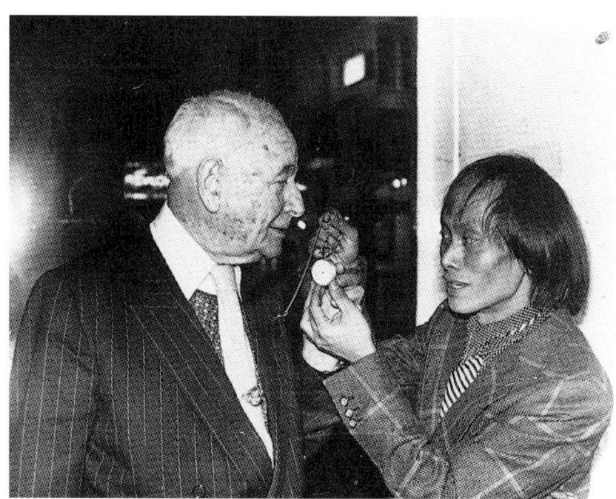

Impromptu with Louis Aragon, **Truth is the Only Daughter of Time**, Paris 1981.

1 9 8 1

Mascaras, Galerie Biren, Paris; at the invitation of the painter Pedro Uhart and the poet Luis Mizon.

Truth is the Only Daughter of Time, impromptu with Louis Aragon, Galerie Biren, Paris.

Vivre c'est l'Envers d'Aimer, a synoptic-realist performance, text by Aragon, incorporating poems by Hamid Fouladvand, Galerie Biren, Paris.

Voyages and Somersaults of the Pilgrim Monkey, synoptic-realist performance, Accademia di Venezia, March; at the invitation of Lovato Guerrino and Emilio Vedova.

The Conquest of Fear: Tales from the T'ang, synopticrealist performance series; Alpignano, near Turin; L'Artistique, Nice, at the invitation of Ben Vautier; Gare de Narbonne; Parc Guell, Barcelona.

3 Extracts, Screen on the Green, Islington, London.

Encounter with the Phoenix at Mayall Road, Brixton Festival, London.

La Sibylla Equatoria, Guild of Transcultural Studies, London.

1 9 8 2

Pentimenti parabolici, Giardino della Memoria, Venice.

Subrisio saltat ('A Smile Soaring'), synoptic-realist performance on love, death and the healing powers of memory, Palazzo Barbarigo della Terraza, Venice; 'Picasso and the Theatre' exhibition, South Hill Park, Bracknell; Old Court Theatre, Windsor Arts Centre; South Hill Park, Bracknell.

1 9 8 3

Night and Day, a suite of synoptic-realist performances, First Festival of Performance, South Hill Park, Bracknell, June. One performance a day for seven days:

Parables of Friendship, prelude, at the old fountain above the Italian garden.

The Rise and Fall of Mamelles Look!, on the concrete staircase by the wooden bridge.

Matisse in Moscow, in the small garden beside the nursery.

Next! Tantalizers, by the bridge near the lake.

Samba Samurai, to introduce the all-night cabaret in

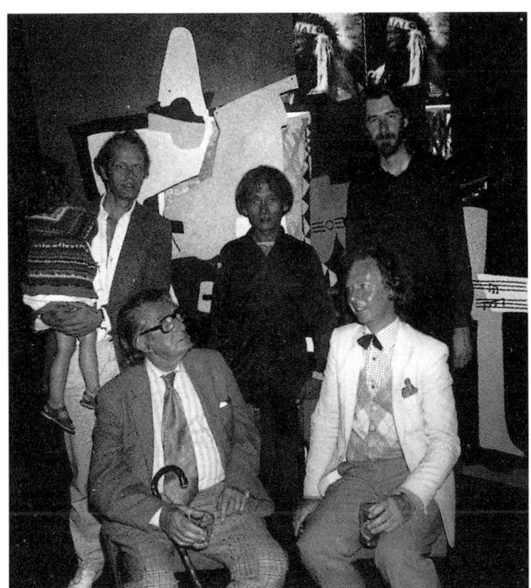

After the performance of **Subrisio Saltat** at South Hill Park, Bracknell, 1982. L. to r: Luciana Brett, GB, Sir Roland Penrose, DM, Gavin Henderson, Alistair Snow.

the Cellar Bar.

La Sibylla Equatoria, in the grotto of the Italian garden.

Icy Door du Cash, nocturne/postlude, inside and outside the artist's studio.

The Hand of Marie Curie, Perfo 1, Theater de Lantaren, Rotterdam; at the invitation of Wink van Kempen and Fred Hilst.

Octetto Ironico (with James Acheson, Lesley Butler, Kevin Goss, Sonia Knox, Roberta Kravitz, Carlyle Reedy, Alistair Snow, Anna Thew), a suite of synoptic-realist performances, Air Gallery, London, August 1983.

Psychic Self-Defence, impromptu at Westminster, London.

Bellini in Burundi, Brixton Art Gallery, London.

1984

Metamorphoses of an Enigma, synoptic-realist performance "consisting of an imaginary voyage between two quotations", Perfo 2, Theater de Lantaren, Rotterdam, May.

Performances and Impromptus in collaboration with Kai Hilgemann as 'The Signs and Wonders of David and Kai':

The Magic Coelacanth, with Marcelle van Bemmel, finale of Perfo 2, Theater de Lantaren, Rotterdam, May.

A Toast to the Baroque Buddha Brotherhood, Kai's studio, Jan van Avenesstraat, Rotterdam, May.

Remembering Man Ray, impromptu at Jan van Avenesstraat, Rotterdam.

Nocturnal Promenade, Piazza San Marco, Venice, June.

The Red Door, portico of the Scuola San Rocco, Venice, June.

All-Day Kayak Event for Two, Bacino di San Marco, Venice, June.

A Dream of Filippo de Pisis Dreaming, Zattere, Venice, June.

The View from Creazzo, Enrico Oliviero's house, Creazzo, Vicenza, June.

Is it Love or is it Sex?, Professor Tom Duddy's house, Guidecca, Venice, June.

Painting Event at Spiaggia Alberoni, Lido, Venice, June.

Libations at the Tombs of Stravinsky and Diaghilev, Isola San Michele, Venice, June.

Parables of Friendship, finale of 2nd International Festival of Performance, South Hill Park, Bracknell, June.

The Moon and Arliquinno at Portobello, St Peter's Hall, Notting Hill Gate, London, July.

The Mirror of Changes, St. James's Institute, Bethnal Green, London, July.

Impromptu at Kew, Kew Gardens, London, July.

Rimbaud in Reading, Reading, Berkshire, July.

Wanderlust in Windsor, Eton and Windsor, July.

Tunnelling through the Thames, Greenwich, London, August.

Gathering Rhododendrons in the Moonlight, Bracknell, August.

Aquerelles, Crowthorne, Berkshire, August.

Mozart in London, Air Gallery, London, September.

From Londonbrücken to Saarbridges, the Thames, London, September.

Gay Galaxy (part one), Het Apollohuis, Eindhoven, September.

A Celebration of World Mythologies in Rotterdam,

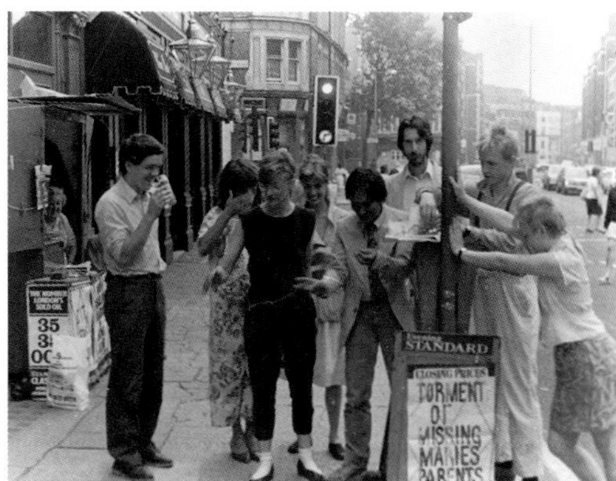

Octetto Ironico, initial get-together in Grays Inn Road, London, 1983.

Midlaanstraat and the Blaak, Rotterdam, October.

Suspensions, Willemsbrug, Rotterdam, October.

Sunset Reverie, the old port, Dordrecht, October.

Gay Galaxy (part two), Doornroosje, Nymegen, November.

Gay Galaxy (part three), Shaffy Theatre, Amsterdam, November.

Card Players from Java, The Devil's House, Arnhem, November.

Gay Galaxy, Hall of Mirrors, ancient palace of the Belgian kings, International Cultureel Centrum, Antwerp, December.

Dawn Walk, Bagno, Steinfurt, Germany, December.

The Maginot Line, impromptu at Verdun, New Year's Eve.

1 9 8 5

Reflets-Regards, impromptu in a room in the rue Bonaparte, Paris.

Conversations à l'Ombre du Sphinx, Louvre, Paris, January.

Dream Tigers, Delacroix's studio, Paris, January.

Hommage à Watteau, Pont Alexandre III, Paris, January.

Hommage à Rodin, Jardin du Musée Rodin, Paris, January.

A Night at Premabuba, Congress Halle, Saarbrücken, February.

The Song of Milarepa, impromptu at Saarbrücken.

Grundrisse Zum Gluck, Goethe Haus, Frankfurt, March.

Mr Casanova International, Impromptu at Frankfurt, March.

Zurichzugsecret, Spiegelgasse, Zurich, March.

This is not the Cabaret Voltaire, Neiderdorfstrasse, Zurich, March.

Gay Galaxy, Halle Sud, Centre Culturelle de Genève, Geneva, March.

Allez-Retour: Pluie-Soleil, Rotterdam-Amsterdam motorway, April.

Brancusi and Tatlin in Berlin, International Festival of Video and Performance, Leeuwarden Filmhuis, Leeuwarden, Holland, May.

Les Problèmes des Deux Corps/Coeures, International Festival of Performance, Kulturhaus Palazzo, Liestal, Switzerland, May.

A Hard-On at Harderwijk: Homage to Rimbaud, Harderwijk, Holland, May.

Zeitung: Duet for James Joyce, Basel, May.

Homage to Matthias Grünewald, Museum Unter der Linden, Colmar, May.

A Snake in Strasbourg, Cathedral Square, Strasbourg, May.

A Dream of Filippo de Pisis in Venice, synoptic-realist performance, Camden Arts Centre, London, October.

Immoderato Incantabile, impromptu at the organ of San Agustin Church, Manila, New Year's Eve.

1 9 8 6

Laban, m/v Xinta, Manila Yacht Club, Manila; yacht courtesy of Ray K. Ilusorio, January.

Kislap at Kilusan, with Rommel and Jerome Suico, Kalentong Market, metro Manila, January.

Alay Kay Malakas at Maganda, with Joe Estrella and Job Alarcon, Kalis Island, Coron, Palawan Province, Philippines, February.

David Smelling Forget-me-nots and Black Tulips, impromptu at Finsbury Square, City of London, April.

Luz. Vi. Minda, Galerie J. et J. Donguy, Paris, June.

Baron Corvo and the Baroque Buddha Brotherhood, with Lovato Guerrino and Alessandro Fiorella, Mondonovo, Rio Tera Canal al Ponte dei Pugni, Venice, July.

Impromptu at Cremona: for Paganini, for Stradivarius, Palazzo Communale di Cremona, July.

Il Re Pastore, Villa Bice, Treviso, Veneto, July.

Bronze di Riace, with Giorgio Spiller, in the river in front of the poet Chimasso's house in Treviso, July.

Ascension, impromptu in the old Palazzo Communale of Conegliano, Veneto, July.

The Desire and Pursuit of the Whole, synoptic-realist performance with Alessandro Fiorella, Diorama, Regent's Park, London, September.

Eloge de l'Exotisme (subtitled *Rupture/Rapture*, and part of a projected larger work to be called *The Encyclopaedia of Exoticism*), "dedicated to the memories of Arthur Rimbaud and Agustín Barrios", Chisenhale Dance Space, London, October.

1987

The Elixir of Immortality, with Simon and Nicholas Parish, Finborough Theatre, London, July.

A Shot in the Dark, a series of performance art works with Brian Morgan. The audience were invited to bring cameras of all kinds to film the performances. The first, subtitled *The Heist Man Cometh*, was premiered at Finborough Theatre, London, in September. Subsequent parts included:

The Dream of Don Piranha, Zap Club, Brighton, October.

Better than the Real Thing, October Gallery, London.

The Rembrandt Room, Open Hand Studios, Reading, June 1988.

1989

The New Voyages of Baron Allergie de Tackyville in America, with Brian Morgan, Clocktower Gallery, New York.

Palimpsests of Poets' Passions, Clocktower Gallery, New York.

1991

Song of Songs of Solomon, with Adam Nankervis. At the 'Lost our Leash' event, M.K. Nightclub, New York, December; Madison Square Park, July 1993.

1992

Five Immortals at Drop-Dead Prices, a transcendental hedonist performance, Cooper Union Great Hall, New York, March.

Shark Attack, with Adam Nankervis. A surreal burlesque for APICHA (Asian and Pacific Islander Coalition on HIV/AIDS), World Aids Day, Art in General, New York.

1993

Three Ghost Plays about Michel Foucault, recitation of the prologue at Café Nico, 101 Avenue A, New York, December.

The Ecstatic Mode, declamation, 'Diatribe - an Archaeology of Discourse', Tomoto Liguori Gallery, New York, December.

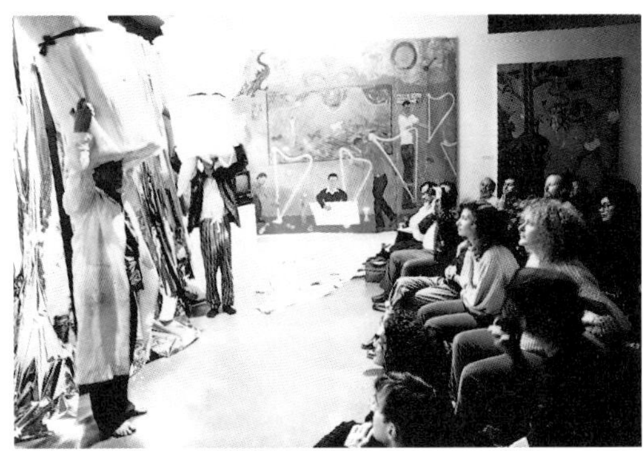

Medalla (left) and Brian Morgan performing **The New Voyages of Baron Allergie de Tackyville in America**, Clocktower Gallery, New York, 1989.

1994

Unfinished Business, "living is an unfinished business" (Medalla), a transcendental hedonist performance, terrace of the Belvedere Castle, Central Park, New York, March.

Plankton Corazon, event with bioluminescence, Brooklyn Bridge, New York.

Mondrian in Excelsis, as part of *The Secret History of the Mondrian Fan Club, Part 2: Mondrian in London*, 55 Gee Street, London, New Year's Eve.

Appendix II

David Medalla's notes on *Parables of Friendship: Myself and Lovato Guerrino at Castello in Venice,* 1985.

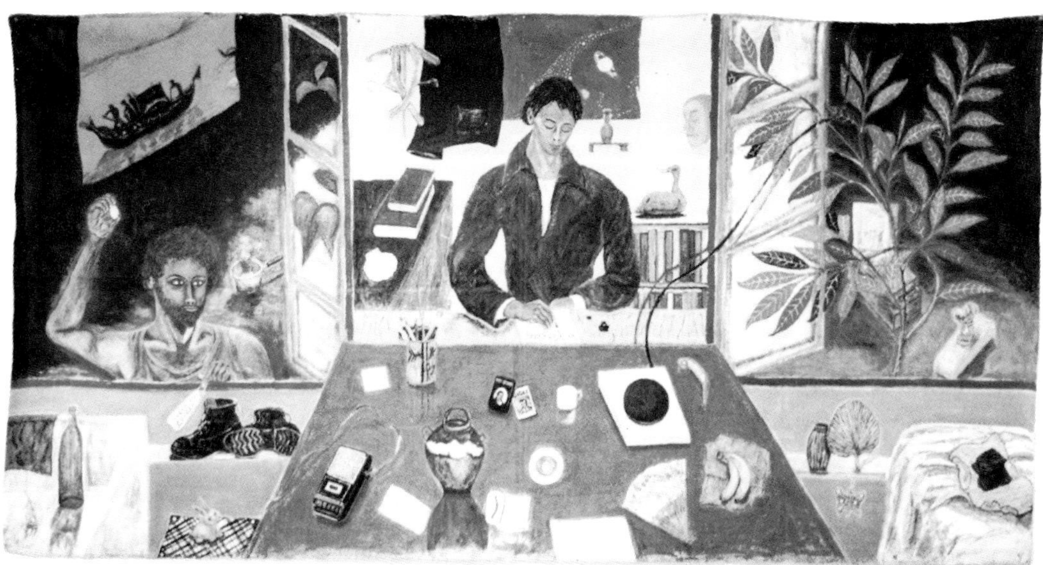

The painting of Lovato Guerrino and myself is the first work in the series I have collectively entitled *Parables of Friendship.* I began it in 1983 and it was first exhibited as a work-in-progress in the one man show I gave in June 1984 at South Hill Park Arts Centre in Bracknell, Berkshire, England, to celebrate the end of my two-year stint as artist-in-residence there. I did not resume work on the painting again until the summer of 1985, as I spent most of the rest of 1984 touring Europe with Kai Hilgemann.

The subject of the painting was inspired by an actual incident which occurred when I was in Venice in 1980, on the eve of a synoptic-realist performance I gave at the Accademia di Venezia. I was the guest of Lovato Guerrino, a brilliant young artist from Vicenza (the hometown, incidentally, of the architect Palladio and of the historian Pigafetta who accompanied Magellan on his voyage to the Philippines). Guerrino lived for a while on Barbaria de la Tole in the district of Castello in Venice, a few minutes walk away from the celebrated equestrian statue of Colleone by Andrea Verrocchio (the teacher of Leonardo da Vinci). Guerrino's tiny room was above a workshop which produced masks for the Venetian carnival. It was the night of the full moon. I was seated in front of Guerrino's desk finishing the text of my performance, entitled *Voyages and Somersaults of the Pilgrim Monkey* which I began in the study of the French poet Louis Aragon in Paris. Guerrino entered the room from the garden of memory at the back of the house, holding aloft in one hand an egg in the moonlight. He had brought me the egg from his parents' farm in Vicenza. I thought the moment had a magical quality to it, and I imagined a similar scene could have taken place several centuries ago in Venice between Antonello da Messina (a Sicilian artist who stayed for a while in Venice) and the great Venetian painter Giorgione di Castelfranco.

I decided to make the incident between Guerrino and myself the subject of the first in my projected series *Parables of Friendship*.

The painting was done after a sketch which I made almost immediately after the incident. Most of the objects depicted in the painting I used as props for my performance at the Accademia di Venezia.

In composing the painting, I consciously tried to resolve synoptically, two different plastic compositional devices: the 'horizontal/vertical opposition' pursued by Mondrian to create what he called 'dynamic equilibrium' and the 'lyrical arabesque' of Matisse, their vitality and unmistakeable lilt (as in jazz and *bel canto* music). Matisse and Mondrian are two of my favourite painters of the first half of our century. In my painting I utilised a kind of orthogonal perspective similar to the ones used in Indian painting and by Chinese masters, for I wanted above all to respect the flatness of the picture surface. Volume and depth I created by means of 'tonal orchestration' of the colours of the figures and objects depicted. In a black and white photograph, this kind of colouristic tonal orchestration will not be evident – so, one has to see the original painting with all its chromatic colours. In fact, I conceived the different elements of this painting in the same spirit that different instruments in a *gamelan* orchestra contribute rhythmically and melodically to the texture and structure of an essentially improvised form of music.

The figure (person) writing at the desk, reflected in a mirror, in the centre of the painting, is myself. The tip of the brush I am holding in the picture is the centre of the actual painting. There are other focal points in the picture such as the egg which Guerrino is holding. Above Guerrino, on the upper left hand side of the picture, is a cloth banner or hanging, on which is depicted a monochromatic representation of the funerary gondola which conveyed the dead body of the great Russian impresario Sergei Diaghilev to his grave on the island of San Michele in Venice. The image was based on a photograph of the event, taken in 1925. The egg is a universal symbol for birth; the connection between life and death is therefore symbolically stated in the corner of this painting. The connection is restated differently through the other window, on the right-hand side of the painting by means of a branch of the laurel-tree, with one or two decaying leaves. The laurel-tree is also a western (Greek and Roman) symbol for glory and fame. Most of the leaves of the laurel-tree in this painting are luxuriant, fresh and green.

By the laurel-tree, there is a toy monkey serenading a polychromed plaster angel in a wooden frame. This is to symbolise the interconnection between the animal world (the monkey) and the sacred or divine world (the angel). I found both these objects in Venice, a few doors away from Guerrino's old room, and I used these objects in my performance at the Accademia di Venezia. Incidentally, in the title sequence of the film *Rebel Without a Cause*, the actor James Dean (whom I knew in New York in the early 1950s) is seen winding a toy monkey similar to the one in my painting. I mentioned this beautiful sequence to the director of that film, Nicholas Ray, when I met him in Amsterdam in the 1960s, and he said that idea came originally from Jimmy Dean himself. The sequence of Jimmy and the toy monkey which moved me deeply when I first saw the film must have lodged in the inner recesses of my memory; it surfaced again, in a metamorphosed way, in my own performance of *Voyages and Somersaults of the Pilgrim Monkey*, which in some ways was an oblique homage to James Dean and other friends in my past.

Behind me in the painting is an old school star map: a representation of the sky at night. Guerrino found this star map on the *fondamenta* (embankment) near the Corte de Milion, the site of the house of Marco Polo, the most celebrated of many intrepid Venetian voyagers. To the left of the star map, beside the jacket, is a kinetic construction I made out of three pieces of old wooden hangers. I joined the hangers together in such a way that they become letters of the alphabet as the hangers are moved about in various positions. I used this portable kinetic sculpture in another performance which I gave in Venice, at the seat of the German Academy, on the magnificent terrace of the Palazzo Barbarigo della Terraza on the Grand Canal. That particular performance was inspired by the *Fifth Duino Elegy* of Rainer Maria Rilke, in which the German poet compared the spatial disposition of the *saltimbanques* of a Picasso painting to the initial letter 'D' of *dasein* or 'Thereness'. My articulated coat-hangers were fairly polyglot and created the initials in German, Dutch, French and Italian!

Behind me in the painting, above the bookcase filled with many colourful books (Guerrino is an indefatigable reader and collector of art books) is a Sung dynasty celadon incense burner in the shape of a ceramic duck. The duck, for the Chinese, is a symbol of fidelity and friendship. Above the duck is a small vase carved from a pine cone and the death mask of the great Venetian lover Giacomo Casanova. On the table to my right are two books: the sonnets of Aretino (the friend of Titian) and the poems of Baffo. Casanova, Aretino, Baffo and the playwright Goldoni (symbolically represented in the painting by the dark green jacket) are my favourite Venetian writers. The seashell near the books is the scallop sacred to Venus. I feel a great kinship with Venetian writers, painters and composers, for they shared a cosmopolitan outlook (like me!) and were passionate lovers of sensuous beauty.

Some of the objects in the painting (such as the two toothbrushes in a glass, the face towel over the kitchen sink, the pair of socks and the pair of underpants on the bed) were articles which Guerrino and I used in everyday life. The pair of black leather boots were the ones I wore when I stayed in Venice. The earthen pot on the table contained red Veneto wine, while the empty green bottle in the sink was used for white Vicentine wine. There is a fresh *ciambella* (Italian doughnut) on the saucer below the small white cup. The two fresh bananas on the brown tissue paper refer, quite obviously, to the sense of taste as does the brown *ciambella*. There are several objects in the painting which refer to the sense of hearing: the little paper whistle used in carnivals and fêtes, the small paper concertina between the earthen pot and the *ciambella*, the small cassette tape recorder which I used in some of my previous performances in Italy, and two cassette tapes of operatic arias sung by Tito Schipa and Beniamino Gigli. Schipa and Gigli were two great tenors who expressed admiration for each other's art. For me, Schipa's voice was like velvety white wine, while the voice of Gigli was like rich red wine. I have often used songs by them in my performances.

The white object with a black disc is a hot plate which Guerrino and I used for making coffee and cooking pasta. There are two fans in the painting: a foldable Spanish type fan and a Filipino straw fan leaning on a small gourd-shaped vase. Below the straw fan is a stuffed silk object from India in the shape of a butterfly, the symbol of rebirth. On the other side of the table is a small handcase in which I used to carry the toy monkey and the ceramic angel. Above this small case with red stripes is a tiny porcelain rabbit, the symbol of fertility. Behind Guerrino in the moonlight is a small saucepan; in it is a pot of blossoming flowers.

There are distinct though distant echoes of past artworks in the painting of the figures. While painting my self-portrait, I thought of the portraits of young men by Lorenzo Lotto, the great Venetian painter of the Renaissance. In the treatment of my worker's jacket, I was very conscious of the way Cézanne achieved volume in his paintings through an architectonic use of tones and contrasts. In painting the figure of Lovato Guerrino, I recalled a beautiful detail of an Adoration by Savoldo which I saw in Venice; that of a young shepherd framed in a window. In the Savoldo painting, the shepherd is looking into the interior of a stable from the right hand side. In my painting, Guerrino is looking into the interior of his room from the left hand side. I had to paint Guerrino in *contre-jour*, or, rather, in this case, *contre le clair-de-la-lune* (against the moonlight).

Painting this work presented me with several challenges: problems of composition, symbolism and figuration. For me, painting this picture was an exhilarating experience, for it enabled me to capture in a relatively stable form an ephemeral and beautiful moment in my life. I painted myself in the act of writing, in a state of contemplation; and I painted Guerrino in the act of calling my name and calling attention to the egg he is holding: a dream-like moment akin to trance. The bamboo container with old brushes on the table reflected in the mirror, is a joint statement of our love for art.

Biography

1942 Born March 23, Manila, Philippines.

1952 Attended schools in various parts of the Philippines. Lived for a time with the Igorots, a Filipino indigenous tribal mountain people, learned their language and translated some of their epic songs into English.

1953 Invited to give special lectures at the University of the Philippines.

1954 Attended Camp Rising Sun, Rhinebeck, New York. Invited by Professor Mark van Doren to attend Columbia University as a special student studying modern philosophy and Greek drama. Spent much of his time in Greenwich Village, meeting artists and writers. Started to paint.

1957 Returned to the Philippines. Attended lectures on art by Fernando Zobel de Ayala at the Ateneo de Manila. Founded the Poetry Club of Manila and the Blue Bamboo studio. Organized poetry readings and performances. Held first solo exhibition of paintings, drawings and sculptures at La Cave D'Angely. Selected as the youngest artist in the 500-year survey of Philippine art organized by UNESCO and shown in the Social Hall of the Department of Foreign Affairs of the Philippines.

1960 Travelled to Europe by ship, via Indochina, Singapore, Sri Lanka, India, Pakistan, East Africa and Egypt. Arrived Marseilles and made his way to Paris. Crossed the Channel and visited London for the first time. Gave his first performances in Paris at the Raymond Duncan Academy. Met many artists and writers, including Man Ray, Georges Braque, Gaston Bachelard, Meret Oppenheim, Lourdes Castro, Yves Klein, Takis, Tinguely, Fontana, Giacometti, Ad Reinhardt, Max Ernst, Magritte, Arp and Hans Richter.

1963 Organized, with Paul Keeler, 'Soundings One', an international art exhibition at the Ashmolean Museum, Oxford. Held a solo exhibition of his paintings at the Mayflower Barn, Jordans, Buckinghamshire. Made first kinetic works in Paris, London and Amsterdam.

1964 Founded the Centre for Advanced Creative Study (later Signals London) with Paul Keeler, Guy Brett, Marcello Salvadori and Gustav Metzger. Opened the flat in Cornwall Gardens he shared with Paul Keeler as a showroom of the avant-garde. Launched *Signals Newsbulletin*, which he edited and designed (1964-66). Participated in 'Structures Vivantes: Mobiles/Images' at the Redfern Gallery, the first exhibition of kinetic art in Britain, and the 'Noctural Show of Kinetic Art' at Villa La Malcontenta, near Venice.

1965 Signals moved to a three-storey showroom in Wigmore Street, mounting a series of large-scale shows of experimental and kinetic art. Special issues of *Signals Newsbulletin* published to accompany exhibitions by Takis, Camargo, Lygia Clark, Soto, Otero and other artists. Exhibited ensemble of monumental bubble-machines at the Daily Mail Ideal Home Exhibition.

1966 Exhibited bubble-machines in 'Weiss auf Weiss', curated by Harald Szeemann at the Kunsthalle, Bern. Exhibited kinetic works in 'Art and Movement', curated by William Buchanan at the Royal Scottish Academy, Edinburgh, and Kelvingrove Art Gallery, Glasgow; the kinetic art exhibition curated by Cyril Barrett, Herbert Art Gallery, Coventry; and 'In Motion', a touring exhibition of kinetic art curated by Guy Brett for the Arts Council of Great Britain. Closure of Signals.

1967 Initiated the Exploding Galaxy, "a kinetic confluence of transmedia explorers", on January 1. Based in a house at 99 Balls Pond Road, Dalston, the Exploding Galaxy devised and performed dance-dramas in many public places in London, Britain and the Continent, as well as in formal venues such as the Round House, London (*The Bird Ballet*, 1967). Solo exhibition of kinetic works at Indica Gallery, London.

1968 Inaugurated *The Buddha Ballet* with John Dugger, a weekend participatory event at Parliament Hill, London. Break-up of the

Galaxy. Travelled with John Dugger and other Galaxy members to France, Italy, Spain, Senegal, South Africa, Kenya, Pakistan, India, Sri Lanka, Singapore, Thailand, the Philippines and Nepal, (1968-70). Stayed with the Kerala Kalamandalam troupe of Kathakali dancers in India and studied Indian dance. Founded the Arts Council of the Philippines while in Manila. Exhibited bubble-machines in 'Air Art', curated by Willoughby Sharp for the University of California Art Museum at Berkeley and other venues in the USA.

1969 Exhibited in 'Live in Your Head: When Attitudes Become Form', the first comprehensive survey of conceptual art, curated by Harald Szeemann at the Kunsthalle, Berne; ICA, London, and other venues in Europe.

1971 Staff-Student advisor at the Slade School of Fine Art, University of London (1971-72). Lecturer on Oriental culture, St Martins School of Art, London (1971-73). Founder and Secretary of the Artists Liberation Front (1971-74). Exhibited in 'Pioneers of Participation Art' at the Museum of Modern Art, Oxford; 'Microcosm', curated by Peter Carey at the Camden Arts Centre, London; '3 > ∞: New Multiple Art', curated by Biddy Peppin and Hugh Shaw at the Whitechapel Gallery, London.

1972 Exhibited jointly with John Dugger at Documenta 5, Kassel, curated by Harald Szeemann, devising and building the *Peoples' Participation Pavilion*. Exhibited *A Stitch in Time* in 'Toeval' (on the random in art), curated by Frans Haks at the Rijksuniversiteit, Utrecht, and in the 'Survey of the Avant-Garde in Britain', curated by Sigi Krauss and Rosetta Brooks at Gallery House, London. Joint exhibition with John Dugger at the ICA, London.

1973 Lecturer in General Studies, Chelsea School of Art (1973-75). Lecturer on Chinese culture and civilization, University of Southampton (1973-74). Chairman, International Committee for Freedom in the Philippines.

1974 Co-founder and Chairman of Artists for Democracy, a broad organization dedicated to "giving material and cultural support to liberation movements worldwide" (1974-77).

AFD's first major project was the International Arts Festival for Democracy in Chile, at the Royal College of Art, London. Enacted *The Porcelain Wedding*, a participation- production-performance, at Edinburgh College of Art, curated by Lynne MacRitchie, and at Arts Meeting Place, London.

1975 AFD opened a cultural centre in Whitfield Street, London. With Medalla as director and Nick Payne as manager, the 'Fitzrovia Cultural centre' staged exhibitions, performances, poetry readings, film shows, lectures and meetings until 1977. Participated in the International Video Encounter, curated by Jorge Glusberg at the Espace Cardin, Paris. Began an intensive development of his performance work (see Appendix 1).

1976 Staged *Thunderous Applause*, a review of three years' work, as part of London Calling, curated by John Sharkey, at Acme Gallery, London.

1977 Exhibited *Eskimo Carver*, a 'participation-production-propulsion' at AFD – Fitzrovia Cultural Centre, the last event before the Centre's closure.

1979 Organized, with Oriol de Quadras and Rino Telaro, 'Mayfair Illuminations 1&2', in which many artists were invited to exhibit and hold events at a large, temporally empty mansion, Hill House, Berkeley Square, London. Exhibited *Rhapsody of the Dagger and Ammonia Boy* and related 'Synoptic-Realist' paintings at the Chenil Art Gallery, London. Left England and began a five-year period of travelling and performing in Italy, Germany, Holland, Belgium, France and Spain, returning occasionally for short stays in Britain.

1980 Performed *Voyages and Somersaults of the Pilgrim Monkey* in the Great Hall of the Academy in Venice. Invited by William Xerra to perform in the 'Vive' festival in Pavia Italy. Performance of *l'Ange du Jour, l'Ange de la Nuit* by Aragon at Galerie Biren, Paris.

1983 Appointed Artist in Residence at South Hill Park Art Centre, Bracknell. Organized, with Gavin Henderson, Director, Alistair Snow, Artistic Director, and Jenni Walwin, the First International Festival of Performance Art at South Hill Park. Participated in 'Perfotijd', curated by Wink van Kempen, at the Theater de Lantaren, Rotterdam. Formed Octetto

Ironico with James Acheson, Lesley Butler, Kevin Goss, Sonia Knox, Roberta Kravitz, Alistair Snow and Anna Thew. Wrote and co-directed with Mark Greaves the film version of *The Hand of Marie Curie*. The film was premiered a few years later at the London Film Co-op during an evening dedicated to Mark Greaves organized by Nick Gordon-Smith. Began his *Parables of Friendship* painting cycle.

1984　Formed a creative partnership with Kai Hilgemann, as The Signs and Wonders of David and Kai and gave many performances together in Europe. Participated in 'Perfotijd 2' in Rotterdam. Co-organized and participated in the Second International Festival of Performance Art at South Hill Park. Performed *Metamorphoses of an Enigma*, at Cirque Divers, Liège, Belgium.

1985　Visited the Philippines with Kai Hilgemann and held a solo exhibition of his work at Pinaglabanan Art Gallery, Manila.

1986　Monumental bubble-machine commissioned by the Auckland City Art gallery, New Zealand for the exhibition 'Chance and Change: a Century of the Avant-Garde', curated by Andrew Bogle. Began his *Luz. Vi. Minda. (Filipiniana)* painting series.

1987　Began a new performance series, *A Shot in the Dark*, with Brian Morgan. The audience were invited to bring cameras of all kinds to film the performances. Began work on his painting *A Memory of Mr Morley's Harp-Shop in South Kensington*.

1989　Performance of *The Dream of Andres Bonifacio*, organized by Hermine Demoriane for the 200th anniversary of the French revolution, at Espace Donguy, Paris. Exhibited in 'The Other Story: Afro-Asian Artists in Post-War Britain', curated by Rasheed Araeen at the Hayward Gallery, London. Painted *A Prophecy in the Shadow of La Grande Arche in Paris*, now in the Arts Council Collection. *A Stitch in Time* also acquired by the Arts Council Collection. Exhibited, and gave performances, in 'Here and There: Travels II', curated by Chris Dercon at the Clocktower Gallery, New York.

1990　Became Artist in Transit at the New York Port Authority. Invited to give a series of five lectures at the Museum of Modern Art, New York, for which his title was 'The Dream of Yadwigha: The Sources in Global Cultures of Modern Art'. Wrote a weekly column for the *Filipino Express*, 'Medalla in Manhattan' (1990-91). Began his painting cycle *New York Epiphanies*. Exhibited in 'Public Mirror: Artists against Racial Prejudice', curated by Tom Finkelpearl, Rebecca Quaytman and Ken Chu at the Clocktower Gallery, New York.

1991　Awarded an Artist's Fellowship by the New York Foundation for the Arts. Exhibited in 'Shocks to the System: Works from the Arts Council Collection', curated by Isobel Johnstone at the Royal Festival Hall, London, and City Art Gallery, Manchester. Started a new collaboration with the Australian artist Adam Nankervis. The duo performed a number of time-based and site-specific events in New York.

1992　Awarded a second Artist's Fellowship by the New York Foundation for the Arts. Exhibited in 'Fluxattitudes', curated by Cornelia Lauf and Susan Hapgood at the New Museum, New York. Awarded a fellowship by the Jerome Foundation of America. Performed *Five Immortals at Drop-Dead Prices* in the Great Hall of Cooper Union, New York, organized by Franklin Furnace.

1993　Lectured on transcendental art in the mid-Manhattan branch of the New York Public Library. Exhibited *New York Epiphanies* and other paintings at the Philippines Center in Manhattan.

1994　Founder and President, The Mondrian Fan Club. A major exhibition of new work held in London, 'The Secret History of the Mondrian Fan Club Part II', at 55 Gee Street, Clerkenwell. For this exhibition he was commissioned by Pulsynetic to produce an ensemble of four monumental perspex bubble-machines, *Cloud Gates*, two new mud- and compost-machines, a neon work, *Kinetic Mudras for Piet Mondrian*, and a suite of paintings and giant chromo-copies. During this exhibition he opened his space to artists, dancers, film-makers, architects, writers and others to exhibit and perform.

Bibliography

Writings and statements by David Medalla

Signals:London, 1964-66.

Medalla edited and designed the *Signals Newsbulletin,* publication of Signals London. Ten issues were produced between August 1964 and March 1966. They were related to the exhibitions in the showroom, with detailed documentation of each artist's work. They also included poems, critical essays, scientific digests, found images and experimental art news. The ten issues of *Signals Newsbulletin* have been reprinted a facsimile and published by inIVA, London, 1995. Medalla also edited and designed invitation brochures (often running to several pages) for 12 exhibitions organised by Paul Keeler as Signals in Wigmore Street, London, between November 1964 and August 1966.

'Marine Valentine for Yves Klein', poem, *Signals Newsbulletin,* vol 1 no 1, August 1964.

'New Projects', *Signals,* vol 1 no 1, August 1964.

'Stele to Takis', *Signals,* vol 1 nos 3/4, Oct-Nov 1964.

'Lygia Clark: an Appreciation', *Signals,* vol 1 no 6, Feb/March 1965.

'Found Poem for Takis' and 'Go to Work on a Poem (reading instructions)', *Signals* vol 1 no 7, April-May 1965.

'MMMMMMM...Manifesto, a fragment', *Signals,* vol 1 no 8, June-July 1965.

'Mira Schendel', *Signals,* vol 1 no 9, Aug-Oct 1965.

'Found Poem for Alejandro Otero', *Signals,* vol 2 no 2, Jan-March 1966.

Statement in *In Motion* catalogue (ed. Guy Brett), Arts Council of Great Britain, 1966.

'Biokinetics and related investigations into the morphology and propositions of art in motion' (extract), *ICA Bulletin,* London, March 1967.

Statement, 'This page is part of your environment - now read on', *International Times* London, March 13-26, 1967.

'The Bird Ballet', ballet script for The Exploding Galaxy, The Roundhouse, London, 1967.

'Participe Present: l'Art de Lygia Clark', *Robho 4,*

Paris, 1967.

'The Exploding Galaxy', *Palatten 1* Stockholm, 1968.

Interview, 'Underground Voices', ed. David Robins and Liza Béar, *Circuit 5,* London, winter 1968.

'From Kathakali to Biokinetic Theatre', interview with Hermine Demoriane *International Times* London, December 13-31 1968.

Interview with Anees Jung, *The Young Statesman,* Calcutta, Autumn 1969.

Letter to dom sylvester houédard, *12 dancepoems from the cosmic typewriter by dsh,* Aplomb Zero no 1 Wiltshire, England, 1969.

'Ephemerals', in *3 -> ∞ :New Multiple Art* catalogue (ed. Hugh Shaw), Arts Council of Great Britain, 1971.

'Some remarks on participation art', *Toeval* ('Chance') catalogue (ed. Frans Haks), Rijksuniversiteit Utrecht, 1972.

Statement, *Tra Rivolta e Rivoluzione* (catalogue), Bologna, 1972.

'Tatlin at the Funeral of Malevich', poem, extract from performance script, *Wallpaper,* London, (ed. Susan Hiller), March 1977.

Interview with Brandon Taylor, *Artscribe* London, no 6, April 1977.

Interview with Rasheed Araeen, *Black Phoenix,* London, no 3, Spring 1979.

'The Spider', poem, *The Filipinas Journal of Science and Culture,* vol 2, Filipinas Foundation, Manila, 1981.

'A Stitch in Time', *South Hill Park Bulletin* Bracknell, July-August 1982.

'Performance' (part 1), *South Hill Park Bulletin* Bracknell, May-June 1983.

'Performance' (part 2), *South Hill Park Bulletin* Bracknell, July-August 1983.

Interview with Jun Terra (part 1), *San Juan* Manila, March 1985.

Interview with Jun Terra (part 2), *San Juan* Manila,

August 1985.

'Conversations with Louis Aragon', *San Juan* Manila, December 1985.

'Paris-London: Memories of the '6os', *And: Journal of Art and Art Education*, London, no 17, 1988.

Interview with Cid Reyes, *Conversations on Philippine Art*, Cultural Center of the Philippines, Manila, 1989.

'Signals', *The Other Story: Afro-Asian artists in post-war Britain*, The South Bank Centre, London, 1989.

'Medalla in Manhattan'. From June 1990, for about a year, David Medalla wrote a regular column in the *Filipino Express*, New York. Something over 20 pieces were written.

A Shot in the Dark, Synoptic Texts by David Medalla and Stories by Brian Morgan, London, 1990.

Statement, *Live Art*, (ed. Robert Ayers and David Butler), AN Publications, Sunderland, 1991.

Statement, (on his painting A Prophecy), *Shocks to the System: works from the Arts Council Collection*, Arts Council of Great Britain, 1991.

Statements in John Strausbaugh, 'The Flying Mondrians: David Medalla's Impossible Art', *New York Press*, New York, vol 7, no 21, May 25-31 1994.

Events poster, Artists for Democracy, Whitfield Street, London, 1977.

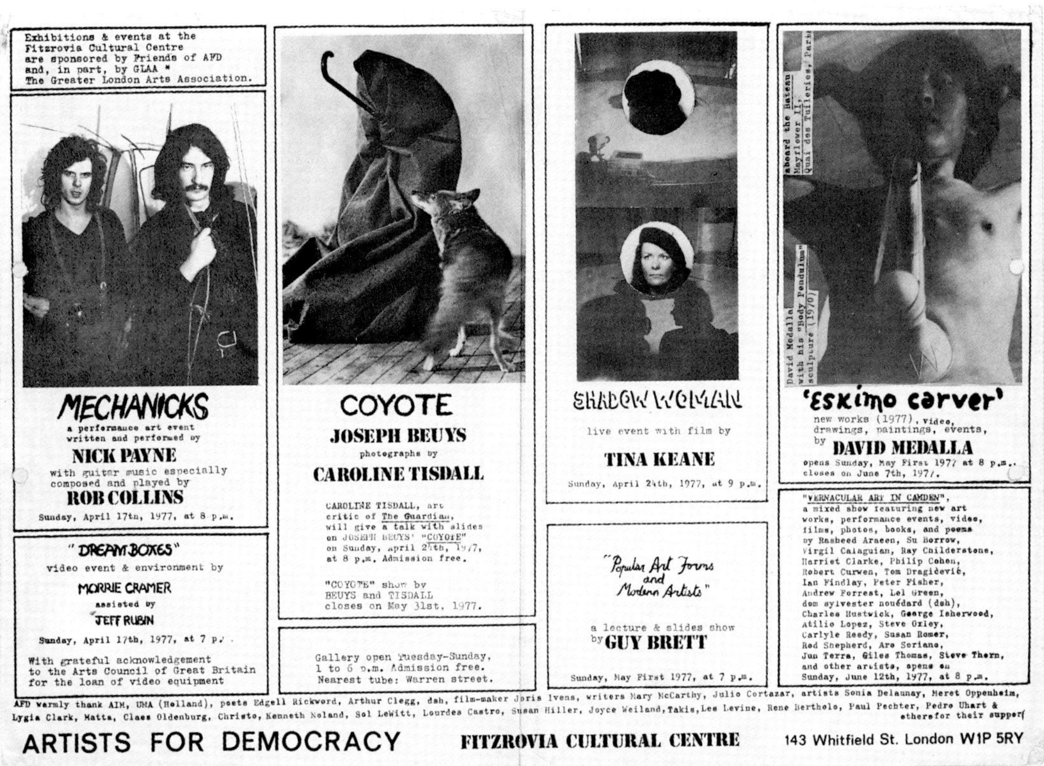

Virtual

Yve-Alain Bois

Though I've known David Medalla for years (we met fairly regularly during the Seventies – each time he came to Paris or I went to London), I've actually seen only a handful of his works. And nothing major at that – a few drawings from his militant period (when he was trying, or pretended to be trying, to lure me into the Maoist faith); a not-so-good sketch of myself in my early twenties (I still have it somewhere, one of the rare evidences that I once had a beard); and then the fragile paper masks, cut out of magazines, that Guy Brett pulled out his travel bag to show them to me and Rosalind Krauss, two or three years ago, in a quaint British-looking tea house near La Madeleine in Paris. Of course I'd seen many photographs over the years – from the bubble machines of the early Sixties up to fairly recent performances – but photographs don't say much about his work (photography can't say much about flux, duration, exchange – the stuff of David's art). Furthermore, these photographs only concerned a limited proportion of his output, indeed a far smaller proportion than I thought before reading the present book.

And yet, contrary to my habit of never writing on anything I have not experienced directly and scrutinised inside out, I would not find it particularly immoral to do so on David's work. This does not mean that I would feel very competent – though, among many other qualities, Guy Brett's study enormously raises the level of my putative competence by the sheer quantity of information it contains. It just means that, in David's case, not having actually seen much of his work does not seem to constitute a confounding handicap, should I have to write about it – and this, for me, despite years of Conceptual Art, is a first.

Before reading Guy Brett's book I had often wondered if David's work, notably his performances, had ever really taken place. But I had concluded that it did not matter much, that language was the true medium of David, that his real performances were his narrations, that it was in relating them, always existing fully in his mind, always replete with multiple layers of allegory, that he performed them. David-Sheherazade: the way he knits his elaborate descriptions, unfolding one after the other the various semantic realms that are intertwined in any of his works, the rhapsodic structure of the tale. This always mesmerised me, as it did others.

In the Seventies David often carried with him a notebook, all scribbled up, filled with the script of one or another of his performances, and would read from it eventually, more often than not extrapolating from it, but always telling about events – past or would-be ones, without distinction. The quintessential oral poet, the story-teller, the seducer.

Guy Brett's study both contradicts such an impression and confirms it at what, for me, is a deeper and more paradoxical level. The book abounds with evidence that testifies to the reality of Medalla's work. Something has existed, and still does, though it is in some way intangible. To be sure, objects have been made (and have been remade, occasionally, if the original was destroyed), performances and intricate participatory pieces have taken place. One of the functions of this book is to attest this, providing a unique eye-witness account.

Yet at the same time, Brett's tale does not diminish, even enhances, Medalla's predilection for fantasy and imaginative projection. Alluding to the ephemeral status of performance as an art form, Brett notes that "even the inventory of over 150 of Medalla's performances evokes something that cannot exactly be verified". The virtual aspect of Medalla's work is underscored everywhere in this book, with numerous examples of unrealised (though not always necessarily unrealisable) proposals dating from the early Sixties to the present: David, the only real conceptual artist, for whom it is enough to think of a project.

One of the structures of Medalla's poetics so perceptively described by Guy Brett is that of the 'meeting'. Accounting for its open-endedness, the sense of infinite unfolding that it entails (the 'and then, and then' of David's narration), Brett also speaks of David's work as vastly metaphoric. But metaphors are usually not open-ended: something stands for something else, something is as something else, yet for a metaphor to work and be recognised as such, the circularity of exchange has to be arrested at some point, the chain of signification has to be broken. Medalla's work, on the contrary, proposes an endless story, that of a *perpetuum mobile*, a universe where particles rebound *ad vitam aeternam*.

In other words, Medalla builds indeed on metaphors, vast amounts of them, but I would say that it is in order to destroy metaphor per se – by excess. It is to annihilate any metaphoric centre by the sheer vastness of possibility. The 'and then, and then' is designed never to stop. Which is why Medalla's participatory pieces are so cogent, why they work – unlike so many other works based on the 'spectator's' participation in the Sixties and Seventies. Which is also why his work, contrary to appearances and, no doubt, to the claims that have been or will be made about it, does not provide an apologetic discourse about identity (national, racial, sexual, social or otherwise). "There is no place for static identities... Everything is in constant flux," Medalla is quoted as saying. In order to cancel any identity, one has to cancel as well the structure of oppositions on which metaphors are grounded: David's strategy is that of superabundance.

This dissolution by excess is perhaps more easily explored in art than in writing,

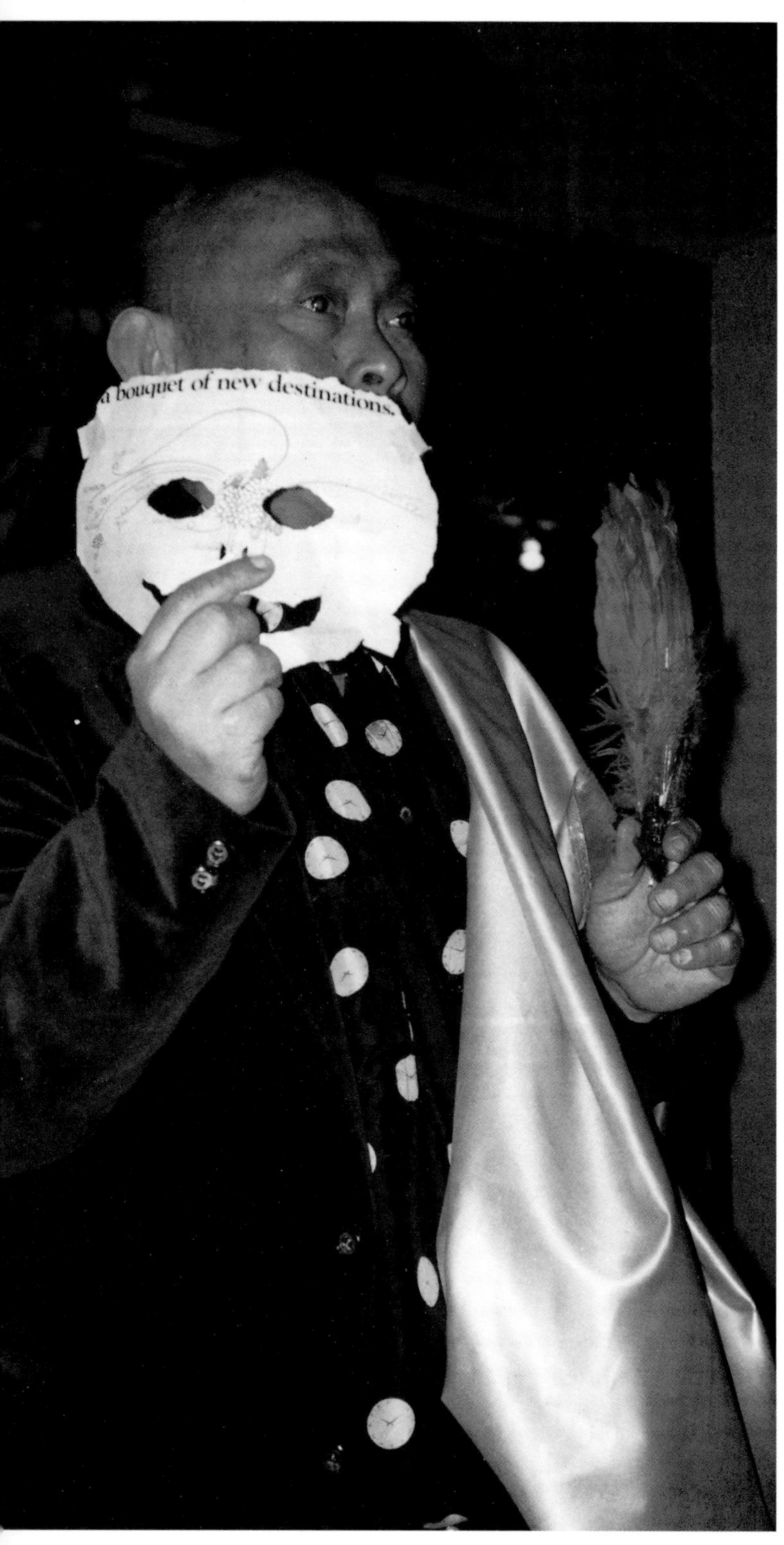

for the infinity of language is daunting once its economical rule is broken loose. David is not the only artist to have engaged in it (one can find traces of such a radical poetic in Duchamp, or in Cage or in Fluxus for example), but to my mind he is certainly the one who carried it further and constantly remained faithful to its liberating principle: his deliberate defaulting of the laws of the art market, his nomadic refusal to remain any bit more than a fleeting moment in any place he might be assigned to by the artistic institution, in sum the casual and (somewhat heroic) detachment with which he managed his career – those were the weapons by which he consciously insured the success of his undermining enterprise.

Nothing was ever allowed to freeze, even if a lack of public recognition was the price to pay for adhering to this axiom.

Medalla invented, for me, the practice of virtuality.

Performing **Mondrian in Excelsis**, the Mondrian Fan Club, 55 Gee Street, London, New Year's Eve, 1994.

Author's Acknowledgments

I would like to thank the many people who, at different times, have given me insight into David Medalla's work and person, among them Gaby Agis, Alejandra Altamirano, Rasheed Araeen, Dore Ashton, Betsy Baker, Anne Bean, Petti Benitez, Yve-Alain Bois, Virgil Calaguian, Sergio Camargo, Lourdes Castro, Lygia Clark, Dan Chadwick, Jean Clay, Michael Colbourne, Hermine Demoriane, David Dickson, John Dugger, Jane England, Rose English, Rose Finn-Kelcey, Jean Fisher, Peter Fisher, Tony Fisher, Boris Gerrets, Matthias Goeritz, Nick Gordon-Smith, Gerhard von Graevenitz, Mark Greaves, Lovato Guerrino, Mona Hatoum, José Herrera, Kai Hilgemann, Susan Hiller, Dom Sylvester Houédard, Kapil Jariwala, Tina Keane, Paul Keeler, Robbie Kravitz, Li Yuan-chia, Victor Lucena, Lynne MacRitchie, Gustav Metzger, James Moores, Brian Morgan, Adam Nankervis, Hélio Oiticica, Roszika Parker, Nick Payne, Clay Perry, Edward Pope, Oriol de Quadras, Carlyle Reedy, Pierre Restany, Cid Reyes, Nick Sawyer, Hugh Shaw, Mira Schendel, John Sharkey, Andy Stahl, Sylvia Stevens, Harald Szeemann, Takis, Caroline Tisdall, Anna Thew, Giles Thomas, Steve Thorn, Tunga, Jean-Luc Vilmouth.

I would particularly like to thank Jun Terra for the interest he took in the progress of this book and his perceptive remarks. I have been indebted too to Petti Benitez's pioneering study 'David Medalla: The 60s and 70s'. Rasheed Araeen commissioned this book; Jean Fisher edited it; Nicola Gray proofed it; Zafar Abbas Malik designed it; Arti Grafiche Roccia, Turin, printed it; inIVA gave a grant towards its publication. Thanks to all of them.

As for my acknowledgement to the artist himself, the reader will realize that that, essentially, is what this book is. I could thank him for several contributions to it, one of which was to find the book's epigram, but these would be small items in 30 years of association and friendship.

Guy Brett was born in 1942 and lives in London. He has been writing on art and organizing exhibitions since the early 1960s. He was Art Critic for the London Times from 1964-1975 and Visual Arts Editor of the London weekly City Limits in the early 1980s. His books include *Kinetic Art* (Studio Vista/Reinholt, 1968), *Through Our Own Eyes: Popular Art and Modern History* (New Society, 1986), and *Transcontinental: Nine Latin American Artists* (Verso, 1990).

Dore Ashton is Professor of Art History at the Cooper Union in New York, and a former Art Critic of the New York Times (1955-60). A distinguished writer on 20th century art and architecture, her many books include *A Fable of Modern Art*, (Thames & Hudson, 1980), *The New York School: A Critical Reckoning* (University of California Press, 1992), and monographs on Philip Guston (Evergreen, 1960) and Mark Rothko (Oxford University Press, 1983).

Yve-Alain Bois has written extensively on many aspects of twentieth century art (mainly abstraction, early and late, but also cubism and Matisse). He was a founder, with Jean Clay, of the revue *Macula* in Paris in 1976. A collection of some of his essays, *Painting as Model*, was published in 1990 by MIT Press. He is the Joseph Pulitzer Jr. Professor of Modern Art at Harvard University.
